Dreams and Visions in Islamic Societies

Dreams and Visions in Islamic Societies

Edited by
Özgen Felek and Alexander D. Knysh

Cover art: H.1702, fol. 12B (Falname); a miniature of Ashab-i Kehf (Sleepers of Ephesus); credit: Topkapi Palace Museum

Published by State University of New York Press, Albany

Printed in the United States of America

For information, contact State University of New York Press, Albany, NY
www.sunypress.edu

Production by Diane Ganeles
Marketing by Fran Keneston

Library of Congress Cataloging-in-Publication Data

Dreams and visions in Islamic societies / Özgen Felek and
Alexander D. Knysh.
p. cm.
Includes bibliographical references and index.
ISBN 978-1-4384-3993-8 (hardcover : alk. paper)
ISBN 978-1-4384-3994-5 (pbk. : alk. paper)
1. Dreams—Religious aspects—Islam. 2. Visions. I. Felek, Özgen.
II. Knysh, Alexander D.

BP190.5.D73D74 2012
297.5'7—dc22 2011010850

10 9 8 7 6 5 4 3 2 1

Contents

Acknowledgments

Some books have remarkable stories behind their creation. This one does not. It was conceived about three years ago, when we realized that there had not been many recent studies of dreams and visions in Islamic societies and that we had something to say about this topic. We decided to collaborate with those who also had the same interest. Initially, we came together in Washington DC, at the annual conference of the Middle East Studies Association, in fall 2008 to share our ideas about this fascinating subject. Carl Ernst and Jonathan Katz expanded our intellectual horizons through their perceptive discussion of the papers presented at our panel. In spring 2009, we had a follow-up conference on this subject in Ann Arbor, and it was then that the concept of this volume took its final shape.

Many individuals and institutions helped us over the course of the past three years. We are thankful for the financial and logistical support provided by the following institutions at the University of Michigan: The Islamic Studies Initiative, Department of Near Eastern Studies, Center for Middle Eastern and North African Studies, Armenian Studies Program, Center for Russian and East European Studies, and Rackham Graduate School. We would like to express our appreciation to Sylvia Meloche of the Islamic Studies Initiative for her outstanding work that ensured the constructive and productive outcome of our conference in Ann Arbor. We also are grateful to Kathryn Babayan who served as a co-chair, along with Alexander D. Knysh, at this conference, Derek Mancini-Lander and Sarah Mirza of the University of Michigan, and Walter G. Andrews of the University of Washington for their insights and suggestions. We extend our heartfelt thanks to the authors of this volume for their commitment to and boundless enthusiasm for this intellectual venture. If this volume has any merits, then the credit for this should be shared by everyone who has made it a reality.

Editors

Note on Transliteration

Because the authors of this volume have made use of Arabic, Persian, Ottoman Turkish, and Urdu texts, the reader should not look for consistency in transliteration. We have adopted a slightly modified transliteration system used by the *International Journal of Middle East Studies* (*IJMES*), a major professional publication in the field of Islamic studies. For example, in the chapters that quote Arabic texts, we use *q* for *qāf,* whereas in the quotations from Ottoman Turkish texts, we use *ḳ* to convey the same letter. Because the *IJMES* chart lacks the nasal *n* and the dot above the letter *ghayn,* we used *ñ* and *ġ* to transliterate words and names in Ottoman Turkish.

Abbreviations

EI[2] *The Encyclopedia of Islam*, Second Edition, Leiden, E. J. Brill, 1954–2000, and Supplements

Elr *Encyclopedia Iranica*, ed. E. Yarshater, New York, 1985–.

EQ *The Encyclopedia of the Qur'an*, ed. Jane McAuliffe, Leiden, E. J. Brill, 2001–2006

ER *Encyclopedia of Religion*, ed. Lindsay Jones, Farmington Hills, Mich., Gale, 2005

MW *The Muslim World*, Hartford Seminary, Connecticut, 1934–

Introduction

Alexander D. Knysh

Writing in the early thirteenth century CE, the great Arab mystic Ibn [al-]ʿArabī (1165–1240) suggests that "The only reason God placed sleep in the animate world was so that everyone might . . . know that there is another world similar to the sensory world."[1] Elsewhere, he states that "Dreams have a place, a locus, and a state. Their state is sleep, which is an absence from manifest sensory things that produce ease because of weariness which overcomes the soul in this plane in the state of wakefulness."[2] By means of the faculty of imagination, Ibn ʿArabī argues, a dreaming individual is capable of seeing disembodied intelligible entities in the form of corporeal, sensory objects.[3] This is the world of dream-imagination in which the mysteries of God and his creation, otherwise impenetrable to the human intellect and sense perceptions, are unveiled. In seeking to substantiate the importance of dreams as a cognitive tool, Ibn ʿArabī frequently invokes the Prophet's saying that "People are asleep, and when they die, they awake."[4] In his interpretation, the implication of this saying is that "[People] will never cease being sleepers, so they will never cease being dreamers."[5] In other words, dreams are an indispensible instrument of cognition: People should dream in order to grasp the true state of affairs in this world and the next and to remain tuned to the ever changing modes of divine self-disclosure in the objects and phenomena of the empirical universe.

Although many Muslims, including some thinkers examined in this volume, may not have agreed with Ibn ʿArabī's assertions, they would no doubt unanimously concede the vital importance of dreams and waking visions for Muslim life. The reasons for this are manifold.

Writing from outside the Islamic tradition, the renowned American historian of Islamic civilization, Marshall Hodgson (1922–1968), offers the following explanation of dreams' importance for premodern Muslim societies:

> Both waking and dreaming visions can form a very fruitful resource for personal mythic formation. . . . Such myth formation need not serve merely the delights of a free fantasy. We are learning that there can be dreams of special urgency which can be pointers to areas of crucial importance to the growth of the personality; and this at all levels of that growth, not merely in its correction of elementary neurosis. Dreams readily take on a colouration, in their symbols and format, from social expectations surrounding the dreamer; but they will give those social expectations a profoundly personal relevance, perhaps more so than can readily be achieved in waking consciousness.[6]

According to Hodgson, premodern Muslims did not consider dreams to be simple expressions of the dreamer's repressed phobias, aspirations, and sexual drives, as well as some other types of neurosis, as asserted by Sigmund Freud in his theory of psychoanalysis.[7] Rather, they were concerned with what dreams could tell them about "the world outside the dreamer, things that could not otherwise be known."[8]

Like Ibn ʿArabī, medieval and modern Muslims have considered dreams to be windows into the hidden mysteries of both this world and the next. In this respect, dreams are akin to, and part of, prophecy itself—a notion based on several prophetic statements to this effect cited throughout this volume.[9] For instance, the Prophet is quoted as declaring that with his death "the glad tidings of prophecy" would cease, whereas "true dreams" would endure. This statement implies that dreams and visions are, in the words of one Western scholar, "a form of divine revelation and a chronological successor to the Koran."[10] This is indeed how they have been perceived by many Sufis. As one of the contributors to this volume argues, by virtue of "having access to a persisting suprasensible and suprapersonal knowledge through the medium of dreams and dreaming," the Sufi master or "friend of God" is but a "transposition" of the Prophet.[11]

This is not to say that veridical dreams and visions are necessarily the prerogative of Muslim mystics or society's spiritual and intellectual elite in general. In principle, "each good Muslim could expect guidance from God in dreams."[12] The amazing pervasiveness of dreams and dream-lore at various levels and among different classes of Muslim society is demonstrated by Part I of this volume. Its chapters discuss the ways in which dreams have been deployed in a variety of non-Sufi contexts: historical, prosopographical, theological, anthropological and multimedia. Given the great importance of dreams and waking visions for mystical Islam, it is only natural that Part II is specifically devoted to their roles in various Sufi communities. As the authors of the chapters in Part II show, the Sufis have put dreams and dream-lore to a broad variety of uses, from training Sufi disciples and prognostication to confirming the special status and authority of individual Sufi masters as well as authenticating spiritual genealogies and mystical orders.

The recognition of the general availability of truthful insights to mystics and nonmystics alike often is offset by the widely held belief that special training and expertise may be required to unravel dreams' subtle symbolism, unless, of course, they are clear and unequivocal.[13] Indeed, very early on, interpreting dreams became a special art, even a profession. Originally, relatively uniform and homogenous, by the end of the tenth century CE the tradition of dream interpretation became fragmented into "a number of competing legacies, each grounding [it] on a distinctive epistemic foundation."[14] Some were strictly Islamic ("*sharīᶜa*-minded") in that they consistently traced their origins back to the beliefs and practices of the first Muslim community under the Prophet's leadership. Such methods of interpreting dreams tended to legitimize themselves by reference to the Muslim scriptures. Others were more cosmopolitan, creatively combining traditional Islamic beliefs with dream-lore derived from non-Islamic sources (Greek, Jewish, Christian, Zoroastrian, and Hindu).[15] Naturally, the Sufis forged their own, distinctive oneirocritic tradition, as the chapters collected in Part II finely demonstrate.

On the whole, dreams and the art of their interpretation are so intimately intertwined that on occasion it is impossible to draw a clear distinction between the two without damaging their organic co-existence in various sociocultural contexts. This is hardly surprising because the very account of a dream or vision by a dreamer or visionary already constitutes their initial interpretation.

As we emphasize the social and cosmological aspects of dreams and visions, we should keep in mind that they were, and still are, seen by Muslims not only as divinations and explanations of outside events, that is, messages from the unseen world of divine mystery, but also as reflections of the inner world of the dreaming person.[16] Dreams and visions thus offer "a constant balance between the private world of latent images, fears and hopes, and outside reality, cosmic as well as social."[17] To divine the implications of dreams and visions for any given individual, Muslim experts on dream interpretation have stressed the necessity of taking into account the dreamer's personality, gender, social status, trade, depth of faith, and other personal circumstances. For, as some of these interpreters have cogently argued, the same symbol may portend different things for different people under different circumstances.[18]

As "expressions of both inner and outer voices," dreams in Islamic contexts are intimately linked to society's aesthetical, ethical, and social values. In a two-way process, these values both mold and are being molded by dreams and dream-lore. Likewise, dreams shape, and are decisively shaped by, personal and collective notions of self and society.[19] The reciprocity of the process of shaping and being shaped cannot be emphasized too strongly.[20] Seen from this vantage point, dreams and visions constitute an essential part of society's functioning and self-perception.

Although "dream cultures"[21] may vary from one Muslim society or epoch to another, the prophetic endorsement just cited and the unequivocal evidence found in the Qur᾿ān itself[22] have assured the continuous relevance of dreams and visions for Muslim communities worldwide. The chapters collected under this cover are an eloquent testimony to both diversity and cultural specificity of dream-lore. At the same time, they show the continuing importance of dreams for Muslims regardless of their social, cultural, and intellectual backgrounds.

Muslims' preoccupation with dreams, visions and their interpretation has successfully withstood the test of time. It is almost as profound at present as it was in the past. No wonder, therefore, that the recent decades have seen the growing interest among academics in various aspects and roles of dreams and dream interpretation in Islamic societies. Beginning with a seminal volume on dreams edited by G. E. von Grunebaum and Roger Caillois in 1966,[23] there has been a constant stream of publications on the subject by Western and Western-trained scholars of Islamic societies and cultures. The most recent ones place special emphasis on dream interpretation as a means of empowerment, education, and spiritual guidance, on the one hand, and subversion of societal conventions and authority contestation, on the other.[24] Although complementing these earlier studies, the chapters gathered in this volume place more emphasis on dreams as such rather than on how they have been perceived and explicated by oneirocritic professionals. Furthermore, the chronological scope of this study is broader in that it encompasses uses of dreams and dream-lore in contemporary Islamic societies and on the Internet.

As already mentioned, Part I deals with dreams, waking visions, and dream interpretation in non-Sufi contexts. Arranged in roughly chronological order, it opens with a discussion by Sarah Mirza of the role of dreams in Ibn Hishām's biography of the prophet Muḥammad. Significantly, in this seminal source, the Prophet is not the only one who sees true dreams and visions. Moreover, a few other dreamers discussed in Mirza's chapter are not even Muslims. Some of them belong to the non-Muslim camp, which makes their dark predictions—obtained through dreams—of the final triumph of the Muslim community ever more dramatic and indubitable. Naturally, the Prophet himself being the protagonist, his revelatory dreams and visions of encounters with the Divine and his messengers occupy the center stage of Ibn Hishām's account of Muḥammad's prophetic mission.

The chapter by Maxim Romanov questions some common assumptions regarding the sternness and sobriety of the Ḥanbalī religiopolitical school that have commonly been contrasted with the "fanciful," "superstitious," and socially "irresponsible" attitudes ascribed to the Sufis. In analyzing biographies of medieval Ḥanbalīs, both leaders and rank-and-file, Romanov brings out the same indulgence in dreams and dream-lore that is routinely associated with Sufi communities. In the Ḥanbalī biographical narratives, dreams play a wide gamut of roles from confirming the veracity and lofty status of certain Ḥanbalī scholars to asserting the supremacy of the Ḥanbalī theological and legal "way" (*madhhab*) as a whole.

That fascination with dreams and dream-lore was not the exclusive preserve of Sunni communities is evident from Omid Ghaemmaghami's illuminating discussion of Twelver Shīʿī dreams about encounters with the Hidden Imām. Drawing a parallel between the tradition describing the Prophet's vision of God in the form of a handsome youth and the numerous Shīʿī stories about appearance of a youthful Hidden Imām in dreams and visions of his followers, Ghaemmaghami concludes that, for the Shīʿīs, the visionary appearances of the Imām represented "the countenance of God upon which His friends have set their affections." Through dreams and visions, argues the author, God's tangible and, on occasion, also visible presence among his faithful servants is maintained, helping the Shīʿīs to cope with their minority status and the historical injustices inflicted on them by the Sunni majority.

With Derek Mancini-Lander's chapter "Dreaming the Elixir of Knowledge," we enter the realm of Persian *belle-lettres*. In examining the life story of a poet from the Safavid epoch (1502–1722), Mancini-Lander shows the critical role that dreams played not only in the poet's artistic evolution and self-perception, but also in how he was viewed by his society and poetic peers. Dreams accompany the protagonist throughout his entire life from early childhood to his eventual promotion, "sanctioned in heaven," to the rank of the foremost poet of his age. Significantly, these dreams appear at and determine the critical turning points of his spiritual and artistic journey. In the words of Mancini-Lander, "they facilitated the transmission of simulacral, yet practical, even somatic, forms of knowing," thereby enabling "total reorientations" not only in the poet's external existence, but in his poetic craft as well. In this way, dreams serve as an effective and indispensible means of the poet's personal and professional growth and self-identity.

In his chapter on "Dreaming ʿOs̠māns," Gottfried Hagen addresses the role of dreams in premodern Ottoman dynastic historiography. He shows that although modern historians of the Ottoman Empire have routinely dismissed dream narratives found in imperial chronicles as "obvious fiction," premodern Ottomans took dreams very seriously indeed. For them, dreams were as real as the historical events they predicted or attempted to explain. Dreams were, in Hagen's words, "taken for real by the actors in the narrative, by [the] author of the account, and, finally, by his audience." As such, dreams possessed "high explanatory value" for both Ottoman chroniclers and their audiences. In attributing meaning to seemingly senseless historical events and catastrophes, they helped the Ottoman populations, or at least the empire's learned elite, to find "orientation in a world that would otherwise be experienced as chaos" and, in so doing, to come to terms with inexplicable dramas (and traumas) of historical process.

With the emergence of Islamic modernist and reformist thought in the latter part of the nineteenth century CE, some Muslim scholars adopted a more cautious or even outright critical attitude toward dreams and dream interpretation. Fareeha Khan's chapter "Sometimes a Dream is Just a Dream" examines the ambivalent approach to dreams characteristic of the reformist Deobandi movement that originated in northern India in 1867. Its major representatives up to the present have felt that Indian Muslims put too much faith in dreams, visions, and all manner of premonitions at the expense of fulfilling their basic religious obligations as outlined in the manuals of the Deobandi school. As long as dreams were conducive toward the overriding goal of improving and reforming the beliefs and practices of the subcontinent's Muslim masses, the Deobandi leaders were prepared to accept them as sources of "absolute guidance." If, however, for one reason or the other, dreams or visions were perceived as an impediment to or distraction from this all-important objective, the Deobandi scholarly elite demanded that they be dismissed as inconsequential or even outright harmful. By espousing this selective view of dreams and visions, the Deobandi leaders have effectively harnessed them to their overarching task of inculcating in their audiences sober reformist attitudes in which the miraculous and fanciful had no major role to play. In a sense, the Deobandi ambivalence toward dreams and visions is articulated in opposition to what they considered the overzealous and uncritical acceptance of dreams within traditional Sufi circles, which are the subject of Part II.

The last two chapters of Part I address the role of dreams and dream interpretation in contemporary Muslim societies. Leah Kinberg's chapter, "Dreams Online," shows how the ancient Muslim belief in the veracity of dreams in which the Prophet appears to the dreamer is played out in the age of the Internet. The vigorous rejection by high-ranking religious scholars of certain dream narratives circulated via Internet blogs and forums indicates that something vital is at stake here. Wittingly or not, such narratives floating in cyberspace can challenge or even undermine the authority of official Muslim scholars as the sole legitimate exponents of "correct" Islam. In this way, dream accounts posted on the Internet become a means and sites of subversion and contestation of the traditional structures of religious authority.

Part I concludes with Muhammad alZekri's chapter on female dream interpretation in present-day Dubai (the United Arab Emirates [UAE]). It shows how the ability to interpret dreams used to be a means of empowering the otherwise disenfranchised female half of the population of this Gulf state, only to be supplanted gradually by male-dominated Salafī TV forums and telephone "hot-lines" seeking to disseminate "politically correct" religious guidance among the UAE's younger audiences. As increasing numbers of Muslims in the Gulf region gain direct, unmediated access to the Muslim scriptures, thanks to the rapid spread of mass education, the art of dream interpretation becomes ever-more deeply rooted in textual sources, such as the Qur᾽ān, *ḥadīth,* and their exegesis. As alZekri vividly demonstrates, this text-based approach inexorably supersedes and marginalizes the folkloric, oral methods of making sense out of people's dreams that were predominant in the not-so-distant past. Nonetheless, the rapid spread of new information technologies and direct access of the public to media outlets have not marginalized or discredited dreams and dream-lore as such. They continue to play a vital role in the Muslim societies of the Gulf and beyond.

In sum, alZekri's and Kinberg's studies show that, as in the premodern and early modern age, nowadays dreams and dream interpretation remain both sites and means of asserting and contesting religious and social authority, with modern information technologies facilitating and "democratizing" the process.

Part II opens with a concise survey by Jonathan Katz of the perceptions of dreams and visions in Islamic mysticism as articulated by its major representatives from the premodern epoch. The author then proceeds to discuss "how reportage of dreams, either by the [Sufi] *shaykh*s themselves or their disciples, was instrumental in securing popular reputations for sanctity" and in validating Sufi "claims to religious and political leadership." Katz's chapter demonstrates that "the most intimate and private of noetic experience—the dream and vision—could also, paradoxically, serve a most public role." This, argues Katz, is particularly true of the dreams in which the Prophet himself appears to Sufi masters to confirm their veracity and their status as guides of their constituencies. According to Katz, such prophetic appearances in Sufi dreams place "the dream at the very heart of communal religious experience."

Whereas Katz's chapter focuses on the dreams of some major Sufi masters from eighteenth- and nineteenth-century North Africa, his conclusions easily can be extrapolated to other parts of the Muslim world. This is made clear by Erik Ohlander's study of the claims to "post-prophetic heir-ship" that the Sufi *shaykh*s of the Muslim East have consistently substantiated by reference to their revelatory experiences in dreams and visions. In sum, as both Katz and Ohlander convincingly show, in Sufi communities worldwide, dreams and visions fulfill the task of indispensible image-, authority- and status-building devices.

The theme of the superiority of Sufi gnosis, often obtained through dreams and visions, is explored in Elizabeth Alexandrin's chapter on the mystical exegesis of the twelfth-century Sufi gnostic Shams al-Dīn al-Daylamī. In al-Daylamī's narrative, the Qurʾān, or rather, a specific selection of Qurʾānic verses, serves as the "primary touchstone" by which the veracity of dreams and visionary experience can be ascertained. For instance, al-Daylamī is fully convinced that the Qurʾān supports the notion that certain elect individuals (such as prophets) can obtain "the vision of God" already in this life. In al-Daylamī's view, this ability does not disappear with the cessation of prophecy. Rather, it is now transferred to Sufi "friends of God" whom God has granted "the vision of the heart." By virtue of this intuitive faculty, the Sufi visionaries can contemplate subtle immaterial entities that ordinary human beings are incapable of seeing, including the light of the Universal Intellect, glimpses of the Afterlife, and even of God himself. Unlike the dreams and visions of ordinary people, the Sufi visionaries cannot err in either their dreams or their interpretation, because they draw their revelatory insights from their meditation on the esoteric aspects of the Qur'ān, which contains nothing but truth.

Shahzad Bashir's chapter on dream narratives from Persian Sufi hagiographies dating back to the Mongol and Timurid periods explores the pedagogical role of dreams in mediating relationship between Sufi masters and their disciples. The appearance of the former in the dreams of the latter fulfills more than the purpose of guidance, admonition, and instruction. It also serves as a means for the disciples to receive and for the masters to provide protection at the time of need. Furthermore, by furnishing sophisticated and often surprising explanations of their disciples' dreams, the *shaykhs* assert their authority as infallible guides of human consciences. Bashir links dreams to the Naqshbandī practice of *rābiṭa* ("bond") that requires the disciple to constantly visualize the master in his mind's eye in order to imprint the master's image on his consciousness. As an essential pedagogical tool and means of communication, Bashir argues that in Naqshbandī Sufism seeing the *shaykh* in reality or a dream is not a passive activity but one that "needs to be cultivated through deliberate practice." Once obtained, this "televisual" communication between the master and his disciple does not cease with the master's death. No longer available in the flesh, the *shaykh* and his guidance can now be accessed through his appearances in the disciple's dreams. In this way, argues Bashir, dreams serve as the vital, incessant "continuation of the relationship as it existed before the master's demise."

The theme of royal dreams with a mystical slant is explored in Özgen Felek's chapter on the self-fashioning of the Ottoman sultan Murād III (r. 1574–1595). In the epistolary accounts of his dreams submitted to his spiritual preceptor, the Sultan portrays himself as a universal Islamic ruler and an accomplished Sufi. The latter identity, argues Felek, is not static—we see the Sultan evolve from a humble novice to the self-appointed deputy of his master followed by his visionary promotion to the rank of the spiritual "pole" of the universe. In a similar vein, he transforms himself into Ḫıżır, Muḥammed, and ʿAlī, thereby asserting his claim to be the supreme spiritual and temporal Muslim ruler of the age and the unifier of Islamdom. As Felek cogently demonstrates, although [self-]image was as important for early modern Muslims as it is for us today, we would hardly take seriously an image built on one's own dreams. This was certainly not how Murād III saw things. For the Sultan, dreams were a powerful and effective way to fashion his image for both his contemporaries and the generations to come.

Meenakshi Khanna's chapter, which concludes the "Sufi part" of the volume, addresses the legacy of Sayyid Ḥasan Rasūlnumā (d. 1692), an Indian Sufi whose principal claim to fame was his ability to maintain constant contact with the Prophet in his dreams and waking visions. No less importantly, he was capable of "showing" the Prophet to his disciples in their dreams—a gift that he had acquired by cultivating the Uwaysi style of mystical experience, namely one that dispenses with long apprenticeship under a living Sufi master by putting its practitioner in direct contact with the Prophet himself. In the context of seventeenth-century India, Sayyid Ḥasan's claims to be able to keep and put others (his disciples) in touch with the Prophet allowed him to compete—successfully it seems—with the traditional Sufi orders that derived their legitimacy and high social standing from their venerable spiritual genealogies and institutions built around them. As the Prophet's direct and unmediated interlocutor, Sayyid Ḥasan's authority was unimpeachable, for, according to the Prophet's often cited saying: "Whoever has seen me in a dream, has seen me in truth, for Satan cannot impersonate me in a dream."[25]

In summary, the reader is invited to enter the fascinating world of dreams and visions as experienced and described by Muslims of vastly diverse intellectual and social backgrounds living in different historical epochs. The contributors hope that their collective study will pave the way for future research on this important and as yet understudied subject.

Notes

1. Quoted in William Chittick, *The Sufi Path of Knowledge: Ibn al-'Arabi's Metaphysics of Imagination* (Albany: SUNY Press, 1989), 119; here and in the quotations that follow I omit the Arabic terms that appear in Chittick's translations.

2. Chittick, *The Sufi Path*, 120.

3. Ibid., 115–16; and idem, *The Self-Disclosure of God: Principles of Ibn al-'Arabī's Cosmology* (Albany: SUNY Press, 1998), 358–59.

4. Although this saying is commonly attributed to the Prophet in Sufi literature, it is not found in any of the standard *ḥadīth* collections; see Chittick, *The Sufi Path*, 396, n. 7.

5. Ibid., 231.

6. Marshall Hodgson, *The Venture of Islam: Conscience and History in a World Civilization* (Chicago: University of Chicago Press, 1974) 3 vols., vol. 2, 466.

7. Ibid.; Anthony Shafton, *Dream Reader: Contemporary Approaches to the Understanding of Dreams* (Albany: SUNY Press, 1995), 51–52; cf. David Shulman

and Guy Stroumsa (eds.), *Dream Cultures: Explorations in the Comparative Aspects of Dreaming* (Oxford: Oxford University Press, 1999), 12.

8. John Lamoreaux, *The Early Muslim Tradition of Dream Interpretation* (Albany: SUNY Press, 2002), 4.

9. See, for instance, Erik Ohlander's chapter in this volume.

10. Lamoreaux, *The Early Muslim*, 4.

11. See Ohlander's chapter in this volume.

12. Lamoreaux, *The Early Muslim*, 4.

13. Louise Marlow, "Introduction," Louise Marlow (ed.), *Dreaming Across Boundaries: The Interpretation of Dreams in Islamic Lands* (Cambridge, Mass. and London, England: Harvard University Press, 2008), 6–7.

14. Lamoreaux, *The Early Muslim*, 76.

15. Ibid.

16. Dror Ze'evi, *Producing Desire: Changing Sexual Discourse in the Ottoman Middle East, 1500–1900* (Berkeley: University of California Press, 2006), 102.

17. Shulman and Stroumsa (eds.), *Dream Cultures*, 6.

18. Ze'evi, *Producing Desire*, 106.

19. Ibid., 104.

20. Marlow, "Introduction," 2.

21. Schulman and Stroumsa (eds.), *Dream Cultures*, 3.

22. Such as the story of Joseph (Yūsuf) in *sūra* 12 that depicts this Biblical prophet as the model interpreter of dreams (see verses 36–55; cf. verses 4–5).

23. *The Dream and Human Societies* (Berkeley: University of California Press, 1966).

24. Marlow (ed.), *Dreaming*; and Lamoreaux, *The Early Muslim*; see also Chapter 4 in Ze'evi, *Producing Desire*.

25. Muslim b. al-Ḥajjāj, *Ṣaḥīḥ bi-sharḥ . . . al-Nawawī* (Beirut: Dār al-kutub al-ʿilmiyya, 1987), 18 vols., 15:22–23.

PART I

Dreams in Biographical, Historical, Theological, Poetical, and Oral Narratives, and on the Internet

CHAPTER 1

Dreaming the Truth in the *Sīra* of Ibn Hishām

Sarah Mirza

There are fifteen distinct dreams narrated in Ibn Hishām's (d. 213/828 or 218/833) redaction of the *sīra* work of Ibn Isḥāq (d. ca. 150/767), our earliest extant biography of the prophet Muḥammad.[1] These dreams usually are narratives given in the form of historical reports (*akhbār*) and placed within the accounts of major events of the Prophet's birth and career in both Mecca and Medina. Here they serve to increase dramatic tension and elaborate the central themes explored by the *Sīra*, including the favored nature of the Prophet's lineage, the miraculous protection of the Prophet, and the Muslim community as falling within the Abrahamic line. A few of these are dreams of the Prophet himself, but a larger number involve members of the Banū Muṭṭalib, the clan of the Prophet, and non-Muslims, including pre-Islamic figures, both men and women. Only a minority of the dreams involves prominent Companions of the Prophet. The *Sīra* is not interested in the act of dream interpretation or in the dreamers' biographies. Regardless of the dreamer's identity, all of the dreams are assumed to be prophetic by their hearers and acted on as such. Here, I explore examples from the *Sīra* of the dreams of Muslims, starting with the Prophet, and of non-Muslims, the second category including both male and female dreamers. These illustrate the distinct use of dreams in the early *sīra*, in which dreaming and dream-telling are communal experiences that serve to activate the community.

The terminology used to refer to dreams and visions in Ibn Isḥāq's *Sīra* corresponds directly with the customary usage in accounts of dreams drawn from Ancient Near Eastern (ANE) texts, as surveyed by Adolph Oppenheim in the introduction to his translation of an Assyrian Dream Book. Akkadian texts commonly use the term *munattu*, from the root n-y-m, and corresponding with Arabic *nāma*, which refer to "early morning," but occasionally also to "sleep" in the sense of "dream."[2] This is an example of the semantic relationship between "sleep" and "dream" in these texts. However, words for "dream" also are derived from roots dealing with visual experiences, such as ḥ-l-m, yielding "dream" in Hebrew, Ugaritic, Aramaic, and Arabic (in Ugaritic meaning "to see").[3] The expression used in Ibn Hishām's redaction of the *Sīra* for all fifteen instances of reported dreams and visions is invariably *raʾā ruʾyā* (he saw . . . a vision). Sometimes there is an additional mention of the dreamer going to bed or being in a state of sleep, although occasionally the experience is described specifically as a "visitation."[4]

In the *Sīra*, the dreams of the prophet Muḥammad occur as symbolic dreams that are immediately translated by the Prophet. According to the reports collected by Ibn Isḥāq,[5] prior to the Muslim engagement with the Quraysh at Uḥud in Year 3 of the Hijra, the Prophet related a dream to his followers that consisted of a series of images: a number of cows, a dent in his sword, and his hand thrust into a coat of mail. Only one image, the coat of mail, is interpreted by the Prophet, who considers it a reference to Medina. Thereafter, the Prophet seeks advice from his followers on whether they should stay in Medina or march out to meet the Quraysh. There is extensive discussion among the Companions, who eventually lean toward leaving the city, although some express discomfort with resisting the Prophet's suggestion to stay in Medina. The believers march out, and the dream and its interpretation are no longer an issue.[6]

A second example of how the Prophet's dreams are subsumed under the drama of the community deals with the battle of Muʾta against the Byzantines in Year 8. Prior to receiving any news of the battle, and with the community's concern growing over the fates of the battle leaders, the Prophet announces the successive martyrdoms of the standard-bearers ʿAbdallāh b. Zayd and Jaʿfar b. Abī Ṭālib, prominent men and early converts. The community's anxiety reaches a climax when the Prophet pauses dramatically before the name of the third-in-command, ʿAbdallāh b. Rawāḥa, a leader of the Medinan Khazrajite tribe. But the Prophet assures the Medinans that he too was martyred and concludes his announcement with a dream in which he saw three thrones of gold carrying the commanders to Paradise, with ʿAbdallāh b. Rawāḥa's throne ascending more slowly than the others because he had hesitated in throwing himself into battle.[7]

As Leah Kinberg has argued, *ḥadīth* (reports on the Prophet's saying and actions) on telling and not telling and on the fabrication of dream accounts are identical with such rules on the transmission of *ḥadīth* about the Prophet.[8] Both *ḥadīth* literature and the *Sīra* emphasize that telling a dream is as vital an experience as the dream itself and the event it foresees. The dreams in Ibn Isḥāq's *Sīra* function as vehicles for authoritative guidance, but only through being points for exploring the drama of the community. Those of the Prophet himself are immediately related to his followers and convey eagerly awaited information to them. This seems to reflect a practice of communal dream-telling as a form of decision making. Along with being related in public, the dreams also are acted on communally, rather than providing information merely for and about the individual dreamer.

Here it is useful to compare the functions of the dreams in Ibn Hishām's redaction of Ibn Isḥāq with the contents and presentation of *Ṣaḥīḥ al-Bukhārī*'s chapter on dream interpretation, the "Kitāb al-Taᶜbīr." Al-Bukhārī's chapter, consisting of sixty *ḥadīth*, has the largest number of *ḥadīth* on dreams in any of the canonical collections' chapters on dreams. The presentation of dreams in this chapter shows that the work is not interested in the chronology related to the dreams, but in models, both for dream interpretation and for Muslim behavior. For example, the Prophet narrates a dream in which a bowl of milk is given to him, the remainder of which he gives to ᶜUmar b. ᶜAbd al-Khaṭṭāb. When asked about its interpretation, the answer is given in one word, *al-ᶜilm* (knowledge).[9] This dream and its interpretation are found under the subsection on seeing milk in a dream, as well as under the subsection on dreaming about a bowl. In another *ḥadīth*, the Prophet sees ᶜUmar wearing a shirt dragging on the ground behind him, which he interprets simply as *al-dīn* (religion).[10] When the Companions relate their dreams to the Prophet, he often interprets them as reflecting their levels of righteousness or anticipated entry into Paradise.

Several of the dreams in both the *Ṣaḥīḥ* of al-Bukhārī and of Muslim concern the status of Abū Bakr and ᶜUmar,[11] whereas these Companions have a minor role in the dreams given by Ibn Isḥāq. In fact, there is very little overlap between the dreams reported in *Ṣaḥīḥ al-Bukhārī* and in the *Sīra* of Ibn Isḥāq. While al-Bukhārī gives two Prophetic *ḥadīth* related to Uḥud, one involving slaughtered cows and the other a broken sword, they are distinct transmissions and interpreted differently from the one in the *Sīra*.[12] In the single instance of the same dream being found in both of these works, the Prophet finds two gold bracelets on his arms that he is told to blow off, and interprets them to represent the defeat of the false prophets al-ᶜAnsī and Musaylima. Although the wording of the dream itself is almost identical in al-Bukhārī and Ibn Isḥāq, they are from entirely different sources, with no common links in their chains of transmitters (*isnāds*).[13]

The *Sīra* has a distinct lesser interest in the dreams of the Prophet himself. Focused on the chronological account of events of the community rather than the Prophet's acts of interpretation, the dreamers in Ibn Isḥāq's *Sīra* are specific, named individuals, unlike some *ḥadīth* in al-Bukhārī where a generic and unnamed "man" or "Bedouin" relates a dream to the Prophet. A significant characteristic of the dreams in the *Sīra* is their relationship with speech acts and audition. Communication within these dreams occurs with unnamed and unidentified individuals, and information is often passed on through conversation and repeated command and response patterns, comparable to the traditional account of the Prophet's first reception of revelation. Most dreams in Ibn Isḥāq's *Sīra* feature disembodied voices.

Thus a more fruitful comparison may be made with dream accounts in Ancient Near Eastern texts, the genres of which are lucidly summarized by Oppenheim. The best attested dream type in the surviving material from the ANE is of the "message dream." In this type, the intentions of a deity are revealed to kings and priests through a vision that always contains a message conveyed as either a command or warning in understandable terms without the need for interpretation. The message dream, which is a privilege to the leader of a social group, occurs under critical conditions, such as the brink of war. This type is commonly found recorded in royal inscriptions that compose a large portion of surviving Egyptian and Mesopotamian texts.[14] This theophany admits only a reaction of submissive consent on the part of the receptor and dreamer, and rarely encompasses dialogue.[15]

Mesopotamian (in Sumerian and Akkadian), Egyptian, Hittite, Biblical, and Greek texts all follow the format of dividing the account of the message dream into two distinct sections. At first, the setting of the dream is described, which includes information on the dreamer, time, location, and noteworthy circumstances. This is followed by the content of the dream, embedded in the descriptive setting that serves as a frame. Following the content of the dream, the account will return to the frame, providing a conclusion that conveys the reaction of the dreamer and/or the actual fulfillment of the prediction or promise.[16] It is common for the first part of the frame to state that the dreamer has gone to bed and is deeply asleep.[17] The same frame system is applied in Ibn Hishām's redaction of the *Sīra*. At the level of verbal expressions it takes the following form: Ibn Isḥāq provides his narrative introduction to the episode in the third person, usually with an *isnād* provided. He introduces the dreamer and the fact that he or she saw some vision using the terminology *raʾā ruʾyā*. Ibn Isḥāq's phrasing in this introductory portion exactly repeats the phrasing used by the quoted report, the *khabar,* that follows, which almost invariably includes the dreamer's words describing the experience in the first person. The *khabar* first provides a description of the circumstances, following Oppenheim's characterization of the first part of the frame, then the content of the dream, usually occurring in the form of quoted speech of the dreamer him or herself, using the phrase *raʾaytu ruʾyā* (I saw . . . a vision). The conclusion to the episode is then given in the remainder of the *khabar*. In the surviving ANE texts of the other dream types, symbolic dreams are recorded only as followed by their (authoritative) interpretation, whereas dreams without interpretation fall under the category of "evil dreams."[18] In Ibn Isḥāq's *Sīra,* each of the dreams experienced by individuals other than the Prophet falls under the category of the message dream.

The Prophet is thus not the only one capable of conveying information to his peers as received through the medium of dreams. The institution of a vocal call to prayer, the *adhān,* is placed within Ibn Isḥāq's discussion of the establishment of the major religious tenets in Medina, which include prayer, alms, fasting, and legal punishments. The Prophet is facing a dilemma. He first considers the use of a horn or trumpet, associated with the Jews, and rejects this idea, settling on using a wooden clapper to call the believers to prayer. At this point ʿAbdallāh b. Zayd comes to Prophet in order to narrate a dream, saying, "Indeed an apparition appeared to me in sleep during this night." In this dream ʿAbdallāh was visited by a "man in two green garments," and through a question and answer method in which ʿAbdallāh first asks to buy the clapper carried by the man, he is instructed on a "better way" as a call to prayer. The item he receives is then recited words, the entire *adhān,* presented line by line including the repetitions. The Prophet calls this a true vision, *ruʾyā ḥaqqin*. The *adhān* is immediately implemented, and ʿUmar b. ʿAbd al-Khaṭṭāb hears it from his house. Suddenly, ʿUmar arrives before the Prophet, "dragging his cloak on the ground," saying: "O Prophet of God . . . indeed I have seen similar to what he has seen." The Prophet responds, "Then to God be praise for this." Oppenheim notes the occurrence in dream accounts from the late classical world and in the New Testament of two dreamers who confirm one another's visions through simultaneous dreaming.[19] In his redaction of Ibn Isḥāq, Ibn Hishām gives an additional report that paraphrases ʿUmar's vision with no mention of ʿAbdallāh b. Zayd. This tradition has ʿUmar himself taking the solution to the Prophet, who in turn refers to the vision as divine inspiration (*waḥy*).[20] The traditions on the *adhān* portray the community as presented with a situation that is worked out communally through dreaming.

As the story of the *adhān* illustrates, correct vision through message dreams is not limited to the Prophet. Indeed, as exemplified earlier, the Prophet's visions as narrated in the *Sīra* are of a different type, requiring authoritative interpretation, more comfortably fitting under the genre of the symbolic dream as given by Oppenheim. Other dreams in Ibn Isḥāq show that true dreaming covers non-Muslims as well. Dream-telling is featured in the very first narrative arc of the *Sīra*, which explores the lineage of the Prophet and the development of the holy sites of Mecca. Ibn Isḥāq introduces this report with the phrase, "Then he saw a vision (*fa-raʾā ruʾyā*)." Rabīʿa b. Naṣr, the polytheist king of the Ḥimyarites, seeks interpreters for a troubling dream in which he has seen a fire coming over the sea and devouring the land. Quoted directly in the report, he states: "I saw a vision which frightened me *(innī qad raʾaytu ruʾyā hālatnī)*." The king insists that a true interpreter will not need to hear the dream from him but will already be aware of the vision. In an extensive narrative given in poetry, two dream interpreters are able to respond to him, and their interpretations concur that the Ethiopians will conquer his land, but will soon be defeated by a true prophet.[21]

The most lengthy presentation of dream experiences in the *Sīra*, however, concerns the discovery of the well of Zamzam by the Prophet's grandfather, ʿAbd al-Muṭṭalib. This experience of an "incubation dream," a type of message dream achieved through sleeping in a sacred locality, is discussed in two different places in the text. The second account first repeats Ibn Isḥāq's introductory statement: "Indeed while ʿAbd al-Muṭṭalib was asleep in the enclosure he was approached and demanded to dig Zamzam."[22] Ibn Isḥāq continues by describing three distinct dreams in which ʿAbd al-Muṭṭalib is verbally commanded a total of four times to dig in a certain site, attempts to obey these commands, and finally succeeds in finding Zamzam. Then follows a report containing the direct speech of the dreamer. ʿAbd al-Muṭṭalib states: "Indeed I was sleeping in the enclosure when a visitor approached me. . . . Then I returned to my bed and slept in it then he came to me . . . (*innī la-nāʾimun fī l-ḥijr idhā atānī ātin. . . . rajaʿtu ilā maḍjaʿī fa-nimtu fīhī fa-jāʾanī . . .*)." This last statement about returning to bed and sleeping in it when the visitor arrives and speaks is repeated exactly each time ʿAbd al-Muṭṭalib relates his dream.[23]

Oppenheim points out that auditory message dreams are common in the Hittite sources in the form of dedication dreams, and that these correspond with the dreams of poets and prophets receiving inspiration and dictation (although such claims to inspiration are rare in ANE texts). These experiences seem to have been auditory only, in which unidentified persons or named individuals require of the dreamer a specific vow to the deity.[24] In a much shorter report than ʿAbd al-Muṭṭalib's, this time concerning a pre-Islamic female figure, the Prophet's mother Āmina bt. Wahb speaks of a dream she had while pregnant, featuring a voice informing her of the name of her son.[25] Message dreams, Oppenheim notes, are commonly given only to men in ANE texts.[26] Although the category of message dream may not be obviously applicable to ʿĀtika's symbolic and mantic dream discussed later, Āmina's "annunciation" dream falls directly under this category. The terminology here concerns not sleeping and visionary experience but expresses that "she was visited" and grammatically emphasizes the passive stance of the receptor. Ibn Hishām's text states: "Indeed she was approached while she was carrying the Prophet of God, God's peace and blessings be upon him, and it was said to her."

Comparable with ʿAbd al-Muṭṭalib's series of informative dreams, another symmetrical structure is created by the dream warnings that predict the Battle of Badr in Year 2 from the vanquished side of the Quraysh. The Prophet's own relatives among the Quraysh, who were non-Muslims at the time, convey these warnings. In one of the lengthiest and most cohesive narrative accounts in the *Sīra*, Ibn Isḥāq relates the dream of another non-Muslim female, ʿĀtika bt. ʿAbd al-Muṭṭalib, the Prophet's paternal aunt. According to most medieval biographers, including Ibn Isḥāq, ʿĀtika did not convert to Islam.[27] "ʿĀtika saw a vision that frightened her *(wa-qad raʾat ʿĀtika . . . ruʾyā afzaʿathā)*." She dreams of a herald on camelback three nights before the news of the Muslims awaiting the Quraysh caravan reaches Mecca. The herald appears in the valley of Mecca and cries out a warning specifying a disaster to occur in three days. He repeats this warning from atop the Kaʿba and then a nearby mountain, whereupon he loosens a rock that shatters and falls on every dwelling in Mecca. ʿĀtika relates the dream in confidence to her brother al-ʿAbbās, introducing her experience, "By God, I saw this night a vision that frightened me." Al-ʿAbbās tells the dream to a friend, who in turn tells his father, and from there the story spreads and is openly discussed among the Quraysh. ʿĀtika's experience is consistently referred to throughout the report as a *ruʾyā*. Abū Jahl, an infamous antagonist of the Prophet, confronts al-ʿAbbās with the taunt, "O Banū ʿAbd al-Muṭṭalib, since when have you had a prophetess (*nabiyya*) among you?"[28] and goes on to state that if the vision fails to come true, the family will be branded as the worst of liars. In three days time, the herald appears, and the narrative delves into the details of the Quraysh preparation to meet the Muslims.[29] Further confirmation of a future disaster comes at the Quraysh camp at Juḥfa, when Juhaym b. al-Ṣalt b. Makhrama b. al-Muṭṭalib, another relative of the Prophet (who converted after the conquest of Mecca in Year 8 but is at the time a non-Muslim), sees (*naẓara ilā*) a vision, just as "what passes during sleep," while in a state "between waking and sleeping," of a herald on camelback who announces, by name, all of the Quraysh who will be killed at Badr. "Juhaym b. al-Ṣalt b. Makhrama b. al-Muṭṭalib b. ʿAbd Manāf saw a vision, and he said: indeed I saw as what passes during sleep while I was between waking and sleeping. I perceived a man." The man in his vision then stabs his camel and sets it loose in the camp, spattering every tent with blood. Abū Jahl again responds, "Here's another prophet (*nabī*) from Banū al-Muṭṭalib!"[30] Oppenheim notes that in ANE texts a symbolic dream may be repeated for the purpose of clarity, done by replacing one symbol without disturbing the trend of the initial dream.[31] This device can be seen clearly in ʿAbd al-Muṭṭalib's successive dreams of locating and digging Zamzam, but also can be seen as occurring across dreamers and patterning the dreams of ʿĀtika and Juhaym.

ʿĀtika's and Juhaym's dreams thus are clearly parallel, featuring a spoken warning by a herald on camelback, and a symbolic destruction which touches every dwelling. Their use to frame the account of the Battle of Badr also reflects the interest of the *Sīra* in the theme of the Prophet's lineage, although the dreamers are not figures that are central to the events foretold. That the warnings are treated with disbelief raises suspense and pushes the narrative forward into the prophesied event. As Abū Jahl's response makes clear, these visions are resisted by the Quraysh because of the family relationship between the dreamers and the prophet Muḥammad. ʿĀtika and Juhaym are not soothsayers known to their people, but unwitting receptors of a type of inspiration that the Quraysh immediately identify with the figure of the Prophet.

There is thus no differentiation in the social function and retelling of Muslim and non-Muslim dreams in the *Sīra*. In both communities, dream narratives serve as points of discussion that lead into action. They galvanize their listeners even if, or perhaps especially if, they are treated with skepticism, as for example when Abū Jahl pokes fun at the Banū Muṭṭalib being known for producing a prophet of God. The type and veracity of the dreams are also not determined by gender, as pre-Islamic female figures and non-Muslim women have visions as true as those of the Anṣār and Muhājirūn men of Medina; although it should be noted that the female dreamers in Ibn Isḥāq are blood relatives of the Prophet. The Prophet's dreams are also no exception to the practice of retelling dreams to an audience as an entry point into decision making, which may leave the symbolic interpretation of the dream behind, as seen in the Prophet's dream prior to Uḥud. The imageries and meanings are less important than the communal activity generated by them.

The trend of the *Sīra's* dream-accounts is thus not a development of the division between true and false, but an elaboration of the orientation of the dreamer. In each of these accounts, the unwittingness of the receptor is key, along with the sociopolitical placement of the dreamer as significant to his or her subsequent communication to the community concerning newly received divine information on near future events. The *Sīra's* lack of concern over authenticating dream accounts and transmission is manifest; ascertaining truth is less a part of its thematic structure than distinguishing between types of inspiration. The *Sīra* thus betrays a distinct attitude toward the concept of *waḥy*, a distinction that can begin to be explained by the early nature of the text and its proximity to pre-Islamic motifs, including oracles and the dreams of ANE figures. Furthermore, Ibn Isḥāq's *Sīra* text wants to forge a relation between the original *waḥy* received by the Prophet and the dreams of community actors and the Prophet's kinspeople, to the point of recreating that trauma and the anxious state of the dreamer. Toufic Fahd points out that the types of inspiration for the prophet, the diviner, and the poet differ only by their intermediaries: the angel for the prophet, the jinn for the *kāhin* (diviner), and the *shayṭān* (satan) for the poet.[32] The verb *waḥā* in the Qurʾān is used for demons (*shayāṭīn*) as well as angels.[33] The comparison between the sources of inspiration for the prophet and oracle is most strikingly expressed through an oracle itself, present in Ibn Isḥāq's text, by which a seer, prior to the Prophet's first revelation, predicts the "confusion of the jinn and their religion."[34] A number of both pre-Islamic and Islamic-era oracles are provided in Ibn Isḥāq/Ibn Hishām, correctly predicting a similar range of occurrences as those covered by the visions discussed in this article. These include Muḥammad's prophethood, his exit from Mecca (the Hijra), the battles of Badr and Uḥud, and the Muslim advance to Muʾta.[35] Significantly, although all are aural, expressed as oracular utterances, none of these are described as having been received through dreams.

The dreams in Ibn Isḥāq's *Sīra* overlap with the classic features of *sīra* narrative, including miracles, the merits of the Prophet and Companions, and establishing a Muslim identity through polemic with Jews and Christians. Each dream and vision recounted in the *Sīra* is a significant station in the narrative comparable to the citation of poetry or the listing of fighters, and serves to emphasize certain themes and events through a shift to a distinct mode.[36] The dreams of ʿĀtika bt. ʿAbd al-Muṭṭalib and Juhaym b. al-Ṣalt have the particular dramatic effect of members of the Prophet's family in the non-Muslim camp foreseeing, and warning of, the victory of the opposing side. These dreams, however, significantly reflect on the Qurʾānic theme of the relationship between listening and inspiration, which is given a pre-Islamic and an Islamic definition in the Qurʾān. For example, in the last few verses of *Sūrat al-Shuʿarāʾ*, "The Poets," the Qurʾān says: "Shall I tell you on whom the Satans come down? / They come down on every guilty imposter. / They give ear, but most of them are liars. / And the poets—the perverse follow them . . ." (26: 221–224).[37] Similarly, in *Sūrat al-Ḥāqqa* the Qurʾān insists, "It is the speech of a noble Messenger. / It is not the speech of a poet (little do you believe) / nor the speech of a soothsayer (little do you remember)" (69: 40–42).[38] Toufic Fahd points out that among the many responsibilities of the Arab *kāhin*, including his roles as performer of sacrifices and guardian of the sanctuary, the duties of augur and seer predominate in nomadic society, whether the terminology applied is *kāhin* or the lower-ranking *ʿarrāf*. The *ʿarrāf* and female *ʿarrāfa* are inspired by a familiar spirit (*tābiʿ* or *tābiʿa*) or an "inspirer for particular occasions" (*raʾiyy* or *riʾiyy*). Thus, the *ʿarrāf* is described as *matbūʿ* ("flanked by a demon"), and his activity sometimes overlaps with sorcery and conjuring.[39]

The dreamers in Ibn Isḥāq's *Sīra* are not demonically inspired, but receive verbal revelations while sleeping or on the verge of sleeping, just as the Prophet himself describes his first encounter with God's word in the report from Ibn Isḥāq through Ibn Hishām, given here with the additional material found in al-Ṭabarī's recension (indicated by: [T.]), which is worth quoting in its entirety.[40] The report is from Wahb b. Kaysān who received it from ʿUbayd b. ʿUmayr b. Qatāda, concerning Muḥammad's custom of undertaking a month of secluded devotion and charity. In Ramaḍān,

> [w]hen it was the night on which God honoured him with his mission and showed mercy on His servants thereby, Gabriel brought him the command of God. "He came to me," said the apostle of God, "while I was asleep, with a

> coverlet of brocade whereon was some writing,[41] and said, "Read!"

This command is repeated twice, and the Prophet continues the narration:

> So I read it, and he departed from me. And I awoke from my sleep, and it was as though these words were written on my heart (T. [1150] Now none of God's creatures was more hateful to me than an (ecstatic) poet or a man possessed: I could not even look at them. I thought, Woe is me poet or possessed—Never shall Quraysh say this of me! I will go to the top of the mountain and throw myself down that I may kill myself and gain rest. So I went forth to do so and then) when I was midway on the mountain, I heard a voice from heaven saying, "O Muḥammad! Thou art the apostle of God and I am Gabriel." I raised my head towards heaven to see (who was speaking), and lo, Gabriel in the form of a man with his feet astride the horizon, saying, "O Muḥammad! Thou art the apostle of God and I am Gabriel." I stood gazing at him, (T. [1150] and that turned me from my purpose) moving neither forward nor backward; then I began to turn my face away from him, but towards whatever region of the sky I looked, I saw him as before.[42]

In ANE reports of such experiences, Oppenheim notes the "towering size" of the messenger, whether the apparition is of a deity or its substitute. In the Sumerian *Dream of Gudea*, the apparition reaches from heaven to earth: "In the dream, the first man—like the heaven was his surpassing (size) / like the earth was his surpassing (size)."[43] Sometimes, besides size, beauty is also the characteristic feature of the divine messenger.[44] Incubation dreams commonly evince what Oppenheim calls a "sudden shift in reality levels" and the shock of meeting the dream apparition, and an emphasis on the passive attitude of the dreamer. In the Old Testament, the phraseology is: "God came to NN in a dream by night."[45] In the Prophet's first revelation, it is noteworthy that the apparition/messenger is not visually described until the sleeper/dreamer awakens. Additional material in al-Ṭabarī's redaction of Ibn Isḥāq's material contains the telling comparison with the ecstatic/inspired poet or possessed individual reflected on by the Prophet himself, immediately following his awakening.

Conclusion

In Ibn Hishām's redaction of Ibn Isḥāq's *Sīra,* the narrative use of dream accounts reveals a thematic concern with distinguishing between types of inspiration, making use of patterns and terminology that directly correspond with the presentation of dream accounts in ANE texts. Dreams should thus be included with, rather than collapsed into, other stock components of early *sīra* narrative along with poetry, lists of individuals involved in key events, and the interpretation of Qurʾānic verses. As demonstrated in their use in the earliest complete *sīra* work, dream accounts serve as narrative units that were clearly integral to the themes of concern to the early transmission of traditions surrounding major events of the emerging Muslim community.

Appendix: Dreams and Visions in Ibn Hishām's *Sīra* in order of presentation[46]

1. Rabīʿa b. Naṣr, polytheist king of the Yemen, dreams of a fire coming from over the sea to devour his land. (W. 10–12)

2. Tibān Asʿad Abū Karīb, predecessor of Rabīʿa b. Naṣr, who converts to Judaism, passes through Mecca and dreams that he should cover the Kaʿba with palm branches, then that it should be with Yemeni cloth, and a third time that it should be with fine Yemeni striped cloth. "He was shown while in sleep (*uriya fī l-manām*) . . . then he was shown that . . . then he was shown that . . . ." (W. 15)

3. ʿAbd al-Muṭṭalib, the Prophet's grandfather, is ordered to dig Zamzam (W. 71), given four successive dream commands identifying the location. (W. 91–94)

4. Āmina bint Wahb hears a voice while pregnant and is commanded to name her son Muḥammad. (W. 102)

5. The Prophet's first revelation while in the cave on Ḥirāʾ occurs while he is asleep ("*wa anā nāʾim*") (W. 152–53; T. 1150)

6. Ṭufayl b. ʿAmr, a poet who converts to Islam, while on an expedition to Yamāma correctly interprets a dream he had as predicting his death. He dreams of his head shaven, a bird coming out of his mouth, a woman taking him into her womb, and his son seeking him in vain. "*fa-raʾā ruyʾā . . . innī qad raʾaytu ruʾyā.*" (W. 254–55)

7. The *isrāʾ* (night journey) and *miʿrāj* (ascent to heaven). These are not described in the customary terms for a sleeping vision, but their relation to revelation received while sleeping is discussed by commentators cited by the *Sīra*. The Qurʾān's mention of a *ruʾyā* (Qurʾān 17: 60) that tests the faith is said to refer to these events, and

is compared with the reference to the *ruʾyā* of Abraham to sacrifice his son (Qurʾān 37: 102, 105). (W. 263–71)

8. ʿAbdallāh b. Zayd b. Thaʿlaba b. ʿAbd Rabbihi, client of the Banū al-Ḥārith of Medina, dreams of "a man in two green garments" passing him with a clapper he asks to buy, and is given something better as a call to prayer, the *adhān*. ʿUmar has a dream corroborating this. (W. 347–48)

9. ʿĀtika bint ʿAbd al-Muṭṭalib, the Prophet's paternal aunt, dreams of a herald on camelback warning the Meccans of a disaster to occur in three days' time. (W. 428–29)

10. Juhaym b. al-Ṣalt b. Makhrama b. al-Muṭṭalib dreams, while in a state between sleeping and waking, of a herald on camelback announcing by name all the Qurayshis slain at Badr. (W. 437–38)

11. The Prophet, taking a light sleep on his bed prior to the engagement at Badr, sees Gabriel holding the rein of a horse. Upon waking he announces God's help to Abū Bakr, referring to the appearance of Gabriel in direct terms: "This is Gabriel." (W. 444)

12. The Prophet dreams of cows, a dent in sword, and his hand in a strong coat of mail prior to Uḥud. An introductory formula from Ibn Isḥāq is not given. Instead, after establishing the context of the Prophet listening to the Muslims discussing the upcoming battle, the report enters into direct speech of the Prophet: "He said, indeed I saw something good, by God. I saw a cow and I saw . . . and I saw . . . So I interpreted it (*fa-awwaltuha*) as Medina." (W. 557–58)

13. Ibn Isḥāq's commentary on the affair at Ḥudaybiya includes the revelation of *Sūra* 48 immediately after the event and as referring to Ḥudaybiya. Verse 28, referring to God fulfilling a vision (*ruʾyā*) of the Prophet about entering the sanctuary is explained as a dream the Prophet had had. (W. 751)

14. Prior to receiving news of the Battle of Muʾta, the Prophet dreams that the three standard-bearers, Zayd b. Ḥāritha, Jaʿfar b. Abī Ṭālib, and ʿAbdallāh b. Rawāḥa, are carried up to Paradise on beds of gold. The martyrdom of the three standard-bearers is introduced by the Prophet matter of factly, as received information, "regarding what has reached me." *Raʾā* is used for the first time in this report in order to introduce the details of the actual vision: "Indeed they were raised up toward me in Paradise, as something that the sleeper sees (*fī-mā yarā l-nāʾimun*), upon beds of gold and then I saw that the bed of ʿAbdallāh b. Rawāḥa was slower than the two beds of his two companions." (W. 795–96; T. 1617, extra vision)

15. The Prophet dreams of two gold bracelets on his arms that he blows away, interpreting them as representing the "liars" al-ʿAnsī and Musaylima. There is no introductory formula by Ibn Isḥāq. The

occasion is a *khuṭba* (sermon) given from the pulpit, during which the Prophet is quoted as saying: "Indeed I saw on the Night of Power but then was made to forget. I saw . . . so I interpreted them as . . . (*fa-awwaltuhuma*)." (W. 964)

Notes

1. These are provided in an appendix to this paper.

2. A. Leo Oppenheim, "The Interpretation of Dreams in the Ancient Near East. With a Translation of an Assyrian Dream-Book," *Transactions of the American Philosophical Society, New Series* vol. 46, no. 3 (1956): 179–373; 225.

3. Ibid., 226.

4. It is interesting to compare the terms for *dream* in the Qurʾān, summarized by T. Fahd and H. Daiber in the *Encyclopedia of Islam*. *Ḥulm* rarely is used "in a pejorative sense with the meaning of dream," *aḥlām* is used twice (Qurʾān 12: 44 and 21: 5), preceded by *aḍghāth*, meaning "incoherent and confused dreams," and once unqualified (Qurʾān 12: 44) "*taʾwīl al-aḥlām*," "the interpretation of dreams." Verbal and nominal forms derived from r-ʾ-y, in contrast, are used for all types of vision, real, intellectual or metaphorical (e.g., *raʾā* and *ruʾyā* for the dream of Joseph [12:4–5], of his fellow prisoners [12: 36], and of Pharaoh [12: 43]; the vehicle for the command to Abraham to sacrifice his son [37: 102, 105]; fulfillment of the dream/desire of Muḥammad to return to Mecca [48:27]; the *isrāʾ* and *miʿrāj* [17: 60]). The Qurʾān uses *manām* (38: 102), referenced as a divine sign (30:23), a summoning to God compared with death (39: 42), and an instrument of divine guidance for the Prophet and believers (8: 43–44). Toufic Fahd and Hans Daiber, "Ruʾyā," *Encyclopaedia of Islam*, Second Edition. Edited by: P. Bearman; Th. Bianquis; C.E. Bosworth; E. van Donzel; and W.P. Heinrichs. Brill, 2009. Brill Online. http://www.brillonline.nl.

5. From a combined *isnād* including traditions from al-Zuhrī, Ibn Ḥibbān, Ibn Qatāda, and al-Ḥusayn b. ʿAbd al-Raḥmān b. ʿAmr b. Saʿd b. Muʿādh.

6. Ferdinand Wüstenfeld, *Das leben Muhammed's nach Muhammed ibn Ishâk bearbeitet von Abd el-Malik ibn Hischâm* 2 vols. in 3 (Göttingen: Dieterichs, 1858–60), 557–58.

7. Ibid., 795–96.

8. Leah Kinberg, "Literal Dreams and Prophetic 'Hadīṯs' in classical Islam—a comparison of two ways of legitimation," *Der Islam* 70 (1993): 290–91.

9. Muḥammad b. Ismāʿīl al-Bukhārī, *Recueil des traditions Mahometanes par abou Abdallah Mohammed ibn Ismail el-Bokhari*, ed. Ludolf Krehl and Th. W. Juynbol. Vol. IV (Leiden: E. J. Brill, 1908), 353. "Kitāb al-Taʿbīr," *bāb* 15 and 16.

10. Ibid., 353–54, "Kitāb al-Taʿbīr," *bāb*s 17 and 18.

11. Ibid., 356–57, "Kitāb al-Taʿbīr," *bāb* 28.

12. From Muḥammad b. al-ʿAlāʾ—Abū Usāma—Burayd—his grandfather Abū Burayda—Abū Mūsā. The Prophet sees a dream in which he emigrates to a land of date-palms and sees cows slaughtered there. He interprets the first image as the good in coming to Yathrib, and the second as the martyrs of Uḥud (Ibid., 360, "Kitāb al-Taʿbīr," *bāb* 39). In another with the same *isnād* as given earlier, the Prophet waves a sword that breaks in the middle, but becomes whole again when he waves it a second time. He interprets this as the losses at Uḥud and the conquest of Mecca (Ibid., 361, "Kitāb al-Taʿbīr," *bāb* 44).

13. Al-Bukhārī has two transmissions. One from Saʿīd b. Muḥammad Abū ʿAbdallāh al-Jurmī—Yaʿqūb b. Ibrāhīm—his father—Ṣāliḥ Ibn ʿUbayda b. Nashīṭ—ʿUbaydallāh b. ʿAbdallāh—Ibn ʿAbbās (Al-Bukhārī, 360, "Kitāb al-Taʿbīr" *bāb* 38); the other from Isḥāq b. Ibrahīm al-Hanẓalī—ʿAbd al-Razzāq—Maʿmar from Ḥammām b. Munabbih—Abū Hurayra (Al-Bukhārī 360–61, "Kitāb al-Taʿbīr," *bāb* 40). Ibn Isḥāq has Yazīd b. ʿAbdallāh b. Qusayṭ—ʿAṭā b. Yaṣār or his brother Sulaymān—Abū Saʿīd al-Khudrī (Wüstenfeld, 964)

14. Oppenheim, 185.

15. An exception here, given by Oppenheim, is Solomon's incubation dream 1 Kgs 3:5 ff.

16. Ibid., 186–87.

17. Ibid., 187.

18. Ibid., 206.

19. Ibid., 209.

20. Wüstenfeld, 347–48.

21. Ibid., 10–12.

22. Ibid., 91.

23. Ibid., 91–94.

24. Oppenheim, 193.

25. Wüstenfeld, 102.

26. Oppenheim, 190.

27. Aḥmad b. ʿAlī Ibn Ḥajar al-ʿAsqalānī, *al-Iṣāba fī Tamyīz al-Ṣaḥāba* (Cairo: al-Maktaba al-Tijāriyya al-Kubrā, 1939), IV: 347.

28. A. Guillaume's translation, in A. Guillaume, *The Life of Muhammad: A Translation of Ibn Ishaq's Sirat Rasul Allah* (Karachi: Oxford UP, 2006), 290.

29. Wüstenfeld, 428–29.

30. Ibid., 437–38; Guillaume, 296.

31. Oppenheim, 208.

32. Fahd, *Divination,* 73.

33. Ibid., 78. cf. Qurʾān 6:121 (Arberry's translation: "And eat not of that over which God's Name has not been mentioned; it is ungodliness. The Satans inspire their friends to dispute with you; if you obey them, you are idolators").

34. Wüstenfeld, 133.

35. Fahd, *Divination,* 81–90; 100.

36. "Story-tellers often interspersed their maghāzī narratives with poetry. This has a function similar to that of speeches; it underlines a point

or emphasizes a dramatic moment by changing to another mode." W. Raven, "Sīra," *Encyclopedia of Islam,* Second Edition. Edited by: P. Bearman; Th. Bianquis; C.E. Bosworth; E. van Donzel; and W.P. Heinrichs. Brill, 2009. Brill Online. http://www.brillonline.nl.

37. A. J. Arberry, *The Koran Interpreted* (New York: Simon and Schuster, 1955) II: 75.

38. Ibid., II: 298. See also Qurʾān 81: 19–25; 21: 5.

39. Toufic Fahd, "Kāhin," *Encyclopedia of Islam,* Second Edition. Brill Online. http://www.brillonline.nl.

40. Guillaume's translation including, in parentheses, the extra material provided by al-Ṭabarī's (T) redaction of Ibn Isḥāq with references in square brackets to the page numbers in the edition by M. J. de Goeje (Leiden: E. J. Brill, 1879–1901).

41. The motif of the revelation of divine will and intentions in writing can be seen for example in Dan 5: 5–30 (the writing on the wall addressed to King Belshazzar that needs to be interpreted by Daniel). Oppenheim, 202.

42. Guillaume, 105–106.

43. Oppenheim, 245.

44. Ibid., 189.

45. E.g., Gen 20:3ff, 31:24, 1 Kgs 3:4 ff, 9:2. Oppenheim, 188.

46. Page references (W) are to the commonly referenced edition by F. Wüstenfeld of the Arabic text of Ibn Hishām (Gottingen: Dieterich, 1858–1860). (T) refers to additional material in al-Ṭabarī's redaction of Ibn Isḥāq's material, in the edition by M. J. de Goeje (Leiden: E. J. Brill, 1879–1901).

CHAPTER 2

Dreaming Ḥanbalites

Dream-Tales in Prosopographical Dictionaries

Maxim Romanov

In Islam, like in many religious traditions, dreams are part and parcel of spiritual life. For centuries, Muslims have taken their dreams seriously, especially those Muslims who belonged to different mystical trends that found their place under the dome of Islam.[1] Here, however, I address the dreams of the Ḥanbalites, a group that for decades has been almost unanimously treated by many students of Islam as the very opposite of Sufism. Nevertheless, despite their differences, the two groups share a fascination with dreams and make extensive use of them in their respective narratives. In fact, some local hagiographies show that a number of rural Ḥanbalī *shaykh*s were treated by their followers as *awliyāʾ* and miracle workers.[2] Moreover, even normative prosopographical Ḥanbalī sources are not devoid of what a Saudi editor of *Ṭabaqāt al-Ḥanābila* called *al-khurāfāt al-ṣūfiyya,* "Sufi superstitions."[3] Examples from both hagiographic and normative sources indicate that it is the very nature of relationship between revered *shaykh*s and their popular following that eventually casts the former as saint guardians of their communities. In other words, being a leader of a popular community, a *shaykh* of any persuasion is very likely to become a local saint. Dreams seem to be one of the mechanisms of the communal process of sanctification. This might be a reason why not all of the dreams passed the above mentioned editor's test of "orthodoxy,"[4] even though they are quite different from those of the Sufis, the alleged archenemies of the Ḥanbalites.

In what follows I address dreams found in the two major prosopographical dictionaries of the Ḥanbalī *madhhab* that cover roughly five centuries and include slightly more than twelve hundred biographies: *Ṭabaqāt al-Ḥanābila* ("Generations of Ḥanbalīs") of *qāḍī* Ibn Abī Yaʿlā (d. 527/1133) and *Dhayl ʿalā Ṭabaqāt al-Ḥanābila* ("Supplement to Generations of Ḥanbalīs") of Ibn Rajab (d. 795/1392).[5] By prosopographical dictionaries, I mean biographical dictionaries in which each individual is presented as part of a particular group.[6] As a scholar of Islamic historiography put it, "prosopographies make individuals members."[7] Quite often, individuals in such sources possess no independent importance. The two sources in question contain a number of "biographies" with no biographical information whatsoever and in most cases these biographies are omitted from biographical dictionaries that are not confined to a particular factional group. One of the examples directly related to the topic of this chapter is the "biography" of Sulaymān b. ʿAbd Allāh al-Sijzī, one of Ibn Ḥanbal's companions.[8] His "biography" consists entirely of a story of Ibn Ḥanbal's interaction with the caliph al-Muʿtaṣim during the *miḥna,* the infamous "inquisition."[9] The significance of al-Sijzī—who most likely was a commoner[10]—lies in his role as transmitter of information about Ibn Ḥanbal.

Both prosopographical dictionaries contain 184 dream narratives with references to dreams and waking visions. Yet some of the dream-tales are repeated and occasionally may involve more than one dream. Overall, dream-tales and references to dreams are found in 95 of 1,259 biographies. Although not comprehensive, my analysis of these narratives has yielded the following results.

First, I address the role of a protagonist—and by protagonist here I mean a person about whom a biographical account is written—in a dream, which varies as follows: (a) he himself had a dream (37 dreams: ~20%); (b) he was seen, mentioned, or alluded to in a dream (127 dreams: ~70%); (c) he transmitted a dream (18 dreams: ~10%). Again, because of the complexity of many dream-tales, these numbers are approximate. Yet, the absolute majority of dreams—127 of 184—are "passive" dreams (i.e., those dreams in which protagonists are dreamt about). Ninety-eight dreams (53%) were seen after the death of the protagonists. What is interesting is that in 62 of 127 dreams, the dreamers are nameless. Most likely, this points to the fact that these dreamers were laity and not the part of the scholarly community. In some cases, especially for the first generation of the Ḥanbalites, even many named dreamers are laymen.[11]

In biographical accounts, dreams are a part of an auxiliary section, which usually is found after main biographical blocks that include name, genealogy, teachers, achievements, students, books, dicta, and death. A comment by Ibn Abī Yaᶜlā suggests that dreams, especially "passive" ones, are one of the "excellent qualities" (*faḍāʾil*).[12] That most dreams are not just a random entertaining element of biographies is supported by the fact that the number of dreams tends to grow together with the importance of a protagonist either for the history of Ḥanbalism in general, or for a particular author. In this respect, Ibn Abī Yaᶜlā favored his father, *qāḍī* Abū Yaᶜlā (d. 458/1066f),[13] whose dream section includes six tales (largest after Ibn Ḥanbal); none of the other people in his generation has dream-tales. Ibn Rajab, on the other hand, seems to have favored two particular families—Banū Qudāma of Damascus[14] and Banū Taymiyya of Ḥarrān. Moreover, there are several people who might have been included in these dictionaries solely because they transmitted certain dream-tales.[15]

Among 95 biographies with dream-related passages there are only 17 with three or more dreams, totaling 96 passages altogether. Most of these 17 *shaykh*s (the elders of the Ḥanbalī School) are famous Ḥanbalites. In chronological order they are: *imām* Ibn Ḥanbal (d. 241/855), Abū Bakr al-Marwadhī (d. 275/888f), ᶜAlī b. al-Muwaffaq (d. 265/878f), Maᶜrūf al-Karkhī (d. 200/815f), ᶜAbd al-ᶜAzīz b. Jaᶜfar, known as Ghulām al-Khallāl (d. 363/973f), *qāḍī* Abū Yaᶜlā (d.458/1066f), Abū Jaᶜfar (d. 470/1077f), Ibn ᶜAqīl (d. 513/1119f), Ibn Hubayra (d. 560/1165f), Ibn al-Mannī (d. 583/1187f), Ibn al-Jawzī (d. 597/1201),[16] ᶜAbd al-Ghanī b. Qudāma al-Maqdisī (d. 600/1203f), plus his brother and two of his sons, Abū ᶜUmar b. Qudāma (d. 607/1210f),[17] Fakhr al-Dīn b. Taymiyya (d. 622/1225f).[18]

Judging by the dreams found in the biographies of the *shaykh*s just listed, they seem to stress a particular kind of importance of the protagonists, namely, their influence over the rank-and-file members of the Ḥanbalite communities:[19] There are 80 of 96 (83%) "passive" dreams and almost 50% of the dreamers are nameless, which, again, suggests that they did not belong to the ranks of Ḥanbalite scholars.

Based exclusively on the materials of these two sources, the significance of dreams is supported by several passages. First of all, the state of sleep is similar to that of death (Qurʾān 39:42), the ultimate experience during which a believer is taken to the presence of God. The importance of the contemplation of death and resurrection, in this regard, is difficult to overemphasize, especially in the context of admonishing preaching (*waᶜẓ*) particularly prominent among the Ḥanbalites.

Furthermore, the importance of dreams is confirmed by a number of sayings of the Prophet with which Ibn Abī Yaᶜlā begins the section on dreams in the biography of his father, *qāḍī* Abū Yaʿlā (d. 458/1066f).[20] Thus, the dream of a believer is the way God speaks to his servant and, even though prophecy has ended with the prophet Muḥammad, it is in dreams that a believer can receive good tidings from God. In one *ḥadīth* the Prophet also says: "Whoever has seen me in a dream, has seen me in reality, for the Devil does not impersonate me!" Ibn Abī Yaʿlā concludes his "theoretical" introduction with a saying of Ibn Sīrīn: "Whatever a deceased person tells you in a dream is true, for he is in the Abode of Truth."[21] This statement of Ibn Sīrīn is very important, especially because the prevailing majority of dreams are those in which protagonists are seen by other people, often posthumously.

The last point in this section is that Ibn Ḥanbal himself seems to have been very appreciative of dreams and even bade his companions to transmit a story that happened to one of his followers. During one of Ibn Ḥanbal's gatherings, a man from his neighborhood came to talk to him, but because he was known for sinful behavior, Ibn Ḥanbal refused. The man begged him to listen to a dream he had had, so eventually Ibn Ḥanbal agreed. As the story goes, the man saw the Prophet surrounded by many people, each of them would get up, approach the Prophet and ask him to pray for him or her, and the Prophet would pray for each of them. In the end, the dreamer found himself the only one left, realizing that he was too ashamed because of his sins. Yet the Prophet said: "I will pray for you, for you do not curse any of my followers." The man later woke up realizing that this intercession had occurred despite his transgressions. Upon hearing this, Ibn Ḥanbal instructed his companions to transmit this story and make sure that it be remembered, for it is beneficial.[22]

This dream-tale takes us to the next important issue: the social consequences of dreams. Although it might be argued that dreams are personal, many of these dreams had far-reaching consequences both for those who saw them and those whom they concerned. Occasionally, dreams may have detrimental consequences for those seen in them. Thus, some Baghdādī commoner dreamt of the Prophet, who told him that if it were not for *shaykh* Ibn Salāma al-Qurashī (d. 592/1195f), they all would have been in trouble. This dream set off a public agitation in which the *shaykh* found himself startled by crowds of people who grabbed him and started throwing him into the air, while praising him. The shocked *shaykh* could only whisper: "I seek refuge with God from this misfortune! . . . What is [wrong] with these people?"[23]

Fear of interrupting someone's dream can influence someone's actions. Thus, *shaykh* Ibn Samʿūn (d. 387/997f) was so appreciative of the elevated status of dreaming that when one of his companions fell asleep during his admonition session, he did not wake him up. Afraid to interrupt his companion's possible communication with the Prophet, Ibn Samᶜūn suspended his session until his companion woke up. It turned out that his companion did indeed see the Prophet in his dream.[24]

Seeing God in one's dream must have been a significant proof to others of the elevated status of a dreamer. Thus, a famous Baghdādī preacher, Ibn al-Jawzī (d. 597/1201), saw God in his dreams three times. Nonetheless, scholars continued to criticize Ibn al-Jawzī, which was somewhat confusing to Ibn Rajab; he seems to have considered these dreams a sufficient proof of Ibn al-Jawzī's correctness.[25]

Aside from these somewhat random but interesting examples, we find that some dreamers were compelled to travel long distances in order to deliver a message. Salama b. Shabīb said:

> We were sitting at Ibn Ḥanbal['s house] when . . . some man came in, greeted [everyone] and asked: "Which one of you is Aḥmad?" Some of us pointed to him. The man said: "I have come from a long way of 1,200 miles over the sea [because] someone appeared to me in my dream and told me: 'Go to Aḥmad b. Ḥanbal['s home]. Ask for him and you will be pointed to him. Tell him: "God, the angels of His heavens and the angels of His earth are pleased with you!"' Thus said, he left without asking him about any *ḥadīth* or legal issue.[26]

Abū Bakr al-Marwadhī transmitted a similar story in which a visitor tells Ibn Ḥanbal that the angels vie with him in piety.[27]

We also find that some dreamers were compelled to repent of their behavior. For example, Ṣadaqa al-Maqāribī, who had harbored a grudge against Ibn Ḥanbal, saw in his dream the Prophet walking with Ibn Ḥanbal. Ṣadaqa tried to catch up with them but failed. After his resentment of Ibn Ḥanbal was gone, he saw the same dream again and almost succeeded in catching up with them. After this second dream he started telling people that they should follow Ibn Ḥanbal.[28] Quite often, dreamers are told to correct their attitudes if they care about their own salvation. There also is a number of dreams in which dreamers are reprimanded for their ill feeling toward protagonists.

Some dreamers change their religious views, but very often the dream itself is followed by some kind of interaction with a person seen or referred to in the dream without which the dream-tale is never complete. This real-life situation confirms the veracity of a dream and concludes a person's conversion. Quite often, the protagonist is aware of an antagonist's dream (this miraculous awareness is a recurring motif). One of these examples is a dream-tale about Ibn Ḥanbal and the caliph al-Muʿtaṣim bi'llāh (r. 218–27/833–42) that took place during the *miḥna* and ended with the caliph's acceptance of the doctrine of the uncreatedness of the Qurʾān. Al-Muʿtaṣim saw a dream (*ruʾyā*) in which two lions attempted to tear him apart but two angels protected him. The angels handed him a letter with a description of a dream that Ibn Ḥanbal saw in his prison cell. In the morning, the Caliph summoned Ibn Ḥanbal so that he could tell him what he saw. Ibn Ḥanbal leaned toward the Caliph and asked him in a quiet voice whether he had the letter. The Caliph responded in the affirmative and said that he wanted to hear Ibn Ḥanbal's version. As the story goes, Ibn Ḥanbal says that he saw himself on the Day of Judgment among other creatures. He was summoned before God Almighty and questioned:

— What is the Qurʾān?—another question followed.
— Your speech, O our God,—he said.
— Where did you take it from?—God asked.
— O Lord, ʿAbd al-Razzāq informed me,—Ibn Ḥanbal said.

Summoned and questioned in the very same manner, ʿAbd al-Razzāq says that he was informed by Muʿammar. Thus everyone and everything in the chain of transmitters is questioned—al-Zuhrī, ʿUrwa, ʿĀʾisha, Muḥammad, Jibrīl, Isrāfīl, the Well-preserved Tablet, and the Pen. When God asks the Pen, it responds: "As You spoke, I recorded." God then affirms the veracity of everyone in the chain and concludes with saying "Truth you said, O Ibn Ḥanbal. My speech is not created (*kalāmī ghayr makhlūq*)." Upon hearing that, the Caliph repented, honored Ibn Ḥanbal, and ordered him to be brought back home.[29]

Another dramatic story describes the conversion from Shāfiʿism to Ḥanbalism of Muḥammad b. Nāṣir (d. 550/1155f), the principal teacher of Ibn al-Jawzī. The story starts with Muḥammad b. Nāṣir saying that he had studied at the Niẓāmiyya Madrasa long enough to absorb the Shāfiʿī teaching, yet he kept pleading God to admit him to the legal and theological school most beloved to Him:

> [Muḥammad b. Nāṣir said]: And when it was the first night of Rajab of the year 494, I saw in a dream as if I entered the mosque of the *shaykh* Abū Manṣūr al-Khayyāṭ. People crowded in front of the gate [to the mosque] and they

> were saying that the Prophet [came to visit] the *shaykh* Abū Manṣūr. I entered the mosque and saw . . . *shaykh* Abū Manṣūr as he went out of his corner and sat in front of some man. I had never seen anyone more handsome than him [and who looked so close to the] descriptions of the Prophet which were transmitted to us . . . I entered and greeted them. [One of them] returned the greetings, but I was not sure exactly who responded to me because of my astonishment at seeing the Prophet. I sat in front of them and inclined towards the Prophet not asking about anything, not even trying to say anything. Then [the Prophet] told me [three times]: "Hold fast to the school of this *shaykh*!" [Muḥammad b. Nāṣir] said: I swear by God thrice . . . that the Messenger of God told me that three times, each time pointing with his right hand towards the *shaykh* Abū Manṣūr. [Muḥammad b. Nāṣir] said: I woke up, my limbs were trembling. I called my mother . . . and told her about what I saw. She told me: ". . . This dream is a revelation [for you], follow it!"
>
> I woke up in the morning and I hurried to [perform the] prayer behind *shaykh* Abū Manṣūr. We finished the morning prayer, and as I was telling him my dream, his eyes filled with tears, his heart humbled, and he told me: "Oh my dear son, the school of al-Shāfiʿī is a good [school], so follow it in legal rulings (*al-furūʿ*), and follow the school of Aḥmad and the people of Tradition (*aṣḥāb al-ḥadīth*) in legal principles (*al-uṣūl*)." I responded to him: "Oh my master, I do not want to be of two colors. God, His angels and His prophets are my witnesses [in that] I declare to you that from this day on I will not rely in my belief and practice on any school except for that of Aḥmad in both legal principles and legal rulings." The *shaykh* Abū Manṣūr kissed my head [and added]: "May God help you." I kissed his hand [in return].[30]

However, in order to dream one has to sleep, and this is where we come across the ambivalent status of sleep in general. The Ḥanbalī community was founded around pious conduct and "mild" asceticism, as Hurvitz characterized it.[31] Yet a number of *shaykh*s are reported to have actively abstained from sleep.[32] Ibn Bashshār (d. 313/925) is reported to have said: "If there is no way you can longer abstain from food or sleep, then sleep as if you were taking a light nap, and eat as if you were sick [and had no appetite]."[33] *Qāḍī* Abū Yaʿlā used to divide his night into three parts: one part for sleep, another one—for devotion, yet another one—for writing about the permissible and the forbidden.[34] Yet another *shaykh* used sleep (*nawm*) and forgetfulness of God and His commands (*ghafla*) as synonyms.[35]

The most interesting examples, however, are found in the biography of the traditionist ʿAbd al-Ghanī al-Maqdisī (d. 600/1203): He would take only one short nap in the night, but most often he would pray straight till the sunrise.[36] Despite such an attitude toward sleep, there are eleven dreams (~6% of all dream-tales) in his biography, which Ibn Rajab uses to confirm his elevated spiritual status. In all of these dreams, however, the *shaykh* is not the dreamer but the one who is dreamt about; in a case like this, these "passive" dreams seem a convenient device.

Except for a few instances, the dreams just examined can be divided into three major categories: posthumous (n=117), affirmative (n=35), and informative (n=27). Because there often are two perspectives in a dream—that of a dreamer and that of the one who is seen in a dream—the same dream may fall into two different categories. Besides, some dream-tales may contain two dreams, so, this division is approximate, yet it is precise enough to present a general picture. According to this morphological pattern, each category also may be divided into subgroups.

Posthumous Dreams

This most prominent category comprises dreams in which a person was seen by somebody else shortly after the death of the former. These dreams must have served as an additional confirmation to the community of the professional achievements and elevated spiritual status of the deceased. Our analysis has yielded the following subsets of the posthumous dreams.

- *Mā faʿala ʾllāh bi-ka*: What has God done to you?

Morphological Pattern: Someone, often nameless, sees himself in some place. He or she sees a protagonist in their dream; the dreamer asks the protagonist: "What did God do to you?"; in most cases the protagonist responds: "He forgave me and granted me Paradise"; his response is often followed by various details.

Themes: Salvation, reward, afterlife, doctrine, intercession.

In many cases, dreamers are given interesting details about what God has granted his servants. Some are granted houses, sometimes with houries; others enjoy the company of angels who serve them; yet others are granted divine permission to continue doing what they did in this life (teaching *ḥadīth*, preaching, reading countless books, etc.), or to do what they desired most of all (e.g., being in the presence of God).[37]

Sometimes protagonists tell dreamers exactly why they were forgiven and, hence, why some things are important and others are not. Thus, one person barely received God's forgiveness because of his interest in speculative theology (*kalām*). Another was reprimanded by God for transmitting *ḥadīth*s from weak reporters only to be forgiven in the end. Often in such dreams traditionalist doctrines are voiced.

> ʿAlī b. al-Muwaffaq said: I had a Zoroastrian neighbor, named Shāhriyār. I used to offer him [to accept] Islam saying that we follow the right path. Yet, he died confessing Zoroastrianism. I saw him in a dream and asked: "What is the news?" He replied: "Our people are at the bottom of Hell." I asked: "Are there any other people below you?" He replied: "Some of your people." I asked: "From what group of ours?" "[They are those] who believe in the createdness of the Qurʾān," he replied.[38]

Dreamers also try to learn about the afterlife, for instance whether the dreamer's relatives are saved, what other famous Muslims are in Paradise and how they spend their time there, how painful the tortures of the grave are, etc. Sometimes dreamers find out from the deceased that they were forgiven due to the protagonist's intercession. Thus, a dreamer saw some righteous man after his death who told him that he had been forgiven because of his love for Ibn Ḥanbal. According to another dream-tale,[39] the funeral procession of a sinner passed by Ibn Ḥanbal's gathering. The *imām* suggested that they pray for him so that God may forgive his transgressions; the next day some pious woman told Ibn Ḥanbal that she saw that man in a dream. The man told her that as soon as Ibn Ḥanbal had prayed for him, God forgave him his sins. Another dream recounts that Ibn Ḥanbal saved some of those next to whom he was buried from the tortures of the grave.[40] Some Khurāsānī man, who came to Baghdad to visit Ghulām al-Khallāl's tomb, did so because the Prophet told him in his dream that whoever visits Ghulām al-Khallāl's tomb would be forgiven.[41]

All these dreams confirm the protagonists' elevated spiritual status. Very close to this category is a subset of 12 instances in which the authors limited themselves to saying that so-and-so was seen in many good dreams (*TOPOS: ruʾiyat lahu manāmāt ṣāliḥa kathīra*).

• On the verge of the protagonist's death (more than ten instances)

MORPHOLOGICAL PATTERN: A dreamer sees (or hears) someone, often unidentifiable; the visitor says that so-and-so passed away; very often, however, the visitor will say some enigmatic phrase or verse of poetry that does not make much sense until the dreamer wakes up and hears about the protagonist's death, hence realizing the true nature of the dream.

THEMES: Prediction, announcement.

Muḥammad b. al-Musabbiḥ heard in his dream that this night Ibn Ḥanbal died and that he should mourn him; several days later he received a letter saying that on that night *qāḍī* Abū Yaʿlā died.[42] Occasionally, these enigmatic announcements are in poetry. So, on the night of Ibn al-Jawzī's death some man dreamt of someone reciting: "By your life, the pulpit has become deserted. And it has become so hard for people to get answers." Later in the afternoon he found out that Ibn al-Jawzī died and realized that this dream was about him.[43]

Fakhr al-Dīn b. Taymiyya's wife saw some garden-like place, where people were building a tall castle. Two exceptionally beautiful women, who turned out to be houries, told her that this was done for Fakhr. The doors of the castle were closed, however. A month before her husband's death, she saw the same dream again, but this time the doors were open.[44]

Occasionally, protagonists themselves see dreams similar to those just described.

• Visiting a deceased (more than five instances)

MORPHOLOGICAL PATTERN: A dreamer sees someone or a group (the Prophet, some religious authorities, angels) either sitting in the local mosque or heading toward the protagonist's town; he then finds out that they came to pay respects to the protagonist.

THEMES: Funeral and tomb visitation.

One Sufi, Saᶜūd al-Ḥabashī, missed the funeral prayer for the deceased *qāḍī* Abū Yaᶜlā, which made him very upset. Sometime later he was approached by some unnamed *shaykh* who said that he saw the Prophet accompanied by his Companions. They came from Madina to Baghdad—to the al-Zūzanī cloister, across the Cathedral Mosque of al-Manṣūr—to pay their respects to *qāḍī* Abū Yaᶜlā.[45] In another story, the Prophet and the archangel Jibrīl came to Ḥarrān to pay respects to Fakhr al-Dīn b. Taymiyya.[46]

Sometimes, a dreamer himself performs visitation. Thus, one Ṣanīᶜat al-Mulk Hibat Allāh b. ᶜAlī b. Ḥaydara was on his way to pray for ᶜAbd al-Ghanī al-Maqdisī and stumbled upon a certain Maghribī man. He tagged along and told Ṣanīᶜat al-Mulk that he was a stranger there but that last night he saw in his dream a wide place with a great number of people wearing shiny white garments. He was told that these were angels who had descended from Heavens to pray for ᶜAbd al-Ghanī. When he asked how he could find ᶜAbd al-Ghanī, he was instructed to wait outside the Cathedral Mosque for a man named Ṣanīᶜat al-Mulk and then follow him.[47]

Affirmative Dreams

Affirmative dreams are those in which a protagonist receives some message that can be regarded as a confirmation of his lofty spiritual status and religious knowledge. Sometimes this message arrives directly to a protagonist in his own dream, sometimes this confirmation comes indirectly, often via a commoner who tells the protagonist about a dream he or she had about him.

- Direct affirmation (more than 10 instances)

Morphological Pattern: Sometimes a dream is preceded by the protagonist's request to see it; the protagonist sees God or some Muslim luminaries; occasionally those seen say something affirmative, but often the protagonist simply enjoys their company; in case of seeing God, the entire dream-tale is often limited to the slight variations of the phrase "I saw the Lord of Majesty in a dream."

Themes: Confirmation of the protagonist's lifetime status and knowledge.

While in the Sacred Mosque in Mecca, ᶜAlī b. [al-]Muwaffaq invoked God: "How long will You be rejecting me? How long will You be exhausting me? Take me to Yourself and give me some rest!" That night, when he fell asleep, God revealed Himself in a dream and invited ʿAlī to His abode.[48] When al-Nāṣiḥ b. al-Ḥanbalī (d.634/1236f) finished one of his books, he dreamt of the Prophet who greeted him, which he took as a sign of approval.[49] Another *shaykh* saw the Prophet who brought him good news that he would pass away in accordance with the Sunna.[50] Ibn Qayyim al-Jawziyya saw Ibn Taymiyya who told him that he had almost reached the elevated status of *shaykh*s like himself.[51]

Sometimes protagonists ask directly for confirmation of their knowledge. Ibn Ḥanbal is reported to have seen the Messenger of God in his dream. "Is everything that Abū Hurayra transmitted from you true?" he asked the Prophet. "Yes," responded the Prophet.[52] Quite often, however, these encounters are just mentioned without any details on what actually happened.[53]

Occasionally, these dreams bring some kind of relief to dreamers. A mystically minded protagonist was terrified of the caliph for some reason; in his dream he was told to write down some verses that turned out to be a message for him not to be afraid.[54] Ṭalḥa b. Muẓaffar al-ʿAlthī accompanied his *shaykh* to a high-ranking official. During the audience there were sweets, but none were offered to them. Consequently, his base soul passionately desired them. Later that night, when he was asleep, sweets were brought to him in a dream and he ate his fill. When he woke up, his base soul no longer had any desire for them.[55] Another dream-tale about ʿAlī b. [al-]Muwaffaq tells us that he used to make the *ḥajj* in a palanquin (*maḥmal*) for years, but once he saw a group of men who were travelling on foot and desired to join them in their endeavor. Exhausted, he was dreaming the following night and saw some slave girls with golden basins and silver vessels who washed his feet. He woke up with no traces of exhaustion.[56]

- Indirect affirmation (more than ten instances)

MORPHOLOGICAL PATTERN: Someone has a dream that somehow emphasizes the protagonist's elevated spiritual status; the dreamer may have had something against the protagonist that provoked the dream, in which case the dream is followed by the dreamer's repentance; a whole set of dream-tales ends with the dreamer's telling his or her dream to the protagonist or the community as a whole.

THEMES: Confirmation of the protagonist's status and knowledge; intercession.

Depending on the perspective, these dreams can be treated either as affirmative—for the protagonists—or as pivotal—for the dreamers (for pivotal dreams, see later), who sometimes have to suffer considerable difficulties to deliver a message to the protagonist.

Dreamers may be told to hold fast on to the protagonist in matters of religion. In the same dreams they are told to communicate a message to the protagonist. I have already mentioned the story of an anonymous man who traveled about twelve hundred miles across the sea to deliver a message to Ibn Ḥanbal.[57] In another story, *shaykh* ᶜImād al-Dīn's wife was told to give her husband a message that he is one of the seven on whom the earth rests.[58]

Occasionally, the dreamer may see a dream in which she or he finds out that the protagonist is a local guardian saint. Thus, a brother of Abū 'l-Ḥasan al-Zāghūnī (d. 527/1132f) saw three angels in a dream discussing whether to destroy Baghdad. Eventually, they decided against it. One of them said: "[We cannot do this] because there are three [pious individuals in Baghdad]: Abū 'l-Ḥasan b. al-Zāghūnī, Aḥmad b. al-Ṭilāya and Muḥammad b. *fulān*[59] in al-Ḥarbiyya."[60]

Another interesting dream-tale concerning intercession is that of Abū Saᶜd b. Abī ᶜUmāma al-Wāᶜiẓ (d. 506/1112f). Ibn al-Jawzī transmitted a dream that was seen at the time of a quarrel between the Caliph al-Mustarshid bi'llāh (r. 512–29/1118–35) and the Saljūq *sulṭān* Maḥmūd (r. 511–25/1118–31).[61] In that dream Aḥmad b. Ḥanbal prayed for the Caliph, which helped him to get the upper hand in the quarrel.[62] What is interesting about this dream is that it demonstrates a fundamental change in the overall attitude of the Ḥanbalī community toward the ᶜAbbāsids.

Sometimes dreamers see dreams about protagonists whom they do not like. In these dreams someone often intercedes for the protagonist, leaving the dreamer ashamed of his or her behavior.[63] Thus, Abū 'l-Fatḥ al-Qawwās (d. 385/995f) was at a *ḥadīth* study group of *qāḍī* al-Muḥāmilī, but he could not hear well, so he got up and squeezed himself between others to get closer to the *shaykh*. The next day, an unnamed man approached him and asked for forgiveness. It happened that he had reproached the protagonist for doing what he did. He then saw the Prophet in his dream telling him that whoever wants to study *ḥadīth* as if from himself, must do as Abū 'l-Fatḥ al-Qawwās does.[64]

Dreamers also may see what fate awaits those who hate pious men. Thus, Saᶜd Allāh al-Baṣrī saw Marjān al-Khādim (d. 560/1165)[65] escorted by two angels—each one of them was holding him by the hand. Saᶜd Allāh asked: "Where are you taking him?" "To the Hellfire, [because] he hated Ibn al-Jawzī," replied the angels.[66]

Sometimes the Prophet sends a dreamer to the protagonist to obtain answers to the questions he may have,[67] or to become the protagonist's apprentice, as in the quoted dream-tale about Ibn Nāṣir's conversion to Ḥanbalism.[68] It is interesting that in the early period the Prophet usually answers the questions of dreamers himself, whereas in the subsequent centuries he delegates this function to the *shaykh*s whose memory is still alive among a given community.

Informative Dreams

Informative dreams are the most diverse, yet their common feature is that dreamers receive some kind of message. Sometimes these messages do not imply any radical, socially tangible consequences.[69] However, sometimes—in the case of pivotal dreams—they are so important that they become turning points in the lives of protagonists. Occasionally, forthcoming events are predicted.

- Pivotal dreams (about ten instances)

  Morphological Pattern: A protagonist does something that provokes a dream; he is told to change his life; he also may be reprimanded for what he has done.

  Themes: Bidding, reprimand.

Unlike the indirect affirmative dreams in which the dreamer and the protagonist are different people, in these pivotal dreams it is the protagonist who sees a dream. The protagonist may be told to do something. Thus, the Prophet may tell a protagonist to perform a *ḥajj*,[70] or give his son another first name.[71] On other occasions, the protagonist is forbidden from doing something, as in the case of Yazīd b. Hārūn whom God forbade to transmit *ḥadīth* from Ḥurayz b. ʿUthmān, because he used to curse ʿAlī b. Abī Ṭālib. Protagonists also may get warnings directly from the Almighty.[72] Thus, al-Fatḥ b. Shukhruf saw God who told him: "Oh Fatḥ, beware lest I catch you neglectful!" Following that dream, al-Fatḥ b. Shukhruf spent seven years living in seclusion in the mountains.[73]

Protagonists may be reprimanded for their arrogance. During his last standing at the Mount ʿArafāt, ʿAlī b. [al-]Muwaffaq asked God to bestow his promised reward for performing the *ḥajj* upon anyone whose pilgrimage had not been accepted. The following night, he saw God saying: "O ʿAlī b. Muwaffaq, you aren't vying with Me in generosity, are you?! For I have already forgiven [them all]."[74] In another dream-tale, after hearing about the sack of Baghdad, Ibn al-Baqqāl al-Ṣūfī condemned this tragedy in his heart and pleaded to God: "Oh Lord, how could this have happened? There were children, there were sinless!" Later in a dream he received a letter saying that he had no right to question God's deeds.[75]

- Predicting the future (fewer than five instances)

MORPHOLOGICAL PATTERN: The protagonist sees someone who delivers a message about the future or some mystery.

THEMES: Prediction, mystery unveiling.

One person saw al-Khiḍr who informed him that he had ten years left to live; he died after nine, however.[76] Another one was informed about the failures and the eventual success of Asad al-Dīn Shīrkūh's conquest of Egypt.[77] Yet another one received a prediction of ʿAbd al-Ghanī al-Maqdisī's forthcoming exile to Egypt.[78] Likewise, it was revealed to Ibn al-Jawzī that the *wazīr* Ibn Hubayra had not died a natural death but was poisoned by his physician.[79]

Conclusion

Fred Donner wrote that "personality in the characters that populate the Qurʾān's narrations are bleached out, because its focus on morality is so intense. The only judgment about a person that really matters, in the Qurʾānic view, is whether he or she is good or evil, and most characters presented in the Qurʾānic narratives fall squarely on one side or other of that great divide."[80] Ideal pietists in the Qurʾān are equally righteous throughout their lives from the day they were born until the day they died. This didactic "dehumanization" seems to have had a profound effect on Arabic biographers and prosopographers, especially in the cases of key figures. However, unlike the Qurʾānic prophets, scholars depicted in biographical dictionaries are far too humane, far too much like the other people of their communities. In this case, dreams appear to be a potent device to perfect their images. The bulk of dreams—posthumous and affirmative—in these Ḥanbalī prosopographical sources require no interpretation. They are clear-cut and straightforward; their main function is to affirm the protagonist's status. As to the posthumous dreams, they are designed to provide the ultimate proof of the protagonist's righteousness. Such a proof is undisputable because it comes directly from the Abode of Truth.

This may explain the relative insignificance of the pivotal dreams in so far as they explain changes in the protagonists' status. Thus, purposefully or not, Ibn Rajab placed the story of Muḥammad b. Nāṣir's conversion to Ḥanbalism in the biographical account of Abū Manṣūr al-Khayyāṭ, the *shaykh* whom Muḥammad b. Nāṣir saw in a dream and was commanded to follow. In all other sources I could find this narrative, it is placed in Muḥammad b. Nāṣir's own biography.[81] Using a pivotal dream as an indirect affirmative one allowed Ibn Rajab to emphasize the loftiness of Abū Manṣūr's status. Were he to use it in Muḥammad b. Nāṣir's biography, the effect would have been different.

There is a certain amount of dream-tales that elude our classification. However, the majority fits into the proposed morphological patterns. Even when it comes to nonclassified dreams, they are still composed of topoi that are found in the ones classified here. The fact that the number of these classificatory patterns is quite limited suggests a conscious effort of dream selection based on the dreams' effectiveness for the purpose of perfecting and solidifying the protagonists' status. On the other hand, sharing posthumous dreams about a respected *shaykh* also could have been a way for the commoners to show their respect to the deceased. This practice of popular spontaneous sanctification is still alive: the day after the great Egyptian preacher ʿAbd al-Ḥamīd Kishk died in 1996, a large crowd gathered to pay respects to the "star of Islamic preaching." "One man exclaimed that the night before he had had a dream in which he had seen Kishk being escorted up to heaven by a group of angels."[82]

Notes

1. For the role of dreams in Sufi tradition, see Part II in this volume.

2. See Daniella Talmon-Heller, "The Shaykh and the Community: Popular Hanbalite Islam in 12th–13th Century Jabal Nāblus and Jabal Qasyūn," *Studia Islamica*, no. 79 (1994), 103–20.

3. Note 2 in *Ṭabaqāt*, iii, 222. This three-volume edition of *Ṭabaqāt* was prepared for the one hundreth anniversary of the Saudi Kingdom. ʿAbd al-Raḥmān b. Sulaymān al-ʿUthaymīn's extensive commentary easily could have taken the entire volume if printed separately. A good share of this commentary is devoted to explaining away a great number of un-Ḥanbalī

elements that Ibn Abī Yaʿlā—to the editor's bewilderment—included in his dictionary of the Ḥanbalites.

4. See, e.g., note 1 in *Ṭabaqāt*, iii, 406.

5. Henceforth, the following abbreviations will be used: *Ṭabaqāt* for Abū al-Ḥusayn Muḥammad ibn Muḥammad Ibn Abī Yaʿlá, *Ṭabaqāt al-Ḥanābila*, ed. Dr. ʿAbd al-Raḥmān b. Sulaymān al-ʿUthaymīn, three volumes. ([Riyadh]: al-Mamlaka al-ʿArabiyya al-Saʿūdiyya, al-Amāna al-ʿĀmma lil-Iḥtifāl bi-Murūr Miʾāt ʿĀm ʿalá Taʾsīs al-Mamlaka, 1999), and *Dhayl* for ʿAbd al-Raḥmān ibn Aḥmad Ibn Rajab, *Al-Dhayl ʿalā Ṭabaqāt al-Ḥanābila*, ed. Muḥammad Ḥāmid Fāqī, vol. 2 ([Cairo]: Maṭbaʿat al-Sunna al-Muḥammadīya, 1952).

6. See Chase F. Robinson, *Islamic Historiography*, Themes in Islamic History (Cambridge, U.K.; New York: Cambridge University Press, 2003), xxv.

7. Ibid., 66.

8. *Ṭabaqāt*, i, 437–43.

9. This "inquisition" was the last attempt of the ʿAbbāsid caliphs to keep the religious affairs under their control. Initiating *miḥna*, the Caliph al-Maʾmūn acted as a proponent of speculative theology and directed his wrath against the traditionalists who despised both the premises and conclusions of speculative theology. A great number of renowned scholars have offered their interpretations of this indisputably crucial event thus making it one of the most complicated issues in Islamic historiography. Major interpretations were elegantly reviewed and analyzed by John Nawas in two articles (see, John A. Nawas, "A Reexamination of Three Current Explanations for Al-Maʾmūn's Introduction of the Miḥna," *International Journal of Middle East Studies* 26, no. 4 (1994); idem, "The Miḥna of 218 A. H./833 A. D. Revisited: An Empirical Study," *Journal of the American Oriental Society* 116, no. 4 (1996).

10. The editor of *Ṭabaqāt* provides a useful note with references to five sources where the details on him can be found. However, all of them are Ḥanbalite sources, and, apparently none of them provides details on when al-Sijzī was born or died (cf. Bakr ibn ʿAbd Allāh Abū Zayd, *ʿUlamāʾ al-Ḥanābila: Min al-Imām Aḥmad al-Mutawaffá Sanat 241 Ilá Wafayāt ʿām 1420*, 1st ed. [al-Dammām: Dār Ibn al-Jawzī, 1422 A.H., 2001], #141). Searching electronic libraries of Arabic sources, *al-Muʿjam al-Fiqhī (al-Mojam)* and *Maktabat al-Taʾrīkh wa-l-Ḥaḍāra al-Islāmiyya*, I could not find al-Sijzī in any source whatsoever.

11. See, for instance, the editor's note 1 in *Ṭabaqāt*, iii, 223. The editor was not able to locate their biographies in other dictionaries, neither did I searching electronic libraries. About the popular character of the nascent Ḥanbalite community see Nimrod Hurvitz, *The Formation of Ḥanbalism: Piety into Power* (London and New York: Routledge, 2002).

12. At the end of a pretty short dream-tales section in Ibn Ḥanbal's biography, Ibn Abī Yaʿlā writes: "Were we to continue mentioning his excellent qualities and dreams that [were seen] after his death, that would have made the book [very] long; besides it was not our intent to [dwell on] his excellent qualities [here], for we wanted to mention those who transmitted from him. So, whoever wants to look into his excellent qualities let him look into

our book *al-Mujarrad* [*fī manāqib al-imām Aḥmad*, which is] about his excellent qualities" (*Ṭabaqāt*, i, 42). Ibn al-Bannāʾ (d. 471/1079) is said to have collected a book of dreams in which Ibn Ḥanbal appeared (*Dhayl*, i, 35).

13. 'f' here means that this is the year of the Gregorian calendar when a Hijrī year started, yet the exact date may fall on the following Gregorian year as well.

14. On some *shaykh*s of this family, see Talmon-Heller, "The Shaykh and the Community: Popular Hanbalite Islam in 12th–13th Century Jabal Nāblus and Jabal Qasyūn," 103–20.

15. E.g., *Ṭabaqāt*, i, 337, 437.

16. Ibn al-Jawzī is also a transmitter of a significant number of dreams in *Dhayl*.

17. A brother of Ibn Qudāma al-Maqdisī (d. 620/1223).

18. An uncle of Taqī l-Dīn b. Taymiyya (d. 738/1328).

19. This list of seventeen *shaykh*s with more than three dream-tales differs remarkably from the one found in Laoust's *Ḥanābila* (EI^2) which is apparently based on the significance of the written output. On the other hand, all Ḥanbalites from Laoust's article that can be found in Ibn Abī Yaʿlā and Ibn Rajab's works have at least one dream related story in their biographical accounts, often posthumous one.

20. *Ṭabaqāt*, iii, 403f.

21. Another story gives us an example of how a nephew, while being between asleep and awake, eavesdropped his uncle's communication with the divine (*Dhayl*, i, 381).

22. *Ṭabaqāt*, i, 338–39. This story and Ibn Ḥanbal's bidding is also a good example of how traditionalists (*ahl al-ḥadīth*) were extending their *ḥadīth*-based worldview by adding piously beneficial precedents to their repository of traditions.

23. *Dhayl*, i, 385.

24. *Ṭabaqāt*, iii, 227.

25. *Dhayl*, i, 414.

26. *Ṭabaqāt*, i, 40. For more details on this morphological pattern, see the category of affirmative dreams (indirect affirmation).

27. *Ṭabaqāt*, i, 151.

28. Ibid., 30.

29. Ibid., i, 440–43, this story is found only in the Ḥanbalite sources.

30. *Dhayl*, i, 98–99.

31. Nimrod Hurvitz, "Biographies and Mild Asceticism: A Study of Islamic Moral Imagination," *Studia Islamica*, no. 85 (1997): 41–65.

32. The editor of *Ṭabaqāt* added critical comments to almost all of these instances.

33. *Ṭabaqāt*, i, 118; cf. ibid., iii, 322.

34. Ibid., 361.

35. *Dhayl*, ii, 70.

36. Ibid., 11–12.

37. *Ṭabaqāt*, ii, 145. There are two other dream-tales, however, in which Bishr b. al-Ḥārith takes the place of Maʿrūf al-Karkhī (*Ṭabaqāt*, ii, 85; *Dhayl*, i, 138).

38. *Ṭabaqāt*, iii, 130.

39. Ibid., iii, 110.

40. *Ṭabaqāt*, i, 41; cf. Ibid., i, 42; *Dhayl*, i, 139.

41. *Ṭabaqāt*, iii, 223; cf. Ibid., i, 60; 159.

42. Ibid., iii, 410.

43. *Dhayl*, i, 429; cf. *Ṭabaqāt*, iii, 408, 463; *Dhayl*, i, 288; ii, 280.

44. Ibid., ii, 160–61.

45. *Ṭabaqāt*, iii, 403–406.

46. *Dhayl*, ii, 160.

47. Ibid., 31.

48. *Ṭabaqāt*, ii, 143–44.

49. *Dhayl*, ii, 199.

50. Ibid., 263.

51. Ibid., 450–51.

52. *Ṭabaqāt*, ii, 357.

53. *Dhayl*, i, 276, 277, 429; ii, 17.

54. Ibid., i, 303.

55. Ibid., 390.

56. Ibid., ii, 146.

57. This dream-tale seems archetypal; one can find other versions of this dream-tale in Abū Bakr Aḥmad b. ʿAlī al-Khaṭīb al-Baghdādī, *Tārīkh Baghdād Aw Madīnat al-Salām*, ed. Muṣṭafá ʿAbd al-Qādir ʿAṭā and Muḥammad ʿAlī Bayḍūn, 1st ed., 14 vols. (Bayrūt: Dār al-Kutub al-ʿIlmiyya [Electronic Database *al-Muʿjam al-Fiqhī*, 3rd ed., 2001, Qumm], 1996), v, 186 and ʿAlī b. al-Ḥasan Ibn ʿAsākir, *Tārīkh Madīnat Dimashq*, ed. ʿAlī Shīrī, 70 vols. (Bayrūt: Dār al-Fikr [Electronic Database *al-Muʿjam al-Fiqhī*, 3rd ed., 2001, Qumm], 1995), v, 315–17. The latter has three versions so that the second is more detailed than the first, and the third is more detailed than the second; in the last two versions it was al-Khiḍr who sent the dreamer on the journey to Ibn Ḥanbal.

58. *Dhayl*, ii, 103.

59. Dreamer forgetting names of one or two of three people he was told about in his dream appears to be one of the dream-tales topoi.

60. *Dhayl*, i, 181; cf. Ibid., i, 8.

61. On their mixed relationships, see Hillenbrand's *al-Mustarshid bi'llāh* (EI[2]), Bosworth's *Maḥmūd B. Muḥammad B. Malik-shāh* (EI[2]) and Eric J. Hanne, *Putting the Caliph in His Place: Power, Authority, and the Late Abbasid Caliphate* (Madison, NJ: Fairleigh Dickinson University Press, 2007).

62. *Dhayl*, i, 109–10.

63. As one of the examples, see the dream-tale of Ṣadaqa al-Maqāribī above.

64. *Ṭabaqāt*, iii, 254; cf. *Dhayl*, i, 17, 29.

65. This Shāfiᶜite swore an oath to exterminate the Ḥanbalites, see Abū 'l-Faraj ᶜAbd al-Raḥmān ibn ᶜAlī Ibn al-Jawzī, *Al-Muntaẓam Fī Ta᾿rīkh al-Mulūk wa-l-Umam (Min 257 A.H.)*, 1st ed., 6 vols. (Bayrūt: Dār Ṣādir [Electronic Library *Maktabat al-Ta᾿rīkh wa-l-Ḥaḍāra al-Islāmiyya*. Version. 1.5 by al-Turāth, Jordan], 1995), x, 213–14.

66. *Dhayl*, i, 429–30.

67. E.g., *Ṭabaqāt*, iii, 218–20.

68. See also *Dhayl*, i, 293.

69. There is a number of dreams in which the Prophet reiterates that the community must follow Ibn Ḥanbal and his school, e.g., *Ṭabaqāt*, i, 8; *Dhayl*, i, 136.

70. E.g., *Ṭabaqāt*, ii, 5; *Dhayl*, ii, 305.

71. Ibid., 70.

72. *Ṭabaqāt*, i, 445.

73. Ibid., ii, 202–203.

74. Ibid., ii, 146. The same story, but with the different protagonist, a famous Sufi Abū Turāb al-Nakhshabī, is found in Ibn ᶜAsākir, *Tārīkh Madīnat Dimashq*, xl, 348.

75. *Dhayl*, ii, 280.

76. Ibid., i, 240–41.

77. Ibid., 308.

78. Ibid., ii, 19.

79. Ibid., i, 285–86.

80. Fred McGraw Donner, *Narratives of Islamic Origins: The Beginnings of Islamic Historical Writing*, Studies in Late Antiquity and Early Islam (Princeton, NJ: Darwin Press, 1998), 75–76.

81. ᶜAbd al-Ḥayy ibn Aḥmad Ibn al-ᶜImād, *Shadharāt al-Dhahab fī Akhbār Man Dhahab (Al-Turāth)*, 1st ed., VIII vols. (Bayrūt: Dār Ibn Kathīr [Electronic Library *Maktabat al-Ta᾿rīkh wa-l-Ḥaḍāra al-Islāmiyya*. Ed. 1.5 by al-Turāth, Jordan], N.D.), iv, 155–56; Muḥammad ibn Aḥmad Dhahabī, *Siyar Aᶜlām al-Nubalā᾿*, ed. Shuᶜayb al-Arna᾿ūṭ and Ḥusayn al-Asad, 9th ed., 23 vols. (Bayrūt: Mu᾿assasat al-Risāla [Electronic Library *al-Muᶜjam al-Fiqhī*, 3rd ed., 2001, Qumm], 1992 (1413 AH)), xx, 269; idem, *Tadhkirat al-Ḥuffāẓ*, 4 vols. (Bayrūt: Dār Iḥyā᾿ al-Turāth al-ᶜArabī [Electronic Library al-Muᶜjam al-Fiqhī, 3rd ed., 2001, Qumm], n.d.), iv, 1290; Muwaffaq al-Dīn ᶜAbd Allāh ibn Aḥmad al-Maqdisī Ibn Qudāma, *Kitāb al-Tawwābīn*, ed. ᶜAbd al-Qādir al-Arnā᾿ūṭ (Bayrūt: Dār al-Kutub al-ᶜIlmiyya [Electronic Library al-Muᶜjam al-Fiqhī, 3rd ed., 2001, Qumm], 1982 [1403 AH]), 232.

82. Charles Hirschkind, *The Ethical Soundscape: Cassette Sermons and Islamic Counterpublics*, Cultures of History (New York: Columbia University Press, 2006), 203.

CHAPTER 3

Numinous Vision, Messianic Encounters

Typological Representations in a Version of the Prophet's *ḥadīth al-ruʾyā* and in Visions and Dreams of the Hidden Imam

Omid Ghaemmaghami

Two of the most central and deeply placed phenomena encountered in Twelve Shīʿī hagiographical sources are visions and oneiric encounters.[1] Initiatory, mystical, and occultist visions also have long played an integral role in legitimizing the Shīʿī institution of *walāya* (guardianship).[2] A recurring and salient substrate in many of the works dedicated to the central figure of Shīʿī eschatology, the twelfth Imam, believed by the Ithnā ʿAsharī Shīʿa to be in perpetual occultation, is the suprarational encounter in visions, dreams, and intuitive experiences between the Imam and the most privileged of his votaries.[3]

The reports of these visions stress the need to receive continued guidance from the Imam and reflect a longing to compensate for the interregnal void caused by his concealment. They, furthermore, represent a unique approach to the challenge of the Imam's absence. They are the testimonies of Shīʿa—and, in particular, prominent *ʿulamāʾ*—who have laid claim to encountering the soteriological "Lord of the Age" prior to his expected appearance and subsequent deliverance. Yet, despite their prominence in Shīʿī sources, they remain a largely neglected body of literature.[4] The proliferation of monographs that include such narratives in Persian and Arabic notwithstanding, the motif has only recently begun to receive attention from Western scholars.

The narratives that describe encounters with the Hidden Imam use a similar stock of themes, conventions, images, and tropes to describe visions of the occulted Imam. In these reports, the Imam is repeatedly described as being a youth (*shābb*) marked by overwhelming, if not ineffable, beauty. His youth, stunning physical features and intoxicating fragrance (not necessarily in that order) often are the first signs that the visionary gives when describing such encounters. A recurring motif in these narratives is the mystical initiation or divine assistance the Imam provides those to whom he appears. This succor takes the form of, for example, leading a lost pilgrim to the Kaʿba, a caravan, or his home; responding to vexing legal or theological questions; or providing a prayer or supplication to be recited to remove difficulties in times of trials and tribulations, often for a specific purpose, such as the healing of an illness. These narratives serve, *inter alia*, to emphasize that the Imam, despite his occultation, can appear to any of his votaries whenever he chooses and is eager to render assistance to those disciples whom he loves.

Yet why does the Hidden Imam appear to his followers in the form of a comely youth? And why does report after report maintain that he will likewise appear as a youth at his *parousia*? These are axioms that are never questioned in the primary sources and, to date, have received no consideration in the secondary literature. The Hidden Imam is believed to have disappeared as a small child, thus one might expect that he would appear as a boy throughout his occultation, or as a venerable *shaykh*, one whose life has been miraculously prolonged by God.

At the same time that the Twelver Shīʿī doctrine of the occultation of the twelfth Imam (*al-ghayba*) was crystallizing, a prophetic Tradition (*ḥadīth*) was circulating in the Islamic lands with potentially far-reaching theological implications. This important *ḥadīth* maintained that the prophet Muḥammad saw God in the most beautiful form possible. Most theologians appear to have accepted this Tradition. However, a different version of the same Tradition, the so-called *ḥadīth al-ruʾyā* (the *ḥadīth* of the vision), went on to describe the most beautiful of forms, claiming that the Prophet saw God in the image of a youth (again, *shābb*). Might there be a connection between this latter Tradition and the narratives that describe encounters with the Hidden Imam?

This chapter follows the scholarly trajectory developed by such scholars as Leonhard Goppelt, Henry Corbin, and Northrop Frye in focusing on issues of spiritual hermeneutics and interpretation rather than historical authenticity. The typological approach invoked by Samuel Amsler, Goppelt, and Frye in their study of the Bible suggests the opportunity to engage these Traditions and narratives phenomenonologically, while synthesizing the literary discontinuities between them.[5]

The typological approach is one of many available methods of interpretation. Employed by Biblical scholars to study the narrative conjunctions in the Old and New Testaments, typology has been described by Frye as "a figure of speech that moves in time: the type exists in the past and the antitype in the present, or the type exists in the present and the antitype in the future." Frye affirms that "[It] is a mode of thought . . . an assumption that there is some meaning or point to history, and that sooner or later some event or events will occur which will indicate what that meaning or point is, and so become an antitype of what has happened previously."[6] Elsewhere, Frye speaks of the types as "the symbols and the antitypes are the realities."[7] The antitypes serve, in the words of Michael Zwettler, "as repetitions, recurrences, or recapitulations of the prefigurative, prerepresentative actualities that constitute their types."[8]

Drawing from this approach, the following thesis is advanced: The prophet Muḥammad's vision of God in the form of a comely youth represents a typological prerepresentation or prefiguration—the type—of which the visions and encounters of the Hidden Imam provide the corresponding realization or recapitulation—the antitype. This study suggests that the famous *ḥadīth* of the vision is a foreshadowing of the encounters with the Hidden Imam. Furthermore, the numerous encounter narratives mark a heightening of the aforementioned type. The most salient elements of these visions that are identified and explored here are youth, beauty, and initiation.

Some introductory remarks are first offered about the *ḥadīth al-ruʾyā*. The second section presents a number of mainly Shīʿī *ḥadīths* that describe the youth and beauty of the Qāʾim. The chapter then explores how these attributes are manifested in a set of eight accounts describing encounters with the Hidden Imam in visions and dreams. Finally, the third part of the study explores the typological implications of the version of the *ḥadīth al-ruʾyā* discussed in the following section and the accounts of visions and dreams of the Hidden Imam mentioned in the second section.

The Ascension of the Prophet and the *ḥadīth al-ruʾyā*

On the more general issue of whether it is possible for humans to see God, the Qurʾān renders possible a number of readings. On the one hand, pericopes speak about the meeting between the believers and God on the Day of Resurrection (e.g., Qurʾān 75:22–23). On the other hand, scholars adduce verses indicating that no created being is capable of comprehending Him (e.g., Qurʾān 6:103). This, of course, is a perfect illustration of what Henry Corbin cogently observed as a *coincidentia oppositorum*[9] in Islamic theology.

For many early Muslims, one of the defining moments of Muḥammad's career was the experience of his ascent to heaven (*miʿrāj*).[10] However, Sunni Traditions suggest that the earliest Companions of the Prophet differed sharply on the question of whether he saw God during this event. For the most part, the negators of a numinous vision interpreted the verses of *Sūrat al-Najm* as being references to Gabriel, maintaining that Muḥammad saw only light.[11] The various positions are summarized by the Egyptian theologian and traditionist Abū al-ʿAbbās Shihāb al-Dīn al-Qasṭallānī (d. 923/1517):[12]

> Some said: He saw Gabriel at the highest horizon; others say he saw Allāh with his heart and his inner view; still others say, he saw Him with his eyes, but all of them speak the truth for they only tell what they have heard.[13]

The Tradition that is considered the weightiest proof that Muḥammad did in fact see God is one which has been narrated on the authority of Ibn ʿAbbās. The *ḥadīth* has several forms and is here mentioned in perhaps its main:

> The Messenger of God said: I saw my Lord in the most beautiful of forms. He said to me, "O Muḥammad! Do you know what the Concourse on High is disputing about?" I answered, "I do not know, Lord." And so He put His hand between my shoulders, and I felt its coolness between my breasts, and I learned all that is in heaven and on earth.[14]

What precisely was the most beautiful of forms that God appeared in? An early and highly contentious Tradition fills in the gap and sheds new light on the issue. According to this version of the *ḥadīth al-ruʾyā*, Muḥammad saw God in the form of a comely and radiant youth:[15]

> On the authority of Umm al-Ṭufayl who said that she heard the Messenger of God say that he saw his Lord in a dream in the most beautiful of forms—[in the form of] a

> youth with abundant hair, His feet in greenery, with golden sandals, and a veil of gold on His face.[16]

There appears to be a *prima facie* case for arguing that this version of the *ḥadīth al-ruʾyā* was well-known in Shīʿī circles of the third and fourth centuries (AH).[17] A reference is made to the *ḥadīth al-ruʾyā* in al-Kulaynī's (d. ca. 329/941)[18] famous canonical collection of Imāmī *ḥadīth, al-Kāfī*. The *ḥadīth* is, furthermore, mentioned and discussed by the Ismāʿīlī Shīʿī philosopher, Abū Ḥātim al-Rāzī (d. 322/933–4)[19] in his *Aʿlām al-nubuwwa*, a book containing the proceedings of a series of debates between Abū Ḥātim and the well-known physician and philosopher, Ibn Zakariyyā al-Rāzī (d. 313/925). Abū Ḥātim considered it a sound (*ṣaḥīḥ*) *ḥadīth* and confidently rejected any anthropomorphic tensions in it through reading Muḥammad's experience as a dream. Because his discussion of this *ḥadīth* is highly original and insightful, it is mentioned here in full:

> Among the sound Traditions are those whose meanings are ambiguous and problematic and those that have been abrogated. (The Traditions) that are ambiguous are numerous. The [scholars] who fail to comprehend their meanings assume that they contradict one another. Among them . . . [is the following *ḥadīth*]: "I saw my Lord in the most beautiful of forms and He put His palms between my shoulder blades till I sensed the chill of His fingers on my chest." (The Messenger of God) maintained that he saw (God) in his dreams and not when he was awake for how would it have been possible for him to say that he saw his Lord while awake when God—the Almighty, the All-Glorious—has said, "No vision comprehends Him, [but] He comprehends all visions, and He is the Subtle, the All-Informed" (Qurʾān 6:103). What (the Prophet) meant is that he saw (God) in a dream. A similar *ḥadīth* has been narrated by ʿUbayd Allāh b. Wahb on the authority of ʿUmar b. al-Ḥārith on the authority of Saʿd b. Abī Mālik on the authority of Marwān ʿUthmān on the authority ʿImārat b. ʿĀmir on the authority Umm al-Ṭufayl Imraʾat Abī b. Kaʿb, who said: "I heard the Prophet mention that he saw his Lord in a dream in the form of a youth in his best years (*shābb muwaffaq*) [seated] on a golden throne with golden sandals on his feet." No one can reject the fact

> that the Messenger of God saw God in a dream. (That the Prophet) said, "I saw [God] in a dream," does not refute (the Qurʾān). Many people see similar dreams. They see their Lord, the angels, the Prophet, the Day of Resurrection or [other] weighty matters. There are many such dreams and they cannot be refuted. No one can deny them and no one can reject their meanings.[20]

As can be seen, the *ḥadīth al-ruʾyā* was being actively discussed by prominent Shīʿī scholars that lived in the same period in which the occultation of the twelfth Imam became a doctrine of the Imāmī Shīʿa. And now we move to discuss the motif of vision and dreams of the Hidden Imam.

Messianic Encounters

In speaking about the Hidden Imam, the landscape of Shīʿī chiliastic literature is marked by a number of seeming contradictions. There are several *ḥadīths*, for instance, that prohibit revealing the name of the Hidden Imam and disclosing the time and place of his appearance. At the same time, other *ḥadīths* ascribed to the Prophet and the first eleven Imams speak openly of the twelfth Imam's name and provide vivid details concerning the time and circumstances of his return.

But one issue about which there is unanimity is the approximate age of the Qāʾim (Riser or Resurrector). In Tradition after Tradition ascribed to the sixth Imam, Jaʿfar al-Ṣādiq (d. 148/765), it is predicted that the Hidden Imam will appear as a young person (usually *shābb* but on occasion, *fatā, ṣabī* or *ghulām*). One such Tradition ascribed to the second Imam, al-Ḥasan b. ʿAlī (d. 50/670) states that, "God will prolong (the Qāʾim's) life in hiding. Then he will cause him to appear, through His might, in the form of a youth (*fī ṣūrat shābb*) less than forty years of age—this that he may know that God has power over all things."[21] In a long Tradition that has been narrated on the authority of al-Mufaḍḍal b. ʿUmar al-Juʿfī (d. ca. 179/795),[22] when the Imam manifests himself at the Kaʿba, "No one will recognize him [because] he will appear as a youth."[23] Another *ḥadīth* recounts the sixth Imam as having said, "The Lord of this cause is the youngest of us in age and the most beautiful of us in appearance." When asked about the time when "the Lord of the cause" would appear, al-Ṣādiq responded allusively, "When travelers set out to pay homage to the lad."[24] When one of his disciples suggested to al-Ṣādiq that he could be the Lord of the Age, the Imam responded with surprise and shock. Pulling his wrinkled skin, he declared, "I have become old, whereas your master is a young man (*shābb ḥadath*)."[25]

A separate Tradition attributed to the third Shīʿī Imam, al-Ḥusayn b. ʿAlī (d. 60/680), uses the same locution that is found in the version of the *ḥadīth al-ruʾyā* cited above: "When the Qāʾim rises, the people will reject him because he will return as a youth in his best years (*shābban muwaffaqan*).[26] No one will remain believing in him except those with whom God made a covenant in [the world of] the first particles."[27] This phrase, *shābb muwaffaq*, is echoed in another Tradition about the Qāʾim: "The Qāʾim is one of my descendants. He will live as long as Abraham (*al-khalīl*), 120 years. He will appear in the form of a youth in his best years (*shābb muwaffaq*) who is thirty-two years old. A band of people will forsake him."[28]

Other *ḥadīths* express a similar expectation. As one *ḥadīth* indicates, the Qāʾim will be persecuted by his own followers for appearing as a youth rather than as an elder: "One of the greatest calamities is that their Lord will appear to them as a young man while they expect him [to appear as] a great *shaykh*."[29]

Another *ḥadīth* ascribed to Muḥammad al-Bāqir states:

> They asked the Commander of the Faithful, ʿAlī, peace be upon him, about the attributes of the Mahdī. ʿAlī responded, "He is a youth with broad shoulders, a beautiful countenance, elegant hair; the hair on his head flows down over his shoulders. The light of his face covers the blackness of his beard and hair."[30]

The physical beauty of the Qāʾim also is referenced in several *ḥadīths* attributed to the prophet Muḥammad. In one such *ḥadīth*, Muḥammad declares:

> At the End of Time, a man will arise from my family—a youth with a beautiful countenance, a broad forehead, and an aquiline nose. He will fill the earth with equity and justice as it had been previously filled with oppression and tyranny. He will rule for seven years.[31]

Another *ḥadīth* ascribed to Muḥammad and found in Sunni sources describes the Mahdī in the following terms: "His face is like a brilliant moon. His (skin) color is the color of the Arabs. His body is like the body of the Israelites. He will fill the earth with justice just as it has been filled with injustice. The denizens of the heavens, the people of the earth and the birds in the air will be pleased with his caliphate. He will rule for twenty years."[32] A rare Shīʿī *ḥadīth* ascribed to al-Bāqir states that in his beauty and magnanimity (*jamālihi wa-sakhāʾihi*), the Qāʾim will manifest the beauty and magnanimity of Joseph, the archetype of comeliness, modesty and beneficence in Islamic literature.[33] Other *ḥadiths* attributed to the Prophet and the Imams describe the twelfth Imam as a youth who is immaculately dressed, whose face is as luminous as the moon, whose eyes are deep black, and whose eyebrows are narrow. The Imam is, moreover, described as possessing a long high nose, a thick beard, and a beauty mark on the right side of his face that is like a brilliant star (*kawkab durrī*).[34] These Traditions emphasize the youth, refinement, and beauty of the Imam, to the point of describing his teeth as equidistant from one another.[35]

Such attributes are among the first things described in accounts of encounters with the Hidden Imam. Most Shīʿī works on the twelfth Imam from the time of al-Kulaynī onward contain accounts of believers who claimed to have met the Imam. Before the death of the eleventh Imam in 260/874, those who claimed to have seen his son and successor as a child described his unusual beauty. One such account states that he had a "broad forehead, white complexion, brilliant eyes, strong palms, bent knees, a mole on his right cheek, and a part of his hair in locks."[36]

Four Accounts of Visions of the Hidden Imam from the Period of Lesser Occultation

Most of the narratives describing encounters with the Hidden Imam from the period of the lesser occultation[37] take place in or around the city of Mecca. The earliest sources affirm that during the pilgrimage season, the Qāʾim "is at Mecca, unrecognized, scrutinizing the hearts of the believers."[38] In what follows, are four typical narratives. We will be keen to look for how the Imam is described in these narratives while keeping in mind the description of the youth in the Prophet's *ḥadīth al-ruʾyā*.

1. A Resident of al-Madāʾin

One of the earliest accounts available is mentioned by al-Kulaynī in his *ḥadīth* compendium, *al-Kāfī*. A chapter of this work is entitled, "The name of those who saw (the twelfth Imam)."[39] Of the small number (fifteen) of reports that are included in this chapter, most simply mention the names of believers who are credited with seeing the son of al-Ḥasan al-ʿAskarī while the eleventh Imam was still alive, that is, while the twelfth Imam was still a young boy,[40] or shortly thereafter, when the twelfth Imam had reached the age of adolescence. The fifteenth and final report in this chapter is noticeably different from all those that precede it. Not only does it contain a clear narrative structure, but al-Kulaynī also does not provide the name of the narrator, mentioning only that he is reporting it on the authority of one of the people of al-Madāʾin[41]:

> I was performing the *ḥajj* with one of my companions. We came to the halting station at the plain of ʿArafāt. Suddenly, [we saw] a youth (*shābb*) sitting down wearing a cloth around his waste and over one of his shoulders. He had yellow sandals[42] on his feet. . . . He did not show any of the strains of travel. A mendicant came to us but we shooed him away. He then went to the youth and begged him [for money]. (The youth) picked up something from the ground and gave it to him. The beggar prayed for him, praying fervently and for a long time. The youth then stood up and disappeared from us.

The narrator and his companion immediately approach the mendicant and inquire as to what the youth has given him. The beggar shows them a piece of gold that they estimate to be twenty *mithqāls*[43] in weight. The two immediately realize that the youth was their master (*mawlā*). Franticly, they begin searching for him but are unable to find him. They ask their fellow pilgrims from Mecca and Medina whether they know anything about this young man. They learn only that he is "a youth and a descendant of ʿAlī (*shābb ʿalawī*) who performs the *ḥajj* on foot each year."[44]

2. ʿAlī b. Ibrāhīm b. Mahziyār

The preceding account may be one of the earliest surviving narratives, but the account from the lesser occultation that is cited perhaps more than any other is the story of ʿAlī b. Ibrāhīm b. Mahziyār.[45] In this account, ʿAlī b. Ibrāhīm b. Mahziyār describes a stranger who appears to him in a dream and commands him to perform the *ḥajj,* for in Mecca he "will surely meet the Lord of the Age." Upon waking, ʿAlī b. Ibrāhīm b. Mahziyār decides at once to set out from his native ʿIrāq for the Ḥijāz. One night in Mecca, while circumambulating the Kaʿba, he sees "a comely and sweet-smelling youth wearing a mantle." The youth guides ʿAlī b. Ibrāhīm b. Mahziyār out of Mecca, riding throughout the night and passing Mount ʿArafāt and Mount Minā until they reach the mountains of Ṭāʾif. The youth proceeds to point to a tent bursting with light pitched on a nearby hill.[46] As the two approach the tent, the unnamed youth turns to ʿAlī b. Ibrāhīm b. Mahziyār and says, "This is sacred space. Only a friend of God (*walī*) enters it and only a friend of God takes leave from it."[47] The youth enters the tent and instructs ʿAlī b. Ibrāhīm b. Mahziyār to do the same. As soon as ʿAlī b. Ibrāhīm b. Mahziyār enters, he beholds the Imam:

> I entered into his presence, may the blessings of God be upon him, and found him sitting on a rug with brown and red-coloured spots, reclining on a pillow. We greeted each other. I looked at him closely and saw a face as luminous as the moon. He was strong yet refined and mild-tempered, not too tall and not too short. He was of medium build and possessed a broad forehead, beautifully arched eyebrows, deep-black and large eyes, an aquiline nose, and two smooth cheeks with a birthmark on the right. My mind was lost in his features as I gazed upon him.[48]

3. ʿAlī b. Ibrāhīm al-Fadakī[49]

> As I was circumambulating the Kaʿba and had completed the sixth *ṭawāf* and was about to begin the seventh, suddenly my eyes fell upon a group sitting to the right of the Kaʿba. A beautiful, sweet-smelling and awe-inspiring youth reverently approached them and began speaking. I have never [heard] words more beautiful than his, nor [heard] a tongue sweeter than his, nor (seen) sitting more exquisite than the manner of his sitting." As al-Fadakī approached the youth, the young man asked him, "Do you know who I am?" When al-Fadakī answered that he did not, the youth declared, "I am the Mahdī. I am the Qāʾim of the Age. I am the one who will fill the earth with justice just as it will have been full of injustice and oppression. Truly, the earth will never be devoid of a Proof. The people will not have [waited] longer than the period in which the Children of

> Israel wandered [the deserts of Sinai] before the days of my advent have been made manifest. This is a trust which I leave in your care. Tell [only] your God-fearing and truthful brothers about it.[50]

4. Muḥammad b. Aḥmad b. Khalaf

In the year 293/906, while on the *ḥajj*, Muḥammad b. Aḥmad b. Khalaf[51] fell asleep near the *maqām ibrāhīm*.[52] A prayer offered in a voice unlike any other he had ever heard awakened him. He looked attentively at the person who was praying. He was a brown-skinned youth (*shābb asmar*). He said, "I have never before seen beauty the like of the beauty of his form, nor a body as well-proportioned as his." After concluding his prayers, the youth left the mosque and began performing the *saᶜy*. Muḥammad b. Aḥmad b. Khalaf likewise began to undertake the *saᶜy* while pondering whether the youth may be the Lord of the Age. He followed the same youth to a valley but as he drew close to him, he suddenly found himself standing before a dark-skinned (*aswad*), awe-inspring man.[53] According to Muḥammad b. Aḥmad b. Khalaf, "he let out the most frightening cry I have ever heard."[54] The dark-skinned man immediately disappeared as Muḥammad b. Aḥmad b. Khalaf stood shaking and distraught from the mighty cry.

The next year, Muḥammad b. Aḥmad b. Khalaf visited the shrine of the Prophet in Medina. While there, in a dream, he saw someone shaking him. He awoke to find the same dark-skinned man he had seen in Mecca the previous year. The man told him that he was commanded to scream in that fashion to Muḥammad b. Aḥmad b. Khalaf. He congratulated him for having been the recipient of such a great blessing and instructed him to render profuse thanks to God for having been enabled to see what he saw. He furthermore commanded him to remain steadfast in his worship of God before adding that "the divine cause/command is near (*inna al-amr qarīb*)."[55]

Four Accounts of Visions of the Hidden Imam from the Period of the Greater Occultation

We now proceed to the period of the greater occultation. The accounts of believers who are alleged to have met the Hidden Imam during the greater occultation are generally more embellished than those from the lesser occultation. Four representative accounts are presented here.[56]

1. Ḥasan b. Mithla

The following narrative is a description of what is believed to be one of the earliest encounters between the Hidden Imam and a follower during the Greater Occultation. In an account that is said to have occurred in the late 4th/10th century, a Shīʿī named Ḥasan b. Mithla al-Jamkarānī[57] reports a dream where a group of people come to his home in the middle of the night and awake him. They cry out, "Arise! Obey the command of Imam Muḥammad Mahdī, the Lord of the Age—may the blessings of God be upon him—for he summons you!" Ḥasan b. Mithla is brought to a nearby field where he finds a throne with fine rugs. Sitting against four pillows on this throne is a young man, thirty years of age. An elder is next to him, a book in hand, reading to the youth. More than sixty men are engaged in prayer around him, some dressed in white and others in green. Ḥasan b. Mithla discerns at once that the elder is the enigmatic al-Khiḍr[58] and that the young man is the Hidden Imam. The Imam instructs Ḥasan b. Mithla to build a mosque on this site, which many today believe to be the Mosque of Jamkarān.[59]

2. Amīr Isḥāq al-Astarābādī

The Safavid era scholar Muḥammad Bāqir al-Majlisī (d. 1110/1698)[60] included five accounts in a section of his encyclopedic *Biḥār al-anwār* entitled, "Rare are the narratives of those who have seen (the Hidden Imam) during the period of the Greater Occultation close to our time."[61] The bulk of this section is dedicated to recounting the story of the Green Island in the White Sea,[62] while the remaining pages are set aside for four other reports al-Majlisī himself has gathered from scholars identified by him as "the most learned and authoritative *ʿulamāʾ*." In each of these accounts, the typological motifs of youth, beauty, and divine assistance are found. Due to constraints of space, only two of the accounts are discussed here.

The first of the accounts al-Majlisī has recorded is one that he heard from his father, Muḥammad Taqī al-Majlisī (d. 1070/1659–1660),[63] a mystically inclined scholar who himself claimed to have encountered the Hidden Imam in a dream and to have received a copy of Imam Zayn al-ʿĀbidīn's (d. c. 95/713–714) *al-Ṣaḥīfa al-sajjādiyya* from him.[64] His father told the younger al-Majlisī that a righteous and honorable man lived in their time by the name of Amīr Isḥāq al-Astarābādī[65] who had performed the pilgrimage forty times. On one of these journeys, Amīr Isḥāq al-Astarābādī was separated from his caravan and was on the verge of dying from thirst. He began crying to the Hidden Imam for assistance, when suddenly, at the end of the road, he saw the shape of a person (*shabaḥ*). He stared at this mysterious figure as he approached him: "I saw a youth (*shābban*) with a beauteous countenance, (wearing) immaculate clothing, brown-skinned, in the form of the most noble of men, mounted on a camel, and carrying a water-skin."[66]

The youth proceeded to provide Amīr Isḥāq al-Astarābādī with water and guide him to Mecca. After departing, Amīr Isḥāq al-Astarābādī realized that the youth was the Hidden Imam.

3. Mīrzā Muḥammad al-Astarābādī

In another account cited by al-Majlisī, we read of the experience of a certain Mīrzā Muḥammad al-Astarābādī (d. 1028/1619)[67]:

> One day, I was circumambulating the Kaᶜba when suddenly a youth (*shābb*) with a beautiful countenance appeared and began likewise to perform the *ṭawāf*. When he approached me, he gave me a bouquet of red roses, even though it was not the season for roses. I received them, smelled the flowers, and said: "Where do these roses come from?" He said, "From *al-Kharābāt*." He then disappeared and I did not see him again.[68]

After the youth disappears, Mīrzā Muḥammad al-Astarābādī realizes that he was the Hidden Imam.

4. A Believer from Kāshān

An unnamed believer from Kāshān[69] sees the first Shīᶜī Imam, ᶜAlī b. Abī Ṭālib (d. 40/661), in a dream. ᶜAlī proceeds to lead him into a tent where he encounters an ineffably beautiful, comely and radiant youth (*javānī dar ghāyat-i ḥusn va jamāl va bahāʾ*). The believer soon learns that this youth is none other than the Hidden Imam, "the Lord of the Age."[70]

Vision of the Lord of the Age, Visions of God

As demonstrated, Shīᶜī sources continually cultivate the image of the Hidden Imam as a comely youth. Each narrative serves to accentuate and foreground the divine promise of the Imam's appearance as a youth at the *eschaton*. The repetition of certain of the Imam's attributes *mutatis mutandis* is a persuasive literary device. The description is especially prominent in the narratives that report encounters between the Imam and the most privileged of his votaries. But what is the connection between these narratives and the report of the prophet Muḥammad's encounter with God?

In order to explore the typologies between the two, we must acquaint ourselves with some of the Imamological principles of Shīᶜī theology. In the earliest Shīᶜī sources, God is spoken of as possessing both attributes apropos of his essence (*dhāt*) and attributes concerning his actions (*fiᶜl*). The attributes of God, "revealed to humanity by the Most Beautiful Names of God," have loci of manifestation: "vehicles of attributes" and "active organs" who are the Prophet and the Imams.[71] Ontologically, therefore, it is impossible for human beings to ever know God. Epistemologically speaking, it is possible to speak of the Imams as God. Amir-Moezzi's study of the earliest Shīᶜī *ḥadīth* collections led him to conclude that for the early Shīᶜī theosophists, "knowledge of the reality of the Imam is the equivalent to knowledge of that which can be known about God."[72] In other words, in the Shīᶜī *weltanschauung*, the Imams are "the perfect manifestation of those aspects of God that can be made manifest."[73]

It may be instructive to consider this in light of the exoteric/esoteric (*ẓāhir/bāṭin*) dichotomy. The esoteric aspect of God is that aspect which completely transcends human understanding and comprehension. The exoteric aspect, on the other hand, finds its manifestations in the theophany of the Imam.[74] This, of course, in no way infringes on the sanctity of *tawḥīd* and the absolute transcendence of God's essence. As Tradition after Tradition attest, the Imams staunchly warn against all manner of anthropomorphism and assimiliationism. Al-Shaykh al-Ṣadūq (d. 381/991), for example, cites the following highly suggestive *ḥadīth* in his *al-Tawḥīd*:

> Abū Baṣīr asked Abū ᶜAbd Allāh (i.e. Jaᶜfar al-Ṣādiq): "Tell me about God—exalted and glorified be He. Will the believers see Him on the Day of Resurrection?" (Jaᶜfar) said, "Yes [just as] they have seen Him before the Day of Resurrection.' I asked him, 'When?" He said, 'When (God) asked them, 'Am I not your Lord?' [And] they said, 'Yes, of a certainty!' " (Qurʾān 7:172) (The Imam) became silent for a while and then said, "Truly, the believers see Him in this world [even] before the Day of Resurrection. Do you

not see Him at this very moment?" Abū Baṣīr said, "May my life be a sacrifice for you! Can I relate this news about you [to others]?" He said, "No, because if you relate it, a denier ignorant of the meaning of what you have said will condemn it. He will then claim that this is anthropomorphism and will disbelieve it. [But] seeing with the heart is not the same as seeing with the eye. Immeasurably exalted is God above that which the anthropomorphists and heretics ascribe to Him!"[75]

Speaking on behalf of all the Imams, al-Ṣādiq affirms in a separate Tradition recorded in the same work, "Were it not for God, we would not be known, and were it not for us, God would not be known."[76] A prophetic *ḥadīth* with an unrelated chain of transmission narrated on the authority of the eighth Imam, ʿAlī al-Riḍā (d. 203/818) states, "He who knows us knows God and he who disbelieves in us has disbelieved in God."[77] Furthermore, al-Ṣādiq reports that when al-Ḥusayn b. ʿAlī was asked about the inner knowledge of God, he responded, "For the people of each age, it is the inner knowledge of their Imam, to whom obedience is due."[78]

The implications of this theology of theophany are quite profound. Since the passing of the eleventh Imam in 260/874, the twelfth Imam continues to be the Imam of the Age for the Shīʿa. It is due to his presence that the world continues to exist. Although devotion and love (*walāya*) for all of the Imams is an unchanging axiom for the Shīʿa, since 260/874, to know and worship God is particularly to know and obey the twelfth Imam and to know and obey the twelfth Imam is to know and worship God. Indeed, as Tradition after Tradition tells us, were it not for the perpetual existence of the Imam, humankind could never know God.

In a *ḥadīth* ascribed to Jaʿfar al-Ṣādiq and narrated by his disciple, Mufaḍḍal b. ʿUmar, the Imam asserts: "When our Qāʾim rises, the earth will shine with the light of its Lord."[79] In a separate but related *ḥadīth*, Jaʿfar avers that "the Lord of the earth is the Imam of the earth." But as Mufaḍḍal's next question reveals, not just any Imam is meant: "What will happen when he appears?" When the Awaited One manifests himself, Jaʿfar responds, the people will have no need for the light of the sun and the moon for the light of the Imam will suffice them.[80]

From these and other Traditions, one can extrapolate that the Imams—but, in particular the Qāʾim—is one with God in that he will cause the earth to become illumined with light. In the famous prayer of *al-nudba,*[81] the Hidden Imam is invoked as "the countenance of God upon which (His) friends (*al-awliyāʾ*) have set their affections."[82] An oft-cited Tradition ascribed to Muḥammad al-Bāqir defines the day [when] the Qāʾim appears as one of the "days of God" mentioned in two verses of the Qurʾān (14:5; 45:14).[83]

Another significant Tradition can be found under the Shīʿī exegete al-ʿAyyāshī's (d. late third/ninth century)[84] commentary on Qurʾān 2:210: "Are they waiting for anything less than that God should come down to them overshadowed with clouds along with the angels? The matter has already been decided and unto God shall all matters return." According to a *ḥadīth* ascribed to the fifth Imam and cited by al-ʿAyyāshī, by God in this verse is meant the Qāʾim, who will descend to earth on a canopy of light on the Day of Judgment in order to separate truth from falsehood.[85] Here, one should bear in mind that the twelfth Imam's most famous epithet, *al-qāʾim,* is also one of the names of God in Shīʿī sources.[86]

As observed by Corbin, in the Shīʿī tradition, "the epiphany of the 'Form of God' responds to the very concept of the Imām. And the whole secret of Shīʿism, its *raison d'être* . . . is first and foremost that there were minds that postulated the form of theophany constitutive of Imāmology."[87] This significant point is further developed in a recent study by ʿAbd al-Hakeem Carney:

> God can only be known in his manifestation, and his perfection manifestation for the Shiʿa theosophists . . . is the figure of the Imām. The Imām becomes the actual beloved, then, because He is the perfect manifestation of the only God that can be loved, the manifest God who makes Himself (albeit incompletely) manifest in the form of the Imām.[88]

Conclusion

It should by now be evident that the visions of the Hidden Imam constitute a figuration, an antitype, "a realized form"[89] of that which has been prefigured in the prophetic *ḥadīth al-ruʾyā*. The antitype represents a heightening of the type. Whereas previously we were presented with a youth (*shābb*) embodying the most beautiful form of God, in the antitype, we find the repeated fulfillment of that experience. The comely youth remains God. As the type, the Divine appears as an unnamed youth. As the antitype, he is the Hidden Imam. The object remains the same. It is the subject that has transformed.[90]

In defining typological exegesis and distinguishing it from other hermeneutical methodologies, Goppelt has averred that "persons, actions, events, and institutions . . . are to be interpreted typologically only if they are considered to be divinely ordained representations or types of future realities that will be even greater and more complete."[91] In this way, we may speak of the encounters with the youthful Imam as confirmations of the *ḥadīth al-ruʾyā* inasmuch as they assist in further appreciating the significance of the Prophet meeting his Lord in the form of a youth. As Frye observed in his analysis of Biblical typology in the Old and New Testaments, "Evidence, so called, is bounced back and forth between the testaments like a tennis ball; and no other evidence is given us. The two testaments form a double mirror, each reflecting the other but neither the world outside."[92]

In contemplating the apocalyptic substrate of the Qurʾān, Todd Lawson observed that "typology frequently erases or collapses time."[93] Lawson's statement could not be more apposite in light of the Shīʿa. History, as is well known, has not often been kind to the Shīʿa, a minority that has at times been ignored and dismissed by the majority of Muslims throughout its history—a history that has been synchronously dominated for more than a millennium by the figure of the Hidden Imam. Reports of encounters with the youtfhful deliverer, the antitype of the Prophet's vision of God, have served to explain this history while simultaneously, explaining *away* this history.

Acknowledgment

This chapter is dedicated in loving memory to Professor Michael Marmura (1929–2009). I would like to record my gratitude to Todd Lawson for his comments on an earlier draft.

Notes

1. The Shīʿī Imams are all believed to have received inspiration and divine guidance through veridical visions. On the superhuman visual capacities of the twelve Imams and their powers to perform vision-related miracles, an important motif in many of the Traditions compiled in one of the earliest extant Shīʿī *ḥadīth* collections, Abū Jaʿfar Muḥammad b. al-Ḥasan b. Farrūkh al-Ṣaffār al-Qummī's (d. 289/902) *Baṣāʾir al-darajāt fī faḍāʾil āl Muḥammad* (Qum: Maktabat Āyat Allāh al-ʿUẓmā al-Marʿashī al-Najafī, 1404/1983–1984), see Etan Kohlberg, "Vision and the Imams," in *Autour du Regard*, ed. É. Chaumont (Paris: Peeters, 2003), 125–57. See also Meir M. Bar-Asher, *Scripture and Exegesis in Early Imāmī Shiism* (Leiden: Brill, 1999), 158.

2. See Hossein Ziai, "Dreams ii: In the Persian Tradition," *EIr*. Cf. Khalid Sindawi, "The Image of ʿAlī bin Abū Ṭālib in the Dreams of Visitors to his Tomb," in *Dreaming Across Boundaries: The Intepretation of Dreams in Islamic Lands*, ed. Louise Marlow (Cambridge: Ilex Foundation, Boston, Massachusetts and Center for Hellenistic Studies, Trustees for Harvard University, Washington D.C., 2008), 179–201; Mohammad Ali Amir-Moezzi, "Visions d'Imams en mystique duodécimaine moderne et contemporaine," in *Autour du Regard*, ed. É. Chaumont (Paris: Peeters, 2003), 97–124; Rainer Brunner, "Le Charisme de Songeurs: Ḥusayn al-Nūrī al-Ṭabrisī et la Fonction des Rêves dans Shiʿisme Duodécimain," in *Le Shīʿisme Imāmite Qurante Ans Aprés*, ed. Mohammad Ali Amir-Moezzi, Meir M. Bar-Asher, Simon Hopkins (Turnhout: Brepols, 2009), 95–115. For Shīʿī conceptions of *walāya*, see Henry Corbin, *En Islam iranien* (Paris: Gallimard, 1972), vol. 4, s.v. index 'walâyat'; idem, *L'homme et son ange* (Paris: Fayard, 1983), 222–28; Hermann Landolt, "Walāyah," *ER*.

3. The eschatological saviour of Twelver Shīʿī Islam, commonly referred to in Shīʿī sources by one of his many epithets, e.g. *al-mahdī* (the rightly guided one), *al-imām al-ghāʾib* (the occulted Imam) *al-muntaẓar* (the expected one), *ṣāḥib al-zamān* (the Lord of the Age), *al-ḥujja* or *ḥujjat Allāh* (the Proof or the Proof of God), *ṣāḥib al-amr* (the Lord of the cause), and in particular, *al-qāʾim* (the rising one or the resurrector). According to the Twelver Shīʿa, he has been in occultation since the late third/ninth century. On this figure, see Abdulaziz Sachedina, *Islamic Messianism: The Idea of the Mahdi in Twelver Shiʿism* (Albany: State University of New York Press, 1981); W. Madelung, "Ḳāʾim Āl Muḥammad," *EI*[2]; J.G.J. ter Haar, "Muḥammad al-Ḳāʾim," *EI*[2]; Mohammad Ali Amir-Moezzi, *The Divine Guide in Early Shīʿism*, trans. David Streight (Albany: State University of New York Press, 1994), 99–123; idem, "Aspects de la Figure du Sauveur dans l'Eschatologie Chiite Duodécimaine," in *Messianismes*, ed. Jean-Christophe Attias, et al. (Geneva: Labor et Fides, 2000), 213–28; idem, "Fin du Temps et Retour à l'Origine," in *Mahdisme et Millénarisme en Islam*, ed. Mercedes Garcia-Arenal (Aix-en-Provence: Édisud, 2001), 53–72; idem, "Eschatology iii. In Imami Shīʿism," *EIr*; idem, "Islam in Iran vii: The Concept of Mahdi in Twelver Shiʿism," *EIr*; Mariella Ourghi, *Schiitischer Messianismus und Mahdi-Glaube in der Neuzeit* (Wurzburg: Ergon, 2008).

4. Among Western scholars, the first person to study the phenomenon was Henry Corbin. See Henry Corbin, "Au Pays de l'Imām caché," in *Eranos Jahrbuch* XXXII (1963): 31–87; idem, *En Islam iranien*, 4: 338–89; idem, "*Mundus Imaginalis*, or the Imaginary and the Imaginal," in *Swedenborg and Esoteric Islam*, trans. Leonard Fox (West Chester, PA: Swedenborg Foundation, 1995), 1–33 and in particular, 20–33; idem, "The Visionary Dream in Islamic Spirituality," in *The Dream and Human Society*, ed. G.E. von Grunebaum and Roger Caillois (Berkeley and Los Angeles: University of California Press, 1966), 381–408. See also Mohammad Ali Amir-Moezzi, "Contribution á la typologie des rencontres avec l'imam caché," in *Journal Asiatique* 284.1 (1996): 109–35; idem, "An Absence Filled with Presences: Shaykhiyya Hermeneutics of the Occultation," in *The Twelver Shia in Modern Times: Religious Culture and*

Political History (Social, Economic and Political Studies of the Middle East and Asia, 72), ed. Rainer Brunner and Werner Ende (Leiden: Brill, 2001), 38–57; Amir-Moezzi, *The Divine Guide in Early Shīʿism*, 115–16. On the social and religious implications of these narratives in the late nineteenth century, see Omid Ghaemmaghami, "Seeing the Proof: Mīrzā Ḥusayn al-Nūrī and the Revivification of the Shīʿī Motif of Encountering the Occulted Imam," paper presented at the Annual Middle East Studies Association Conference (MESA), 25 March 2006, UC Santa Barbara; idem, "Arresting the *Eschaton*: Mīrzā Ḥusayn Nūrī (d. 1320/1902) and Shīʿī Messianism in the Late Nineteenth Century," paper presented at the annual meeting of the Society for Shaykhī, Bābī and Bahāʾī Studies, MESA, 21 November 2009.

5. Typology is uninterested in the accurate reconstruction of texts and narratives. As observed by typologist Samuel Amsler, "Typological interpretation does not deal with the literal historical sense of an event, but with its theological meaning. . . . The theological truth of the events is not placed in doubt even when the historical reconstruction indicates that the event happened in a way different from what is presented in the texts." Samuel Amsler, *L'Ancien Testament dans l'Église: Essai d'Herméneutique Chrétienne* (Neuchâtel: Delachaux and Niestlé, 1960), 221 ff. (cited in Leonhard Goppelt, *Typos: the Typological Interpretation of the Old Testament in the New,* (n. 83) (Grand Rapids: William B. Eerdmans Publishing Company, 1982), 233.

6. Northrop Frye, *The Great Code: the Bible and Literature* (Toronto: Academic Press Canada, 1982), 80–81.

7. Northrop Frye, *Words with Power* (San Diego: Harcourt Brace Jovanovich, 1990), 139.

8. Michael Zwettler, "A Mantic Manifesto: The Sūra of 'The Poets' and the Qurʾānic Foundations of Prophetic Authority," in *Poetry and Prophecy: The Beginnings of a Literary Tradition*, ed. James L. Kugel (Ithaca: Cornell University Press, 1990), 96.

9. Henry Corbin, *Alone with the Alone* (Princeton: Princeton University Press, 1997), 272.

10. See Josef van Ess, "Vision and Ascension: *Sūrat al-Najm* and its Relationship with Muḥammad's *Miʿrāj*," *Journal of Qurʾānic Studies* 1: 1 (1999): 47–62.

11. See al-Sayyid Muḥammad Ibn al-ʿAlawī al-Mālikī, *The Prophets in Barzakh and the Hadith of the Isrâʾ and the Miʿrâj followed by the Immense Merits of al-Shâm and the Vision of Allah*, 2nd ed., trans. Gibril Fouad Haddad (Fenton: As-Sunna Foundation of America, 1999), 145 ff.

12. Regarding him, see C. Brokelmann, "al-Ḳasṭallānī," *EI*[2].

13. Annemarie Schimmel, *And Muhammad is His Messenger: The Veneration of the Prophet in Islamic Piety* (Chapel Hill: University of North Carolina Press, 1985), 163, citing al-Qasṭallānī.

14. Muḥammad b. Jarīr al-Ṭabarī, *Jāmiʿ al-bayān* (Beirut: Dār al-Fikr lil-Ṭibāʿa wa-l-Nashr wa-l-Tawzīʿ, 1415/1995), 27: 64 (no. 2513). The various chains of transmission and text of this Tradition are gathered and discussed by ʿAbd al-Raḥmān b. Aḥmad b. Rajab (d. 1393/1973), *Ikhtiyār al-ūlā fī sharḥ*

ḥadīth ikhtiṣām al-malāʾ al-aʿlā (Damascus: Maktabat Dār al-Bayān, 1985). For a detailed discussion of the implications and controversies surrounding this *ḥadīth* in the Sunni tradition, see W. Wesley Williams, "*Tajallī wa-Ruʾyā:* A Study of Anthropomorphic Theophany and *Visio Dei* in the Hebrew Bible, the Qurʾan and Early Sunni Islam" (Unpublished PhD Dissertation, University of Michigan, 2008), 155 ff.

15. See Hellmut Ritter, *The Ocean of the Soul: Man, the World and God in the Stories of Farīd al-Dīn ʿAṭṭār* (Leiden: Brill, 2003), 365. Several versions of this Tradition are provided in Annemarie Schimmel, *Mystical Dimensions of Islam* (Chapel Hill: University of North Carolina Press, 1976), 290.

16. Abū Bakr Aḥmad b. ʿAlī al-Khaṭīb al-Baghdādī (d. 463/1071), *Taʾrīkh Baghdād*, 13: 312. Variants of this Tradition are provided by the respected Indian scholar, ʿAlī b. ʿAbd al-Mālikī al-Muttaqī al-Hindī (d. 975/1567) in his *Kanz al-ʿummāl fī sunan aqwāl wa-l-afʿāl* (Beirut: Muʾassasat al-Risāla, 1409/1989), 1: 228. Cf. Jalāl al-Dīn ʿAbd al-Raḥmān al-Suyūṭī, *al-Laʾāliʾ al-maṣnūʿa fī 'l-aḥādīth al-mawḍūʿa* (Egypt: al-Maktaba al-Tijāriyya al-Kubrā, n.d.), 1:16. See also Ritter, *The Ocean of the Soul*, 459–61, 484 ff; Pierre Lory, *Le Rêve et ses Interprétations en Islam* (Paris: Albin Michel, 2003), 35, 140; Schimmel, *And Muhammad is His Messenger*, 164. al-Malikī refers to it as "a condemned, disauthenticated" Tradition, *The Prophets in Barzakh and the Hadith of the Isrâʾ*, 138 (esp. n. 254).

17. Jaʿfar Muḥammad b. Yaʿqūb Isḥāq al-Kulaynī al-Rāzī, *al-Uṣūl min al-kāfī* (Tehran: Muʾassasat Dār al-Kutub al-Islāmiyya, n.d.), 1: 100–101.

18. On him, see Etan Kohlberg, "Kolayni," *EIr*.

19. On him, see H. Halm, "Abū Ḥātem Rāzī," *EIr*.

20. Abū Ḥātim Aḥmad b. Ḥamdān al-Rāzī, *Aʿlām al-nubuwwa* (Tehran: Imperial Iranian Academy of Philosophy, 1397/1977), 99–100. Persian translation, Abū Ḥātim al-Rāzī, *Munāẓirah-yi Muḥammad Zakariyyā-yi Rāzī bā Abū Ḥātim Rāzī dar mabāḥis̱-i ilāhīyāt, falsafah, paydāyish-i zabān va ʿulūm* (Tehran: Markaz-i Farhangī-i Intishārāt-i Munīr, 1377(sh)/1998), 97–99. Curiously, the Persian translator has chosen not to introduce the version of the *ḥadīth* that mentions the youth, instead providing this Tradition in a footnote (on the bottom of page 99) with the dismissive comment: "The narrations [of this *ḥadīth*] are Sunnī and this is their belief." See also Josef van Ess, *The Youthful God: Anthropomorphism in Early Islam* (Tempe: Department of Religious Studies, Arizona State University, 1988), 18 (note 78).

21. Abū 'l-Qāsim ʿAlī b. Muḥammad b. ʿAlī al-Khazzāz al-Qummī al-Rāzī, *Kifāyat al-athar fī naṣṣ ʿalā al-aʾimma al-ithnā ʿashar* (Qum: Intishārāt-i Bīdār, Maṭbaʿat al-Khayyām, 1401/1980–1), 226. Cf. different *ḥadīth* attributed to Jaʿfar al-Ṣādiq in al-Ṣaffār al-Qummī, *Baṣāʾir al-darajāt*, 189: "The Lord of this cause does not exceed forty years of age." See also, Shaykh al-Ṭāʾifa Abū Jaʿfar Muḥammad b. al-Ḥasan al-Ṭūsī, *Kitāb al-ghayba* (Qum: Muʾassasat al-Maʿārif al-Islāmiyya, 1425/2004–2005), 419.

22. One of Jaʿfar al-Ṣādiq's foremost disciples on whose authority a number of Traditions of an esoteric nature are narrated. On the works that are attributed to him, see Hossein Modarressi, *Tradition and Survival: A Bibliographical Survey of Early Shīʿite Literature* (no. 146) (Oxford: Oneworld, 2003), 333–7.

23. Muḥammad Bāqir b. Muḥammad Taqī al-Majlisī, *Biḥār al-anwār* (Beirut: Dār Iḥyā᾽ al-Turāth al-ʿArabī, 1403/1983), 53: 6–7. Al-Mufaḍḍal asks al-Ṣādiq a follow-up question: "My master, will he [really] return as a youth or will he appear as an old man?" Affirming that the Qā᾽im can appear as a youth, al-Ṣādiq states that God can manifest him in whatever form (*ṣūra*) He wants.

24. Al-Majlisī, *Biḥār al-anwār*, 51: 38–9. Cf. Muḥammad b. Ibrāhīm b. Jaʿfar al-Nuʿmānī, *al-Ghayba* (Beirut: Mu᾽assasat al-Aʿlamī lil-Maṭbūʿāt, 1403/1983), 123, which has a slightly different version of the first part of this Tradition: "The Lord of this cause is the youngest of us in age and the most obscure of us in appearance."

25. Al-Majlisī, *Biḥār al-anwār*, 52: 280.

26. The expression *shābb muwaffaq* has been translated by van Ess as "youth in his best years" while noting that it "lacks lexicographical parallels." Idem, *The Youthful God*, 18 (note 82). According to Lane, *shābb* means "youthful, or in the prime of manhood; a youth, or a young man; in the state from puberty to the completion of thirty years; or from sixteen years to thirty-two." Edward Lane, *Arabic-English Lexicon* (New York: F. Ungar Publication Company, 1955–6), 1: 1494. Its semantic field encompasses the qualities of briskiness, liveliness, and sprightfulness, but also burning brightly and fiercely. Al-Majlisī comments that the adjective *muwaffaq* in this context may refer to someone who is well-proportioned and mild-mannered or someone who is in the full vigor of his youth. Al-Majlisī, *Biḥār al-anwār*, 52: 287.

27. Al-Nuʿmānī, *al-Ghayba*, 125, 142. Cf. *Biḥār al-anwār*, 52: 287, where the Tradition begins with *law kharaja* in place of *law qad qāma*.

28. Al-Nuʿmānī, *al-Ghayba*, 125–6. A later version of his *ḥadīth* is cited in al-Ṭūsī, *Kitāb al-ghayba*, 420: "The life of the friend of God (*walī Allāh*) will be prolonged as long as Abraham, the friend [of God] (*al-khalīl*), 120 years. He will appear in the form of a youth in his best years (*fatā muwaffaq*), a thirty year old young man." Among the differences between the two is the fact that the latter has the locution *shābb muwaffaq* in place of *fatā muwaffaq*.

29. Al-Nuʿmānī, *al-Ghayba*, 125.

30. Al-Majlisī, *Biḥār al-anwār*, 51: 36. Cf. a similar Tradition cited in idem, 51: 44.

31. ʿAlī al-Kūrānī al-ʿĀmilī, ed. *Muʿjam aḥādīth al-imām al-Mahdī* (Qum: Mu᾽assasat al-Maʿārif al-Islāmiyya, 1411/1991), 1: 113 (citing Sunni works). See also ʿAbd al-Raḥīm Mubārak, *Bashā᾽ir al-imām al-muntaẓar fī al-kitāb wa-l-sunna wa-l-athar* (Mashhad: Mu᾽assasat al-Ṭabʿ wa-l-Nashr al-Tābiʿa lil-Āstāna al-Raḍawiyya al-Muqaddasa, 1430/2009), 305.

32. Al-ʿĀmilī, *Muʿjam*, 1:130.

33. Abū 'l-Ḥusayn ʿAlī b. al-Ḥusayn b. ʿAlī al-Masʿūdī (d. 346/957–8), *Ithbāt al-waṣiyya lil-imām ʿAlī b. Abī Ṭālib* (Beirut: Dār al-Aḍwā᾽, 1409/1988), 280.

34. A useful compilation of *ḥadīths* of this nature that describe the twelfth Imam's physical characteristics is provided in ʿAlī al-Yazdī al-Ḥā᾽irī, *Ilzām al-nāṣib fī ithbāt al-ḥujja al-ghā᾽ib* (Beirut: Mu᾽assasat al-Aʿlamī lil-Maṭbūʿāt, 1422/2002), 1: 419–21.

35. Al-Majlisī, *Biḥār al-anwār*, 51: 80, 96.

36. Ibid., 52: 25.

37. The period of the concealment of the Hidden Imam is divided into two periods: the lesser and greater occultation. According to later Shīʿī sources, during the lesser occultation (from the death of the eleventh Imam in 260/874 to 329/941), the twelfth Imam was in communication with the Shīʿī faithful through a set of four representatives. The last of these representatives in 329/941 was instructed by the Imam to not appoint a successor. At this point, the greater occultation is said to have begun during which there are no direct representatives between the Imam and the Shīʿa. According to the Shīʿa, the greater occultation will continue until the Imam's emergence from hiding at the End of Time. See Said Amir Arjomand, "Ḡayba," *EIr*.

38. D.B. MacDonald and M.G.S. Hodgson, "Ghayba," *EI*².

39. Al-Kulaynī al-Rāzī, *al-Uṣūl min al-kāfī*, 1: 329–32.

40. Ibid., 330.

41. Al-Madāʾin was once a metropolis on the Tigris river that declined in importance after the founding of Baghdad. See M. Streck and M. Morony, "al-Madāʾin," *EI*². Most of the residents were Shīʿī Muslims or pro-ʿAlids during the first to third centuries of the Islamic period. See Ghulām-Muḥsin Muḥarramī, *Tārīkh-i tashayyuʿ az āghāz tā pāyān-i ghaybat-i ṣughrā* (Qum: Markaz-i Intishārāt-i Muʾassasah-yi Āmūzishī va Pazhūhishī-i Imām Khumaynī, 1384AS/2005), 181.

42. Note the similarity between the yellow sandals of the Imam and the golden sandals of the youth encountered by the Prophet.

43. One *mithqāl* is equivalent to approximately 4.8 grams.

44. Al-Kulaynī al-Rāzī, *al-Uṣūl min al-kāfī*, 1: 332.

45. On him, see Said Amir Arjomand, "Imam *Absconditus* and the Beginnings of a Theology of Occultation: Imami Shiʿism Circa 280–90 A.H./900 A.D," *Journal of the American Oriental Society* 117.1 (1997), 6.

46. Cf. the tabernacle or tent of meeting where Moses would meet with God (*Exodus, passim*).

47. Cf. the words of God to Moses as he approached the Burning Bush (*Exodus* 3:4–5).

48. Abū Jaʿfar Muḥammad b. ʿAlī b. al-Ḥusayn b. Bābūya al-Qummī al-Ṣadūq, *Kamāl al-dīn wa-tamām al-niʿma* (Beirut: Muʾassasat al-Aʿlamī lil-Maṭbūʿāt, 1424/2004), 424–27.

49. There is no information in the Shīʿī *rijāl* works about this person other than the account of his having encountered the Hidden Imam mentioned here. ʿAlī al-Namāzī al-Shāhrūdī, *Mustadrakāt ʿilm rijāl al-ḥadīth* (Iṣfahān: Ibn al-Muʾallif, 1415/1994), 5: 275 (no. 9547).

50. Ibid., 444–5. See also Sachedina, *Islamic Messianism*, 75.

51. There again is no information in the Shīʿī *rijāl* works about this person other than the account of his having encountered the Hidden Imam mentioned here. Al-Namāzī al-Shāhrūdī, *Mustadrakāt ʿilm rijāl al-ḥadīth*, 6: 414 (no. 12,481).

52. A small shrine near the Kaʿba that houses a stone believed to bear the footprints of Abraham. See M.J. Kister, "Maḳām Ibrāhīm," *EI*².

53. The dark-colored skin may be an allusion to the fact that the mother of the putative twelfth Imam, according to some accounts, was a black slave. See Amir-Moezzi, *The Divine Guide*, 108. The man is described here as resembling a *fanīq*, a towering, strong male camel of superior breed that is never ridden. Al-Majlisī, *Biḥār al-anwār*, 52: 5.

54. Cf. the eschatological cry (*ṣayḥa*) mentioned in the Qurʾān (e.g. 36:49) that according to Shīʿī Traditions will announce the appearance of the Qāʾim. See Madelung, "Ḳāʾim Āl Muḥammad," *EI*².

55. Al-Ṭūsī, *Kitāb al-ghayba*, 254–7. Cf. Qurʾān 16:1: "God's cause/command comes; so seek not to hasten it." According to a *ḥadīth* ascribed to al-Ṣādiq, the cause or command of God (*amr Allāh*) mentioned in this verse is "our cause/command, meaning the rise of our Qāʾim (*huwa amrunā yaʿnī qiyām al-qāʾim*), (the one who will arise from) the family of Muḥammad. God has commanded us to not hasten (his appearance)." Sharaf al-Dīn ʿAlī al-Ḥusaynī al-Astarābādī al-Najafī, *Taʾwīl al-āyāt al-ẓāhira fī faḍāʾil al-ʿitra al-ṭāhira* (Qum: al-Madrasa lil-Imām al-Mahdī, 1407/1987), 1: 252.

56. A comprehensive, analytic and synthetic treatment of the accounts describing encounters with the Imam from the greater occultation is the focus of the author's PhD dissertation, tentatively titled "Seeing the Proof: The Narratives of Encounters with the Hidden Imam during the Greater Occultation," expected to be completed in 2011.

57. There are no known references to this person in any of the early Shīʿī biographical works.

58. The legendary figure mentioned in Islamic sources and commonly identified as the anonymous spiritual guide of Moses featured in the *Sūrat al-Kahf* of the Qurʾān. See Anna Krasnowolska, "K̲EZR," *EIr*; A.J. Wensinck "al-Khaḍir (al-Khiḍr)," *EI*²; John Renard, "Khaḍir/Khiḍr," *EQ*. In Shīʿī works written to prove the occultation of the Hidden Imam, stories of al-Khiḍr are often adduced as accounts of another holy figure whose life has been miraculously prolonged by God and who is in a perpetual state of concealment. For an analysis of narrative stories about al-Khiḍr that were incorporated into the earliest Twelver Shīʿī works on the occultation of the Twelfth Imam, see the recent article by Kyoko Yoshida, "*Qiṣaṣ* Contributions to the Theory of *Ghaybah* in Twelver Shīʿism," *Orient: Reports of the Society for Near Eastern Studies in Japan*, XLIV (2009): 91–104.

59. Mīrzā Ḥusayn Ṭabrisī Nūrī, *Najm al-thāqib (sic)* (Tehran: Intishārāt-i Masjid-i Muqaddas-i Jamkarān, 1410/1989), 294–300; idem, *Jannat al-maʾwā fī man fāza bi-liqāʾal-ḥujja wa-muʿjazātihi fī al-ghayba al-kubrā*, appended to al-Majlisī, *Biḥār al-anwār*, 53: 230–4. See also See Corbin, *En Islam iranien*, 4: 338–46; Mohammad Ali Amir-Moezzi, "Jamkarán et Máhán: Deux Pélerinages Insolites en Iran," in *Lieux d'Islam. Cultes et Cultures de l'Afrique á Java*, ed. Mohammed Ali Amir-Moezzi (Paris: Éditions Autrement, 1996), 154–61. For a critical study of the provenance of this account and the rising cult of the Jamkarān Mosque in contemporary Iran, see Omid Ghaemmaghami, "Jamkarān: the Absence of Tradition," forthcoming.

60. On him, see Abdul-Hadi Hairi, "Madjlisī, Mullā Muḥammad Bāḳir," *EI*[2]; Etan Kohlberg, "al-Majlisī," *ER*.

61. Al-Majlisī, *Biḥār al-anwār*, 52: 159–80.

62. Ibid., 159–73. See Corbin, *En Islam iranien*, 4: 346–67; Omid Ghaemmaghami, "To the Land of the Promised One: The Green Isle in Akhbārī, Shaykhī, Bābī and Bahāʾī Topography," Paper presented at the conference "Messianism and Normativity in the Late Medieval and Modern Persianate World," Freie Universität, Berlin, 17–18 September 2010.

63. On him, see Abdul-Hadi Hairi, "Madjlisī-yi Awwal, Muḥammad Taḳī," *EI*[2]; Rainer Brunner, "Majlesi, Mollā Moḥammad Taqī," *EIr*.

64. See Kathryn Babayan, *Mystics, Monarchs, and Messiahs: Cultural Landscapes of Early Modern Iran* (Cambridge, Mass.: Harvard University Press, 2002), 458–9.

65. There does not appear to be any information about this figure other than what has been mentioned about him in this account. See al-Namāzī al-Shāhrūdī, *Mustadrakāt ʿilm rijāl al-ḥadīth*, 1: 549 (no. 1998).

66. Al-Majlisī, *Biḥār al-anwār*, 52: 176.

67. On him, see ʿAbbās al-Qummī, *Al-Kunā wa-l-alqāb* (Tehran: Maktabat al-Ṣadr, 1359/1940–1), 3: 220–1.

68. Ibid., 176. ʿAlī Davānī notes that al-Kharābāt is an island in the Atlantic Ocean. Al-Majlisī, *Mahdī-yi mawʿūd*, trans. by ʿAlī Davānī (Tehran: Dār al-Kutub al-Islāmiyya, 1380/1960), 938 (note 1). There may be a connection between it and the Green Island, which was also believed to have been several hundred miles off the coast of Spain.

69. Kāshān is a city in central Iran in the modern province of Iṣfahān.

70. The account is recorded in a tile from the Shrine of the Footprint of ʿAlī. A photograph of the tile is found in Linda Komaroff and Stefano Carboni (eds.), *The Legacy of Genghis Khan, Courtly Art and Culture in Western Asia, 1256–1353* (New Haven: Yale University Press, 2002), 58. Referred to in Abbas Amanat, *Apocalyptic Islam and Iranian Shiʿism* (London: I.B. Tauris, 2009), viii.

71. Amir-Moezzi, *The Divine Guide in Early Shīʿism*, 45. See also idem, "Seul l'Homme de Dieu est Humain. Théologie et Anthropologie Mystique à Travers l'Exègése Imamite Ancienne (Aspects de l'Imamologie duodécimaine IV)," in *Arabica* 45 (1998): 193–214.

72. Amir-Moezzi, *The Divine Guide in Early Shīʿism*, 45.

73. Mohammad Ali Amir-Moezzi, "Cosmogony and Cosmology in Twelver Shiʿism," *EIr*. See also idem, "Seul l'Homme de Dieu est Humain," 193–214; idem, *The Divine Guide in Early Shīʿism*, 44–55, 125–31.

74. Amir-Moezzi, "Seul l'Homme de Dieu est Humain," *passim*.

75. Al-Ṣadūq, Abū Jaʿfar Muḥammad b. ʿAlī b. al-Ḥusayn Bābūya al-Qummī al-Shaykh al-Jalīl al-Aqdam, *al-Tawḥīd* (Qum: Jamāʿat al-Mudarrisayn fī-l-Ḥawza al-ʿIlmiyya, 1416/1995–6), p. 117. Also cited in al-Majlisī, *Biḥār al-anwār*, 4: 34–5.

76. Al-Ṣadūq, *al-Tawḥīd*, 290. Also cited in al-Majlisī, *Biḥār al-anwār*, 3: 273.

77. Al-Ṣadūq, Abū Jaʿfar Muḥammad b. ʿAlī b. al-Ḥusayn Bābūya al-Qummī al-Shaykh al-Jalīl al-Aqdam, *Amālī al-Ṣadūq* (Beirut: Muʾassasat al-Aʿlamī lil-Maṭbūʿāt), 523.

78. Al-Ṣadūq, *ʿIlal al-sharāʾiʿ* (Najaf: al-Maktaba al-Ḥaydariyya wa-Maṭbaʿatuhā, 1385/1966), 1: 9.

79. Al-Ṭūsī, *Kitāb al-ghayba,* 468. Cf. Qurʾān 39:69: Cf. A different Tradition cited in al-Ṣadūq and ascribed to the eight Imam, ʿAlī al-Riḍā: "The Day of the Appointed Time (Qurʾān 15:38, 38:82) is the day of the advent of our Qāʾim . . . When he appears, the earth will shine with *his* light . . . Truly, God is with him and in him." idem, *Kamāl al-dīn,* 346.

80. ʿAlī b Ibrāhīm al-Qummī, *Tafsīr al-Qummī* (Najaf: Maṭbaʿat al-Najaf, 1386/1966–7), 2: 253 (under the commentary for Qurʾān 39:69). Cf. Abū Jaʿfar Muḥammad b. Jarīr b. Rustam al-Ṭabarī al-Ṣaghīr, *Dalāʾil al-imāma* (Qum: Muʾassasat al-Baʿtha, 1413/1992–3), 462. See also Bar-Asher, *Scripture and Exegesis in Early Imāmī Shiism,* 138, who correctly identifies this *ḥadīth* as being eschatological and comments that it "places the Imam on an equal footing with God."

81. The *Duʿāʾ al-nudba* (lamentation prayer) is a famous Shī'ī supplication attributed to Jaʿfar al-Ṣādiq. The prayer is recited on the Shī'ī *aʿyād* (holy days) and as part of the visitations to mosques and other places of worship associated with the twelfth Imam.

82. Al-Majlisī, *Biḥār al-anwār,* 99: 108.

83. Ibid., 51: 46, 50.

84. On him, see B. Lewis, "al-ʿAyyāshī," *EI²*; I. K. Poonawala, "ʿAYYĀŠĪ," *EIr*; Bar-Asher, *Scripture and Exegesis in Early Imāmī Shiism,* 54–63.

85. Muḥammad b. Masʿūd al-ʿAyyāshī, *Tafsīr al-ʿAyyāshī* (Tehran: al-Maktaba al-ʿIlmiyya al-Islāmiyya, n.d.), 1: 103.

86. See William C. Chittick, trans. *A Shiʿite Anthology: selected and with a Foreword by ʿAllāmah Sayyid Muḥammad Ḥusayn Ṭabāṭabāʾī* (London: Muhammadi Trust of Greater Britain & Northern Ireland, 1981), 28. Cf. Al-Majlisī, *Biḥār al-anwār,* 43: 351; 87: 194; 95: 78.

87. Henry Corbin, *Alone with the Alone,* 277.

88. ʿAbd al-Hakeem Carney, "Imamate and Love: The Discourse of the Divine in Islamic Mysticism," in *Journal of the American Academy of Religion* 73:3 (2005): 705–730, 729. This concept of "manifestationhood" is certainly not exclusive to the Shīʿa. Non-Shīʿī mystics, for example, have interpreted the sound Prophetic Tradition, "Whosoever has seen me, has seen God" (*man raʾānī fa-qad raʾā al-ḥaqq*) [al-Bukhārī, *Ṣaḥīḥ al-Bukhārī* (Istanbul: Dār al-Fikr lil-Ṭabāʿa wa-l-Nashr wa-l-Tawzīʿ, 1401/1981), 8: 72] "to mean that Muḥammad was indeed the perfect mirror of Divine Beauty, the locus of manifestation for all Divine names and attributes, through whose beauty one can understand the Divine Beauty and Perfection." Schimmel, *And Muhammad is His Messenger,* 131; idem, *Mystical Dimensions,* 223.

89. Northrop Frye, *The Great Code,* 79.

90. It may be instructive to trace the motif of initiatory encounters with a mysterious, comely youth in visions and dreams throughout the course of Islamic history in a separate study. We can mention four accounts here: 1) Shihāb al-Dīn Yaḥyā al-Suhrawardī's (d. 587/1191) tale, "The Crimson Archangel," of a visionary who finds himself in the presence of a youth who announces himself to be "the first-born of the children of the Creator." Henry Corbin, "*Mundus Imaginalis,* or the Imaginary and the Imaginal," 3. 2)

Ibn al-ʿArabī's (d. 638/1240) encounter with a mysterious youth (*fatā*) at the Kaʿba whom he describes in the *Kitāb al-isrāʾ* of his *al-Futūḥāt al-Makkiyya* as being "of a spiritual essence" and endowed "with lordly attributes." Ibn al-ʿArabī, *The Meccan Revelations*, ed. Michael Chodkiewicz, trans. Cyrille Chodkiewicz, Denis Gril (New York: Pir Press, 2004), 2: 20. 3) A tale from the Safavid period of the Archangel Gabriel's encounter with a majestic youth, presumed to be ʿAlī, on the shores of the Sea of Reality, who proclaims that he is the Mystery of God and initiates Gabriel into the knowledge of 700,000 sciences. Alessandro Bausani, *Religion in Iran: From Zoroaster to Bahá'u'lláh*, trans. J.M. Marchesi (New York: Bibliotheca Persica Press, 2000), 308–9. 4) Shaykh Aḥmad al-Aḥsāʾī (d. 1241/1826), who experienced numerous visions of the Imams, records that his earliest initiatory dream was of a mysterious youth who taught him the esoteric interpretation of Qurʾān 87: 2–3. Henry Corbin, "Visionary Dream in Islamic Spirituality," 402.

91. Goppelt, *Typos*, 17–8.

92. Frye, *The Great Code*, 78.

93. Todd Lawson, "Duality, Opposition and Typology in the Qurʾan: the Apocalyptic Substrate," *Journal of Qurʾanic Studies* 10:2 (2008), 39–40.

CHAPTER 4

Dreaming the Elixir of Knowledge

How a Seventeenth-Century Poet from Herat Got His Name and Fame

Derek J. Mancini-Lander

This chapter examines the narration of dreams as a key instrument of knowledge transmission in the training of an early seventeenth-century poet, ʿAbd Allāh Bihishtī Haravī, who was born and raised in the city of Herat during the Safavid era. Bihishtī's mid-seventeenth-century *masnavī* (long poem in rhymed couplets), *Nūr al-Mashriqayn* ("The Light of the Two Easts"),[1] describes the cities the author visited in the course of his travels; however, it also contains an autobiographical account of his rise to fame as a poet, focusing explicitly on his training and coming into knowledge. At the heart of this account is a dream, which, according to Bihishtī's narrative, plays a pivotal part in his education. When the poet speaks of his education he alludes to several classes of knowing: His emphasis is not simply on the acquisition of intellectual knowledge, but rather on a combination of intellectual knowledge, technical know-how, knowledge of ethical behavior, and above all, the kind of understanding that is necessary for devotion to one's masters, and through them, to the *Imāms*, and ultimately to God. According to the narrative, it is his dream that seals this bundle of noetic material and ultimately allows him to become an eloquent and prestigious poet. Moreover, his account makes explicit the connection between knowledge and status within a "society" of poets. In focusing on this single case study of a poet's process of coming to know, I aim to prompt a new discussion, not only about the character of knowledge transmission among poets in the early modern Persianate world, but also about the role that dreams and their narration may have played in transmitting knowledge among all vocations and circles of affiliation in the Persianate context, of which poets were one. Most importantly, continuing the work of Jonathan Berkey and Michael Chamberlain, who have pioneered the study of knowledge as social practice in premodern Islamic societies, I aim to use this case study on dreams as an opportunity to reconsider the ways in which we think about the concept of knowledge in vocational training, and particularly its entrenchment in the social practices and ritualized activities that surrounded the process of learning and attaining status in Islamic societies. Attention to such practices should help us shift our understanding of Islamo-Persianate learning away from exclusively propositional forms of knowing (knowing that) to practical forms of knowing (knowing how).

From early on in Islamicate societies dreams were understood to function as one of the only channels of access to divine knowledge for ordinary Muslims, a means of communication that was analogous, although not equivalent, to the kind of contact associated with prophecy itself.[2] As such, dreams were understood to sanctify and render authoritative the claims of the dreamer. Accordingly, as many contributors to this volume note, since premodern times dreams presented Muslims with a powerful means of acquiring authority and leadership in highly competitive environments.

In the Safavid period, dream narratives appear at pivotal moments in all varieties of texts, including biographical works, travel writings, memoirs, and histories.[3] We also find documentary materials, such as *ijāzāt* (licenses) and *vaṣāyā* (testaments), in which dreams are presented as playing a pivotal role in the transmission of esoteric and nonordinary kinds of knowledge.[4] These types of sources reveal that dreams and their narration were not only valuable tools for social competition among the highest echelons, they also proved to be key for less powerful members of society, such as craftsmen or local preachers. For these folk, the acquisition of knowledge and authority was as critical as it was for princes and great *shaykh*s and was no less contentious.[5] Accordingly, adepts of any given vocation often cited dream experiences as the source of their superior knowledge or skill and as both the cause and proof of their preeminence. The authors of all manner of sources report that at crucial moments in their training or initiation, young apprentices and pupils in almost every vocation (from sovereigns to handicraftsmen) encountered prophets or saints who transmitted vital (sometimes secret) knowledge to them in their dreams.[6] In such literature from the Safavid period, dreams and visions seem to have functioned as common, initiatory mechanisms by which novices from all disciplines and trades came to acquire key elements of their training. Their public narration, oral or literary, attested to the fact that such acquisition had occurred.

As a complement to studies of knowledge transmission and dreams among the *ʿulamā,* mystics, kings, and craftsmen, it would be productive to consider the role of dreams and their narration in the vocational training of poets; for in the early modern Persianate world, poets were ubiquitous and participated in a network of social practices that have been largely understudied in favor of those of princes, religious scholars, and Sufis.[7] Moreover, even though—thanks to the authors of myriad *tazkirahs* (biographical dictionaries)—we know much about the poets writing in the Safavid, Mughal, and Ottoman realms,[8] particularly their literary projects, we know little about the practices by which these versifiers came to learn their craft and acquire prestige in their own circles of affiliation and beyond. Although dreams regularly appear in works of almost every genre during the early modern period, no scholarly work has looked systematically at dreams as key rhetorical devices in the Persianate literary idiom.[9] More specifically, there is no general study on dreams in the early modern Persian poetic tradition, much less one examining dreams that taught poets how to master their craft.[10] By examining the education of ʿAbd Allāh Bihishtī Haravī, one poet from the Safavid age who centered his account of his education on a dream narrative, I intend to encourage further inquiry into the role of dreams in Persianate vocational training, as well as into dreams as rhetorical devices in Persian verse.

In the absence of scholarship on the dream motif in Persian verse tradition, it is yet too early to say how frequently initiatory dreams, such as Bihishtī's, appear in self-narratives (versified or not) from the early modern period. Given what I have mentioned about the import of dreams in literature about other vocations, Bihisthī is most likely far from unique; still, until a more systematic study of the literature is performed we will not know for sure. In the meantime, by sketching the important thematic topography and rhetorical figures in this one case study, I gesture toward an analytical paradigm for studying other such Persianate dream narratives that can be used later in more systematic studies of a greater body of literature. Although Bihishtī was a relatively minor poet,[11] his *Nūr al-Mashriqayn* proves a particularly fruitful text for the type of scouting project undertaken here, for the author explicitly and rather deliberately makes his dream narrative pivotal in his account of his own rise to fame and in fact places it in the very center of his work as a whole. Moreover, in the course of his writing, Bihishtī quite intentionally theorizes about the role of dreams in vocational training and about their place in the literary genre of self-narrative. Consequently, this text is an important source for social historians, for although we cannot assemble a complete picture of how poets actually learned their craft and attained their status simply by reading one account, because Bihishtī's dream-centered narrative is rather engaged with a yet unsettled, philosophical discussion about knowledge and its various categories, and because he has organized his self-narrative around this very discussion, we can provisionally use his work to identify some of the epistemological frames through which contemporaries conceptualized knowledge in Safavid societies. At the very least, we can infer where these ideas about knowledge might have been contested. Although we can only cautiously imagine how individuals may have come to acquire knowledge in practice, by examining these ideas as they are construed in a narrative about vocational training, we can begin to comprehend how individuals obtained the symbolic capital necessary for success in a given vocation.

Other than what Bihishtī himself relates, we know rather little about his life; it appears that his biography can be found in only two *tazkirahs*, Mālik Shāh Ḥusayn Sīstānī's early seventeenth-century work, *Khayr al-Bayān*,[12] and ʿAlī Ibrāhīm Khān's eighteenth-century *Ṣuḥuf-i Ibrāhīm*.[13] Bihishtī himself explains that he was born in Herat in 1006/1597–1598 and both of his biographers concur that he studied versification there under Faṣīḥī Anṣārī Haravī (d. 1049/1649), an important figure in Bihishtī's text.[14] After composing verses for a time in a salon patronized by Ḥusayn Khān Shāmlū, like many Safavid literati in this era, Bihishtī migrated to India. He spent time in Lahore and eventually travelled to Gujarat where he entered the service of the adolescent Prince Murād Bakhsh, the fourth son of the Mughal Emperor Shāh Jahān, who was governor of that region until his imprisonment and death in 1068/1658 after the Battle of Samugarh.[15] It was for that prince, Bihishtī tells us, that he began composition of his *masnavī*, *Nūr al-Mashriqayn*, which he composed as a response to Khāqānī's twelfth-century work, *Tuḥfat al-ʿIraqayn* ("The Rare Gift of the Two Iraqs").[16] Curiously, the work contains a panegyric section for Shāh ʿAbbās II among the introductory verses,[17] which indicates that his loyalties had shifted some time before he completed the work. We know neither the date of the work's completion nor that of Bihishtī's death; nonetheless, the colophon in the only extant manuscript is dated 1067/1657 in the Gujarati city of Aḥmadābād. The copyist describes himself as a servant of Bihishtī and mentions his hope that God will extend his master's life and fortune; hence, Bihishtī was likely still alive in India at the time of this codex's production.[18]

Nūr al-Mashriqayn begins with a series of panegyric pieces and eulogies for the twelve *Imāms*, which are followed by descriptions of the holy cities of the Ḥijāz. The latter half of the work consists of descriptions of the many cities that Bihishtī himself visited in the course of his travels from his hometown of Herat through Iran and India. In between these two halves of the work we find the poet's brief account of his own rise to success and greatness entitled "On the explanation of his own circumstances and his coming to be from nothingness and description of his grief and the wretchedness of the days of his childhood until the time of his growing up and coming of age."[19] The poet's self-narrative begins at his birth, which he tells us occurred in 1006/1597:

> When one thousand and six years had passed
> in good fortune since Muṣṭafá's migration,
> the Creator of the world sent me
> from the realm of nonexistence to the city of being.[20]

He writes that he was born two months prematurely and afterward remained at death's door. Once forty days had passed, he developed a debilitating rash, which, "due to the grace of the Creator of the world," vanished after six months.[21] Still, he remained blind in one eye, lame, and quasi-mute. With this metaphor of the infirm body, literally unable to see, speak, or move properly, in the opening lines Bihishtī sets up his progress toward eloquence and preeminence as a process of bodily healing and links his inability to speak with his inability to see and move. The implication is that these faculties will have to be nurtured together. Furthermore, by presenting his life as beginning in such a state of disability, the poet implies he was disqualified from work in any vocation or from participation in society.[22] He was literally a nobody.

Bihishtī then relates that in order to cure his suffering, his father became a *mujāvir*[23] of Herat's many graveyards, where the "mirrors of the face of desires [i.e., the *imām-zādahs* and *sayyids*] . . . lie tranquil."[24] After a time these acts of devotion finally paid dividends:

> For forty nights altogether, my old father
> got up at dawn to perform a circumambulation.
> When the forty-day visitation was finished
> fortune came out the door for me.[25]

The poet then recounts that shortly afterward he was riding on his father's shoulders through the bazaar and seeing freshly baked breads for sale, he miraculously spoke for the first time saying, "Papa, get me some bread / because my soul feels the weakness of hunger."[26] Overjoyed, his father bowed to the ground and thanked God (*ẕū al-mann.*) The miracle continued:

> I jumped from my place without anyone's help.
> By the grace of the Bestower (*dādār*), a paralyzed leg
> miraculously attained the power of walking.[27]

Whereas the boy's initial healing had come by God's grace, without intercession, here his muteness and lameness are cured only after his father performs these devotions at saints' tombs.[28]

> Learning of this miracle, a respected, learned man
> declared:
> Even though this boy is not fortunate,
> it has become clear to me that he is not without
> discernment (*naẓar*).
> If he is to go to school, it is time.
> Let his tongue be unloosed in praise of God.
> His age has turned from four to five
> if he is to become an eloquent one (*navā-sanj* [melody-weigher]), it is time.[29]

Recognizing a trace of discernment in the young Bihishtī's nature and wishing to help him turn his newfound ability to speak toward praise of God's glory, this man decided to become his teacher. By implying that eloquence relies on the ability to see (to discern) the proper subject for speech, this passage is furthering the connection between speech and sight introduced earlier, in this case through the concept of "discernment," an intermediary sort of faculty that yokes together sight, reason, and judicious action and effects a kind of knowledgeable seeing and knowing-in-action.[30] Although at this point the young Bihishtī already possessed a discerning nature, this faculty still required refinement. For this reason, he studied with this master for twelve years or so until the man died.[31] At that point he explains:

> After the death of this teacher
> my temperament (*ṭabīʿat*) studied a different lesson.

Since I had always had a relish for poetry
my passion for poetry [now] increased.[32]

Bihishtī then remarks that after his turn toward versification he became a student of Faṣīḥī, one of Herat's respected versifiers, whose pen name literally means "the eloquent one." Next, the author recounts that while under Faṣīḥī's tutelage he met another poet, a *qalandar,* or wandering mystic, from Shīrāz, known as Ahlī, who was:

Free from the snares and shackles of ignorance (*jahlī*)
The verses of all the poets of the world
he knew by heart, all the way back to Ādam.[33]

Upon hearing Bihishtī's poetry, this poet realized that Bihishtī was "just a neophyte (*mubtadī*) /trained [only] by the grace of God (*luṭf-i īzadī*)."[34] The *qalandar* then gave the young poet an assignment:

I beg of you a poem
out of sincere interest, not as a trial of natural talent.
In this way, [compose] a poem such that the eight hemistiches,
have a single rhyme from the beginning.[35]
By way of allusions (*īmā*) in the eighth hemistich
bring up the name of a *rubāᶜī.*
When that treasure comes to the hand of your thought,
through that *rubāᶜī,* you will become discerningly eloquent (*sukhan-sanj*).[36]
In this way, in praise of whomever,
by necessity, your nature will smooth the pearl [speak eloquently].[37]

This passage is particularly instructive. The *qalandar,* Ahlī, suggests that it is by composing a poem in this particular form (called "*musamman-rubāᶜī*") that the novice Bihishtī will achieve eloquence. Moreover, by compelling him to honor a predecessor's work in the final line—that is, the line that is generally the place reserved for the poet's own pen name—Ahlī's exercise offers the young poet an opportunity to practice a deferential attitude. Furthermore, the prestigious Ahlī humbly speaks in *taᶜāruf* with the novice poet; by saying, "I beg of you a poem (*az tū shiᶜrī marā gadāʾī-st*)" the master is rendering himself a supplicant before his student. By inverting social roles, Ahlī models exactly the lesson that his exercise intends: Mastery comes only through humility.

Here we might pause to consider the significance of Ahlī's *takhalluṣ,* for Bihishtī uses it to set up a principal set of oppositions that run throughout his self-narrative. Moreover, with our musing on this name's etymology we can begin to compose a clearer picture of the poet's epistemology of learning, which is one of our key concerns. Ahlī derives from the word *ahl,* meaning tame, temperate, or domesticated.[38] The related, abstract noun, *ahlīyat,* which comes up later in the text, has a range of meanings that include domesticity, worthiness, capability, and expertise, particularly the kind that is attained through exercise, discipline, or training. As such, these terms also have resonances that imply a sense of social refinement, etiquette, and manners, that is to say, habituated bodily practices that serve as both a means toward social ascendancy and a sign of its attainment. The seemingly contradictory range of meanings that these terms index reveals a structural relationship between the concepts of temperance, self-restraint, and servitude on one hand—each signifying a submissive attitude of the self with respect to the social hierarchy—and on the other hand, expertise and capability, that is, the means toward and mark of advancement within a social hierarchy. The signification of the name "Ahlī" is further restricted here by the fact that Bihishtī describes Ahlī as a *qalandar*, that is, a mystic whose particular brand of temperance is characterized by piety, devotion to the *Imāms* and God through the restraint of his nature or carnal self.[39] As a devotee of *Imām* ᶜAlī, Ahlī has made himself a domestic in the Prophet's household, and in doing so has acquired not only status, but knowledge as well. Bihishtī is clear about exactly the kind of knowledge Ahlī possesses: freedom from "the snares and shackles of ignorance." This is nothing other than the discernment (*naẓar*) or knowledgeable seeing that he mentioned earlier, i.e., the kind of practical knowledge that both results from and gives rise to habituated and embodied acts of piety, humility, and ethical behavior.[40] Here, we note again that for Bihishtī, knowing is not strictly cognitive, but somatic as well. Knowing is a form of seeing, and by extension, a form of doing.[41] To this characterization, Bihishtī adds that Ahlī is a master poet, having knowledge of all the poets "back to Ādam." Thus, Bihishtī links discernment to knowledge/capability in his craft, namely versification.

With the figure of Ahlī, Bihishtī has provided a paradigm for a perfect, or rather, a perfected man whose name signifies a balance between three different, although interrelated and indissoluble classes of knowing, the intellectual, technical, and social-spiritual,[42] each of which, must be cultivated in tandem with the others. As a way of fleshing out what this social-spiritual knowledge might entail, we may provisionally consider these three categories of knowing in relation to Plato's linked concepts of *episteme* (intellectual knowledge), *techne* (technical knowledge), and *poiesis* (engendering knowledge). Poiesis, which mediates between episteme and techne on one hand,[43] and between knowledge itself and actual deeds on the other hand, resonates with this notion of a social-spiritual kind of knowing.[44] Essentially, poiesis describes the process of transmitting (or engendering) knowledge in the context of a hierarchical relationship, which, in Plato, occurs in the love between an older man and a beautiful youth.[45] In the Islamo-Persianate context, the same social categories apply, but are expanded to comprise any relationship between an individual of a higher rank with one of a lower rank, including those between holy beings and ordinary men.[46] In this sense, poiesis refers primarily to the form or process by which knowledge comes to be transmitted rather than to noetic content itself; moreover, it is a process that occurs first in the bodily realm and only later becomes objectified in the mental realm: It orients the student in a particular (deferential) posture with respect to his masters.[47] In so doing, the interaction itself focuses the recipient's attention on his relative status and compels him to inhabit and embody that posture.[48] Beyond the content transmitted in the course of the relationship, a knowledge of the whole order of things comes to be transmitted/generated in the very body of the student.[49] In turn, this embodied knowledge predisposes the student to act in accordance with particular habits. For Plato, this kind of knowledge engenders "the Good" in acts of justice and temperance (*sophrosune* and *dikaiosune*); temperance, it should be recalled, is a key element of Ahlī's name.[50] However, in Bihishtī's world it is specifically a sense of the social/cosmological hierarchy and one's proper orientation in it—that is to say, habituated devotion to the social-cosmological order—that leads to such acts of goodness, enables the integration of technical and intellectual knowledge, and ultimately, realizes vocational expertise (knowledge-in-practice). As an intermediary sort of knowing—between knowing of and knowing how and between knowing and doing—poiesis simultaneously comprises and engenders intellectual knowledge, technical knowledge, and the capacity for action in the world; as such, it gives rise to a way of being and compels both knowledgeable seeing and discerning action.[51] As Bihishtī later demonstrates, in accordance with its liminal and therefore extraordinary nature, social-spiritual or poietical knowledge is often transmitted in extraordinary ways in intermediary spaces—in dreams.[52]

For now we may simply observe that even in name Ahlī stands in contrast to our poet: At this point in the narrative, Bihishtī remains unnamed and his nature is yet untamed (*vaḥshī*). It is exactly this state of indiscipline and lack of piety that has prevented him from achieving the eloquence and prestige that he seeks. He has not yet learned to see or speak because he lacks the crucial kind of knowledge and experience.

After his encounter with Ahlī, the youth relates that he set about his assignment. He struggled throughout the night, yet was unable to produce the verses Ahlī had assigned. Just before dawn the young poet experienced a powerful dream, which forms his narrative's climax:

> For a while, I was at war with myself.
> I fell asleep near dawn.
> I saw in a dream (*dīdam dar khvāb*) a certain gathering
> and a place like the garden of paradise.
> All those present were beautiful like the sun:
> the light from their cheeks was glittering,
> clad in white from head to toe,
> sun-like, the cloak upon their shoulders.
> One among them, who had the voice of David,
> stood up; he was a eulogizer [of the martyred *Imāms*].
> Those who were listening to his tune
> opened the vein of weeping from the heart.
> I too, because of my tears of burning sorrow,
> was caught between fire and water.
> All of a sudden, one of these [noble] youths
> said: O, you who has no ability [*nātavānān*] to speak!
> Did you compose what Ahlī asked of you
> and pierce that jewel of the jewel box of verse?
> I said: this type of poetry is difficult.
> Uttering it won't be easy.
> I am merely a beginner and my temperament (*ṭabīʿat*) is still raw (*khām*).
> How will the wildness of my sensibility (*vaḥshī-yi maʿnīyam*) be tamed?
> In praise of whom shall I utter such verses?
> From whose blessing shall I seek such verses?
> He said: O you who are ignorant of the spring of divine-bounteousness (*bahār-i fayż*)!
> don't take upon yourself difficult labor.
> In praise (*manqabat*) of ʿAlī, the sublime,
> a pearl-weighing finely imagined poem—

Listen, listen to how Masīḥā[53]
tells praises of Murtażá [ʿAlī].[54]

After these words of advice from these luminous beings, Bihishtī awoke and, falling to the ground in gratitude and prayer, composed some verses in praise of ʿAlī in the *muṣamman-rubāʿī* form that Ahlī had told him to employ. Bihishtī does not include this *rubāʿī* in his narrative, but paraphrases it, presumably because it would not have fit with the meter and rhyme scheme of the *masnavī*:[55]

From the beneficence of God, the teacher of Wisdom
and from the miracles of the Enemy-Burning King,
in praise (*manqabat*) of the Shāh of Sacred Authority
(*valāyat*)
The secrets of eternity showed their face (*rū dād*).
Now, in my name (*bih nām-i dāʿī*),
the *muṣamman-rubāʿī* is famous.
On account of his calling it forth, Ahlī, the *qalandar*
increased the kindness of the family of Ḥaydar [ʿAlī][56]

Here Bihishtī explains that it is through this pronouncement of devotion that he accomplished his first truly eloquent utterance, exactly as Ahlī had told him he would. Ahlī had given him the form (poetry as memorial/supplication), but it was the luminous beings in his dream who totally reoriented the poet's nature and, by perfecting his sight, gave him the physical capacity to versify eloquently. In so doing, he acquired the "secrets of eternity." Still, he gives special credit to Ahlī for having been instrumental in bringing this devotional poem to ʿAlī out of him. Moreover, in the line I have translated, "in my name . . . the quatrain is famous" in place of the possessive-adjective "my" he actually uses the word "*dāʿī*," which literally means "the caller" but in this context translates something like "the one calling for your attention." This is a kind of apophastic circumlocution, an "un-saying" through which he can name himself (and invoke his own fame) without literally doing so; any explicitly ego-centered utterance would have broken his posture of humility and would have invalidated any claims to knowledge. In this way, Bihishtī is implying that without the knowledge he received from his benefactors, his name and fame would be empty.

Upon composing this *rubāʿī*, Bihishtī rushed to the Faṣīḥī's *majlis* where he recited it before his master and peers. Faṣīḥī exclaimed:

You have gathered flowers from the blessed gardens of
paradise!

You have pierced many royal pearls.
Why don't you say your *takhalluṣ*?[57]

Faṣīḥī is referring to the poet's pen name, which in the Persian verse tradition, customarily appeared in the last distich of the poem, the signature verse. Bihishtī's closing verse had apparently lacked this *takhalluṣ*; because he was just a novice at the time, he hadn't yet acquired one. He respectfully responded that a devotee must only receive his *takhalluṣ* from his master.[58] Commenting that the *takhalluṣ* should spring from a particular incident (*bāb*), Faṣīḥī wrote a *qiṭ*ᶜ*ah* on a slip of paper and handed it over to his student:

Tonight in our salon, one burning at heart,
by means of a fine temperament,
drove the ship into the watery depths of thought
on the subject of the virtues of the Commander of the World.
The heavenly-natured ones of the world of sanctity (*riżvān-manishān-i* ᶜ*ālam-i qudus*)
gave him his *takhalluṣ*, "Bihishtī (Heavenly One)."[59]

Bihishtī's *takhalluṣ* possesses a magical, refractive quality: The heavenly nature it describes refers not only to his own person, but also to those heavenly beings who had perfected him in his dream.[60] Thus, speaking or signing his own name became an act of remembrance and deference and of self-aggrandizement simultaneously.[61]

Bihishtī reports that afterward his skill continued to improve until he reached great fame. Before closing his narrative, he concludes with a short eulogy for his own master, Faṣīḥī, the last lines of which reads:

One can find the elixir of knowledge (*aksīr-i* ᶜ*ulūm-rā tavān yāft*)
in companionship (*ṣuḥbat*) with Mīrzā Faṣīḥī;
Bihishtī became famous in his time
owing to Mīrzā Faṣīḥī's expertise (*ahlīyat*).[62]

We should note that this last distich continues to play on allusions, as Ahlī had recommended earlier, and in doing so, the poet both lays out his genealogy and illustrates his devotion to his master, Faṣīḥī. Moreover, in the midst of this poetic tribute, the poet secretly slips in equal credit for his success to Ahlī by means of a pun: in this final distich, Faṣīḥī's very "expertise," which allowed him to "become famous in his time," is his *ahlīyat,* his expertise or pious-temperance, a word that, as explained earlier, is etymologically related to Ahlī's own *takhalluṣ*. If Faṣīḥī, "the Eloquent," had provided Bihishtī with his poetic technique, the outward tools of his trade, Ahlī, "the Temperate," gave him the spiritual/ethical knowledge to perfect those gifts by giving him an exercise that prepared him for a meeting with the dream-beings. Bihishtī's recognition of two guides, one who imparts the outward knowledge and one who imparts inward knowledge, is typical of Persianate craft circles and is analogous to the conception of training in the *futuvvat* fraternities for craftsmen (which often included poets alongside handicraftsmen.)[63] In that context, the novice was initiated into the brotherhood and craft in the presence of both a craft master (*ustād*) and a spiritual guide (*pīr*). The former taught the technical craft knowledge; the latter taught its esoteric meaning.[64]

It is just at the point when Bihishtī is struggling most that he finds himself in this dream-*majlis* of heavenly beings, whom Faṣīḥī later calls the "heavenly-natured ones of the world of sanctity."[65] These beings, having observed Bihishtī's "raw" (*khām*) and "wild" (*vaḥshī*) nature, do not actually teach him any techniques of versification. Instead, while in *ṣuḥbat* with these saintly beings the poet receives a quasi-tangible sort of knowledge, an "elixir of knowledge:" It is a burst of information, compressed into ᶜAlī's name, which, in being transmitted, orients Bihishtī in a posture of humility and temperance. The concept of *naẓar* (gaze/discernment) is fully developed here: As he gazes with admiration on his masters, he thus *discerns* a pious subject for versification—praise of the Imām and obeisance to his masters.[66] The dream-beings impart a poietical sort of knowledge: in helping him into a posture of submission and in focusing his attention on the social hierarchy inherent to teaching itself, they succeed in engendering in him the knowledge of his own status relative to his benefactors/superiors, and thereby prompt him to embody that orientation in action. In seeing/knowing, he perfects his speech. In speaking his poem he perfects what he knows and sees.

The exclusion of his *takhalluṣ* in the last distich of his *rubāᶜī* serves to mirror the poet's own, newly habituated, pious orientation; in full devotion to ᶜAlī (vis-à-vis Faṣīḥī and Ahlī), his own words appear empty of selfness. In discerning the proper object of veneration from the improper, he also has acquired the ability to discern the eloquent from the ineloquent. With this reverence for his masters, and through them, devotion to the *Imām,* the poet rids himself of the last traces of his childhood infirmity that had formerly stiffened his tongue. The knowledge he receives from the dream-beings (through Faṣīḥī and

Ahlī's mediation) immediately transforms both his attitude vis-à-vis his superiors and his technical mastery. It is a true elixir.

As already mentioned, initiatory dream experiences like Bihishtī's were not uncommon features of vocational training in Islamicate societies, or at the very least, of literary accounts of such training.[67] Interestingly, Bihishtī sets up his passing from "nothingness" to "coming of age"—beginning with his encounter with Ahlī and concluding with his acceptance as a great poet—as a typical rite of initiation:[68] At the outset, Bihishtī describes himself as a neophyte who cannot yet compose elegant verses. After receiving Ahlī's assignment he enters a period of separation from the company of his fellow poets, where he spends all night working on the *rubāᶜī*. Having thus prepared himself for an encounter with the sacred beings, he enters into a dream state in which he finds himself in a world betwixt and between ordinary realities. In *ṣuḥbat* with these liminal beings, he receives, nested in ᶜAlī's name, the "elixir of knowledge," i.e., the special orientational knowledge he needs to advance. After awakening he returns to society from the dream world and comes before his master, where he undergoes an initiatory ordeal in which he performs his devotional *rubāᶜī*. Upon passing this test of skill he receives his all-important *takhalluṣ*, that is, his new identity as a member of the society of ranking poets.[69] His name, Bihishtī, heavenly one, stands as an authentication and explanation of both the origin and quality of his mastery.

Moreover, the officiator of this ritual of incorporation and naming, Faṣīḥī, seals Bihishtī's passage into a higher rank by inscribing it onto a slip of paper in the form of a *qiṭᶜah,* which simultaneously describes the occasion of his performance, bestows his new pen name on him, and explains the name's origins. As a certificate of Bihishtī's passage into a higher social status, this *qiṭᶜah* functions like an *ijāzah*. After this episode Bihishtī tells us he spins verses with ease and achieves great fame.

Further proof of this accomplishment is the short eulogy for his master that concludes this autobiographical section of the work. In these final lines, this entire narrative of coming of age closes with the signing of his *takhalluṣ* in its proper place. With this signature, the poet fills the void left by his apophastic "un-signature," which we observed earlier in his initiatory poem. In so doing, he performs, manifests, and seals his transformation into a real poet, assumes his new rank among great versifiers, and finally heals the infirmity with which he began his life narrative. Furthermore, by coupling his own name (itself, linked to the dream-beings) with those of his two masters in this key verse, he is performing the fact of his newfound deference and devotion, postures, which he has learned are essential for mastery in his craft. He thus succeeds in mitigating the traces of any egotism that might result from impressing his verses with his own name; at the same time, he is placing himself squarely in both Faṣīḥī's and Ahlī's authoritative lineage, having inherited their eloquence and mastery, their *faṣāḥat* and *ahlīyat*. Most importantly, Bihishtī has become an "Ahlī," both a humble servant and an honored master. The proof is in the poem itself, which is a metapragmatic performance of both his humility and mastery perfected.

Conclusion

After reading this single representation of a poet's coming into greatness, we should not too enthusiastically conclude that poets of the Safavid realm, like contemporary legal scholars, or members of confraternal organizations, participated in ritualized initiatory procedures that incorporated them into more prestigious ranks. We do not have enough data with which to make such claims. Nevertheless, we certainly do sense the ways in which Bihishtī's audience must have read such schematic literary representations of self. Moreover, Bihishtī's work provides clues as to how his audience conceived of different categories of knowledge, their means of circulation, and the interrelationship between such a system of knowledge acquisition and the social order. Whether or not Bihishtī was ever formally initiated into a society of poets is not my concern; his recounting of the story—and in particular his recitation of the dream narrative and versified eulogy—served to verify (albeit informally) his position as a poetic master, whose talents and piety had been certified and authenticated by his association with great poets, spiritual adepts, and heavenly beings.

With regard to the role of dreams in this process of social elevation, the appearance of dream encounters at key moments of social transformation in the life narratives of people from diverse professions, such as scholars, craftsmen, princes, and poets, suggests that dreams were standard devices in the literature that were meant to reaffirm the sociocosmological hierarchy, and simultaneously, to recall that practicing one's place in that order was a key aspect of both mastering one's craft and ascending the social ladder; these were promotions sanctioned in heaven, and as such, rendered the subject's authority in holding those ranks indubitable. However, to recognize the social function of these dreams is not to deny their efficacy as real vehicles of knowledge transmission; because dreams possessed a special ontological status, betwixt and between worlds,[70] they facilitated the transmission of simulacral, yet practical, even somatic, forms of knowing, which I have been calling poietical-knowledge. These forms of knowing, like dreams themselves, had no stable reality, but in mediating between knowing and doing, they nonetheless engendered total reorientations in being, which in turn enabled mastery in one's craft.

Notes

1. ʿAbd Allāh S̱ānī Harāvī Bihishtī, *Nūr al-Mashriqayn: Safar-Nāmah-i Manẓūm az ʿAhd-i Ṣafavī*, ed. Najīb Māyil Haravī (Mashhad: Bunyād-i Pizhūhish-hā-yi Islāmī, 1998). (Hereafter, *Nūr*.) This edition is based on the only extant manuscript: ʿAbd Allāh S̱ānī Harāvī Bihishtī, "Nūr al-Mashriqayn fī Javāb Tuḥfat al-ʿIraqayn-i Khāqānī min Taṣnīf Makhdūmī Khudāygānī ʿAbd Allāh S̱ānī al-Mutakhallaṣ bi-Bihishtī al-Haravī," in *Kitāb-khānah-i Millī Malik* (Tehran: 1067/1657). I have not seen this codex but the colophon in the printed edition states that this copy was made in 1067/1657, 270.

2. John C. Lamoreaux, *The Early Muslim Tradition of Dream Interpretation*. (Albany: State University of New York Press, 2002), 4. Many scholars have cited the famous *ḥadīth* that ascribes true dreams to one forty-sixth part of prophecy, including Katz, Ohlander, and Khan's chapters in this very volume.

3. One important study on dreams accounts in the Safavid period is Sholeh Quinn, "The Dreams of Shaykh Safi al-Din and Safavid Historical Writing," in *Iranian Studies*, vol. 29, 127–42.

4. Dreams serve as the key mechanism for the transmission of knowledge/authority in Muḥammad Taqī Majlisī's *ijāzah* to his son, Muḥammad Bāqir Majlisī: Muḥammad Taqī ibn Majlisī, "Ijāzah Muṭawwila Ibn al-Majlisī al-Awwāl liʾl-Thānī," in *Muʿarrif-i Islāmī: Yād-nāmah-i Majlisī* (Tehran: 1379 h.), 184–85.

5. The best survey of craftsmen and guilds in Safavid period is: Mehdi Keyvani, *Artisans and Guild Life in the Later Safavid Period* (Berlin: Klaus Schwarz, 1982).

6. İlhan Başgöz writes about this common motif in folktales about *aşıklar* or Anatolian troubadours, where the capacity to sing and to perform magic could only be acquired through initiatory dream encounters with sacred beings. İlhan Başgöz, "Dream Motif in Turkish Folk Stories and Shamanistic Initiation," in *Turkish Folklore and Oral Literature: Selected Essays of İlhan Başgöz*, ed. Kemal Sılay (Bloomington, Indiana: Indiana University Turkish Studies, 1998). On dream motif in the *aşık* poetic tradition in general, see Umay Günay, *Âşık Tarzı Şiir Geleneği ve Rüya Motifi* (Ankara: Türk Tarih Kurumu Basımevi, 1986), especially 107–15.

7. I do not wish to imply that poets formed a social circle totally separate from *ʿulamā* or Sufis; many poets were also experts in law or theology, belonged to a Sufi *ṭarīqah*, simply practiced a mystical form of Islam

without formal membership in an order, or some combination of all of these. Moreover, I should stress that the ʿ*ulamā* and Sufis were *not* mutually exclusive categories of affiliation; there was a great deal of overlap.

8. Poets often traveled between imperial realms within long established networks of social affiliation that connected the cities of ʿIrāq, Khurāsān, Central Asia, the Indian subcontinent, and Asia Minor, where Persian poetry and the more universal elements of Persian and Islamic culture were predominant. Imperial borders and designations of space did not limit the itineraries of poets.

9. Shahzad Bashir and Omid Ghaemmaghami's articles in the present volume make forays into this field.

10. For such a study on Anatolian troubadours see Başgöz, "Dream Motif." Günay, *Âşık.*

11. As demonstrated by the fact that he is found in only two extant *tazkirahs*.

12. Mālik Shāh Ḥusayn ibn Mālik Sīstānī, "Khayr al-Bayān," in British Museum, *Ms. Or. 3397* (London), 401a-b. (Hereafter, *KB.*) The colophon in this copy (folio 467a) states that the work was completed 1041/1631. Thus, this copy was made before Bihishtī's death, which occurred after 1068/1657.

13. ʿAlī Ibrāhīm may have conflated Bihishtī with his contemporary, the poet Darvīsh Vālah Haravī. Both studied under Faṣīḥī. ʿAlī Ibrāhīm Khān Khalīl, *Ṣuḥuf-i Ibrāhīm*, ed. ʿAbad Riżā Baydār (Patna, India: Kitāb-khānah-i Khudābakhsh, 1978), 136. (Hereafter, *ṢI.*)

14. Sīstānī, "KB," 401a. Faṣīḥī receives a long notice in Sīstānī, 300b–301b.

15. According to Bihishtī, Murād Bakhsh was only sixteen when they met. Bihishtī, *Nūr*, 268.

16. ʿAlī Ibrāhīm mentions that Darvīsh Vālah also wrote a *javāb* (response) to the *Tuḥfat* of Khāqānī. Khalīl, *ṢI*, 136. The most famous Safavid-era response to Khāqānī is *Muḥīṭ-i Kawnayn* (completed 1061/1651) by Sālik Qazvīnī (yet another migrant to Hindustan.)

17. Bihishtī, *Nūr,* 64–6. That Bihishtī would single out this Safavid monarch for praise even though he had lived in India and served Mughal princes for so long is suggestive.

18. Ibid., 270.

19. Ibid., 180–95.

20. Ibid., 180.

21. Ibid., 181.

22. A contemporary *futuvvat-nāmah* emphasizes that only men with perfect bodies should be allowed to join *futuvvat* circles. Craftsmen with deformities, lameness, blindness, and even ugly faces, should be barred from membership. Mīrzā ʿAbd al-ʿAẓīm Khān Qarīb Gurgānī, "Futuvvat-Nāmah-i Mīrzā ʿAbd al-ʿAẓīm Khān Qarīb," in *Chahārdah Risālah dar Bāb-i Futuvvat va Aṣnāf*, ed. Mihrān Afshārī and Mahdī Yadānī (Nashr-i Chashmah, 1381), 88–92.

23. *Mujāvir* literally means "near" or "neighboring." Used substantively, it refers to a devotee who remains perpetually near to a shrine.

24. Bihishtī, *Nūr,* 182.

25. Ibid.

26. Ibid., 183.

27. Ibid.

28. Ritual tomb visitation for the sake of healing was widespread, and stories of such healings were common narrative devices in works from this period.

29. Bihishtī, *Nūr,* 184–85.

30. "*Naẓar*" also means, quite simply, "gaze." This concept of knowledgeable seeing will be developed further below.

31. Bihishtī, *Nūr,* 186.

32. Ibid.

33. Ibid., 187. This edition of *Nūr* notes that this is the famous Ahlī Shīrāzī of the fifteenth and sixteenth centuries. But this cannot be the same Ahlī because that poet died in 942/1535–1536, and most likely never went to Herat. (See Paul E. Losensky, *Welcoming Fighānī* [Costa Mesa: Mazda Publishers, 1998], 24.) Another Ahlī, called Ahlī Khurāsānī or Turshīzī did go to Herat but also lived too early. Ahlī was not an uncommon pen name; Bihishtī's Ahlī must have been yet another poet by that name.

34. Bihishtī, *Nūr,* 187.

35. The editor notes that this type of *rubāʿī,* the "*musamman-rubāʿī*" is distinguished by eight metrical feet per *bayt* (rather than the usual six.) However, this explanation differs from Bihishtī's rather ambiguous description in the text.

36. *Sukhan-sanj* translates "eloquent one" or "poet," but literally means "a weigher of speech." As such, it signifies a person whose eloquence stems from a refined, discerning nature.

37. Bihishtī, *Nūr,* 188.

38. The editor of Ahlī Shīrāzī's *dīvān* offers a handful of etymological explanations for his *takhalluṣ*. The first is that it derives from a word meaning "*rām* . . . the opposite of *vaḥshī*." He also suggests that it might come from "*ahl allāh*" or "*ahl al-bayt*." Ahlī Shīrāzī, *Kullīyat-i Ashʿār-i Ahlī Shīrāzī,* ed. Ḥāmid Rabbānī (Tehran: Kitāb-khānah-yi Sanāʾī, 1344/1965 or 1966), 1.

39. In *futuvvat* or chivalric confraternities for craftsmen, the initiatory ritual of binding-the-loins signified restraint of the carnal self for the sake of devotion to the craft master, *pīr,* and family of ʿAlī. The widely transmitted, late fifteenth-century *Futuvvat-Nāmah-i Sulṭānī* of Vāʿiẓ Kāshifī asserts that apprentices' craft-training also necessitated initiation into *futuvvat,* which imparted ethics and mystical secrets. Ḥusayn Vāʿiẓ Kāshifī, *Futuvvat-Nāmah-i Sulṭānī,* ed. Muḥammad Jaʿfar Maḥjūb (Tehran 1971), 94–138. A survey of wandering dervish groups such as the *qalandars* can be found in Ahmet T. Karamustafa, *God's Unruly Friends: Dervish Groups in the Islamic Middle Period 1200–1550* (Oxford: Oneworld Publications, 2006).

40. In his *Āʾīnah-i Shāhī* ("Mirror for Princes"), Bihishtī's contemporary, Fayż Kāshānī writes extensively on the subjugation of the lower elements of the self (the *ṭabʿ* [natural-disposition,] *hawā* [caprice or lust], and *ʿādat* [habit]) as a key step in the development of discernment, which he characterizes as a kind of seeing with the intellect (*ʿaql*). This work is essentially a vocational

manual for princes, whose ability to rule justly depends upon their development of this intellect. In the course of this work, Fayż develops a theory of self that explains how the quality of one's thoughts and deeds is determined by a set of five "commanders" (*ḥākim/ḥukkām*). Two of these are internal (*ʿaql, ṭabʿ*), two external (*sharʿ, ʿurf*) and one both internal and external (*ʿādat*). The king learns justice by developing the higher commanders and habituating attention to them. Mullā Muḥsin Fayż Kāshānī, "Āʾīnah-i Shāhī," in *Rasāʾil* (Shiraz: Chāp-khānah-i Mūsavī, 1320).

41. "When that treasure comes to the hand of your thought . . ." evinces the active, manifest, nature of Bihishtī's notion of cognition.

42. This term is unsatisfactory but it speaks to the fact that in the Islamo-Persianate system the praxis-oriented kinds of knowing (embodied knowledge), such as morals, manners, and even masterful craftsmanship were represented as being inseparable from acts of piety and devotion.

43. We may further correlate episteme and techne with propositional and practical forms of knowledge.

44. As presented in Plato, *The Symposium*, trans. Christopher Gill (New York: Penguin Books, 1999), 43–50. Plato elaborates on Techne and Episteme in the Republic: Plato, *The Republic*, ed. G.R.F. Ferrari, trans. Tom Griffith (Cambridge: Cambridge University Press, 2000), especially 19–36, 186, 224, 317, and 321.

45. This is outlined in the dialogue between Socrates and Diotima: Plato, *The Symposium*, 48–49.

46. In the Islamicate context, the hierarchical master–disciple relationship itself (often called *ṣuḥbat* =companionship) is sacred, and thus both a site of heightened ritualized activity and the conduit through which nonordinary types of "material" such as *barakah* are transmitted. I would suggest that is precisely this "social-spiritual" significance, and not solely the curricula themselves, that separates *ʿilm-i naqlī* from *ʿilm-i ʿaqlī* (the transmitted and rational sciences.)

47. The genealogy of thought concerning embodied knowledge and social practice has been developing among sociologists and anthropologists since the work of Marcel Mauss (see Marcel Mauss, "Body Techniques," in *Sociology and Psychology Essays* [London: Routledge, 1979]) and has been elaborated on by such important thinkers as Bourdieu, who popularized the notion of "habitus" (see Pierre Bourdieu, *Outline of a Theory of Practice*, trans. Richard Nice [Cambridge: Cambridge University Press, 1977]). More recently, Thomas Csordas, one of the leading phenomenologists of the body, has proposed a paradigm in which knowledge comes to be learned first in the body, and only then in the mind, particularly in the context of ritualized activity. (See in particular: Thomas Csordas, "Words from the Holy People: a case study in cultural phenomenology," in *Embodiment and Experience: The Existential Ground of Culture and the Self* (Cambridge; New York: Cambridge University Press, 1994 269–90.) Talal Asad and his student, Saba Mahmood have adapted this complex of theories for Islamic Studies, shifting the domain of Islamic piety and the locus of its acquisition from the mind to the body and from the realm

of ideas to that of practice. See Talal Asad, *Genealogies of Religion* (Baltimore: Johns Hopkins University Press, 1993) and Saba Mahmood, *Politics of Piety* (Chicago: University of Chicago Press, 2005). My analysis here draws from models of social-practice theory as well as phenomenology.

48. Poiesis' ability (as an engenderer of and an intermediary between knowledge and action) to compel the subject to embody a habituated, ethical orientation parallels the higher role Fayż Kāshānī gives to the intermediary "*ᶜādat*" (habit), the "commander" of the self that mediates between the internal and external commanders as well as between actual thoughts and deeds. Although for Fayż, habit is actually a lower faculty, he implies that the goal is to *habituate* attention to *ᶜaql* and *sharᶜ*. See note 40.

49. Scholars have discussed the homoerotic resonances of Plato's theory exhaustively. On this theme, we may indulge in drawing a tenuous parallel to homoerotic elements in some master–disciple relationships observed in the Islamicate world. For example, Abdellah Hammoudi has studied the exchange of bodily fluids (including semen) between Sufi masters and their disciples in the course of their instruction/habituation. In this case, literal insemination facilitates the gestation of knowledge. See Abdellah Hammoudi, "The Path of Sainthood: Structure and Danger," in *Princeton Papers in Near Eastern Studies* (Princeton: The Department of Near Eastern Studies, Princeton University, 1994), 79–84. On the connection between semen and knowledge in Islamic learning circles, see the discussion of *bulūgh* in Brinkley Messick, *The Calligraphic State: Textual Domination and History in a Muslim Society* (Berkeley: University of California Press, 1992), 77–80.

50. The elder (lover) thus "reproduces" himself in the mind and bodily practices of the younger (beloved). Plato, *The Symposium*, 46–47.

51. Habituated discernment becomes a "commander" of the self in Fayż Kāshānī's sense of the term. See notes 40 and 48.

52. One also might observe the ways in which the liminal nature of poetic language engenders knowledge by means of poiesis. Poetic language actually *does* something ordinary language cannot.

53. Another allusion, probably to the poet and physician, Rukn al-Dīn Masᶜūd Masīḥ Kāshānī, Bihishtī's contemporary, who spent time in Shāh ᶜAbbās's court before moving to India. Masīḥ wrote numerous poems in praise of the *Imāms*, and also one in praise of Herat, which suggests he could possibly have met Bihishtī either in Herat or in India. I am grateful to Paul Losensky for these insights.

54. Bihishtī, *Nūr,* 189–90.

55. The *rubāᶜī* is not extant.

56. Bihishtī, *Nūr,* 190–91.

57. Ibid., 191.

58. Ibid., 192.

59. Ibid., 192–93. Sīstānī provides an abbreviated account of this dream and quotes Faṣīḥī's *qiṭᶜah.*

60. Furthermore, in the seventeenth century, "*khiṭṭah-i bihisht*" was a common epithet of Herat, the poet's hometown.

61. Furthermore, the naming ritual itself is one that performs and actualizes hierarchical relations of power between the master and disciple, the namer and the named. By investing his subordinate with a name, the master manifests his power over him. In turn, the *takhalluṣ*, a souvenir of this naming ritual, preserves and perpetuates the memory of the named person's subordination. For this reason, in addition to memorializing the luminous beings, Bihishtī's name also recalls his master, Faṣīḥī, who ritually bestowed the name on him.

62. Bihishtī, *Nūr*, 195.

63. Kāshifī deals explicitly with the craft of poets on pp. 280–97.

64. Kāshifī, *FNS*, 131–38. This continues a long tradition, going back at least to the Ismāᶜīlīs in which mystically inclined Muslims considered Muḥammad to have been the bringer of outward revelation (law), whereas ᶜAlī was the bearer of the law's esoteric meaning.

65. Bihishtī, *Nūr*, 193.

66. The concept of *naẓar*, in the sense of "gaze" had a specific and technical usage in some mystical circles: It referred to the disciples' practice of gazing with passionate adoration on the face of the master. In such a posture of adoration, the disciple prepared himself to receive his master's blessing/knowledge/authority. See, for example, Bashīr's explanation of sight and Naqshbandī *rābiṭah* in this volume, p. 243. Also see the discussion in Omid Safi, *The Politics of Knowledge in Premodern Islam: Negotiating Ideology and Religious Inquiry* (Chapel Hill, NC: University of North Carolin Press, 2006), 134. It is no coincidence that *naẓar* is a key term in Bihishti's piece; I am proposing that the mechanisms by which poets and Sufis, as well as the other vocations, came to acquire knowledge, expertise, authority, and prestige all comprise part of a single episteme.

67. As in the Anatolian *aşık* traditions: Başgöz, "Dream Motif;" Günay, *Âşık*.

68. Recalling the separation, liminal, and incorporation stages of van Gennep's prototypical, albeit embattled, "rite of passage." Arnold van Gennep, *The Rites of Passage* (Chicago: University of Chicago Press, 1960), 11.

69. "*zumrah-i shāᶜirān*" in Sīstānī's words, 401a.

70. Dreams and visions were thought to occur in the *ᶜālam al-mithāl* (the imaginal world, or the world of likenesses). See discussion in Henri Corbin, "The Visionary Dream in Islamic Spirituality," in *The Dream and Human Societies*, edited by G. E. Von Grunebaum and Roger Caillois (Berkeley, University of California Press, 1966), 381–408.

CHAPTER 5

Dreaming ᶜO͟smāns

Of History and Meaning

Gottfried Hagen

Ottoman historical consciousness as manifested in a distinct historiography appears surprisingly late. Heroic narratives of the rise of the House of ᶜO͟smān appear in the late fifteenth century. They were increasingly readjusted according to Islamic concepts and to literary conventions of emerging Ottoman classicism. The initial framework of the dynastic history arranged chronologically is joined by world histories, which gain prominence from the late sixteenth century onward, whereas local or special histories remain rare. Just as the typical Ottoman historian is a scholar or an official of the Ottoman state (or both), the dynasty as the embodiment of statehood is the fundamental unit of historiography. Narratives typically progress as an additive sequence of events, with very little interpretive interference on the part of the historian.[1]

Dreams as intrinsically individual and personal events at first glance do not appear to have a place in the strictly state- or dynasty-centered world of premodern Ottoman chroniclers. Yet, dreams were a regular, although not necessarily frequent theme in Ottoman historiography. Throughout the premodern era, and probably much longer, people in the Ottoman Empire were firmly convinced of the reality of dreams. Dreams narrated in Ottoman historiography were taken for real by the actors in the narrative, by author of the account, and finally by his audience. Yet, historians reading Ottoman chronicles, typically in search of factual information on the course of events of

Ottoman history, have chosen to neglect the dreams as improbable at best, and more often as obvious fiction.

In this chapter, I analyze selected dream accounts contained in Ottoman chronicles from the fifteenth through the seventeenth century, focusing on two in particular, and drawing on another dozen or so. My goal is to make a contribution to both the study of dreams in Islamic cultures, and to Islamic historiography. I am not concerned with the factuality of the dreams: Every dream, as soon as it is remembered, is already a construction, and its veracity is unverifiable by definition. Rather, I am interested in the fact that chroniclers and their audiences saw a place for the dream in the narration of historical events. My reading of their accounts will show how dream narrations reveal an intentional or implicit interpretive dimension of their historiographical endeavors. Dream narratives can function as historiographical devices to put forward particular understandings of events that otherwise would have remained hidden. They can reveal an unspoken "philosophy of history," which I take with Karl Löwith as "systematic interpretation of universal history in accordance with a principle by which historical events and successions are unified and directed toward an ultimate meaning."[2]

In his small but insightful book, *Meaning in History. The Theological Implications of the Philosophy of History*, published in German as *Weltgeschichte und Heilsgeschehen* ["World history and the manifestation of salvation"],[3] Löwith demonstrates how modern notions of universal historical teleology such as Marxism have their origins in medieval and early modern theology. Löwith contrasts this concept to that of the ancient Greeks, who saw history as a consistent recurrence of the ever same patterns. As a result, for the Greeks history had a meaning within its own horizon, whereas medieval (Christian) and modern (secular) teleologies see a goal beyond history, salvation from the evils of this world, be it in the fulfillment of the cycles of history, doom and resurrection, or by the advent of communism and the end of class differences.

I argue that several theological aspects of an Islamic interpretation of history can be determined in a careful reading of Ottoman narrations of dreams in historiographical contexts. The general notion of a God-centered model for history manifests itself in three distinct complexes:

1. The concept of divine guidance of events toward a goal that can lie within the horizon of history, or beyond it. A temporal goal would be primarily sociopolitical, whereas a *telos* beyond history would be eschatological.[4] Such a historical "plan of salvation" would not only

shape universal histories as a whole, but might become apparent also in works of limited geographical and chronological scope.

2. Predestination is closely related to the previous point, in that supposedly the predetermined events are guided by a divine intention. By projecting the act of predetermination back to the time before creation, it is as far removed as possible from the actual event.

3. A theological understanding of history also may focus on divine interference in particular events, in order to establish or restore justice, by punishing or rewarding human actors.

The study of dream narrations therefore can serve to overcome the extreme dearth of self-exegesis in Ottoman historiography. A more literary analysis, as opposed to strictly historical or psychological, of dream narratives in contexts outside of oneirocritical literature also will help to shed additional light on discourses of dreaming and thus on the understanding of reality in Islamic societies.

Narration

In what follows, a dream of Sultan ᶜOs̱mān II (r. 1618–1622) will serve as the central case study. I draw on a number of other examples from different sources for comparison, most importantly the more famous auspicious dream of his ancestor, ᶜOs̱mān I (d.1324?). Between them, the two narrations of dreaming ᶜOs̱māns, I and II, share most of the crucial features of Ottoman historical dream accounts.

ᶜOs̱mān II's dream is first reported by a rather noncanonical source: Ḥüseyn Tūğī was not only an eyewitness to many of the events that led to the downfall of ᶜOs̱mān II in 1622, he also was an officer of the janissary corps, which was instrumental in bringing those events about.[5] The auspicious dream of ᶜOs̱mān I on the other hand is a stock element of the opening section of many Ottoman chronicles. Here I focus on what seems to be the oldest version in the chronicle of ᶜĀşıḳpaşa-zāde, who was a dervish close to the Ottoman court, and must have died after 1484.[6]

Tūğī begins his narrative with the catastrophic outcome of the affair, then backs up and lists causes and premonitions which—in hindsight—were leading to the young Sultan's downfall.[7] The dream I am interested in forms a part of this sequence that constitutes a prelude to the dramatic events that form the main part of Tūğī's narrative. Although the Sultan was ostensibly planning to make a pilgrimage to Mecca, rumors sprang up that the real plan was to move the capital to Anatolia, and recruit new troops to get rid of the janissaries. In the subsequent protests, and on the advice of several influential persons at his court, the Sultan first abandoned his pilgrimage plans, but then, as the riots continued, he had a dream. Tūġī explains:[8]

> You should also know that a few days before this crowd gathered, [Şeyḫülislām] Es‘ad Efendi and the grand vizier had talked the *Pādişāh* out of his plans to go to the Ka‘ba. One night, His Majesty the *Pādişāh* in his dream saw himself sitting on the imperial throne, reading the Noble Qur’ān he was holding in his hand. His Excellence the Prophet, Pride of all Creation, and Intercessor for the Disobedient—peace be upon him—appeared. He took the Qur’ān from his hand, [took his armor and coat of mail from his neck, slapped him in the face][9] and dragged him down from the throne. As the *Pādişāh* wanted to rub his face in the dust of [the Prophet's] glory, he did not find the audacity to do so; it was not granted. At this moment the *Pādişāh* woke up. The following morning he sent for the *ḫoca* [‘Ömer Efendi, his tutor], and requested an interpretation of the dream.

It is worth pointing out that the dream is narrated as an objective reality. There is no indication that doubts were raised about either the veracity of the dream or the legitimacy of an interpretation in the political context of the moment. Oneirocritical literature sometimes appears to preempt criticism from society, indicating that the practice was not uncontested, but such objections do not seem to have affected chroniclers' reliance on the explanatory value of these dreams.[10]

Our account fits a general pattern of dream narratives in historiography inasmuch as it is an actor on the political scene who dreams.[11] Because the Sultan was the representative of the ruling house, and as such, the embodied "state," it is most fitting that he should be the person to receive inspiration and guidance through a dream.

One can only speculate in which way the dream became public, but once it was communicated to the Sultan's instructor, probably submitted in written form, its dissemination in the nearer and farther environment of the Sultan is not really surprising. Narration of the dream to others is the first, necessary element of any dream mentioned in the chronicles. Not every dream, not even every dream of a sultan, becomes public, let alone its being recorded by Ottoman historians.[12] This is true even when the boundary between personal and public persona was blurred, and some most trivial events were preserved for posterity.[13] Any dream, in order to be recorded and communicated to others, orally or in writing, has to be considered meaningful in some respect, although we know of a number of dream narratives where the significance is not clear, like the dream books of Āsiye Ḫātūn or Sultan Murād III, which consist of dreams written down in order to consult an expert interpreter.[14] A dream that finds its way into the historical record must have been considered significant in the most literal sense. Although some of them appear detached from the larger narratives, more as curiosities,[15] historians have repeatedly employed dream narratives in their work at crucial junctures in the unfolding drama of political events.

There are two fundamental forms of conveying meaning through dreams. In a number of instances, the message is conveyed explicitly by an authoritative person, who appears in the dream to address the dreamer. This may be a former sultan or a sheikh, but most frequently, it is the prophet Muḥammed who communicates with the dreamer. Evliyā Çelebi (1611–after 1683), the great traveler and even greater storyteller, opens his ten-volume book of travels with a dream, in which he sees the prophet Muḥammed and all his Companions praying in a mosque in Istanbul. Having served the community as *müʾezzin*, he approaches the Prophet, but erroneously asks for *seyāḥat* (travel) instead of *şefāᶜat* (intercession); the Prophet smiles, and grants both.[16] Kātib Çelebi (1609–1657), after having spent most of his life writing on historiography, geography, and biography, that is, on secular knowledge, was admonished at the end of his life by the Prophet to dedicate more attention to the name Muḥammed.[17] Similarly, Ferīdūn Aḥmed (d. 1583) was inspired to compile his diplomatic work, *Münşeʾāt-ı selāṭīn*, by a dream of the Prophet.[18] Certainly, more examples can be found. This kind of dream, which from a narratological and literary point of view is rather banal, also can be found in other sources, such as hagiographies. A dream by the seventeenth-century popular preacher and Puritan activist Ḳāḍīzāde Meḥmed Efendi, found as a short separate text in a collection of treatises, also includes an encounter with the Prophet, in which the Prophet encourages Ḳāḍīzāde to proceed on his path of enjoining right and forbidding wrong.[19]

Classical oneirocriticism labels such dreams theorematic, as opposed to allegorical dreams, which code the message in symbolic objects and sequences of events. There was ample literature available to the Ottomans for determining the meaning of allegorical dreams, ultimately going back to Greek heritage.[20] The individual dreams, however, which are recorded in chronicles, do not easily fit the categories established by oneirocritical literature, because dream books tend to isolate key symbols in a dream that carry the meaning and usually do not account for sequences and processes, while the dreams recorded in chronicles usually are described as consisting of more than a single symbol.

A good example of the symbolism is found in a dream related in virtually every chronicle since the late fifteenth century, attributed to the future eponym of the House of ᶜOs̱mān, while staying in the house of the pious and wealthy sheikh Edebalı:[21]

> ᶜOs̱mān Ġāzī prayed, and wept for a while. Then sleep overcame him, so he lay down and slept. Among them there was a saintly sheikh, from whom many miracles had become manifest, and all the people believed in him. He was a dervish, but his dervishhood was an inner dervishhood: he had many possessions, goods, and animals. He also had torches and banners. Never was his guest house empty, and ᶜOs̱mān Ġāzī came from time to time to visit. When ᶜOs̱mān Ġāzī slept he saw in his dream how from the chest of this saint a moon rose, and came towards him and entered his [ᶜOs̱mān's] chest. The moment that the moon entered his chest a tree sprang up from his navel, and its shadow covered the earth. There were mountains in the shadow, and water sprang from the foothills of the mountains. Some people drank from these waters, and others watered their gardens, and yet others caused fountains to flow. Then he woke up.

This dream, like that of ᶜOs̱mān II, warrants interpretation, to which we turn next.

Interpretation of the Dream

In contrast to theorematic dreams, allegorical dreams carry a more complex and more ambiguous message and therefore require expert interpretation. The meaning attributed to the symbols in the allegorical dream is accessible to those with superior knowledge, such as saintly persons who often act as dream interpreters. As such, interpreters and their work regularly become part of the narration in the chronicles. Characteristically, the interpreter is not a person outside of history, an impartial figure whose only task it is to unveil a hidden but existing meaning. More often than not, the interpreter also is somebody involved in the event, so that the meaning of the dream emerges in the interaction of two persons. This applies to the dream of ᶜOsmān I, which was interpreted by sheikh Edebalı in whose house it occurred:[22]

> He came and told the sheikh. The sheikh said: "ᶜOsmān, my son! Good tidings to you: God Most High has given sovereignty to you and your descendants. May it be blessed. And my daughter Malḫun is to be your wife." He immediately gave his daughter in marriage to ᶜOsmān Ġāzī.

What makes the case of ᶜOsmān II so interesting is the fact that there are multiple and competing interpretations presented in the course of events, both of which turn out to be valid and efficacious in some form. The first one is provided by the Sultan's instructor, as indicated at the end of the preceding quote. The excerpt from Tūġī continues:

> The *ḫoca* interpreted it as follows: "My *Pādişāh*! Initially you had the noble intention to go to the Kaᶜba, then you rescinded, although holy warfare and pilgrimage are commanded by the Word of Glory. You are reading the Word (of the Qurʾān), why are you not acting upon its noble decree? This is why the Noble Qurʾān was taken from your blessed hand. As you did not have a chance to rub your face against His Majesty's blessed foot, you should make a sincere decision. After you have performed the pilgrimage, you will rub your face against the Pure Garden [the Prophet's tomb]." The *Pādişāh* was very pleased by this interpretation, and this time, most firmly insisted on making the pilgrimage.

On the preceding pages, Tūġī had accused ᶜÖmer Ḫoca of being part of the faction that wanted the Sultan to go on the pilgrimage for very personal reasons: to use the Sultan's presence in Mecca to wreak revenge on the *şerīf* and governor of Mecca who was blocking ᶜÖmer's brother's ascension to the prestigious judgeship of Mecca.[23] ᶜÖmer Ḫoca is thus blamed for providing a fateful interpretation, as any reader was aware, as the Sultan's insistence on making the pilgrimage would only hasten his downfall. It would have been obvious to any reader of Tūġī that ᶜÖmer Efendi interpreted the dream so as to suit his own purposes. ᶜÖmer Efendi presented being dragged down from the throne as punishment for abandoning a decision to perform a religious act (*niyet*, Ar. *niyya*).[24] By putting the blame on ᶜÖmer, Tūġī exonerates the Sultan; in other words, Tūġī is giving his version of a favorite trope of any kind of political criticism in Islamic historiography, the sultan and his corrupt advisor.

Despite the partiality, nothing in the account indicates that the interpretation of the dream as such could have been considered fraudulent or manipulative, although, as we will see, Tūğī himself favored a different understanding, which was confirmed by the events. On the contrary, interpretations in accordance with one's interest were legitimate. Simple manuals of dream interpretation often give a number of different meanings of each symbol to choose from; the choice of interpretation actually had the power of influencing the outcome of the prediction. Evliyā Çelebi, an invaluable source for dreams in Ottoman society, had his own vocational dream interpreted by two authorities, back to back.[25] He also narrates the death of the wife of his patron Melek Aḥmed Paşa as the dramatic climax after a series of ominous dreams, partly by Melek Aḥmed Paşa, partly by the wife, princess Ḳaya İsmiḫān herself. Each of these dreams consists of an extended vision with numerous protagonists, of a complex symbolism, and each of the dreams is interpreted by a person present: Evliyā as the knowledgeable boon companion, Melek Aḥmed Paşa, a dervish, or Ḳaya İsmiḫān herself. True to dramatic form, each time a more or less contorted positive interpretation is put forward, only to be negated either by another interpretation, or by another, equally ominous dream. Melek Aḥmed Paşa refuses to allow another interpretation to contradict his own, auspicious one, but of course, to no avail. The entire passage documents how several competing interpretations were possible according to the interpreters.[26]

In the case of ʿOs̱mān I and Edebalı, the narrative resumes after a commenting passage in verse with the story of a follower of Edebalı, who asked and received a modest appanage from ʿOs̱mān in gratitude for the good tidings.[27] The reward demanded and granted also shows that a correct interpretation of the dream and its coming true are intimately linked, so that the bearer of the message also has a share in the event itself.

Allegorical dreams lacking the figure of an interpreter are rare but not unheard of. The oldest Ottoman chronicles tell a *ġāzī* legend of the taking of Aydos Castle in Bithynia. According to its oldest version in ʿĀşıḳpaşa-zāde, the daughter of the lord of this Byzantine frontier castle had a dream in which she found herself in a pit, unable to climb out, until a handsome young man (*yiğit*) appeared, to help her out, take her old clothes off, and dress her in new silk clothes. It would probably have disrupted the dramatic arc of the narrative had the author given away the interpretation at that point, which later on becomes clear enough: The dream is a symbolic annunciation of conversion. Instead, the narrator only declares that the young lady immediately knew what the situation was, and when the Turks under Orḫan laid siege to Aydos, she proceeded without hesitation to hand over the castle to the Turks, one of whom she eventually married.[28]

This example, in which the young lady took inspiration for action immediately from a dream, leads us to the next point to be discussed, the impact of the dream on the events, by motivating certain actions by the protagonists.

Motivation by the Dream

Typical dreams in historiographical contexts have two dimensions, one motivating, the other interpretive. Although the balance between them may shift, in most cases both of them are present to some degree. Just as the dream of the young lady of Aydos motivated her to abandon her paternal heritage and religion, ᶜOs̱mān I's dream led sheikh Edebalı to conclude a marriage between his daughter Malḫun and ᶜOs̱mān. The imperial Ottoman dynasty was to descend from this alliance between the tribal leader and the dervish lodge.[29] Finally, ᶜÖmer Efendi's interpretation of the dream of ᶜOs̱mān II also immediately motivated a decision of immense impact for the future: The Sultan tried to avoid the divine punishment by rescinding his decision and by insisting on the pilgrimage. This would then be understood as the decision to follow through with his secret plans to get rid of the janissary corps, and thus reignited the janissary rebellion that in the end overthrew him.

From the narratological point of view, in the dramaturgy of the unfolding tragedy, ᶜÖmer Ḫoca's problematic interpretation is a first *peripeteia* before the final catastrophe, naturally known to the Ottoman reader. It is here that the entire episode reaches the quality of a classical tragedy: As he seeks to avoid the announced fate, the Sultan only hastens its advent, by taking fatal decisions, and becoming entangled deeper and deeper in the morass of sin and oppression.

It cannot be emphasized enough that these historical dreams are read and understood through the outcome they forebode. The familiar outcome serves as validation for the dream, while the dream helps the historian to render a historical event intelligible by supplying a motivation for an action or an event that otherwise might remain unexplained in an understanding of history as a series of human choices.[30] Readers of Ottoman chronicles certainly did not read them as open-ended, but with a teleological perspective, as leading up to, explaining, and ultimately legitimizing, their own present. Aydos Castle was taken by the early Ottomans, and there may have been a memory of it falling through treason rather than in battle. An etiology based on the legend of the lady's dream would provide a compelling explanation of how this event came about. The imperial dynasty must have not only enjoyed divine favor (discussed in the following section), but also had a special relation with Sheikh Edebalı and his descendants. ᶜOs̱man's dream legitimized this alliance by attributing it to divine inspiration. Even more urgent might have been the question why, against the advice of several of his senior statesmen, and despite a *fetvā* declaring the *ḥajj* not mandatory for sultans, ᶜOs̱mān II insisted on going to Mecca. The fact that dreams were able to explain what otherwise might have been unexplainable reinforces the readers' trust in them, and their inclination to believe in their meaning in historical contexts.

The modern historian might call motivation by dreams a psychological explanation, claiming that ᶜOs̱mān II, for instance, was motivated by feelings of guilt, whether those were manipulated by ᶜÖmer Efendi, or "genuine." For the Ottoman reader, however, the dream indicates just the opposite: Dreams that simply emerge from the individual's fears and desires are worthless. Dreams that have a meaning come from elsewhere, they are external, caused by a higher authority, by God, although they may be understood as responding to the dreamer's fears and desires.[31] As a historiographical device the dream explains the ultimate reason of an action, from where it cannot be traced any further back. Moreover, the motivation is associated with divine authority.

Conversion is one of the most inscrutable phenomena that the historian can face. Modern historians consequently have more and more shifted their focus from the individual to the social context and power relations in which conversion is performed and negotiated. This route being unavailable to the premodern Ottoman historian, it is not surprising that more than one conversion narrative is grounded in a dream narrative. Not only the lady of Aydos, but also a legendary contemporary of ᶜOs̱mān I, and ancestor of an important lineage of the Ottoman aristocracy, is said to have converted due to a dream. The fifteenth-century historian ᶜOruc tells how the day after the consummation of ᶜOs̱mān's marriage with Edebalı's daughter ᶜOs̱mān went out to hunt, and encountered Köse Miḫal, who had that same night seen the prophet Muḥammed in his dream. The Prophet had ordered him to become Muslim, and given him the new name ᶜAbdullāh, so Miḫal came to publicly convert in the presence of ᶜOs̱mān and then join him in the Holy War. Besides the motivating aspect of the dream, it is noteworthy how the conjunction of the two dreams enforces the notion of divine blessing on the Ottoman enterprise.[32]

Divine inspiration for rulers can also be sent in the form of dreams: This is what gave Meḥmed II the idea to have his fleet hauled over the hills from the Bosphorus into the Golden Horn, the ultimate measure that gave the besieged city of Constantinople into his hands in 1453.[33] Special customs and rituals can also be established because of dreams: The custom to attach the key of the Kaᶜba to the shaft of the Holy Banner when going on campaign goes back to a dream by the *şerīf* of Mecca in the era of Murād IV.[34] The motivation of authors to write a book, as discussed before, belongs to the same category.

Annunciation: Catastrophe

As mentioned earlier, the dream of ᶜO̱smān II—different from almost any other historiographical dream narrative—does not end with the Sultan's insistence on performing the pilgrimage as a consequence of ᶜÖmer Efendi's interpretation. Instead, a second interpretation is sought, with a very different result:

> One day he [the Sultan] invited his imam after prayer, and told him this dream. The imam said: "The Pride of Sheikhs, Üsküdarī Maḥmūd Hüdāyī—holy be his secret—is the one who prays for you—may his prayer be answered. You should ask him for his judgment." The *Pādişāh* wrote the dream down in detail, and sent it to the sheikh. In his interpretation of the dream, the sheikh wrote: "My *Pādişāh*, the Word of Glory is the divine judgment, and it has to be obeyed. The throne on which you were sitting is the armor of existence.[35] This dream is most frightening and noteworthy. God knows, this dream will come true very soon. Do penitence, ask forgiveness, and in accordance with the word 'Seek help from those in the grave,' ask for help from the noble tombs of the holy friends of His Majesty Most High. Let us hope that this will drive away evil." The *Pādişāh* went to visit the tomb of Ebū Eyyūb el-Anṣārī—may God be pleased with him.

This time, Maḥmūd Hüdāyī, a famous mystic of great influence with the house of ᶜO̱smān,[36] interpreted the dream in a very different manner. It is striking that the second interpretation took a much more symbolic and less literalist approach than the first. The sequence of the two interpretations suggests that the second is assigned higher value in the eyes of the chronicler. This impression is supported by the fact that, due to the intimate connection of dreams with Sufism, a Sufi like Maḥmūd Hüdāyī would command a higher authority on such matters by default.

This second interpretation of the dream also provides a motivation, as Hüdāyī's advice to do penitence is the reason why the Sultan went to Eyyüb. Eyyüb is a highly symbolic site outside Istanbul, where Ottoman lore locates the tomb of Abū Ayyūb al-Anṣārī, the Prophet's standard bearer, as a saint of conquest and holy warfare. Holding a prominent place in the Ottoman accession rituals, the site is considered one of the holiest in Islamdom. The Sultan's visit, however, instead of assuaging divine wrath, made things worse because the Sultan's guards in search for animals to sacrifice committed numerous grave injustices. Injustices by servants are entirely the responsibility of the king, according to traditional notions of justice.[37] This reverse effect of the attempt to avoid the catastrophe, constituting the transition from peripeteia to denouement, certainly adds to the quality of tragedy in the event.[38]

For Hüdāyī, this dream is not so much a call for a particular action but an annunciation of the catastrophe to come: the downfall and murder of the Sultan at the hands of his own servant-soldiers. From a religious point of view, this narrative highlights the problem of divine justice. Tūġī more than once suggests that the Sultan suffered injustice by calling him *maẓlūm*, but he also points to very real political mistakes committed by the Sultan, which would have justified deposition, but not murder. However, he finds the justifying explanation in the curse pronounced by the Sultan's brother, when ᶜO͟smān II had him strangled to safeguard his throne according to the Ottoman "Law of Fratricide." The rebellious soldiers, he says, have become the means to fulfill this malediction.[39]

For Kātib Çelebi the situation is more difficult to explain, because he takes more pains to exonerate the Sultan. The unresolved dilemma persisted as his version of the events became the standard account, and may at least partly explain the lasting trauma resulting from ᶜO͟smān II's downfall. With the divine wisdom that preordained this catastrophe presumed but not revealed, the episode stands as a reminder to resign to God's will. I do not see an Ottoman parallel to the Mamlūk historian al-Nuwayrī al-Iskandarānī, who went to great lengths to explain the calamities that befell his hometown, especially with the conquest and pillaging by a crusader army in 1365, as divine intervention that would ultimately work to the benefit of the Muslims, and thus as a necessary "detour to salvation."[40]

Annunciation of suffering and evil, such as Princess Ḳaya İsmiḫān's death, through dreams is reported as deeply disturbing, understandably, by Evliyā Çelebi, but arguably functions as a reminder that death is ordained by God, and therefore should not only be accepted, but ultimately is a redemption from this world, and a step toward salvation. Predestined fate cannot be changed, as all annunciations demonstrate. Penitence as recommended by Maḥmūd Hüdāyī to ᶜOs̱mān II was intended only to avoid that the Sultan would die as a sinner, as another sign of resignation to the predicted catastrophe. Similarly, a dream by the court astrologer Sāᶜatçi Ḥasan, which predicted the death of Murād III, also recommended sacrifices as penitence, without being able to influence the course of events, and to avert the Sultan's death.[41]

The inevitable character of the announced fate reminds us again that dreams are understood in hindsight, through the lens of the catastrophe that the audience of the historian knows to have happened. Annunciation in dreams thus becomes a commentary not so much on the moment of the dream, but on the subsequent events. From the perspective of the protagonists, the dreaming Sultan, and his entourage, this dream is directed toward the future, but its importance for the historian is that it lends meaning to the past that had unfolded since, and that he records for his own time. It shows that the events were divinely ordained, and, as such, inevitable and obvious: The dream interpreter was able to see what was to come.

The divine wisdom that has remained hidden in our main example can be revealed in the dream as well. Peçevī (d. 1649?) relates the following about the eve of a disastrous Ottoman defeat at Hatvan in the Long Turkish War in 1593:[42]

> The following I heard from Naṣreddīn-zāde Muṣṭafā Efendi, who was well-known and recognized in Budin. The night when we took position with the army of Islam vis-à-vis the camp of the infidels, a pious man from the Muslims of Pest had a dream: "In a wide plain in a beautiful meadow a large group which didn't resemble our contemporaries in either clothing or composure and attitude was sitting in a large circle. Persons, some known, some unknown to me, were led to the ruler who presided over the assembly. He compared with a register and to most of them said: 'This one, too, is a martyr.' "

The dreamer inquires and is told that the person presiding is none other than the prophet Muḥammed, flanked by the Rightly-Guided

Caliphs, and is busy predicting which Muslim is going to be martyred in the upcoming battle. When the dreamer realizes that among them are most of the notables and commanders of the frontier region, he tries to plead with the Prophet, because he fears that without its protectors the area will fall to the infidels. His plea is not relayed to the Prophet by the person on his left, Abū Bakr, but by ʿAlī, who sits to the Prophet's right, and immediately, the dreamer is brought to him:

> [He continued:] "As soon as he looked at me he said: 'You, too, belong to Paradise, and are one of the martyrs of this battle. These have been recorded in the register of martyrs in the Divine Council, *the ink has dried*,[43] it is impossible to change it. This is the most beneficial for the people of the frontier lands. If these oppressors won, my community would be crushed by their injustice.' " As soon as he woke up he spread word about his dream and bid farewell to everybody. And of those people [he had seen as martyrs] he warned several. Sheikh Naṣreddīn said: "I asked about myself, and beseeched him not to hide anything. He swore an oath, saying: 'I saw how they brought you to the council of the Prophet. He said: 'This one, too, is a martyr, but not a martyr in this battle.' " It came true: he later attained martyrdom, innocent and without justification, through the tyrannical sword of Murtaḍā Paşa.

So the infidel enemies turned out to function as tools in the hand of God, as they help to punish the tyrannical and unjust, and to save the community of the righteous. Divine justice does not have to wait until Judgment Day but is enacted in the course of history itself. Thus, dreams reveal a mechanism of historical causation that goes beyond individuals and power to include a dimension of morality and divine justice, as manifest in the divine wisdom (*ḥikmet-i ilāhī*) inherent in historical events.[44]

Annunciation: Bright Future

However, not every dream directed toward the future necessarily pronounces a bad omen; the interpretation of an event as announced in dreams could also be positive. Sultan Murād III (r. 1574–1595) learned of his imminent ascension to the throne through a dream, which his spiritual advisor sheikh Şücāᶜ interpreted for him.[45] Meḥmed II was foretold his unlikely victory over his nemesis Uzun Ḥasan in a dream:

> A strange dream is told of the Sultan when he set out to fight against [Uzun] Ḥasan Beg. He saw himself wrestling Ḥasan Beg in the arena, both of them dressed like wrestlers. At first, Ḥasan Beg reached a partial victory over the Sultan by pushing one of his shoulders to the ground. But then the Sultan hit him in his belly with the side of his fingers, split his belly open, ripped part of his liver out, and threw it on the ground. The Sultan woke up, and pondered the dream, and was frightened by the vision of the initial victory [of Ḥasan Beg]. As he was pondering, a scholar from among his companions came to him, and he related his dream, and he [the scholar] interpreted it as [an annunciation of] total victory. He said: "I obtained an omen regarding the victory from the Mighty Qurʾān this morning, and what came out was the verse 'We gave you a great victory,'[46] and I calculated the value of the letters, and the sum gives the year 878 [i.e. the current year], so I am absolutely certain of victory." The Sultan asked: "What is your evidence to attribute the victory to our side?" He said: "My evidence is twofold. One is the omen [from the Qurʾān] in front of you, and the other is that the 'we gave you victory' is addressed to our Prophet, with whom you share the name." The Sultan was very pleased with this and bestowed generous gifts upon this companion. However, he kept thinking about the initial victory; when the incident of Murād Paşa occurred, he thought of it and consoled himself with it.[47]

Not only does this episode demonstrate how annunciation through dreams was part of a whole system of prognostication, in which the different oracles were used to confirm each other. It again provides an explanation for an unlikely event; Uzun Ḥasan, together with his Venetian allies, had inflicted heavy losses on the Ottomans and defeated an Ottoman army led by Ḫāṣṣ Murād Pasha only days before Meḥmed was able to gain a decisive victory against him.[48] Ultimately, therefore, it is a particularly powerful confirmation of the divine approval and support that the House of ᶜOsmān enjoyed in general, and under the reign of Meḥmed II in particular. This divine support for the Ottoman dynasty had in turn been granted and assured in ʿOs̱mān I's dream as quoted before:

> The sheikh said: "ʿOs̱mān, my son! Good tidings to you: God Most High has given sovereignty to you and your descendants. May it be blessed. And my daughter Malḫun is to be your wife."

Later chroniclers had a number of variants to report, all of which predicted future glory and conquest. This aspect, too, constitutes a prediction of the future for the protagonists in the narrative, but at the hands of the chronicler, it becomes a key to the past that he records and that his audience remembers. Because the prophecy is open-ended, it comprises all of this past, and transcends it. The Ottoman success story, which lies between the time of the prophecy and the present of the reader, validates the dream and the prediction it made. Thus, it suggests to interpret all of Ottoman history in the light of this prediction, as a divinely ordained success, and to project it further into the future. This is made explicit by a late historian, Müneccimbaşı (d. 1702, also an expert in prognostication, to be sure), who took this and other related omens of Ottoman greatness out of their chronological context, and prefaced his chapter on the Ottoman dynasty with them. Müneccimbaşı thus made it clear that, in the divine plan of history, this dynasty had special blessing and was destined to rule until the end of time. Appropriately, he placed the account of the Ottomans at the very end of his world history, as if all world history was about to ultimately converge in it, and there could be no history after it.

The dream, which announced a particular course of history, becomes part of the event itself, and helps to make its goal transparent. In Löwith's words:

> Single events as such are not meaningful, nor is a mere succession of events. To venture a statement about the meaning of historical events is possible only when their *telos* becomes apparent. When a historical movement has unfolded its consequences, we reflect on its first appearance, in order to determine the meaning of the whole, though particular, event—"whole" by a definite point of departure and a final point of arrival.[49]

We have seen how dreams reveal an understanding of history as divinely ordained course of events, and how God, commenting on, or explaining his interference in history in dreams, revealed it to protagonists and observers in dreams. Löwith continues:

> If we reflect on the whole course of history, imagining its beginning and anticipating its end, we think of its meaning in terms of an ultimate purpose.

If world history from an Ottoman perspective also had such an ultimate purpose, can it be discovered in the dreams? While there is no explicit statement on this aspect, ᶜOs̱mān I's dream seems to point toward a promise of world domination by the Ottomans. A dream attributed to ᶜOs̱mān's father Ertuğrul speaks of a fountain springing up from his hearth and flooding the entire world, expressing a similar idea, but in less idyllic and more violent images.[50]

The assumption of an ultimate goal is based on a sense of unidirectional development in history. It is thus distinct from the cyclical notion of history that was most elaborated by Ibn Khaldūn, and familiar to the Ottomans most likely since the sixteenth century.[51] Ibn Khaldūn's cycles could repeat themselves forever, were it not for an end of time arbitrarily imposed by God. Promises of Ottoman world domination would remain within the horizon of history, even when a historian like Müneccimbaşı prays and predicts that the Ottoman Empire would last until the end of time.

Löwith perceived in modern notions of progress as well as in Christian salvation history a teleology that transcended history, with an ultimate goal or *telos* beyond history. The concept of salvation history (or *Heilsgeschichte*) implies that history itself is part of the path to salvation. In our cases, and elsewhere in Muslim historiography, as far as I can see, history is what separates man from salvation, in other words: Salvation occurs when history is over, but history does not bring man closer to the end of time. Moreover, God's interference in history in order to reward justice and punish oppression is, strictly speaking, incompatible with a salvation history in which justice is done at the end of time.

A pattern that divides the course of world history into distinct phases, in a descending order, like medieval Western historiography did, based on the vision of Daniel, is generally absent in Islamic historiography. Although historians certainly were cognizant of an imminent end of time, they usually did not attempt to compute the remaining time to Judgment Day, or explicitly determine the relation of their own time to turning points and the end.[52] Works that explicitly connect their own present to the imminent end of time are rare; a noteworthy example is Mevlānā ᶜĪsā's (wrote between 1529 and 1535) *Cāmiᶜü 'l-meknūnāt*, a sixteenth-century history, which Barbara Flemming described as both a narrative of the campaigns of the Ottomans (*ġazavāt-nāme*), and a work on the battles (*melāḥim*) at the end of time, combining pragmatic didactic thrust with an apocalyptic one.[53]

The way prominent world historian Muṣṭafā ᶜĀlī (d. 1600) made use of it can be considered characteristic, as he did not adopt the apocalyptic basis when he cited the *Cāmiᶜü 'l-meknūnāt* in his vast world chronicle *Künhü l-aḫbār*. More frequently, he uses history as a series of events memorable for their moral lessons, called *ᶜibret* (ar. *ᶜibra*, pl. *ᶜibar*). Tūġī's work, on which I have relied heavily here, is entitled *ᶜibret-nümā*, and it should not be forgotten that Ibn Khaldūn's famous *Muqaddima* is part of his *Kitāb al-ᶜibar* ("The Book of Admonitions"). As Robinson points out:

> To say that God's will was the engine of history is not to suggest that men were considered mere puppets strung from His hands. According to a theology worked out during the tenth and eleventh centuries, men were given to act as agents of their own free will by acquiring the responsibility of acts created by God. They were rewarded and punished accordingly, always in the Next World, and often in this one too. . . . This explains why so many historians presented their work as a record of human choices, from which their readers were to draw the appropriate lessons. History taught these lessons (or "admonitions," Ar. *ᶜibra*, pl. *ᶜibar*), a word that appears frequently in titles, such as those of Usāma b. Munqidh, Ibn Khaldūn and al-Dhahabī, and an idea that appears even more frequently in introductions to historical works.[54]

Islamic historiography in the Ottoman era remained thoroughly this-worldly in terms of its applicability and *Sitz im Leben*, although it did not rule out extra-worldly causation and interpretation. A common expression of this relation is expressed in the formula: "If God wills a thing, he arranges its causes."[55] Tūġī makes this point when he concludes his discussion of the decisions that brought about the end of ᶜO̱smān II with a verse:

> God avenges his servants by means of his servants in turn—only those ignorant of divinely inspired knowledge think the servants did it.[56]

Conclusion

In an earlier article I took the functional distinction between motivation and annunciation as the basis of a typology of dreams in historiographical contexts.[57] This chapter argues, instead, that the functional distinction is valid, but that both functions are present in most episodes of dreams, although one can certainly take precedence over the other.

Dreams are windows onto another layer of meaning, but require much context outside of the dream narration, and even the chronicle of which these are a part, to be decoded. Dreams have high explanatory value for the observer of history, both the active chronicler, and his audience. They suggest motivations for actions that otherwise remain inscrutable, they help to cope with catastrophes by suggesting deeper meanings due to divine wisdom (*ḥikmet-i ilāhī*), and they promise brighter times ahead. As they help to attribute meaning to historical events, they function as orientation in a world that would otherwise be experienced as chaos. They even reveal perspectives on history in its entirety up to the end of times, but not a goal beyond the horizon of historical time.

My discussion of dreams in chronicles is not exhaustive; numerous variants may still be hidden between the folios of texts I haven't had a chance to study. I have not been able to determine a development (e.g. from the "credulous" Middle Ages to more critical modernity, or from the highly educated sixteenth- and early seventeenth-century chroniclers to the less educated "popular" ones). Yet, we can take the current discussion of dreams in historiography as a reminder in the political-minded and all-too-secular field of Ottoman studies, how religion is not just a piece of political propaganda, or opium for the people, but a powerful means for individuals as well as society as a whole to understand and give meaning to their experience in this world.

Notes

1. Colin Imber, Colin Heywood, and more recently Baki Tezcan and Gabriel Piterberg have pioneered a more cultural reading of Ottoman chronicles.

2. Karl Löwith, *Meaning in History: the Theological Implications of the Philosophy of History* (Chicago: University of Chicago Press, 1949), 6.

3. Karl Löwith, *Weltgeschichte und Heilsgeschehen; die theologischen Voraussetzungen der Geschichtsphilosophie*, 2. Aufl. ed. (Stuttgart: Kohlhammer, 1953).

4. Löwith, *Meaning in History.*

5. Fahir İz, "Eski Düzyazının Gelişimi: XVII. Yüzyılda Halk Diliyle Yazılmış Bir Tarih Kitabı. Hüseyn Tûğî. Vak'a-i Sultan Osman Han," *Türk Dili Araştırmaları Yıllığı Belleten* (1967).

6. N. Atsız, ed. *Aşıkpaşaoğlu Ahmed Âşıkî. Tevârîh-i Âl-i Osman* (Istanbul: Türkiye Yayınevi, 1949).

7. The event and the subsequent historiography are discussed in detail by Gabriel Piterberg, *An Ottoman Tragedy: History and Historiography at Play*, Studies on the History of Society and Culture 50 (Berkeley, CA: University of California Press, 2003). Piterberg provides an elaborate analysis of the narrative procedure in Tūğī's chronicle and its subsequent transformation at the hands of later historians.

8. İz, "Hüseyn Tûğî," 127.

9. This part is missing in the Dresden ms. of Tūğī edited by İz (otherwise the best edited text), but is found in other manuscripts (quoted from Flügel #1044 by Piterberg, *An Ottoman Tragedy: History and Historiography at Play*, 24), in Kātib Çelebi, *Fez̲leke-i Kātib Çelebi* (Istanbul: Cerīde-i Ḥavādis̲ Maṭbaᶜası, 1869–70), II, 11, based on a version of Tūğī, and also referred to below. Piterberg seems to read *cüppe* "cloak," but since Kâtib Çelebi pairs it with *cûşen* "chain mail," I prefer to read *cebe* "armor."

10. Justification by a *ḥadīth* in the opening section of an oneirocritical manual, quoted in Gottfried Hagen, "Träume als Sinnstiftung—Überlegungen zu Traum und historischem Denken bei den Osmanen (zu Gotha, Ms. T. 17/1)," in *Wilhelm Pertsch—Orientalist und Bibliothekar. Zum 100. Todestag*, ed. Hans Stein (Gotha: Forschungs- und Landesbibliothek Gotha, 1999), 109.

11. We will, however, encounter some exceptions to this rule.

12. The collection of dream narratives by Sultan Murād III, *Kitābü l-menāmāt*, seems to be a special case. It is preserved in only one manuscript, and does not seem to have circulated in any significant degree. I thank Özgen Felek for sharing many insights during our prolonged discussions of this work.

13. Muṣṭafā II (r. 1695–1703) famously asked his court chronicler if his very eating spinach would be recorded for the afterworld—and the chronicler obliged (Cemal Kafadar, "Self and Others: The Diary of a Dervish in Seventeenth Century Istanbul and First-Person Narratives in Ottoman Literature," *Studia Islamica* 69 (1989): 136, citing R. A. Abou-El-Haj, "The Narcissim of Mustafa II (1695–1703): A Psychohistorical Study," *Studia Islamica* 40 (1974): 115–31; see p. 120).

14. On both of these see Kafadar, ibid. Fındıḳlılı Meḥmet Ağa Silāḥdār, *Silâhdar Tarihi*, 2 vols., Türk Tarih Encümeni Külliyatı (Istanbul: Devlet Matbaası, 1928), II, 614, mentions a dream by Meḥmed IV which was recorded only years later when the Sultan suddenly understood its meaning.

15. See for instance Jan Schmidt, *Pure Water for Thirsty Muslims: A Study of Muṣṭafā ᶜĀlī of Gallipoli's Künhü l-aḫbār* (Leiden: Het Oosters Instituut, 1991) on curious events and mirabilia (*ᶜajāʾib*) in Muṣṭafā ᶜĀlī's chronicle.

16. Çelebi Evliyā, "Seyāḥat-nāme," in *Evliyā Çelebi Seyāḥatnāmesi*, ed. Aḥmed Cevdet (Dersaadet (Istanbul): Iḳdām Maṭbaᶜası, 1896–1938), I, 28–32. This story is a reminder that although dreams were certainly accepted as objective reality, not every dream narrative had to be taken at face value.

17. Kātib Chelebi, *The Balance of Truth.* Transl. with an introd. and notes by G. L. Lewis (London: Allen and Unwin, 1957), 145–46.

18. Excerpt quoted in Moriz Wickerhauser, *Wegweiser zum Verständniss der türkischen Sprache: eine deutsch-türkische Chrestomathie* (Wien: Kaiserlich-Königliche Hof-und Staatsdruckerei, 1853), 211.

19. Hagen, "Träume als Sinnstiftung," 124–27. Interestingly, the dream is dated precisely, to the 17th of Rabīᶜ II, 1039, which makes it predate the unrest caused by Ḳāḍīzāde and his followers as recorded in the chronicles. On the legal reasoning see Michael Cook, *Commanding Right and Forbidding Wrong in Islamic Thought* (Cambridge, U.K.; New York: Cambridge University Press, 2000).

20. T. Fahd, *La divination arabe; études religieuses, sociologiques et folkloriques sur le milieu natif d'Islam* (Leiden: Brill, 1966), is still the most comprehensive overview; but see also Leah Kinberg, *Morality in the Guise of Dreams: a Critical Edition of Kitāb al-manām / Ibn Abī al-Dunyā* (Leiden; New York: Brill, 1994). On one of the most popular, frequently consulted up to this day, by ᶜAbdalghanī al-Nābulsī, see Elizabeth Sirriyeh, *Sufi Visionary of Ottoman Damascus. 'Abd al-Ghani al-Nabulusi, 1641–1731,* RoutledgeCurzon Sufi Series (London: Routledge, 2005).

21. Atsız, ed. *Aşıkpaşaoğlu Ahmed Âşıkî. Tevârîh-i Âl-i Osman,* 95. I am indebted to Robert Dankoff, who made his unpublished translation of this section available to me. My translation differs from his in some instances.

22. Ibid., immediately following the section quoted before.

23. İz, "Hüseyn Tûğî," 125. The entry on ᶜÖmer Efendi in ᶜAṭāʾī's *Zeyl-i Şaḳāʾiḳ* (in *Şakaik-ı Nu'maniye ve Zeyilleri* / [Taşköprizade Ebülhayr İsamüddin Ahmed Efendi], ed. Abdülkadir Özcan, Istanbul: Çağrı Yayınları, 1989, III, 728–29) highlights ᶜÖmer Efendi's particular interest in the Holy Sites, but does not specifically address his involvement in the downfall of ᶜOsmān II.

24. Islamic law insisted that the *niyya* immediately precede the act, lest it should lose its character and become simple decision (*ᶜazm*). It must accompany the act until the end. So the *niyya* became a legal act of its own. (Wensinck, A.J. "Niyya." *Encyclopaedia of Islam,* Second Edition. Edited by: P. Bearman, Th. Bianquis, C.E. Bosworth, E. van Donzel and W.P. Heinrichs. Brill, 2009. Brill Online. <http://www.brillonline.nl>).

25. Evliyā, "*Seyāḥat-nāme,*" I, 31.

26. Robert Dankoff, *The Intimate Life of an Ottoman Statesman: Melek Ahmed Pasha (1588–1662): As Portrayed in Evliya Çelebi's Book of Travels (Seyahat-name),* SUNY series in medieval Middle East history (Albany: State University of New York Press, 1991), 221–36. On multiple meanings of symbols see also Dror Ze'evi, *Producing Desire: Changing Sexual Discourse in the Middle East, 1500–1900* (Berkeley: University of California Press, 2006), 106–107.

27. Atsız, ed. *Aşıkpaşaoğlu Ahmed Âşıkî. Tevârîh-i Âl-i Osman,* loc. cit.

28. See Paul Wittek, "The Taking of Aydos Castle: A Gazi Legend and its Transformation," in *Arabic and Islamic Studies in Honour of H. A. R. Gibb,* ed. George Makdisi (Cambridge, Mass.: Dept. of Near Eastern Languages and Literatures of Harvard University, 1965). More on the folkloric aspects in

Hasan Özdemir, *Die altosmanischen Chroniken als Quelle zur türkischen Volkskunde* (Freiburg im Breisgau: K. Schwarz, 1975).

29. As such, this dream is at the core of the Ottoman dynastic myth: see Colin Imber, "The Ottoman Dynastic Myth," *Turcica* 19 (1987) and Colin Imber, "The Legend of Osman Ghazi," in *The Ottoman Emirate*, ed. Elizabeth Zachariadou (Rethymnon: 1993).

30. Chase F. Robinson, *Islamic historiography*, Themes in Islamic history (Cambridge, U.K.; New York: Cambridge University Press, 2003), 129.

31. Kappert's characterization of motivation by dreams as psychologizing conflates the two options, which however, for the historian are clearly distinct (Introduction to Muṣṭafā D̲jelāl-zāde, "Ṭabaḳāt ul-memālik we dered̲jāt ül-mesālik," in *Geschichte Sultan Süleyman Kanunis von 1520 bis 1557*, ed. Petra Kappert (Wiesbaden: Reichert, 1981), 34). Ze'evi has argued that Ottomans did recognize dreams as results of psychological processes, but, in my opinion, he neglects that although Ottomans recognize that dreams may result from the individual psyche, they typically dismiss those as meaningless (Ze'evi, *Producing Desire*, 99–103). Evliyā Çelebi's vocational dream discussed above shows the interference of psychology, as his desire to travel causes him to misspeak in the dream, but it does not cause the dream as such (Evliyā, "Seyāḥat-nāme," 28–30).

32. Edirneli ᶜOruc, "[Tārīkh]," in *Oruç Beğ Tarihi (Giriş, Metin, Kronoloji, Dizin, Tıpkıbasım)*, ed. Necdet Öztürk (Istanbul: Çamlıca Basım Yayın, 2007), 8b–9a. Some variants may be noted: ᶜOruc calls Edebalı's daughter with a pious Muslim name Rābiᶜa; he attributes the foundational dream of the Ottoman dynasty to ᶜO̱smān's father Ertuğrul, although the eventual marriage is still concluded between ᶜO̱smān and Edebalı's daughter (6a); Köse Miẖal, according to other sources, had long been a companion of ᶜO̱smān, while still a Christian. Colin Imber pointed out that the legend of Köse Miẖal's dream also helped ᶜOruc's contemporaries to understand the status of the Miẖaloğlu family in their time (Colin Imber, "Review of: Heath W. Lowry, The Nature of the Early Ottoman State," *The Turkish Studies Association Journal* 27, no. 1–2 (2003): 112).

33. Aḥmed b. Lüṭfullāh Müneccimbaşı, "Jāmiᶜ al-Duwal," in *Müneccimbaşı Ahmed b. Lütfullah. Camiü'd-düvel. Osmanlı Tarihi (1299–1481)*, ed. Ahmet Ağırakça (Istanbul: Insan Yayınları, 1995), 175 (text), 242 (translation).

34. Recorded by Silāḥdār, *Silahdar Tarihi*, II, 15.

35. Something seems to be missing here; Kātib Çelebi has: "And the armor is the world of (physical) existence."

36. Hüdāyī died in 1628 at a very old age. See Beldiceanu-Steinherr, I. "Hüdāʾī, Maḥmūd b. Faḍl Allāh b. Maḥmūd." *Encyclopaedia of Islam*, Second Edition. Edited by: P. Bearman, Th. Bianquis, C.E. Bosworth, E. van Donzel and W.P. Heinrichs. Brill, 2009. Brill Online. <http://www.brillonline.nl>.

37. Gottfried Hagen, "World Order and Legitimacy," in *Legitimizing the Order: Ottoman Rhetoric of State Power*, ed. Maurus Reinkowski and Hakan Karateke (Leiden: Brill, 2005), especially 61–73.

38. Ottoman observers clearly were aware of it, although Ottoman literary theory did not have a concept of 'tragedy'; Piterberg's translation

of the heading used by chroniclers, *vaqᶜa-i hāʾile-i ᶜOsmānīye* as "Ottoman Tragedy" is misleading.

39. İz, "Hüseyn Tûğî," 140.

40. About him see Otfried Weintritt, *Formen spätmittelalterlicher islamischer Geschichtsdarstellung: Untersuchungen zu an-Nuwairī al-Iskandarānīs Kitāb al-ilmām und verwandten zeitgenössischen Texten* (Beirut: In Kommission bei Franz Steiner Verlag Stuttgart, 1992).

41. Schmidt, *Pure Water for Thirsty Muslims,* 127–28. ᶜĀlī points out that the warning contained in the dream was heeded only as stomach aches plagued the Sultan. This could mean that men had failed to understand the warning at the right moment, so that the blame falls on them. It is remarkable that the dreamer in this case is the court specialist for prognostication, but the annunciation did not come to him through the stars.

42. İbrāhīm Peçevī, *Tārīḫ-i Peçevī* (Istanbul: Maṭbaᶜa-i ᶜĀmire, 1283), II, 143–45; see also Hagen, "Träume als Sinnstiftung," 121.

43. This phrase is in Arabic in the original.

44. The phrase, regularly implied, is used explicitly in the account of a dream in Muṣṭafā Efendi Selānikī, *Tārīḫ-i Selānikī* (Istanbul: Maṭbaᶜa-i ᶜĀmire, 1281), 212.

45. Schmidt, *Pure Water for Thirsty Muslims,* 127.

46. Qurʾān XLVIII, 3.

47. Müneccimbaşı, "Jāmiᶜ al-Duwal," 207 (text), 282 (translation).

48. See the account in Colin Imber, *The Ottoman Empire, 1300–1481* (Istanbul: The Isis Press, 1990), 213–18.

49. Löwith, *Meaning in History,* 5.

50. Müneccimbaşı, "Jāmiᶜ al-Duwal," 6–9 (text), 53–57 (translation). Fantasies of world domination have been read into other sources as well: see prominently Osman Turan, *Türk Cihân Hâkimiyeti Mefkûresi Tarihi: Türk Dünya Nizamının Millî, İslâmî, ve İnsanî Esasları,* 2 ed., 2 vols. (Istanbul: Nakışlar Yayınevi, 1978).

51. Cornell Fleischer, "Royal Authority, Dynastic Cyclism, and "Ibn Khaldûnism" in Sixteenth-Century Ottoman Letters," *Journal of Asian and African Studies* 18 (1983); Gottfried Hagen, "Überzeitlichkeit und Geschichte in Kātib Čelebis Ğihānnümā," *Archivum Ottomanicum* 14 (1995/1996).

52. See Schmidt, *Pure Water for Thirsty Muslims.*

53. Barbara Flemming, "Ṣāḥib-Qirān und Mahdī: Türkische Endzeiterwartungen im ersten Jahrzehnt der Regierung Süleymans," in *Between the Danube and the Caucasus. Oriental sources on the history of the peoples of Central and Southeastern Europe,* ed. György Kara (Budapest: Akademiai Kiado, 1987), 5252, see also Barbara Flemming, "Der Ğāmiᶜ ül-meknūnāt. Eine Quelle ᶜĀlīs aus der Zeit Sultan Süleymans," in *Studien zur Geschichte und Kultur des Vorderen Orients. Festschrift für Bertold Spuler,* ed. H.R. Roemer and A. Noth (Leiden: Brill, 1981).

54. Robinson, *Islamic Historiography,* 129–30.

55. *Idhā arāda llāhu shayʾan hayyaʾa asbābahū,* quoted for instance in Kātib Çelebi, *Cihān-nümā* (Istanbul: Müteferriḳa, 1732), 9.

56. İz,"Hüseyn Tûğî," 140. The term used here for mystical knowledge is ᶜ*ilm-i ledünnī*, knowledge that is directly imparted to the mystic from God (through dreams?).

57. Hagen, "Träume als Sinnstiftung."

CHAPTER 6

Sometimes a Dream Is Just a Dream

Inculcating a "Proper" Perspective on Dream Interpretation

Fareeha Khan

The Contradictory Approach of Deobandis to Dreams

When reading through the spiritual discourses of the renowned Sufi-jurist Mawlānā Ashraf ʿAlī Thānawī (d. 1943), one finds versions of the following statement often: "I do not consider dreams to be an authoritative thing in this spiritual path." Often aspirants will write in their dreams to him, seeking his guidance on the purport of their night visions, only to be told that their spiritual focus should lie elsewhere. For instance, when one individual wrote in asking for any special prayer that would help him reach his desired goal of seeing the Prophet in a dream, Thānawī answered, "A more needed prayer than this is that Allāh makes you active and attentive towards the essentials [i.e., one's religious obligations, including the daily prayer]." One can sense in such responses a clear disdain for dreams and dream interpretation; they are not as important as what lies before one in terms of practice and conduct in the real, physical world.

At the same time, however, there are instances recorded in these same spiritual discourses where obvious weight *is* given to the meaning of dreams. Often, but not always, these dreams will have some mention of the prophet Muḥammad. One man relates a lengthy dream to Thānawī, in which he sees the Prophet giving him a seat of honor. He is elated that the Prophet is treating him so well, but when he approaches the Prophet and tells him details about his spiritual practice, the Prophet becomes angry. "Indeed you are a *murīd* (disciple) of an innovator!" the Prophet proclaims. The man becomes alarmed at his sudden anger, and by the fact that he was being spurned by the blessed Prophet himself. He begs and pleads with the Prophet to pardon him, only to be kicked in the ribs! The man relates the entire dream to Thānawī, and instead of dismissing it, Thānawī takes the dream very seriously. He writes back, "This dream is absolute guidance. It is essential (*wājib*) to leave the spiritual guide who acts against the Prophetic practice (*sunna*) and to establish contact with the people of truth. I have no hesitation in giving instructions regarding the spiritual path [i.e., taking on the role of spiritual mentor]. Start acting on the legal rulings as outlined in the books *Bihishtī Zewar* ("Heavenly Ornaments") and *Iṣlāḥ-i Rusūm* ("Reforming Customs") [both texts written by Thānawī]. Take the spiritual litanies from *Qaṣd al-sabīl* [also by Thānawī] and the general advices contained in my spiritual discourses. Full instructions in detail will be discussed when we meet in person."

In light of the seemingly contradictory attitudes toward the importance of dreams, how does one know when an apparently spiritual dream is really of consequence? Sometimes a dream is written off as inconsequential to the spiritual path; other times it is considered "absolute guidance." Is the tension due to the contents of the dream itself, or due to some spiritual element within the dream that only the spiritual master can detect? Are dreams of those who have committed themselves to a spiritual path more important than those of mere lay people, who have no interest in perfecting their inner practice? Or could it be that the spiritual master wishes to inculcate a certain attitude toward dreams in the aspirant, and only when he or she reaches an understanding of the real place of dreams in spiritual life does the master begin to explain?

In this chapter, I address these questions in light of the accounts and writings of modern Sufi *ᶜulamā* (religious scholars) from South Asia such as Thānawī and others who received training at Deoband or Deoband-affiliated schools. Given the fact that they were *ᶜulamā*, and trained in the various Islamic sciences (including *taṣawwuf*), I argue that these scholars promoted what was in their view a "balanced," and not excessive, interest in dreams and dream interpretation. Yes, dreams were important—they were considered to be a portion of prophecy (*waḥy*) itself—but their meaning and import for one's own life necessarily had to be weighed against other considerations, both legal and spiritual in nature.

The Importance of Dreams in Deobandi Thought and Lore

The renowned scholars whose work I examine in this chapter trace their intellectual lineage to the theological seminary (*madrasa*) formed at Deoband, a town in north India, in 1867. The *ʿulamā* of Deobandi lineage see themselves as inheritors of the classical Sunni tradition of scholarship and spirituality. In line with what Tim Winters calls a tripartite orthodoxy of "the four schools of *Sunnī* jurisprudence . . . the major Sufi orders (*ṭuruq*), and . . . the three great *Sunnī* theological schools [*Ashʿarī, Māturīdī,* and *Ḥanbalī*],"[1] these *ʿulamā* were and continue to be careful to encourage learning in the Ḥanafī school as well as allegiance to a mixed *ṭarīqa* lineage (with many of them claiming primary allegiance to the Chishtī order). Often labeled "reformist," the founding scholars of the Deoband school were not reformist in the sense of wanting to abolish Sufi practice, because they not only saw benefit in Sufism but actively encouraged its practice. They were, however, acutely concerned with "improving" (making *iṣlāḥ* of) the religious practice of the Muslims of India, and even were willing to curb such practices as the *mawlid* (the celebration of the birthday of the prophet Muḥammad, a common religious event) if the particular form of these practices encouraged polytheistic belief, adoption of Hindu practices, or immoral behavior.

Biographical accounts of the Deobandi *ʿulamā* are replete with references to dreams, indicating the fact that they viewed dreams to be of considerable importance. The founding of their *madrasa* was itself accompanied by numerous dreams indicating its special status, even pointing out the site at which the school should be built. Instead of citing family connections to the town of Deoband, which were in fact present among the early founders, or the town's other particular amenities, the *ʿulamā* laid more emphasis on the spiritual indications that guided them toward this site. As Barbara Metcalf writes:

> Both Shaikh Ahmad Sirhindi in the seventeenth century and Sayyid Ahmad Barelwi in the early nineteenth were said to have commented that an "odor of learning," *bū-yi ʿilm,* came from the very ground of the town. Maulana Rafiʿuʾd-Din dreamed of seeing the Kaʿba located in Deoband's garden;

> of Hazrat ʿAlī [ʿAlī was the Prophet's cousin and son-in-law] founding a school whose pupils he later recognized as Deoband's; and of the Prophet himself giving milk to students there. Such dreams not only endowed the location of the school with sanctity, but gave the founders a self-fulfilling confidence in their mission.[2]

Dreams can be found indicating the close relationship between Deobandi teachers and their students. They functioned as a mode of communication and instruction between not only Deobandi spiritual masters and great figures of the past (such as *awliyā* and the Prophet himself), but also between novice disciples and their spiritual guides, who would use the interpretation of dreams to direct the *murīd* toward the proper "next steps" on the spiritual path.

The Origin of Dreams

By reading the various historical accounts of the formation of Deoband and of the lives of these most prominent South Asian scholars, it is clear that dreams held for them special significance. But why did they see dreams to be of significance in the first place? What place did dreams have in the metaphysical conception of Deobandi *ʿulamā*?

Citing from the early nineteenth-century *Tafsīr al-Maẓharī*, a commentary of the Qurʾān written by one of the students of Shāh Walīullāh, Muḥammad Shafīʿ ʿUthmānī, mentions in his own Qurʾānic commentary that dreams are of three types. The first type are those that include images and situations from one's everyday, waking life; the second type are those that are influenced by the devil—dreams that introduce forms and situations that can be either pleasing or terrifying; and the third final type, a kind of *ilhām* or inspiration, "which is activated to warn a servant of Allāh or to give him glad tidings."[3]

To explain the existence of this third inspirational type of dream, Shafīʿ ʿUthmānī states:

> The Sufis say that everything, before it comes to exist in this world, has a particular form in another universe called *ʿālam al-mithāl*, a universe where, not only the substantial objects and physical realities, but also the attributes and noncorporeal meanings, have particular shapes and forms. When the human self is freed from the concerns of body management while dreaming, it sometimes gets connected

> to the universe of *ᶜālam al-mithāl*. There one would see the representative forms. Then, these forms are shown from the universe of the Unseen. At times, it would so happen that temporary disturbances would cause false imaginings to mix up with the real. Therefore, it becomes difficult for the interpreters to interpret the dream soundly. However, when free of discordant elements, they are real.[4]

It is this third type of dream, the true dream, which falls under the *ḥadīth* or saying of the Prophet in which he states that a dream is 1/46th of prophecy (*nubuwwa*). Shafīᶜ ᶜUthmānī cites not just this percentage, but says that there are in fact other numbers given within *ḥadīth* literature as well; while some *aḥadīth* mention a dream to be 1/46th, others mention 1/40th, 1/49th, 1/50th, and 1/70th of *nubuwwa*. ᶜUthmānī says that there is in fact no contradiction between these various fractions, because "each narration is correct in its place."[5] What they indicate is the spiritual state of the dreamer. One who manifests the traits of "truth, trust, honesty and is perfect of faith" shall be the one whose dream will be a fortieth of prophecy. Whoever has a lower degree of perfection of these traits, his or her dream will reflect the smaller percentage, with the true dream of someone at the weakest spiritual level being 1/70th. However, Shafīᶜ ᶜUthmānī warns his reader that, as seen in the dream accounts within the Qurʾānic chapter on Joseph (Yūsuf), it is sometimes possible for a sinning disbeliever to have a true dream, so one who has a true dream must not be accorded respect simply for this reason.[6]

Dreams, and their interpretation, have a certain control over the course of life events according to Shafīᶜ ᶜUthmānī. This is the reason why one is instructed to only disclose one's dreams to people whom one trusts. As Thānawī, who had been ᶜUthmānī's teacher, also mentions, a dream negatively interpreted may bring about the occurrence of negative events. According to Shafīᶜ ᶜUthmānī, this is because a dream "when related, and interpreted by the listener . . . actualizes as interpreted. Therefore, one should not relate the dream to anyone, except to a person who is knowing and wise, or is, at the least, a friend and well-wisher."[7]

ᶜUthmānī takes this idea of suspended or conditional destiny from a *ḥadīth* found in al-Tirmidhī. To offer an explanation for this possibly unusual-seeming concept of destiny, he cites again from *Tafsīr al-Maẓharī*[8] ("The Commentary of Maẓharī"), in which it is stated that "certain matters of destiny are not absolutely pre-decided but instead remain in a state of suspension." One way to understand how this could be so is to reflect on the *ḥadīth "Anā ʿinda ẓanni ʿabdī bī,"* "I am as My servant thinks of Me." If one believes that good will come from Allāh, then one's life will be full of blessing, and if one fears that one will only receive misfortune from Allāh, then that is what one will see in one's life. Receiving a bad interpretation will cause an incorrect spiritual orientation toward God, so that instead of having *tawakkul* and high hope with Allāh, one will begin to fear impending harm. This implanted fear would likely eventually result in the actualization of bad events in one's life.

In explaining the nature of dreams and dream interpretation, Shafīʿ ʿUthmānī's commentary has allowed us to see some hints as to why a "proper" orientation toward dreams is necessary according to these *ʿulamā*. A dream can be meaningless, when influenced by the Devil for instance. It also can be quite meaningful, with this being contingent not only on the interpretation given, but also on the character and spiritual traits of the dreamer, thus requiring a righteous comportment internally and externally in one's life.

Dreams in Light of the Sharīʿa

Deobandi scholars stress the fact that one should never act on a dream in a way that contravenes the Sharīʿa or the accepted opinions of the scholars on religious matters. An auspicious dream, such as one where a person sees himself in Paradise, should be seen as a good omen, but it should not bring about complacency in a person in terms of his religious practice, such that one abandons the Sunna and believes "that he has been exempted from doing anything."[9] A dream that indicates something good for a person, whether the fact that he will excel in a field or task, or that he will be of the dwellers of Paradise, only communicates the idea that one has *the potential* to have these things realized. Such dreams do not serve as a guarantee, but only are a source of encouragement for one to begin to act in the appropriate manner.[10]

One should not go against religious law because of a dream, nor discount a *ḥadīth* because of it, nor use a dream as a form of evidence in a legal court case. One *may* act on a warning contained in a dream: for instance, if one sees that someone is about to commit murder or cheat another, one may alert the one to be victimized. However, a dream cannot act as proof. Muḥammad Taqī ʿUthmānī, the son of Shafīʿ ʿUthmānī and currently the leading Sharīʿa scholar of Pakistan, relates an interesting story to emphasize the necessary separation of matters of law and the dream world:

There was a Qadi (Judge) who used to decide cases referred to him for judgment. A case was submitted to him for decision. The Qadi heard the case, examined the witnesses and made up his mind about the final judgment to be announced in a day or two. In the meantime in the night he saw the Holy Prophet (s) in a dream. The Holy Prophet (s) did not, so felt the Qadi, concur in the Qadi's judgment but advised him to change his judgment. When the Qadi awoke from sleep and reconsidered the details of the case thoroughly, he felt convinced that the Holy Prophet's judgment did not fit with the framework of the Sharīᶜa. The issue took a very serious turn. The Qadi could not decide what to do. He called on the Caliph and told him in detail his predicament due to this strange dream. In order to resolve the difficulty, a meeting was arranged of all the *ᶜulamā* of the capital and the problem was put before them. The *ᶜulamā*, feeling convinced of the genuineness of the dream, were inclined to decide the case according to the direction of the Holy Prophet (s) received through the dream. A great savant and learned man of his age Hazrat ᶜIzzuddīn bin ᶜAbdus Salām was also present at the meeting. He was regarded as a *mujaddid* (the promised restorer of the religion) of his time. He stood up and addressed the meeting as follows:

> It is my considered opinion that the case should be decided according to the provision of the Sharīᶜa. . . . I take all responsibilities for the sins, if any, involved in this judgment. It is not lawful to decide a case in light of indications contained in a dream. We are required to obey only those directions of the Holy Prophet (s) which have come to us through reliable authorities.[11]

By highlighting this story within his exposition on "dreams in light of the Sharīᶜa," Taqī ᶜUthmānī stresses the point that although dreams have a certain importance, they cannot enter the public space in a way that serves to adjudicate serious matters. Deobandi scholars held the esoteric dimensions of Islam in high regard, but, like other *ᶜulamā* before them, maintained a separation between that realm and the exoterically known and confirmed aspects of the religion. The Prophet had left behind only the Qurʾān and his Sunna, and the Sunna, for the purpose of worldly application, had been preserved in the apparent, physical world through sensorially verifiable chains of narration, and not through the more elusive dimension of dreams.

One could not let the dream world interfere with the legal management of society, because the form of evidence was simply not one that could "hold up in court."

Who Can Have True Dreams, and Who Can Interpret Them?

Anyone can have a true dream; one does not have to be a pious Muslim or even a believer to have a dream that contains truth. This fact is established from the Qurʾān itself: In the Chapter on Joseph, there are four true dreams related, and three of them are seen by unbelievers (the one seen by the king of Egypt, and the two dreams seen by Joseph's fellow prisonmates). Along with these examples, Shafīʿ ʿUthmānī in his commentary on the Qurʾān mentions that the prophet Daniel (Ar. Dāniyāl) had interpreted the dream of the "disbelieving King of Babylon, Nebuchadnezzar," that Chosroe (Kisrā) had seen a dream about the coming of the Prophet, and that the Prophet's aunt ʿĀtika had seen a true dream about the Prophet as well before she accepted Islam, as noticed by Sarah Mirza in her contribution in the present volume.[12]

However, Deobandi scholars give warning that one should not get confused about matters of belief just because an unbeliever can see true dreams. Dreams are only one type of intuitive experience; even unbelievers can experience illumination (*kashf*), where they come to know of imminent events by way of visions while in a waking state. As Thānawī states: "Often it so happens that due to engagement in *dhikr* (remembrance of Allāh; chanting) and spiritual exercises (*shughl*), one experiences a type of spiritual focus (*yeksūʾī*) that may result in occurrences of *kashf*, and so on. This is not any exceptional feat, but the spiritual aspirant (*dhākir*) may incorrectly assume that reaching the Divine Presence (*wuṣūl ilā Allāh*) may be arrived at without Islam, when in fact *wuṣūl* has nothing at all to do with such matters (i.e., *kashf*, etc.)."[13] As seen here, dreams, illumination, and such matters fall under spiritual states (*aḥwāl*) for the Deobandis, and like other Sufis, they do not believe these things to be the goal of the spiritual aspirant, as spiritual arrival and reaching the Divine Presence are separate from the mere experience of spiritual states.

As one contemporary Deobandi scholar states, "The non-Muslim can get some hint from the *lawḥ al-maḥfūẓ* (the Sacred Tablet), since it is at the first level of the heavens. They need *īmān* (faith) to go beyond this, since the angels will pelt all else away." His explanation is in line with the most common Qurʾānic exegetical explanations of how soothsayers and other unbelievers are able to access sometimes true information about the future: The jinn are able to listen in on the conversations of angels by approaching the lowest level of the heavens, but the angels pelt them away so that they cannot reach higher heavenly realms. Therefore, a Muslim's faith should not be affected by "gurus or Christians"[14] having dreams that contain truth, because this is not proof of their being spiritually and religiously sound.

Obviously, for these Deobandi scholars, dreams are important, and have "consequences both eventually [in this world, in the *dunyā*] as well as consequentially [in the Afterlife or *ākhira*]."[15] But for a non-Muslim who sees a true dream, his dream only contains this-worldly consequences.[16] As for what the Sufis term *true dreams* (*ruʾyā ṣaḥīḥa* or *ruʾyā ṣādiqa*), these have both this-worldly and next-worldly consequences. One of the most often quoted *ḥadīth* about dreams is "Nothing remains of prophethood (*nubuwwa*) except true dreams (*al-mubashshirāt*)." It is these latter dreams, the ones that hold meaning for both the *dunyā* and the *ākhira*, and the ones that require faith in Islam as a prerequisite, that fall under "*al-mubashshirāt*."[17]

Although anyone could potentially experience a true dream, not everyone has the ability to interpret them. According to Shaykh Amīn Kholwādia, the contemporary Deobandi scholar mentioned here who is "authorized" to interpret dreams, one's ability to understand the meaning of dreams correlates directly with one's understanding of revelation. He says in his commentary on the Chapter of Joseph:

> Yūsuf (*ʿalayhi al-salām*) as a child is being prepared to understand that dreams have a significant role to play in people's lives. Just as dreams have a significant role to play in a prophet's portfolio, [since] it is part of revelation, likewise dreams have a significant role to play in the lives of human beings. . . . Your subconscious is alive, and what happens inside impacts what happens outside. Except, not everyone has the knowledge and ability to understand the subconscious. Who has the ability to do the latter? People who understand *waḥy* and revelation.[18]

According to Kholwādia, one can develop the state needed to see and interpret true dreams. "Not that we seek them," he says, because "they are secondary. But we work to get to the state needed (through *dhikr*, *ʿibāda*, etc.)"[19] To interpret dreams, one needs to understand that dreams are intrinsically linked to the idea of revelation. Just as it took Joseph years to understand the full implications of a dream that he sees as a young boy, so revelation can take the whole lifetime for a prophet such as Muḥammad to truly understand. It is by way of revelation that God communicates to humanity via His prophets (*nabī*, pl. *anbiyā*), and once they are gone, God continues to send messages to human beings that hold meaning and import for their lives. The more comprehensive one's knowledge of revelation, that is, of the Qurʾān, and the deeper one's understanding of the teachings of Muḥammad, the more able one becomes in seeing the meanings of true dreams. It is, after all, the consequences of the Afterlife that are of most significant import for the human being, and in the view of scholars such as Kholwādia, how can one truly understand the depth of meaning contained in a true dream unless one has a truly broad view of reality that is not limited just to the finite nature of the events of this world?

For Kholwādia, dream interpretation is a "science like any other," and requires both spiritual resolve as well as direct training under one who is already qualified to interpret dreams. Some Deobandi scholars, however, believe dream interpretation to be more akin to a "gift." Although Ashraf ʿAlī Thānawī was himself a Sufi master (and therefore one might assume that he possessed the proper spiritual state), and although he was trained in the other Islamic sciences as well, he would often say that he was "simply not predisposed to dream interpretation." He mentions others of his contemporaries who have a natural gift for interpreting dreams, and their understanding of dreams seems to be intuitive in nature. He cites an occasion, for instance, when another Deobandi scholar, Muḥammad Yaʿqūb, was approached by a man seeking an interpretation for a disturbing dream. In this dream, the man had seen himself holding a heavy girl-child in his lap. She is so heavy that he resolves to find a place to put her down. He sights a female dog on the road, cuts open the dog's stomach, and places the girl inside. The dog begins to walk alongside the man, and the man keeps turning to check on it since it is carrying the girl inside, and he is afraid the dog may run away. After going some distance on the road, the dog vanishes. When Muḥammad Yaʿqūb is first told this dream, he turns the man away saying he does not understand its meaning. "Come again some time, and if I come to understand it, I will tell you its interpretation." When the man returns a second time, Yaʿqūb "receives" the interpretation while standing in prayer (*namāz mein qalb par wārid huʾi*). He tells the man: "You experienced sexual desire and you had illicit relations (lit. "blackened your face") with a street girl. She became pregnant with your daughter and due to the child's birth you became even more involved with this woman. Then the woman was unfaithful to you." Thānawī praises the interpretive ability of his contemporary and says that one could never have guessed what the dream meant unless one had special intuitive ability.[20]

The Spiritual Place of Dreams

In his writings on *taṣawwuf,* Thānawī places the true dream (*ruʾyā ṣāliḥa*) under the category of *aḥwāl,* sing. *ḥāl.* According to Thānawī, the *ḥāl* is a temporary spiritual state that comes about involuntarily, without choice (*ikhtiyār*). This is why *aḥwāl* do not count as being part of *dīn* or religion, since what is required by religion is the results of one's own toil and effort.[21] To be placed in or to be granted one of these states (among them he lists illumination [*kashf*], the true dream [*ruʾyā ṣāliḥa*], or inspiration [*ilhām*]) is not something one should seek or be proud of; these states are in fact a form of *dunyā,* this-worldliness, and they are merely natural internal states as are more familiar ones like joy and happiness (*farḥ wa surūr*).

Aḥwāl are by their nature inconstant, and one should not become upset and worried when such a state is lifted from one. In fact, what causes spiritual harm is not the lifting of the state, but the despair individuals often fall into when their state is lifted.

To explain this further, Thānawī says that certain preliminaries must first be understood. The entire point of *sulūk* or spiritual discipline is to become annihilated in the Divine (*al-Ḥaqq*). That is, one's own attributes (*ṣifāt*) are annihilated, and one instead begins to be shaped via the attributes of God (*mutakhalliq bi akhlāqi'llāh*).[22] There are two aspects to the attributes of the human being: the first being causes (*mabādī,* sing. *mabdā*) and the second being effects (*muntahāt,* sing. *muntahā*). If one is still at the level of causes, then he requires a cause to bring about a particular effect. For example, for a person to manifest the attribute of mercy, he must first see that another human being is suffering, and by experiencing that cause, the effect of him being kind to the one who suffers comes about. At this level, the person is still acting by way of his own attributes, since for him to manifest mercy there need to be both causes and effects present.

God's attributes are without cause; with respect to Him there are only ends and effects (*ghāyāt aur muntahāt*). True spiritual perfection comes about when the human being acts without the need for any cause. He is not overcome (*maghlūb*) by any human emotion, regardless of these emotions being considered "good" or "bad" in the view of human beings. Rather, he gains complete control over his self, such that he can "switch on" and "switch off" internal states as they are required, in order to conform to the Divine decree. When a person begins to avoid sin and does good deeds without any cause, such as fear of punishment or even love of the Divine being present, but instead has an existence that is in constant conformity with the Divine Will, then he has reached a level of spiritual perfection (*kamāl*), and he is said to now be shaped through the attributes of God Himself.

It is helpful here to revisit the concept of "reaching the Divine Presence" (*wuṣūl ilā Allāh*) that was mentioned earlier. Because specific spiritual states are not brought about through choice or the will of the human being, they cannot be the goal of the spiritual seeker. According to the Deobandi scholars (although of course, this idea is not unique to them), the goal of the Sufi is to do what is pleasing to Allāh, by conforming both his external and his internal states to the teachings of the Prophet. It is this effort at shaping his will to the will of Allāh that eventually leads to proximity (*qurb*), until one who finally gains complete control of his self may taste true knowledge of God and thereby reach the Divine Presence.

It is for this reason that spiritual states such as true dreams, although not rejected or avoided, also are not things to be sought out by the spiritual seeker. It is good if they bring benefit, such as helping to increase one's religious practice, but in and of themselves they are not considered a spiritual goal. They are like flowering trees along the spiritual path Thānawī says; if one is able to spot these along the way and admire them and take benefit from them, fine, but even he who does not notice any flowers can still traverse the path and reach the desired Goal.[23] The reason why the spiritual seeker must be careful of such spiritual states is the danger of being diverted; if one stops to smell the flowers but does not move on, one will have essentially lost the way.

Conclusion

As mentioned earlier, the Deobandis are known for their reformist or *iṣlāḥī* concern. For them, one of the primary missions of the *ʿulamā* is to be aware of the state of the masses, the *ʿawāmm,* and to impart knowledge that helps toward improving their religious practice and to reorient them toward a correct attitude toward religious matters.

When Thānawī downplays the role of dreams in the quotes mentioned at the start of this chapter, it is because he wishes people to look to dreams *only if* they know their proper place and value. The masses, he believed, put too much emphasis on ideas such as *kashf* (waking visions of true events) and *ilhām* (inspired knowledge of the truth). Visions and premonitions are given too much importance, when primary importance should be given to those concrete things that the Prophet has left behind. When asked about dreams, it is said that Thānawī often would quote a Persian couplet as follows: "I am neither the night nor the worshipper of the night that I should tell things about dreams. I am the slave of the Sun [i.e., the Prophet, *ghulām-i āftābam*] and can only speak of the Sun." For him, spiritual distinction could only be marked out by evidence of one being in conformity to the Sunna or practice of the Prophet, which meant for him both the external and internal aspects of the Prophetic reality. One's access to true dreams was not necessarily an indication that such a pious state had actually been reached.

Taqī ᶜUthmānī relates a similar sentiment in his own, more contemporary to us, spiritual discourses. He says that there are two going opinions about dreams amongst the masses: one opinion assigns no value at all to dreams; the other overemphasizes their value, thereby elevating the recipient of a true dream to the rank of saint, even if that person's piety and righteousness cannot be attested to. Often, a spiritual traveler may become distracted by his own true dreams; they may contain truth, but be simultaneously a test from God, to see whether the servant will begin seeking true dreams for their own sake or recognize them to be a veil to the True, *al-Ḥaqq*, Himself.[24]

With this analysis, one can see why it is that Thānawī, when conversing and corresponding with his disciples in the early twentieth century, would sometimes completely reject their requests for dream interpretation, and other times look to their dreams with great reverence. In the *iṣlāḥī* orientation of the Deobandi *ᶜulamā*, everything must be measured according to the ultimate religious benefit it will have for the believer, even if that means that seemingly accepted religious forms and practices must be abandoned to fulfill this purpose. What must be remembered is that even a "true dream" could be a test and not necessarily a sign of one's spiritual or religious status. The benefits of true dreams can only be reaped by those who are willing to conform their will to the will of God, and to heed the messages brought by dreams but not become obsessed with the fact that they are "special enough" to see such things. For these scholars, it is only through such an understanding that a proper perspective on dreams and dream interpretation can be reached.

Notes

1. Tim Winter (ed.), *The Cambridge Companion to Classical Islamic Theology* (Cambridge: Cambridge University Press, 2008), 7.

2. Barbara Metcalf, *Islamic Revival in British India: Deoband, 1860–1900* (Princeton: Princeton University Press, 1982), 92.

3. Muhammad Shafīᶜ, *Maᶜārifu'l-Qur᾿ān*, (trans. Shamim Muhammad) (Karachi: Maktaba-e Darul-Uloom, 2005), vol. 5, 28. Also see Leah Kinberg's and Jonathan Katz' contributions in this volume.

4. Muhammad Shafīᶜ, *Maᶜārifu'l-Qur᾿ān*, 28.

5. Ibid., 29.

6. Ibid., 31. For a similar notion, see Sarah Mirza's chapter in this volume.

7. Ibid., 32.

8. This *tafsīr* or Qur᾿ānic commentary is well known in South Asia. It was written by Qāḍī Thanā Allāh Pānipatī (d. 1810) and was named in honor of his teacher Mīrzā Maẓhar Jān-i Jānān (d. 1780).

9. Muḥammad Taqī ᶜUsmānī, *Discourses on Islamic Way of Life*, trans. Iqbāl Ḥussain Anṣārī (Karachi: Dāru 'l-Inshā᾿āt, 1999), vol. 5, 101.

10. Shaykh Amīn Kholwādia on Dārul Qāsim website, "Sūra Yūsuf (12:1–6) (Mar 29, 2009)" http://www.darulqasim.org/Tafseer.aspx.

11. ᶜUsmānī, *Discourses on Islamic Way*, vol. 5, 102–103.

12. Muḥammad Shafīᶜ, *Maᶜārifu'l-Qur᾿ān*, 31.

13. Ashraf ᶜAlī Thānawī, *Malfūẓāt Ḥakīm al-Ummat*, comp. Maḥmūd Ashraf ᶜUsmānī (Multan: Idāra-e Ta᾿lifāt Ashrafiyya) vol. 1, 44.

14. Amīn Kholwādia, phone interview by Fareeha Khan, April, 27, 2009.

15. Ibid.

16. Ibid.

17. Ibid.

18. http://www.darulqasim.org/Tafseer.aspx.

19. Kholwādia, interview.

20. Thānawī, *Malfūẓāt Ḥakīm al-Ummat*, vol. 1, 235.

21. Ashraf ᶜAlī Thānawī, *Sharīᶜat wa ṭarīqat*, comp. Muḥammad Dīn (Lahore: Idara-e Islamiyyat, 1981), 298.

22. One Deobandi Sufi guide explained this statement of Thānawī's by making reference to a *ḥadīth* in which ᶜĀ᾿isha is asked about the character of the Prophet, to which she replies, "His character was the Qur᾿ān" ("*Kāna khuluquhu al-Qur᾿ān*"). Thānawī 's phrase "*mutakhalliq bī akhlāqi'llāh*" should not be understood as meaning that the person begins to *partake* in the attributes of God, as this would be considered *shirk*, or associating others with God (the

cardinal sin of Islam). Rather, the phrase is meant to emphasize that upon reaching this level, the spiritual seeker begins to exist exactly in the way God requires him to be. (Phone interview with Mansoor Ali Khan, August 2009)

23. Thānawī, *Sharīʿat wa ṭarīqat*, 298.

24. ʿUsmānī, *Discourses on Islamic Way*, vol. 5, 95–96.

CHAPTER 7

Dreams Online

Contemporary Appearances of the Prophet in Dreams

Leah Kinberg

Although prophecy came to an end with the death of Muḥammad, the seal of the prophets, the Islamic community was not left without guidance. In his farewell sermon, the Prophet reportedly explained that as long as the people follow the two sources that he had left for them, the Qurʾān and the Sunna, they would not go astray.[1] On a different occasion, he is quoted as saying: "Mission and prophecy have come to an end; there is no messenger after me and no prophet."[2] According to the *ḥadīth*, these words troubled the people, so to encourage them, the Prophet added: "But the tidings remain." For "tidings" the text uses the term *mubashshirāt* and defines it as "dreams revealed to pious Muslims" and as "part of prophecy." Affirming dreams as an extension of prophecy, this *ḥadīth* provides the people with the comforting notion of everlasting guidance that is to be revealed to righteous Muslims of all generations in their sleep.

The other world, *al-ākhira*, which is considered the abode of truth *(dār al-ḥaqq)*,[3] and its dwellers, the Dead, the bearers of truth, are regarded as "those who know" (*yaʿlamūn*), whereas the Living are those who can act (*yaʿmalūn*).[4] This belief created a special interaction between the Living and the Dead: The Dead, who have become aware of the value of duties, appear in dreams to instruct the living on how to act; the Living, on the other hand, turn this knowledge into deeds. Because the delivered message originates in the realm of truth, it is considered to be sound and genuine, and the advice may be followed safely (although not in judicial matters[5]). The ability to have such instructive dreams (*manāmāt ṣāliḥa*) is limited to the righteous and is therefore considered to be a virtue.[6]

Consequently, one may think that the appearance of the Prophet is not deemed as crucial, and that the communication with any deceased through the medium of dreams is sufficient to instruct the community. However, the large number of reports about the appearance of the Prophet in dreams, adduced in various classical works, is an indication of the existence of a real need to see the Prophet in dreams. This can be explained by the urgent need to answer unsolvable crucial issues,[7] where dreams function as a balance pivot. In addition to providing answers to major questions, the Prophet also appears in dreams that deal with personal issues and trivial matters. The abundance of these dreams implies love for the Prophet and full trust in the medium of dreams. This is supported by the following words ascribed to the Prophet, "He who has seen me in a dream has (or 'will') certainly seen (see) me in wakefulness."[8] This pronouncement comes in different versions, usually with the assuring ending: ". . . for the devil does not take my form,"[9] and encourages the dreamers to trust their visions. The notion behind this *ḥadīth* is twofold: On the one hand, it protects the dreamer from any devilish or self-illusions that may result from his own eagerness to see the Prophet. On the other hand, it allows the dreamer to experience direct contact with the Prophet. In so doing, the dream is elevated to the degree of an authentic *ḥadīth*.

Unsurprisingly, the infinite confidence in dreams, especially in those reinforced by the appearance of the Prophet, could have been, and indeed was, used to fulfill a variety of needs, and not necessarily innocent ones. The desire (sometimes need) to promote ideas and to justify acts, either on a personal level or for the sake of the whole community, led to a long line of fabricated dream narrations. The traditionalists of classical times were well aware of the phenomenon, and took preventative measures to avoid it, especially in relation to the appearance of the Prophet. This stands at the basis of the following saying, ascribed to the Prophet: "He who lies about his dream [deliberately] will have to tie a knot in a small barley corn on the Day of Judgment."[10] (Because the act cannot be performed, the message becomes a threat of Hell.)

In previous studies, I examined the central role of dreams in classical Islam, and I often dealt with dreams as a convenient tool of legitimization. However, I have never studied contemporary dreams. As a matter of fact, until recently, personal contemporary dreams were inaccessible. This has changed with the Internet revolution. In the past few years we have observed an enormous increase in the number of Web sites built by and dedicated to Islamic communities. In the past ten years, and mainly within the past three to four years, we have witnessed an ongoing interest in this new phenomenon and a constant increase in academic studies dedicated to the examination of the function of the Web as a platform for Muslims to disseminate knowledge.[11] These studies focus on the most central portals, those that adduce wide databanks that contain religious, judicial, and historical texts on Islamic heritage, such as islamweb[12] and islamOnline.[13]

Smaller communal forums and individual blogs have yet to be examined; these nonofficial and nonselective sites grant their members a welcoming and familial feeling, and in so doing, encourage them to open up and express their ideas and sentiments. As such, many of these sites have become channels to communicate private emotions, beliefs, and genuine fears. Hence, a survey of the information accumulated in these sites allows us to go beyond normative and official records and to actually penetrate into the most hidden areas. Not surprisingly, among the topics discussed in these online sources, we often find dreams.

In this study, I examine several blogs and communal forums that have gone unnoticed until now and show that the proliferation of online dream narrations suggests that contemporary dreams have not lost the status they held in the early days, but rather continue to be an integral part of life among modern Islamic communities. Out of a large assortment of dreams, I focus on those in which the Prophet appears, and I show the correspondences between classical and modern dreams of this kind. I mention the link from which every dream was retrieved and provide basic information about the sites consulted, including the date they were registered online. All the links were accessed on July 31, 2009.

The study is divided into two parts: the first presents and analyzes two types of dream narratives, and the second examines a chain-letter dream that was circulated through email.

Dream Narratives

Personal Dreams with Private Implications

Thou Shall Not Lie

ʿAynī wa-ʿaynak is one of thousands of Arabic language Islamic sites on the Net. There is nothing special about this site. Like others of its kind, it has forums *(muntadayāt)* divided into themes that are chosen by its members. One such forum is dedicated to dreams, where members join to seek explanations and interpretations of their daily dreams. The following, paraphrased from Arabic, is merely one example, posted on the Net in December 2006 by a person from Salé, Morocco, under the name Layal.[14]

> As a matter of fact I am going to tell you two dreams about the same topic: In the first I was standing in a garden; its grass reached my shoulders; I heard people telling me to step aside to let the Prophet approach, but out of curiosity I remained in my place. When the people drew near, I saw them carrying a person wearing white clothes; his face, however, was not clear. I woke up and shared the dream with my family and friends, but I was worried that it was not the Prophet and that I might be considered a liar to the extent that the [threatening] *ḥadīth* about those who lie in their dreams[15] will apply to me. After a few days I saw myself walking through a long passage. I saw a man of magnificent appearance, who began to walk with me. He then addressed me and said: I am the messenger of Allāh whom you have seen [before].

Having been informed of the Prophet's arrival, but with no way to verify the fact, leaves this dreamer puzzled about the actual vision and worried of being trapped in an unintentional lie about the Prophet. The duty to provide accurate reports, especially when it comes to dreams, has not lost its binding power, and the relevant prophetic warnings are still attached to the report. Judging by the fear conveyed in the first dream and the relief in the second, we may assume that this sense of responsibility has not disappeared over the course of history, but has rather become part of the believer's conscience, being revitalized once and again with every contemporary appearance of the Prophet in a dream.

Piety Earns the Appearance of the Prophet

The actual appearance of the Prophet in dreams always has been viewed as a sign of piety and high morals, not to mention evidence of the Prophet's love and care. This notion is the core of the next two dreams, experienced by the same person. The dreams are presented as taking place six years apart. They were posted on the Net in July 2001 in Riyāḍ.[16]

> [Paraphrased from Arabic] When I was little, before I became fourteen, I had some disagreements with my parents. I loved Qurʾān reading, I loved to listen to the *ḥadīth*, and I worshipped Allāh and obeyed Him, all this despite my young age. . . . Among a variety of *ḥadīth* sayings, the one about sweetness of faith (*ḥalāwat al-īmān*)[17] captured my mind. I was sure that this sweetness was something tremendous that seizes the believer's soul and elevates him. . . . I wished I could understand it, taste it, and live by it. Those were the dreams of a teenager. It seems that Allāh, with His compassion, decided to teach me the essence of this sweetness and led me into that strange night. I fell asleep and had a dream. In my dream, the Prophet entered our house and slept in my mother's bed. ʿUmar slept in my bed. The room was dark and the Prophet covered his body with a sand-colored cover, which hid his face. ʿUmar also covered his face. I wanted to see their faces, but could not. I cried and woke up in a panic. I kept crying for a whole week. My family worried. I was hysterical. I felt that it was either a punishment or a message—don't you want to see me? I pray so much, and love you so much, I love you oh *Rasūl*, why, why, why do you cover your face? I decided to begin a new life, that of obedience and devotion, of fasting, Qurʾān reading and *Fiqh* (Islamic jurisprudence) learning. I then began to live piously. I turned twenty. It was the tenth of the month of *Dhū al-Ḥijja,* and I was fasting the whole day. I had a dream. I was walking to the mosque next to our house and a man drew my attention and said that the Prophet was behind me. I turned my head and saw him; I saw his face; I swear to God; I was standing in front of him; he looked at me; he smiled at me. . . . He entered the mosque. A piece of wood was blocking the way. I took it away to keep the Prophet safe. I looked at him again while he was in the mosque, and a third time when he left. He smiled at me and left. I woke up, and now I can tell you—I can feel the sweetness of faith . . . total love toward Allāh and His messenger.[18] The smile that he gave me was interwoven with such tenderness and affection that

> since that day, whenever I came across anger or any kind of rudeness I thought to myself: "Had you been here with me, you would not have let it happen."

The sequence of the two dreams emphasizes the idea that the ability to see the Prophet in a dream is a reward that can be earned—after six years of piety and devotion, the Prophet finally revealed his face to the dreamer. Trusting that the appearance of the Prophet in a dream comes as a grace bestowed on the devout may explain why—over the Net—people keep asking about possible ways to be blessed with such dreams, and why various forums dedicate long chapters to answering this need.[19] An analysis of the methods used to attempt to see the Prophet in dreams will take us beyond the scope of this chapter. However, the reasons for this recurrent inquiry are my main concern. They are imbedded in yearnings for the Prophet, accompanied by the old traditional confidence that his appearance in dreams is the epitome of celestial bliss. This may suggest that such feelings have remained unchanged throughout Islamic history and continue to provide comfort, or positive feedback, to use a more modern expression.

Personal Dreams with Communal Implications

Although the two aforementioned dreams focus on morale and piety in general, they are private and with minimal relevancy to the entire community. The next dreams are different; they are typical of dire times and usually occur during wars. They demonstrate the love and care of the Prophet for the believers in the battlefield, and serve as a means of motivation and encouragement. To understand their enormous influence we must keep in mind that the inspiration for these dreams lies in the Qurʾānic idea regarding the angels' assistance during the battle of Badr.[20]

From a large assortment of dreams, I chose to focus on those that were formed in the Middle East during the Gaza war in early 2009.

> [Paraphrased from Arabic]: My dear brothers, I am going to tell you about my dream with the Prophet during the first day of the Gaza war: I saw myself going to the mosque for the Morning Prayer. We performed the prayer and afterwards remained to read the Qurʾān, me and a few more brothers. When we finished, one of the brothers drew my attention to a person with a white glowing face, wearing a

> turban,[21] and identified him as the Prophet. I left my seat and went to sit beside him. There was a Qurʾān in front of him. The Prophet approached me and said: "You will win the war!" I swear to God, this is what he said. I swear, this is the dream that I had and this is what the Prophet promised us.[22]

Although this dream is mentioned by only one online site, other dreams related to the Gaza war have been widely disseminated over the Web.

A mother relates that her son woke up smiling and told her that he had seen the Prophet in his dream. The Prophet informed him that in two days he would become his companion in Paradise.[23] Still in the dream, the man/boy told the Prophet that he was a soldier in the troops of ʿIzz al-Dīn al-Qassām, and asked whether they were on the right path. The Prophet answered in the affirmative and added: "If *you* are not on the right path, then who is?" (italics added)[24]

Of a different nature is a text that associates the appearance of the Prophet in a dream with three flags held by the fighting warriors: the flag of Khālid (hinting at Khālid b. al-Walīd), the flag of Saʿd (hinting at Saʿd b. Abī Waqqāṣ), and the flag of Ḥusayn (hinting at Ḥusayn b. ʿAlī).[25] Yearning for victory, the text places the present war among the central battles of early Islam, and identifies its warriors with Islam's most distinguished military commanders.

Another frequently quoted dream is transmitted by Sheikh Aḥmad al-Qaṭṭān[26] from a sheikh in Mauritania, who transmitted it from a sheikh from Riyāḍ (notice the *isnād*). The Riyāḍī sheikh saw the Prophet in a dream wearing a "turban of war."[27] He asked him where he was going and the answer was to Gaza.[28] Aḥmad al-Qaṭṭān defined the dream as genuine, and interpreted it as indicating the people of Gaza's future victory.[29] A different version, or maybe a dream in its own right, tells that Aḥmad al-Qaṭṭān saw the Prophet fighting with the warriors *(mujāhidīn)* of Gaza.[30]

In relation to the same war, we find other dreams, each relating a different sheikh's vision of the Prophet. In one dream, the Prophet is seen angered and drawing his sword,[31] explaining that he was going to Gaza. In another dream, the Prophet is heard saying that the gates of Heaven have opened to receive the warriors of Gaza, and in another in this series the Prophet mentions that the martyrs (*shuhadāʾ*) of Gaza will enter Paradise.[32] Another version mentions that the Prophet was seen fighting with Gaza's weak and oppressed people *(mustaḍʿafīn)*.[33]

Following the same pattern, or rather being presented in different literary layouts, the root of the referenced Gaza dreams is hardship and an urgent need for encouragement and validation.

The Gaza war is not unique in producing such dreams; previous wars in the Middle East, as well as in Egypt,[34] Iraq,[35] Chechnya,[36] and Afghanistan,[37] all bequeathed a long line of dreams that tell of the Prophet assisting the warriors. This motif is not new to Islam. A case in point occurred in the year 92/711, when Ṭāriq b. Ziyād reached the southern shore of Spain and had a dream. He saw the Prophet and the four Caliphs walking on water. They reached him and announced Ṭāriq's expected victory.[38] Another case is mentioned in the records of the seventh/thirteen century. Reportedly, Quṭuz the *Mamlūk* (d. 658/1259) saw the Prophet in a dream. Through his dream he learnt that he was about to defeat the Mongols and rule Egypt.[39]

Summary

Although the Web supplies a voluminous number of texts that deal with the appearance of the Prophet in dreams, they basically all break down into a small number of complete texts similar to those just presented. The remainder are presented in broken language, half-sentences, vague phrases, and poor content, if any at all. This is typical of blogs and communal forums, and can be excused as the online language syndrome. However, in our case, the general process of language deterioration is not the only explanation for the poor quality of the texts. Emotional involvement carries at least an equal share. Facing the Prophet in a dream is likely to produce anxiety, hesitation, and fear—symptoms that often contribute to the incoherency and disorientation of the report. The more exclamation marks, broken lines, half words and three dots (. . .) used, the more excitement is conveyed. Hence, despite the fact that these incomplete fragments do not tell a full story, they enable us to discern that when the Prophet is involved in a dream, people experience difficulties controlling their feelings and readily let themselves be carried away. A disguise of cynicism or sophistication, so typical of our present time, is not evident here. Pious Muslims and warriors do not remain indifferent at the sight of the Prophet in a medium that has always been considered a source of the ultimate truth.

This notion is reinforced in the next section.

The Enigma of the Attendant of the Sacred Shrine in Madina

In support of my assumption regarding the unceasing impact of the Prophet's appearance in dreams among contemporary Muslims, I present here an Arabic version of an admonition related to a certain Sheikh Aḥmad, the attendant of the Sacred Shrine of the Prophet in Madina. No further details about his personality or time are given, but the text is widely distributed and can easily be traced by Google in different languages. However, I limited my search to Arabic.[40] Most of the versions are presented in the format of a chain-letter delivered by email, even though this very letter was in circulation long before emails became so popular. There is no reason to doubt that the Arabic version already existed in the seventies, probably a few years before Ibn Bāz[41] disapproved of it in his *fatwā*, or juridical opinion (see discussion later).

The following is a paraphrase of an Arabic version that appeared on the Web on February 20, 2007:

> Late Friday night, reciting the Glorious Qurʾān, I was about to go to bed when I saw Muḥammad the Apostle of Allāh: "O Sheikh Aḥmad . . . I am so ashamed of the people's despicable deeds that I could face neither Allāh nor the Angels, since from Friday to Friday, 160,000 people died without faith in Islam; none of them went to Heaven. Women do not obey their husbands, those who have money do not help the poor, and others do not perform their pilgrimage as prescribed, nor say their prayers regularly. Present them with this admonition, O Sheikh Aḥmad; it is transmitted by the Pen of the Almighty from the Guarded Tablet. He who writes and communicates it from country to country and from place to place will have a palace built for him in Heaven; but in case he does not, he will be deprived of my intercession *(shafāʿa)* on the Day of Judgment. He who copies [and sends] it, Allāh will enrich him if he is poor, settle his debts if he is indebted, or pardon him and his parents if sinful. He who does not write it, his face will blacken both in this world and in the Hereafter."[42]

This warning ends the Prophet's message. Before presenting the rest of the text, I emphasize some of the measures that the text uses to make the admonition more appealing and persuasive.

Immorality and disrespect of basic duties are acts that bring about divine punishment. Those who witness its results must learn a lesson from the misfortune of the sinners and must warn their brothers about it. For their endeavors they will be rewarded with the Prophet's intercession. This is the main idea of the present admonition. It reiterates the Islamic traditional concept of divine remuneration, a fundamental and well-known issue within devoted Muslim communities. Recurrence of familiar ideas presented in such a simplified manner, stylistically similar to classical dreams, captivates the audience and enables the preacher to penetrate their hearts and persuade them to act. To further remove doubts as to the reliability of the message, the text finds recourse in sensitive, indeed sacred, concepts, to which no pious individual can remain indifferent. One such sensitivity is the issue of remuneration in the next world and the fate that awaits the believer on the Judgment Day. Another is the recourse to the eternally guarded tablet and pen. By extending its source beyond the Prophet to eternal authorities (". . . it is transmitted by the Pen of the Almighty from the Guarded Tablet . . ."), the message is elevated to the degree of *ḥadīth qudsī*.[43] Thus, although prophetic words are considered genuine when delivered in dreams, the eternal authorities of the present admonition go beyond and create an overwhelming communication that is likely to touch upon the believer's deepest emotions and fears.

Upon listening to the Prophet, Sheikh Aḥmad swears three times by the name of Allāh that he is relaying the truth and that in case he is lying, he will die as an infidel.[44] He then concludes that the one who sends twenty copies of this admonition will be delivered from Hell Fire, and conversely, those who disregard the letter will be severely punished. The message ends with a list of individuals who sent copies of the letter and prospered, and another list of those who ignored it and consequently encountered misfortune and even death.

This ending is typical of chain letters. However, the text contains elements that are not characteristic of this popular means of communication. In most cases, contemporary chain letters avoid dealing with fundamental religious issues, and do not occupy the minds of respected scholars. This case is different. The amount of online inquiries addressed to sheikhs about how to treat this message,[45] may lead us to believe that in many cases the average recipient of the letter does not dare pass judgment as to the value of this admonition nor take any measures before consulting with a learned sheikh regarding the letter's substance. The sheikhs' answers vary in length and seriousness. Some are popular and bland, some are rude, yet others use Qurʾānic verses and prophetic *ḥadīth* to back up their opinions. Despite the differences, all aim to present the letter as fraudulent.[46]

The following is the oldest and most detailed response ever given in this matter. It contains all of the components of a *fatwā,* and indeed was meant to be one. It was written in the seventies by Sheikh Ibn Bāz.[47] The printed text of the *fatwā* can be found in a collection of four *fawtās* by the name *al-Taḥdhīr min al-bidaʿ*, published by *al-Jāmiʿa al-Islāmiyya of al-Madīna al-Munawwara* in 1398/1978 (17–22). Almost three decades after its first publication, with the recent reappearance of the same admonition, this time in the form of an online chain letter, Ibn Bāz found it necessary to respond again.

The following are fragments of the new online version (from Arabic). The *fatwā* begins with an explanation:

> "Having been informed about this recent letter," says Ibn Bāz, "I hesitated whether to write about it, due to its apparent falsehood and because of the audacity of its fabricator. I could not imagine that such a deceit could fool anyone of minimal insight or sound commonsense. Yet, several brothers informed me that the letter circulated among the people and that some even trusted it. I thus understood that fighting it is the duty of a person of my standing, and decided to write about it to show its senselessness, and in so doing to stop people from being deceived by it."[48]

Having explained his reasons to react, Ibn Bāz presents several arguments to prove the letter's futility. First, he deals with the appearance of the Prophet. According to the report, Sheikh Aḥmad had seen the Prophet before he fell asleep (". . . I was about to go to bed when I saw Muḥammad the Apostle of Allāh . . ."). To this Ibn Bāz reacts as follows:

> The defamer claims to have seen the Prophet while preparing to go to bed and not while actually sleeping . . . After his death, the Prophet has never appeared in a vision to a wakeful person.[49]

Ibn Bāz then chastises the letter's creator for being a Sufi; "Ignorant Sufi," as he says, "guilty of an obscene error."[50]

When dealing with the call to reproduce copies of the letter with the hope to gain happiness and grace in this world and the next, Ibn Bāz reproaches the author for attributing false words to the Prophet and charges him of trying to start a new religion:

> The calumnious inventor of this admonition came in the fourteenth century with a desire to start a new religion. Whoever adopts this new religion will be admitted to Paradise, while he who does not, will reside in the Fire. This fabricator wants to assign this false admonition a

> status higher than the Qur ͗ān by claiming that he who writes and communicates it from place to place will have a palace built for him in Heaven, whereas those who ignore the letter will be deprived of the intercession of the Prophet on the Day of Judgment. Truly, it is the most repulsive lie and the clearest deception.

Other rewards promised to those who produce copies of the letter are wealth, discharge of debts and forgiveness. To this, Ibn Bāz furiously replies:

> This is the most obvious proof that the fabricator of the admonition is a shameless liar and insolent toward Allāh and His worshipers. The three virtues cannot be achieved even by copying the Glorious Qur ͗ān. So, how can they be awarded to someone who copies this deceitful admonition?

Another issue that distresses Ibn Bāz is the pretense to treat unseen matters *(͑ilm al-ghayb)*. He explains that since revelation came to an end with the death of the Prophet, he could not know how many people died and how many entered Hell (". . . From Friday to Friday, 160,000 people died without faith in Islam; none of them went to Heaven . . ."). This information belongs to Allāh alone, declares Ibn Bāz: "Say: None in the Heavens or on earth, except Allāh, knows what is hidden . . ." (Q 27:65).[51] He concludes his *fatwā* with a fervent warning:

> O brothers, be careful and avoid believing such lies, do not let it circulate among you. . . . Do not let yourselves be deceived by the oaths of liars . . . do not be like Adam and Eve. They trusted the Devil, but he turned to be the greatest of all deceivers.[52]

Ibn Bāz clearly expresses his motivation to write this *fatwā*. As we have seen, in his careful examination of the letter, he touches on the most sensitive issues and creates a significant edifying piece for members of the Muslim community to follow. Nevertheless, I wonder: Is it likely that a chain letter could create such a strong reaction? Is it likely that a figure of Ibn Bāz's standing will be occupied with a chain letter due only to some people's decision to take the letter seriously? What made Ibn Bāz so determined and infuriated?

In answer to this question I suggest that Ibn Bāz saw a real danger in this letter, although not because it was delivered as a chain letter. The danger lies in its content. As previously mentioned, the notions introduced in the letter touch on delicate and precarious issues, which are likely to move every pious Muslim. Is it reasonable to assume that a devout individual, raised with a clear conviction of the significance of the Prophet's appearance in dreams, will be able to disregard such a message? I believe that no matter how sophisticated one may deem himself to be, ignoring a text that follows fundamental concepts and touches on the divine remuneration is not an easy task. Ibn Bāz is aware of dreams' influence on Muslims, especially those that deal with the appearance of the Prophet. He also understands that challenging the idea by solely focusing on the Qurʾān and the *ḥadīth* will prove incomplete, particularly because these very sources put a lot of trust in dreams and hold them in the highest regard. Consequently, Ibn Bāz chooses to produce an inculcating *fatwā* that, on the one hand, respects the traditional views and reveres the medium of dreams, but, on the other hand, highlights the message's false elements. While reiterating the ridiculous, deceptive, and misleading nature of the text and elaborating on its manipulative arguments, Ibn Bāz tries to divert the people from their natural inclination to follow the admonition. He then conveys a harsh warning against anyone who might take advantage of the powerful nature and irresistible appeal of dreams in order to lead the community astray.

If success is measured by results, then in the case of Ibn Bāz's *fatwā*, the Web leads us to two opposite conclusions. On the one hand, we witness a heavy usage of this *fatwā*. On several occasions, through a variety of sites, we come across questions addressed to local sheikhs regarding the chain letter. In their answers, the sheikhs generally say a few words of their own and then continue with direct citations from the Ibn Bāz's *fatwā*, using it as the ultimate guideline.[53] On the other hand, there is no sign that the admonition has disappeared. As recently as May 2009, I came across three emails from three different sources with the same dream attached.

Conclusion

The sites that have been consulted are neither selective nor meticulous. Their material hardly attests to local affiliation and their purposes are often obscure. We seldom know who stands behind the blogs and have no way of deciphering the motivation of forums' members. Using these sources as the sole foundation for academic studies, therefore, is problematic. Nevertheless, on the assumption that the Web deals with material "on demand," the large number of Islamic sites that deal with dreams signifies a high level of interest in this medium among Islamic communities in general and among their devoted members in particular. Moreover, the nature of blogs and communal forums frequently exposes us to private feelings toward dreams and thoughts that we cannot always identify otherwise. As a result, they open up new avenues into the research on the contemporary usage of traditional Islamic metaphors and conventions, among which dreams play a significant role.

The impact of dreams on the life of a contemporary individual who is a devout Muslim is not noteworthy on its own, as people in any given community dream. However, the dreams presented in this study possess an additional element that constitutes the very core of our discussion: Whether personal, with individual messages, or more general, with applications to the entire community, each one of the aforementioned dream narrations relates to the actual appearance of the Prophet and demonstrates the notion that his support can benefit the believers in any given time and place. This very idea is embedded in Islamic history since its very beginning and has not faded away in modern times.

While describing his own private experience, the contemporary Muslim who relates his dream finds recourse in the Qurʾān and the *ḥadīth*, and in so doing creates some sort of a neo-classical text. It is difficult to know whether this phenomenon is part of the contemporary intensive usage of classical Islamic material to justify and validate various arguments and views, or rather a reflection of the special hidden sentiment preserved for dreams in general and for the ability to see the Prophet in dreams in particular. In trying to decide, it is imperative to take both suppositions into account and conclude that due to the recent revival of the Islamic legacy and its application to current affairs, dreams, and especially the appearance of the Prophet in dreams, have regained their ever-significant function, which dates back to the very beginnings of Islam.

Notes

1. A widely circulated tradition, delivered in many versions, either as a separate *ḥadīth* or integrated into the text of *khuṭbat al-wadāʿ*. See Ibn Hishām,

al-Sīra al-Nabawiyya (Egypt 1355/1936), 4/251; Mālik b. Anas, *al-Muwaṭṭa*ʾ (Beirut, 1407/1987), 2/752; Abū ʿAbd Allāh al-Ḥākim al-Naysābūrī, *al-Mustadrak ʿalā al-ṣaḥiḥayn* (Beirut, 1968), 1/93; ʿAlī al-Muttaqī al-Hindī, *Kanz al-ʿummāl fī sunan al-aqwāl wa al-afʿāl* (Beirut, 1399/1979), 1/1/954. See also Wensinck and Mensing, *Concordance et indices de la tradition musulmane* (Leiden, Repr. 1988) (=Wensinck), 6/222 (m.s.k), 4/350 (ʿa.ṣ.m), 5/534 (k.t.b).

2. For a list of references see L. Kinberg, "Literal Dreams and Prophetic Ḥadīth in Classical Islam—a comparison of two ways of legitimation," *Der Islam*, Band 70 Heft 2 (1993), 279–300 (= "Literal dreams"), notes 10–12.

3. Ibid., note 26.

4 Leah Kinberg (ed.), *Morality in the Guise of Dreams: Ibn Abī al-Dunyā's K. al-Manām* (Leiden: Brill, 1994), Nos. 89, 307; Ibn Abī al-Dunyā, *Kitāb al-Qubūr*, in Leah Kinberg (ed.), *The Book of Death and the Book of Graves by Ibn Abī al-Dunyā* (Haifa: Al-Karmil Publications Series, 1983), No. 4.

5. See the arguments presented by Ibn al-Ḥājj in his *K. al-Madkhal* (Cairo, 1401/1981), 4/292–93, under the title "Juxtaposing Dreams with the Qurʾān and the Sunna of the Prophet." Cf. *Manām*, introduction 4.4 "*K. al-Manām* and juridical works *(fiqh)*," 36–37. See also the online *fatwā* in http://www.islamonline.net/servlet/Satellite?pagename=IslamOnline-Arabic-Ask_Scholar/FatwaA/FatwaA&cid=1140333531497.

6. See Kinberg, "Literal dreams," note 40.

7. For debates over the supremacy of the Qurʾān over the *ḥadīth*, see L. Kinberg, "Qurʾān and ḥadīth: A struggle for Supremacy as Reflected in Dream Narratives," Louise Marlow (ed.), *Dreaming Across Boundaries: The Interpretation of Dreams in Islamic Lands* (Boston: Ilex Foundation, 2008), 25–49; the struggle between the schools of law in L. Kinberg, "The Legitimation of the Madhāhib through Dreams," *Arabica* XXXII (1985), 47–79; the struggle over the canonization of the Qurʾān readings in L. Kinberg, "The Standardization of Qurʾān Readings: The Testimonial Value of Dreams," *The Arabist*, Budapest Studies in Arabic: 3–4 (1991), 223–38; and the question of the reliability of *ḥadīth* transmitters in L. Kinberg, "Dreams as a Means to Evaluate Hadīth," *Jerusalem Studies in Arabic and Islam* 23 (1999), 79–99.

8. For a detailed list of references see "Literal dreams," note 16. See also the *fatwā* in http://www.islamweb.net/ver2/fatwa/ShowFatwa.php?Option=FatwaId&lang=A&Id=22154, and note 49.

9. See Kinberg, "Literal dreams," notes 16 and 18.

10. Ibid. notes 19–23, and note 15. For a study of this *ḥadīth* see G.H.A. Juynboll, *Muslim Tradition, Studies in Chronology, Provenance and Authorship of Early Hadīth* (Cambridge: Cambridge University Press 1983), 96–133.

11. See, for example (in chronological order): Gary R. Bunt, *Muslims: Rewiring the House of Islam* (Chapel Hill: University of North Carolina Press, 2009); Mohammed el-Nawawy and Sahar Khamis, *Islam Dot Com: Contemporary Islamic Discourses in Cyberspace* (New York: The Palgrave Macmillan, 2009); Bettina Gräf, "IslamOnline.net: Independent, interactive, popular," *Arab Media & Society* 2008, issue 4 (can be accessed in http://www.arabmediasociety.com/?article=576); idem, "Sheykh Yūsuf al-Qaradāwī in Cyberspace," *Die Welt*

des Islams, 2007, 47, 403–421; Gary R. Bunt, "Defining Islamic Interconnectivity" in Miriam Cooke and Bruce B. Lawrence (eds), *Muslim Networks: From Hajj to Hip Hop* (Chapel Hill: University of North Carolina Press, 2005), 235–51; Muhd Rosydi Muhammad and Marjan Muhammad, "Using Information and Communication Technology (ICT) to Disseminate the Understanding of Islamic Jurisprudence (Fiqh) and Juridical Opinion (Fatwā): A View of a Technologist." Paper presented at the Seminar on Understanding Islam through Techno-daie, Kuala Lumpur, 2003 (can be accessed at http://kict.iiu.edu.my/rosydi/article_jea/techno_daei.pdf); Gary R. Bunt, *Virtually Islamic: Computer-mediated Communication and Cyber Islamic Environments* (University of Wales Press, 2000); Dale F. Eickelman and Jon W. Anderson (Eds.), *New Media in the Muslim World: The Emerging Public Sphere* (Indiana: Indiana Series in Middle East Studies, 1999).

12. Bettina Gräf, 2007, note 14; Using ICT, 14.

13. Bettina Gräf, 2008; Using ICT, 13.

14. http://www.3iny3ink.com/forum/t100304.html, Saudi-based (2006).

15. The text adduces the *ḥadīth "Man kadhdhaba ʿalayya mutaʿammidan fa-l-yatabawwaʾ maqʿadahu min al-nār,"* usually aimed at those who lie while transmitting *ḥadīth*. For the *ḥadīth* used to threat those who lie in their dreams, see note 10.

16. http://bafree.net/forums/showthread.php?t=17403, Yemeni-based (2001), defined as "a net for Self-Help and Self-Improvement since 1999."

17. See note 18.

18. Referring to the *ḥadīth* "three are capable of feeling the sweetness of faith . . ." For classical references see Wensinck, 1/210 (a.m.n). On the sweetness of faith in a feminine form (English), see http://www.islamweb.net/womane/nindex.php?page=readart&id=149552.

See also the *fatwā* (Arabic) in http://www.islamic-fatwa.com/fatawa/index.php?module=fatwa&id=763.

19. See, for example, http://www.sunniport.com/masabih/showthread.php?t=4833 and http://www.turntoislam.com/forum/archive/index.php/t-1025.html.

20. Q 3:123–125. The link http://www.omania2.net/avb/archive/index.php/t-396210.html raises a question about the participation of angels in Muslims' wars: *"hal tushāriku al-malāʾika fī ḥurūb al-muslimīn."* Search on Google for *"malāʾika yuqātilūn"* (in Arabic) comes up with approximately 167,000 sites.

21. See notes 27 and 35.

22. http://forum.hawaaworld.com/archive/index.php/t-1550025.html, Saudi-based (2000), taking special interest in women.

23. The same motif is used in the dreams of ʿUthmān b. ʿAffān. As he was besieged by the mutineers, ʿUthmān had two dreams that predicted his imminent death. In one, the Prophet invited him to break his fast in Paradise (*Manām* no. 112), and in the other, the Prophet, together with Abū Bakr and ʿUmar, told ʿUthmān that they were waiting for him [in Paradise] (*Manām* no. 265).

24. http://www.shababna.net/forum/showthread.php?p=332675. Egyptian-based (2005).

25. http://www.arabicdream.com/forums/--t51804.html. American (California)-based (2004).

26. A famous preacher *(khaṭīb)* of Kuwait. See his teachings on http://www.ashefaa.com/files/sharit/kataan.html. Lebanese-based (2004).

27. In the battle of Badr, the angels had white (or yellow) turbans; Gabriel had a yellow turban (Ibn Kathīr, *al-Bidāya wa-'l-Nihāya* (Beirut 1398/1978), 3/281), and so did Zubayr b. ʿAwwām (Ibn Saʿd, *al-Ṭabaqāt al-Kubrā* (Beirut 1405/1985), 3/103). When the Prophet entered Mecca, he had a black turban on (Ibid., 4/292–93). See also Wensinck, 4/348 (ʿa.m.m.), and note 35.

28. http://www.al-yemen.org/vb/archive/index.php/t-330873.html. Egyptian-based (2005).

29. http://safeena.org/vb/showthread.php?t=100208087. Swiss-based (2001).

30. http://www.ikhwan.net/vb/showthread.php?t=75465. Saudi-based (2001).

31. The expression used is "*shāhir*[an] *sayfahu*," namely "standing with his unsheathed sword." The term is widely used in classical sources to describe warriors taking part in battles in general and in the *ḥurūb al-ridda* in particular (*al-Bidāya wa 'l-Nihāya*, 5/249). The term often occurs to describe the angel who protects al-Madīna or Bayt al-Maqdis from the *Dajjāl* (the deceiver, Antichrist) with an unsheathed sword. See Ibn Abī al-Shayba, *Muṣannaf* (Riyāḍ, 1409/1988), 6/405; Yāqūt al-Ḥamawī, *Muʿjam al-Buldān* (Beirut: Published, 1376/1957), 5/167, respectively. Also, the *shuhadā*ʾ will come back to life with unsheathed swords: ʿAbd Allāh Ibn al-Mubārak, *al-Jihād* (Tunis 1391/1972)). Regardless of the differences in meaning, whether in classical sources or contemporary texts, the term indicates endless determination to act against the enemy.

32. https://www.d1g.com/forum/show/2565941.

33. http://www.almsloob.com/vb/showthread.php?t=22060. Yemeni-based. In using this Qurʾānic term (Q 4:97, 8:26) the narrator associates the fate of the people of Gaza with that of the oppressed that Allāh will not neglect and places the dream among good tidings that assure alleviation of hardship.

34. During the October war (1973), people reported dreams about the appearance of the Prophet smiling among the troops. See Glenn E. Perry, *The History of Egypt* (Connecticut: Greenwood Press, 2004), 121. At least one dream was ascribed to Sheikh al-Azhar of that time, Dr. ʿAbd al-Ḥalīm Maḥmūd, who—reportedly—saw the Prophet crossing the canal with the warriors (http://www.eltsawofelislamy.com/Archive/357/article4-3.html). Egyptian-based (2005).

35. The Prophet is seen in a dream, and his turban (see note 27) surrounds the area of Fallujah. The scene is interpreted to indicate prophetic care and victory (http://www.ahewar.org/debat/show.art.asp?aid=29094).

36. Sheikh Manṣūr Ushurma fulfilled the orders of the Prophet who appeared in his dream in waging *jihād* against the Russians. See Elizabeth

Sirriyeh, *Sufis and anti-Sufis: The Defense, Rethinking and Rejection of Sufism in the Modern World* (Richmond, Surrey: Curzon Press, 1999), 38.

37. Throughout an American attack in Afghanistan, the Prophet and the four righteous Caliphs reportedly appeared in a dream. The Prophet appointed each one of the Caliphs to lead a battle in a specific area, and took upon himself the northern part, which turned to be the harshest battlefield: http://www.alajman.ws/vb/showthread.php?t=13174.

For more Afghani dreams see http://hafsallah.multiply.com/notes/item/81, and the long dream about the Prophet helping the Taliban, translated into English by the site of the revolutionary association of the women of Afghanistan http://www.rawa.org/dream.htm.

38. Abū 'l-ʿAbbās Shams al-Dīn Ibn Khalikān, *Wafāyāt al-aʿyān wa-anbāʾ abnāʾ al-zamān* (Beirut 1387/1968), 5/320; cf. a longer version in Ibn al-Athīr, *al-Kāmil fī 'l-taʾrīkh* (Beirut 1385/1965), 4/562.

39. Abū 'l-Falāḥ al-Ḥanbalī, *Shadharāt al-Dhahab fī akhbār man dhahab* (Beirut 1399/1979), 5/293. See also P. M. Holt, "The Position and Power of the Mamlūk Sultan," *Bulletin of the School of Oriental and African Studies*, Vol. 38, No. 2 (1975), 245–46; Annemarie Schimmel, *Die Träume des Kalifen* (München: C.H. Beck 1998), 232.

40. Search on Google for "*ḥāmil mafātīḥ ḥaram*" (in Arabic) comes up with approximately 30,000 sites that present the dream. The text comes in variations with regard to the number of people who died and the number of copies of the letter that must be circulated.

41. ʿAbd al-ʿAzīz b. ʿAbd Allāh b. ʿAbd al-Raḥmān b. Muḥammad b. ʿAbd Allāh Ibn Bāz, born in Riyāḍ in 1330/1909 and died there in 1420/1999. He served in a variety of central judicial institutes in Saudi Arabia, and his *fatwās* were followed by millions. From the early 1960s, he was the head of the Council of Senior Islamic Scholars, served as the head of the Committee for "Commanding Right and Forbidding Wrong," and during the years 1993–1999 reached the highest rank in Saudi Arabia as the grand *muftī*. See his official site on http://www.binbaz.org.sa/.

42. http://www.islamhouse.com/p/6034. One of the official, multi-language Islamic sites, created by the Islamic propagation office in Rabwah, Saudi Arabia (2000), which considers itself to be "a perfect site for teaching the correct Islam."

43. See J. Robson, "*Ḥadīth Ḳudsī*," *EI*[2] 3/28–29. The authorities of the pen and the guarded tablet are used in crucial matters: the formula of the *istiʿādha* (seeking refuge in Allāh from the Devil: "*aʿūdhu bi-Allāh min al-shayṭān al-rajīm*") was established on the authority of the Prophet, who had learned it from Gabriel who transmitted it from the pen that transmitted it from the guarded tablet. Cf. al-Bayḍāwī, *Tafsīr* (Cairo: 1305/1887), 366; Abū 'l-Qāsim al-Zamakhsharī, *al-Kashshāf ʿan ḥaqāʾiq al-tanzīl* (Cairo: 1392/1972), 2/428; al-Fayḍ al-Kāshānī, *Tafsīr al-Ṣāfī* (Beirut: 1402/1982), 3/155; Abū 'l-Faḍl al-Alusī, *Rūḥ al-Maʿānī fī Tafsīr al-Qurʾān* (Beirut: 1408/1987), 7/228, each in his commentary on Q 16:98. Abū ʿAbd Allāh al-Qurṭubī, *al-Jāmiʿ li-aḥkām al-Qurʾān* (Beirut: 1407/1987), 1/87 quotes the same *ḥadīth* but mentions the guarded

tablet *before* the pen. The sequence "guarded tablet—pen" appears also in a report, according to which the Prophet received the revelation from Gabriel, on the authority of Mīkāʾīl, on the authority of Isrāfīl, on the authority of the guarded tablet on the authority of the pen (Muḥammad ʿAbd al-Raʾūf al-Munāwī, *al-Tawfīq ʿalā muhimmat al-taʿārīf* [Beirut: 1989/1410], 1:589). The Shīʿī *ḥadīth* that defines ʿAlī's *wilāya* as the divine protection against Hell Fire (*"wilāyat ʿAlī ḥiṣnī man dakhalahu amana nārī"*) is based on a "golden *isnād*" that runs as follows: ʿAlī b. Mūsā al-Riḍā on the authority of his ancestors—ʿAlī—Rasūl Allāh—Gabriel—Mīkāʾīl—Isrāfīl—guarded tablet—pen—Allāh. See: Muḥammad Bāqir al-Majlisī, *Biḥār al-anwār* (Beirut 1403/1983), 39:237; cf. ibid., 236.

44. About lying in dreams, see the first section of this chapter.

45. Limiting the results given in note 40 by adding the word *suʾāl* (in Arabic), comes up with more than 20,000 sites. See for example, http://www.islamweb.net/ver2/Fatwa/ShowFatwa.php?Option=FatwaId&lang=A&Id=2026.

46. See, for example, the reaction of *Muftī* Ebrahim Desai (English) on http://askimam.org/fatwa/fatwa.php?askid=ae11a619f71f2d3a80900b31628cd75e, and al-Qaraḍāwī's words (Arabic) on http://www.qaradawi.net/site/topics/article.asp?cu_no=2&item_no=6158&version=1&template_id=232&parent_id=17. See also the only case where graphics are attached to the aversive feelings toward the letter, http://sista2sista.wordpress.com/2008/08/23/do-not-send-hoax-chain-letters-about-islam/ (English).

47. See Ibn Bāz's biography in note 41.

48. http://www.islamhouse.com/p/6034. For the nature of the site see note 42.

49. Cf. http://www.binbaz.org.sa/mat/17216, where Ibn Bāz elaborates on the subject in his *fatwā* about the *ḥadīth "man raʾānī fī al-manām fa-qad raʾānī fī al-yaqẓa"* (cf. note 8).

50. Cf. http://www.binbaz.org.sa/mat/10236, where Ibn Bāz blames the Sufis for introducing innovations to Islam. In http://www.binbaz.org.sa/mat/10026, Ibn Bāz elaborates on the ceremony held for the Prophet's birthday (*mawlid al-nabīyy*) and defines it as innovation (*bidʿa*); in http://www.kuwaitchat.net/msgs/archive/index.php/t-61624.html he blames those who celebrate the *mawlid* for being infidels.

51. Cf. Ibn Bāz's *fatwā* on the subject http://www.binbaz.org.sa/mat/4201.

52. Refers to Q 7:21–22.

53. Of the 30,000 occurrences (see note 40), about 20,000 sites attach the *fatwā* of Ibn Bāz immediately after the dream. See, for example, http://www.3iny3ink.com/forum/t240540.html http://www.zainq8.net/vb/archive/index.php/t-2834.html http://www.islamtoday.net/questions/show_question_content.cfm?id=119017 Saudi-based (2000).

CHAPTER 8

Transforming Contexts of Dream Interpretation in Dubai

Muhammad alZekri

In this chapter, I examine the shifting contexts of dream interpretation in Dubai over three generations, beginning with the generation that witnessed the pearling economies in the Arabian Gulf. I then compare it to the two generations that have followed, which have been highly impacted by changes brought about by the discovery of oil and the emergence of a contemporary multimedia society. My study has been motivated by the absence of any examination of the shifting social power relations constituted through dream interpretation in East Arabia and neighboring Islamic societies. This study examines aspects of dream-lore in power relations and gender empowerment, the emergence of new social and economic structures, and gradual shifts from unmediated to mediated forms of dream-lore as well as oral forms toward textual contexts of dream interpretation and communication. In my comparison of these three generations, I point to the rising tensions between folk and formal beliefs and the mainstreaming of a formalized and standardized male-dominated interpretation. These tensions are relevant markers enabling us to better evaluate the social and cultural consequences resulting from these transgenerational and gender shifts in the framework of dream interpretation.

Background research in Dubai for the benefit of this chapter was conducted in two phases. During the first phase in 1996–1997, I focused on the latest pearling generation and the social relations and interpretations established in the wider context of female folk beliefs. Later, based on research visits in 2008–2009, I gathered new information on the two latter generations under consideration here, but I also have provided some additional information on the first generation. My qualitative research was conducted primarily via face-to-face open interviews that were recorded and later transcribed. Through content analysis interpreted in the framework of local social and cultural codes, I present here a discussion of my conclusions.

Generation A: Empowerment of Women during the Pearling Era

Definition and Contextualization of Generation A

Generation A (further referred to as GA) is characterized by a largely shared understanding of and adherence to traditional Islam, community values, and norms and belief systems that also included a significant amount of dream-lore. Such dream-lore created spiritual and emotional bonds among community members and paid tribute to the shared economic experience of the close-knit community of Dubai. My primary sources of information on the dream-lore of GA are female respondents raised during the time when the pearling industry of Dubai was undermined by the introduction of Japanese cultured pearls in the 1930s.[1] It was a period of transition in which the economic reality had to be adjusted through a gradual shift to new industries or through relocation in order to participate in the early oil exploitations of the neighboring Gulf states.[2]

The shared value base of the community was affirmed by a number of factors such as the *farīj* system,[3] as well as the strong social bond of *Banī Yās*[4], the main Arabian families that characterized historic Dubai. Strong ties and community values were maintained by disallowing marriages outside family alliances, by geographical proximity resulting from settling within the same *farīj*, and by social discourses nurtured by the reaffirmation of shared religious and cultural values. In this chapter, I examine in particular the social discourses that resulted from dream interpretation and dream-lore.

Legitimacy and Context of Dream Majālis in Generation A

The *majālis* (gatherings) for dream interpretation in GA are not only gender-dominated, but also gender-restricted, an exclusively female domain. Male dreamers who wished their dreams to be interpreted had to first disclose the narrative of the dream to a female family member who would then visit the dream interpreter on their behalf. Due to this gender restriction, interpretations have to be examined in light of female education systems and provisions for religious instruction to girls at the time.

Female members of GA were educated by a *muṭawwa*ᶜ (male teacher) or a *muṭawwa*ᶜ*a* (female teacher) who were, in addition to the *Shuyūkh* (plural of *Shaykh*, religious authority), the source of traditional religious and moral knowledge in Dubai society. The *muṭāwi*ᶜ*a* (plural, teachers) provided unmediated knowledge that was presented orally in classroom settings that were either gender-mixed (girls ages six to nine were allowed to attend the mixed-learning classes) or gender-separated. All the women I interviewed attended these classes, which imparted the basic skills of writing and reading, especially of the Qur᾽ān, but many women like Umm Manṣūr, a sixty-nine-year-old Arabian grandmother from al-Ḥamriyya-Dubai, later lost her ability to read and write due to lack of practice: "I was taught to read basic Arabic words but because I could not practice, I have now become unable to do so."[5]

Due to the lack of relevant language books, even reading and writing instructions were oral,[6] as was the transmission of knowledge of society through religious traditions, narration, ceremonies, and poetry. Researchers on orality in Arab traditional cultures confirm that even "up to the present, orality has continued to be a well-known method of preserving Arab culture and transmitting it to succeeding generations."[7] The only book mentioned during my interviews was the Holy Qur᾽ān[8] and it can be assumed that the women of GA were not familiar with any other written resources that could be applied to the interpretation of dreams.

By relying on oral modes of transmission, the boundaries separating the knowledge base of traditional Islam and popular folkloric practices of the local population were blurred. For example, over time, the representatives (*Shuyūkh* and *muṭāwi*ᶜ*a*) of traditional Islam were compelled to accept folk healing methods and rituals unrelated to "scriptural" Islam. The result was an intertwining of folk practices and traditional Islamic beliefs whereby the *muṭāwi*ᶜ*a* were themselves applying folk healing rituals to cure various ailments. Umm Muḥammad, now a seventy-nine-year-old Arabian grandmother from Deira-Dubai, described a practice—which had no Islamic roots or references—in which the *muṭawwa*ᶜ, accompanied by a few children, performed a *ṣalāt al-mayyit* (a funeral prayer) to cure another person from the power of the "evil eye." In the absence of modern medicine, folk practices and cures provided meaning, when none seemed to exist, such as why good people get sick, why things go wrong, why a young person would die, and so forth. In the absence of scientific explanations, folk beliefs not only render meaning to the hardships of life, but also become the basis for a shared "logical" way of thinking for everyone in the community, by "explaining the unexplainable."[9] These examples show that female members of GA grew up in an unmediated environment of oral education in which traditional religion was enriched by folkloric norms and knowledge. More importantly, this usage of folk tradition by religious authorities served to legitimize the role and importance of female dream interpretation.

Dream interpretation was a female domain with several levels of sophistication. Each small family unit usually had its "dedicated" dream interpreter, usually a grandmother who was considered most trustworthy and spiritually guided.[10] Within a neighborhood or larger family unit, the designated interpreter was the woman judged to be the most competent, with the most sophisticated interpreters often known far beyond their own *farīj*. They qualified because of their "eloquence, wisdom, social respect, a commanding personality, devoutness, the possession of a repertory of colloquial proverbs and a large inventory of folk dream lore [as well as] a widespread reputation and recognition in the community."[11] These women in particular are consulted in what I refer to as dream *majālis*.

The institution of the dream *majālis* was accepted by both males and females, who put trust in its advisory value and thus legitimized it. Young boys no older than age nine usually accompanied their mothers to dream-interpretation sessions. By doing so, they experienced the social legitimization of this tradition and, later, remembered that their fathers had permitted their mothers to participate. With the establishment of this social habit and traditional right, they were less likely to disapprove of participation by their wives,[12] even if the *majlis* was located outside the *farīj*, which women hardly ever left for other reasons. The superiority of women in the field of dream interpretation continues to remain unquestioned.

Dream *majālis* were a common practice in Dubai, and each dream interpreter had a regular clientele. Monetary compensation was received only in rare cases, but all interpreters would accept expressions of appreciation, such as gifts and food items. These dream *majālis* can be interpreted as social institutions that contributed to the preservation and reaffirmation of traditional community values on at least three different levels. First, they confirmed the worldview of the local community by supporting its practices and values through dream interpretation. Second, the dissemination of dream-related lore among women and men was essential for maintenaning authority of the dream interpreter and strengthening female superiority in this respect. Third, the presence of children in the *majālis* secured the intergenerational transmission of dream-lore and its continuity in future generations.

The Practice of Dream Interpretation in Generation A

Dream interpretation *majālis* were usually arranged by prior consultation as to the most appropriate visiting time. Rather than specifically asking for a dream interpretation, the client would arrange an appointment to meet for coffee or a social gathering. This was a suitable introduction to the important social activities surrounding the rather short interpretation session itself. Many of my respondents described the successive etiquette of conduct in the *majālis*. For instance, Umm Muḥammad relates the following:

> I was nine years old [in the year 1939] when I accompanied my elder sister to visit a dream interpreter. It was about 9 a.m. My sister knocked on her door, and we were welcomed to enter. We walked straight into the *majlis* [name of gathering but also room where the gathering takes place]. After the welcoming pleasantries, we sat down on mats and rested our backs against the wall cushions. We exchanged greetings with the other visiting ladies who had already gathered in the *majlis*. In the center of the room were a coffee pot and dates. We were served coffee and ate a few dates. After this the dream interpreter approached us and said "May Allāh welcome you!" My sister expressed her thanks. She told the lady that she had had a dream a few nights earlier and asked her to explain its meaning to her. Everyone was listening to my sister's words as she was recounting her dream. After my sister had completed her narration, the dream interpreter, who had carefully and silently listened, commenced her interpretation with the standard salutation: "That is good. The result shall also be good and shall overcome everything bad with Allāh's Blessing on His messenger Muḥammad, Peace Be upon Him." Then she gave meaning to my sister's dream. I remember that my sister was happy and joyful for the rest of the *majlis* which the women spent chatting.[13]

However, not all dream accounts and interpretations would be given in public, because respect of the dreamer's right to confidentiality and privacy was an essential moral principle of conduct at that time. In particular, dreams that could be considered dishonorable or contained socially unacceptable acts would be disclosed in a private *majlis* attended by the dreamer and interpreter. On this ethical point, Umm Muḥammad reports about the same *majlis*:

> I remember on that day when I was with my sister, another lady with a young boy wanted to have her dream interpreted. But she did not want anyone to know the content of her dream. After the dream interpreter completed her explanation of my sister's dream, she turned to this lady and said "May Allāh welcome you!" She replied equally "May Allāh welcome you!" Then she paused for a short moment and said "*Wallāh*" and paused again. The dream interpreter responded by asking her to follow her to the adjacent room. There I assume she received her interpretation. After a short time they both returned to the *majlis*.[14]

Dream interpretation in GA was an occupation that ensured esteem and a respected social status in the community. The interpreter was respected for her wisdom and for her empathy in rendering dream explanation. Her ability to decipher Allāh's messages contained in dreams underlined her spiritual maturity, her connectedness, and her ability to generate a positive meaning for enigmatic and disturbing dreams, which made her popular as a source of good news. Moreover, the standing of the dream interpreter went beyond enjoying honor and respect; she also had strong influence on moral and ethical discourses in the community and could influence behaviors as well as religious interpretations and rulings.

Dream Lore in Generation A: Source of Freedom and Empowerment

Dream interpretations were always given in a particular context and to a specific person by allowing the interpreter to tailor an explanation to the personal needs and expectations of the dreamer. To ensure the relevance of the information, dreams could only be decoded if the interpreter was familiar with the dreamer's life and family history. This requirement appears in the earliest Islamic treatises on dream interpretation. For example, Ibn Sīrīn (d. 728 AD) required a dream interpreter be aware of the genealogy, habits, and customs of the dreamer both at individual and community levels, in addition to knowing the local proverbs and idioms used by the community.[15]

Knowledge of the dreamer's personal context enabled the interpreter to offer practical advice relevant to the individual situation of the dreamer, including male dreamers whose dreams were narrated to her, or male family members who were actors in the dreams or could be understood to have been impacted by the dream. Because of the exclusiveness of female mediation and interpretation, the discourse of giving meaning to dreams indirectly became the female version of *fiqh* (Islamic jurisprudence). Dream interpretation always started with small talk and socialization that usually disclosed further information relevant to the current situation of the dreamer. Umm Manṣūr explains:

> When women visit me for dream interpretation, we speak about many social issues, the well-being of the children and mothers, diseases of family members, and other family affairs. Of course I am concerned if I hear that a woman is not fairly treated by her husband, of which I disapprove. I am trying to understand the context, and give advice to both the woman and her husband if they did wrong.[16]

Based on such conversations, the dream interpreter determined the kind of advice her client needed. Umm Manṣūr shared with me one such example: "Dreams about dead relatives were in general considered to mean that the departed was in need of *ṣadaqa* (charity or alms donation) from the dreamer to benefit the relative in his/her afterlife." But the dream interpreter might alter the meaning of symbols in a dream to take into account the additional knowledge she had of the dreamer, as shown by the following incident:

> A woman came to me to seek the interpretation of a dream that her husband had. I knew for quite some time that he had not been treating her well and that he used to shout at and sometimes beat her. In his dream he visited his dead father. When his father saw him, he kept staring at him with a frozen and serious look. The husband got worried and wanted to know the reason for this frightening look of his father. He asked his wife to come and see me. I told her to tell her husband that his father disapproved of the way he treated her, that his serious look disapproved of his son's anger, and that his frozen stare condemned his

> son's physical violence toward his wife. I added that it was a warning from his father for him to become a loving and understanding husband. I then suggested that he give charity for the purpose of benefiting his dead father and in appreciation for his advice.[17]

With a dream-lore dominated by women, a female power base was established that helped to counter the traditional power base dominated by the male *shaykh* and *muṭawwa*ᶜ. Through the interpretation of dreams, the interpreter was able to uphold women's rights and facilitate the fair treatment of women in her community. With the female power base established through dream interpretation, dream-lore became a tool used to "reprogram" those value systems of traditional communities that restricted or subjugated women in various ways; moreover, dream interpretation constituted a subtle counter-hegemony in a male-dominated society. Dream *majālis* provided empowerment and freedom to the women of GA and were therefore cherished social institutions. Dream *majālis* gave women an opportunity to move around freely without male objection and participate in social gatherings, and to maintain social relationships and female authority in a knowledge domain that rendered an important service to society. In addition, it empowered the interpreters—who also were the mediators of male dreams—to introduce, in their role as interpreters of Allāh's messages in dreams, a female perspective on moral and ethical questions related to male rule and conduct. The discourses of male *shaykh*, *muṭawwa*ᶜ, and tribal leaders that were communicated through speeches in mosques and public gatherings were counterbalanced by a female, semipublic sphere created via folk belief-based interpretation of supernatural messages. The balance between the male hegemony of religious interpretation and the female counter-hegemony of interpretation of dreams that was peculiar to GA resulted in an often unacknowledged holistic social construction with important contributions from both genders.

Generation B: Secondary Orality in an Industrialized Society

Definition and Contextualization of Generation B

Generation B (GB) did not personally experience the pearling era but is still familiar with its customs, its moral and ethical codes and understandings, and its stereotypes and proverbs through childhood participation in GA gatherings. The members of GB experienced the oil discovery in Dubai (1966) in their late childhood and the independence of the United Arab Emirates (UAE) from British colonial rule (1971) in their adolescence.[18] GB is a generation strongly characterized by transition in many aspects of life, resulting from the development of an industrialized society, as well as changes in community belief systems that moved from folk-belief to more formalized versions of Islam, and from a predominantly oral society to one based on textual resources. An important aspect of this transition was the introduction of a government school-based education system.[19] The new government school provided formalized and partly secularized education and introduced widespread literacy through the use of language textbooks and exercises. Parallel to the new government school system was the emergence of new discourses in cross-generational religious education in mosques and male gatherings, in which a new generation of religious scholars, often from Saudi Arabia, introduced the concept of *qāl Allāh qāl Rasūluh*. This concept can be described as referenced teachings[20] supported by the Sunna of the prophet Muḥammad and the Qurʾān. This was contrary to the traditional knowledge system that normally did not refer to written sources for religions positions. Over time, the "referenced teaching style" gained the reputation of being the means to convey true knowledge as it was supported by the most authoritative religious sources. It became even more predominant after the introduction of a new "secondary orality"[21] (late 1970s to mid-1990s) in the form of religious lectures and speeches by the Saudi scholars that were recorded on audiocassettes that were widely distributed and could be found in almost every household.

The new writing and reading[22] ability of GB was in this context a means of empowerment as it also allowed its female members, at least on a theoretical level, to support their opinions through religious referenced texts. Not surprisingly, it was not books that became the medium of self-education but rather the broadly disseminated audiocassettes that could be consulted by both male and female members of both generations. Religious interpretations and rulings could now be given by both genders, who could refer not only to the primary Islamic resources but also to the content of audiocassettes. This development allowed women to gain access to male religious discourses that would have previously reached them only in mediated form.

In this new context, the knowledge body of GA was undermined for it was declared to be "popular" and thus deviating from the mainstream teachings of "formal" Islam. The newly introduced concept of *qāl Allāh qāl Rasūluh* (referenced teachings) also paved the way for those who were most competent in religious referenced teaching techniques to assume the role of dream interpreters. This led to a reduced role of traditional dream interpreters of GA who, due to their lack of knowledge of scriptural Islam, could not compete with referenced teachings, because their dream-lore was based on orally transmitted folklore.

Overlapping Discourses of Dream Interpretation in Generation B

Over time, given increasing doubts over the legitimacy of the folk beliefs that were the basis of dream interpretation, GB had to gradually adjust to alternative methods of interpretation that were in the process of being established. This need was soon addressed when the so-called Islamic Guidance Centers (IGC) opened in the UAE in the late 1970s. These institutions for consultancy on religious issues were introduced and operated by Saudi *ʿulamāʾ* (scholars of religion). Not only did they propagate formal Saudi *Salafī* Islam,[23] but also they aimed to eventually abolish what they perceived to be "non-Islamic" local traditions based on folk beliefs.

The expanding influence of the IGCs was helped by access to telephones that was spreading rapidly in the region. Not only was the telephone now becoming available at home, but also there emerged phone-based religious guidance "call centers." Through distance communication with religious authorities, even women were able to seek advice directly from the scholar. Given what must have been high demand, the scholars in the call centers soon developed some basic expertise in dream interpretation and included this service in their services.

The dream interpretation offered by the IGC phone services lacked all the traditional social aspects of the dream *majālis* and became faceless and impersonal. The requirements outlined by Ibn Sīrīn that the interpreter be familiar with the dreamer's life and family context were abandoned and replaced by the more general interpretations mediated by the Sunna and the Qurʾān. This element of impersonality often led to dissatisfaction with the unfamiliar style of dream interpretation now on offer. It encouraged women to return to the *majālis* of GA. Fifty-year-old Umm Ibrāhīm, a member of GB from Umm Ḥrīr-Dubai, describes her experience:

> In my dream, I was laying on my bed. I was alone in my bedroom without my husband, and in the far left corner of

> the room I saw a spider with her spider babies. I simply tried to forget it but after two days later I could not get the dream out of my mind. I decided to call the IGC. I asked for *Shaykh* Abū ʿAbd al-Raḥmān and related to him my dream. He assured me that a spider is a good insect because it had covered the cave of the Prophet when he had to hide from his enemies. He said I should not worry, make *ṣadaqa* [charity] and pray two *rakaʿa* [prayer units] to Allāh. One day later, I called Umm Saʿīd [a dream interpreter from GA] whom I know well and who has good reputation for dream interpretations. She told me that it was a good dream because it was an early warning that things were about to go wrong. She told me to take better care of my husband and to ensure that I should not be stubborn, and I should resolve disagreements peacefully. She told me that the spider could stand for me being left alone in a corner with my children but that with the love of my husband that would not happen. Umm Saʿīd knew that I was having arguments with my husband at that time, and I felt that her advice was very relevant to my situation. I followed her advice and, *alḥamdulillāh* [all praise be to Allāh], my relationship with my husband is now much more peaceful.[24]

Despite the campaign by the *Shuyūkh* (religious scholars, now from Saudi Arabia) who introduced the concept of *qāl Allāh qāl Rasūluh* (referenced teachings) to undermine traditional dream interpretation, the GA interpreters could still produce explanations that were accepted by those from GB who consulted them. The inability of GA to compete on the basis of referenced teachings because of their reliance on folkloric knowledge did not seem to negatively impact GB. Rather, what mattered to GB was the ability for GA dream interpreters to relate the interpretation of dreams to the personal circumstances of dreamers.

Dreams in Generation B: Toward Impersonal and Formalized Interpretations

The phone services established by such institutions as the IGCs intruded into the folk belief-based female domain of dream interpretation and imposed a new type of interpretation based on the texts of the scriptures. In the former balance of male hegemony and female counter-hegemony, this new method of asserting authority basically discredited both gender discourses by establishing a new formal superstructure. Although equally accessible to women and men, this superstructure is exclusively male-generated, as the experts of the IGC had a formal religious education that was not accessible to women. Although young women of GB may have experienced a temporary strengthening of their social status thanks to their participation in the new discourses (due to their reading and referencing ability and the legitimatization of their positions through direct communication with renowned scholars), the new male dominance gradually dislodged female contributions to moral and ethical discourses that had emerged from the dream *majālis* of GA.

The traditional *majālis* continued for a while, but began to change their character for a number of reasons. First, the *Shuyūkh* succeeded in planting the seeds of doubt among GB about the legitimacy of dream interpretation of GA, for it was heavily impregnated with folkloric elements rather than religious references. Moreover, the women of GB who had consulted traditional dream interpreters were now also proffering alternative references to themes and contexts they had learned through instructions via audiocassettes or the phone. Second, the standing of the *majālis* was further reduced because men no longer had to rely on their female family members to communicate with the interpreter; instead, they could simply telephone the call center. Third, the women of GB no longer had to attend the *majālis* of GA as they could now use the telephone, and did so increasingly over time as the population shifted to the outskirts of the historic centers and markets of Dubai city. Fourth, the interpretation of dreams became highly impersonal as there was no longer the direct, physical meetings and gatherings of women in the home of the dream interpreter. Last, the *majālis* were further weakened by the perception that basing dream interpretations in GB on the Sunna and Qurʾān was superior to the emotional and subjective discourses of the female folk tales of GA.

Generation C: Male Dominance in Formalized Multimedia Discourses

Definition and Contextualization of Generation C

Generation C (GC) refers to the generation of people currently in their thirties. They were raised in a transformed, Westernized Dubai, where fashion, lifestyle, consumption, and convenience have replaced much of the traditional, moral, and ethical ties that characterized the local community in the past. Members of GC often reside in increasingly anonymous high-rise complexes and new artificial cities and spend their leisure time in shopping malls, health clubs, and cinemas. Their identities are frequently characterized by sociocultural discontinuity and a sense of cultural estrangement. After they have become a small minority in their own city and country, now so dominated by expatriates, and with the former GA residence neighborhoods turned into business and entertainment cores of the new multimedia society, they experience a subtle, often nonvocalized sense of dislocation. This does not mean that they have lost Islamic values and are no longer religious, but with the disappearance of a close-knit community environment and strong family alliance bonds, piety and its outward demonstration are progressively more of an individual choice.

The GC was educated either in fully secularized government schools or private schools providing foreign curricula education (mostly U.S. and U.K. schooling systems). With a strong emphasis on literacy and textual acquisitions of knowledge, these education systems have enabled GC to seek information in books and in the now most popular resource, the Internet. The new multimedia opportunities—a third phase of orality—such as web forums, satellite television, mp3 files, and podcasts also have influenced the process of dream interpretation, which now is a completely public and, at least at first glance, strictly male domain.

Dream Interpretation on Television and the Internet

Dream interpretation in GC like in GB is practiced on multiple levels. Although the resources of dream interpretation of the earlier generations (the dream *majālis* of GA and the call centers of GB) are still available, they are no longer popular among GC, which has fully embraced new and alternative practices. The dream *majālis* are the distant remains of an old-fashioned generation and are largely incomprehensible to members of GC who no longer understand the discourses, proverbs, idioms, and folk belief-based values used in traditional dream interpretation. Additionally, IGC centers had to close down after 9/11 for fear they would promote radical tendencies, but phone interpretation services are still being used through the *Awqāf* (religious endowment) authority of Dubai. Its reputation among GC, however, seems limited, as a twenty-nine-year-old mother from Bar Dubai-Dubai, Fāṭima, daughter of Umm Ibrāhīm and a member of GB, explains:

> There is no point in calling them. Once I had a dream, and mummy asked me to call; but it takes ages for them to answer and then they constantly made me feel as if I had interrupted them from something, and that they were doing me a big favor to interpret my dream. . . . Mummy sometimes still calls her *Shaykh* from the former IGC line on his private number.[25]

The three most popular sources of dream interpretation of GC in Dubai are (a) self-initiated interpretation based on a variety of dream-interpretation books in Arabic; (b) the *Ruʾyā,* a dream interpretation show on Nūr Dubai TV; and (c) web forums on dream interpretation that are either linked to the *Ruʾyā* show or separately explore and exchange ideas on the meaning of dreams. I have so far been unable to characterize which age or gender groups favor which of the aforementioned media as the experience of my interviews showed very diverse references to all three sources. Further research will shed more light on this subject.

ʿAlī and Saʿīd, Arab brothers from Dubai in their early twenties whom I interviewed at Burjumān Mall in Dubai, explained that, usually it is not a question of preferring one source over the other, but rather one of sequence in light of the dream's complexity. The first option for them is to relate their dreams to their sister, who has a collection of dream-interpretation books and who consults these to investigate the potential meanings of a dream. "Only if the books do not help, and she is very uncertain with regard to the interpretation, she may approach others for clarification."[26]

Another source is the *Ruʾyā* show produced by Nūr Dubai TV and broadcast on Fridays and Saturdays from 9:30 to 11:00 p.m. (Dubai local time). Every weekend, a large number of people watch as Wasīm Yūsuf, a young Jordanian *Salafī Shaykh,* with a Qurʾānic Studies degree from a Jordanian university, interprets dreams that are related to him by the callers. In my interview with *Shaykh* Wasīm Yūsuf, he explained his objective as follows:

> It is important, my brother, to understand that dream interpretation that follows Sharīʿa is lacking nowadays. I am trying to reintroduce the medieval Islamic tradition of dream interpretation based on *qāl Allāh qāl Rasūluh* from the Qurʾān and the Sunna. Dream interpretation is a religious subject as any other that introduced important legal practices in the past. You know that the introduction of

> the Islamic *adhān* (call for prayer) was based on a dream confirmed by the prophet Muḥammad (May God's prayer be upon Him). At present, there are a lot of commercial and folkloric dream interpretations that throw people into an ocean far from religion. Re-establishing *sharīᶜa*-based dream interpretation is important because the dreamer receives Islamic instruction for future guidance based on his nightly vision.[27]

Additionally empowered by a religious edict *(fatwā)* from a former, foremost student of *Shaykh* Muḥammad Nāṣir al-dīn al-Albānī (d. 1999) and a second *fatwā* from another foremost student of the late *Shaykh* Ibn Bāz (d. 1999) (these *Shuyūkh* are highly regarded authorities among contemporary *Salafīs*), this young Jordanian TV presenter and his dream interpretation show have been widely accepted by the GC generation because they comply closely with current Islamic teachings.

Of more than 2,000 calls to each show, approximately 45 callers receive a dream interpretation. The following interpretation given to a female caller during a show in February 2009 is a typical example of Islamic guidance:

> "I dreamt that I was standing on a dam at the seashore. It was a stormy day with high and rough waves. I observed the waves but they did not reach me. Inside one of these waves I saw youngsters engaged in surfing and jetting activities and I felt they would drown soon. *Shaykh*, can you please tell me the meaning?" The *Shaykh* responded, "In the name of Allāh and may peace and prayers be upon His Messenger. If this is a true vision, the dam is a barrier, so Almighty God said in the Holy Qurʾān 'and we have put a barrier before them and a barrier behind them'[28] and God will protect you from mingling with the people of leisure. You shall stay away from them, and Almighty Allāh knows better."[29]

The third source of dream interpretation in GC is web-based, in the form of forums and blogs. The writers are predominantly female, and they exchange dreams that have been brought to their attention and share ideas on their interpretation. This has the advantage that each dream under discussion may have several interpretations, and the interpretation found to be most interesting and promising is then conveyed to the dreamer. These discussions take place in response to individual requests or to formal male interpretation sources, such as the *Ruʾyā* show, to which they offer alternative, and often more creative, interpretations.[30] The sources mentioned in these discussions reflect the various sources of knowledge peculiar to the three generations examined here: elderly family members are cited as folk-belief authorities; books of both medieval Islamic and translated Western authors; and TV interpretations of *Shaykh* Wasīm Yūsuf. Additionally, an increasing number of quite innovative individual interpretations with reference to the Qurʾān and the Sunna are introduced by the new, self-educated, female dream-interpretation community.

Dreams in Generation C: Public Interpretation and Critical Expertise at Home

With the disappearance of the GA dream interpretation *majālis* and the GB dream interpretation call centers, GC has created two new parallel settings for dream interpretation. On the one hand, there is the increasingly isolated core family at home; on the other, there is the extreme public media environment that broadcasts to millions of viewers. The first setting resembles most closely the personal and case-specific interpretations of the GA *majālis*, although interpretations are now based on books rather than the proverbs of folk traditions. The second setting is TV shows that are totally impersonal. Although the interpretation at home provides emotional support, the public show offers entertainment to the masses.

In terms of gender contribution, a very sharp divide can be observed. Whereas in the TV show *Shaykh* Wasīm Yūsuf functions as a representative of formalized, male-dominated, *Salafī* Islam with elements of Islamic instruction and doctrine, the vast majority of callers are women from Dubai. There also are the granddaughters of women from GA. Because they are considered to be the most competent dream interpreters in their family, they maintain an expertise in dream interpretation within their households. Additionally, as ʿAlī and Saʿīd explained earlier, dreams that cannot be easily interpreted by a female interpreter within the family may then be referred to the TV program by female family members on behalf of their male relatives. Men seem to be uncomfortable submitting their dreams for interpretation. Therefore, they delegate this task to their female relatives.

The postmodern situation that has emerged presents some difficulties from the vantage point of Islamic ethics: Women communicate publicly on TV with a male representative of formal *Salafī* Islam, which, in turn, serves to reconfirm female hegemony over dream interpretation. At the same time, the religious authority that promotes this TV program is using dream interpretation to communicate formal religious doctrines to an audience that otherwise would not be motivated to seek such instruction.

Last but not least, Internet forums seem to have become an important means to achieve a balance between the public, formal, male interpretation of dreams and the more private, personal, and informal dream-lore of women. As the new means of mass communication takes hold, interpretations by women are becoming more popular, and new sites featuring virtual dream interpretation *majālis* have emerged as the latest alternative for the upcoming generation. With these forums and blogs, dream interpretation may return to its traditional female dominance, reinstate its independence from religious authorities (while remaining faithful to the discourse of Qur'ān and Sunna) and close the shifting cycles of the last three generations. It is certainly worth observing the evolution of dream interpretation in the coming years.

Conclusion

A comparison of the three consecutive generations in Dubai has illustrated the shifting hegemonies and counter-hegemonies, in the sense explained by Gramsci, of dream interpretation as a cultural phenomenon.[31] Within this cultural framework, the focus on dream interpretation shifts from content to context, and, in my study, from the symbolic images of the dream texts toward the intergenerational power relations and shifting perspectives of mediation and formalization.[32] The relations of power established through the control of dream interpretation derive from hegemony-establishing discourses as proposed by Foucault.[33] The meaning given to dreams inevitably generates moral and ethical guidelines, with the "new" dream interpreters seeking to impose their moral and ethical authority on their audiences. For instance, a *Salafī* interpretation of a dream inevitably conveys the overall *Salafī* vision of the world as well as the *Salafī* value system. If, on the other hand, the interpreter is a family member, her interpretation conveys a more personal, family-related world outlook.

The current generation is coming of age with the skills to research, collect information, and cross-reference new interpretations, all the while lacking the historic and cultural connections to the value systems and means of expression of the three preceding generations. With the ever increasing availability of referenced, textual resources, the future challenge for dream interpreters will not be to link a dream to the Qur᾿ān, the Sunna of the Prophet, or proverbs, but rather, to make sense out of them in a personal, family, and community context on the basis of faith.

Notes

1. Frauke Heard-Bey, *From Trucial States to United Arab Emirates* (Ajman-U.A.E.: Motivare, 2004), 219–22; K. G. Fenelon, *The United Arab Emirates, an Economic and Social Survey* (London: Longman, 1973), 56.

2. Cf. al-ʿAbdūlī al-Sharhān in: ʿAbd Allāh ʿAbd al-Raḥmān, *Al-Imārāt fī dhākirat abnā᾿ihā* (Shāriqa: Ittiḥād kuttāb wa-udabā᾿ al-Imārāt, 1989), 235ff, 195.

3. *Farīj* is an Arabic colloquial word used by Arabs of East Arabia to denote the traditional urban quarter with narrow lanes and attached houses with common walls. See, Heard-Bey, *From Trucial States*, 242.

4. Ibid., 27–34, 239.

5. Umm Manṣūr, interview/majlis in al-Ḥamriyya-Dubai, 1996.

6. ʿAbd AllāhʿAlī al-Tābūr, *al-Taʿlīm al-Taqlīdī al-Muṭawwaʿa fī al-Imārāt* (al-ʿAīn: Zayed Centre for Heritage and History, 2000), 46ff.

7. Issa J. Boullata, *Arabic Oral Traditions*, 1: [http://journal.oraltradition.org/issues/4i-ii/editors_column] (accessed 27 July 2009).

8. Dream interpretation in the Qur᾿ān legitimizes the interest in dreams and dreams' interpretation. In this regard see cf. Mohammad J. Mahallati, "The Significance of Dreams and Dream Interpretation in the Qur᾿ān: Two Sufi Commentaries on Sūrat Yūsuf," in L. Marlow (ed.), *Dreaming Across Boundaries: The Interpretation of Dreams in Islamic Lands* (Boston: Ilex Foundation, 2008), 32ff.

9. Clifford Geertz, *Islam Observed: Religious Development in Morocco and Indonesia* (Chicago: The University of Chicago Press, 1968), 94; M. B. Hamilton, *The Sociology of Religion: Theoretical and Comparative Perspectives* (London: Routledge, 1995), 160–61.

10. Heard-Bey, *From Trucial States*, 150.

11. Muhammad al-Zekri, "Folk Beliefs of Arab Women of Dubai Prior to Oil Discovery in 1966" (University of Exeter: Unpublished MA Thesis, 1998), 36.

12. Ibid., 137.

13. Umm Muḥammad, interview/majlis in Deira-Dubai, 2009

14. Ibid.

15. Ibn Sīrīn, *Tafsīr al-Aḥlām al-Kabīr* (Beirut: Dār al-Kutub al-ʿIlmiyya, 1982), 7ff.

By consulting *al-Fihrist* by Ibn al-Nadīm (d. 1046 AD) who attributed *Taʿbīr al-Ru᾿yā* to Imām Ibn Sīrīn and by further using al-Ẓāhirī (d. 1468 AD) who attributed *al-Jawāmiʿ* to Imām Ibn Sīrīn, we are persuaded that Ibn Sīrīn had written texts, but without using *tafsīr* in the title in any of his writings. Ibn al-Nadīm, *al-Fihrist* (Cairo: al-Maṭbaʿ al-Tijāriyya al-Kubrā), 543–45.

16. Umm Manṣūr, interview/majlis in al-Ḥamriyya-Dubai, 2009.

17. Ibid.

18. Cf. Ebrahim al-Abed, et al. *Chronicle of Progress* (London: Trident Press, 1996), 15.

19. Nūr ʿAlī Rāshid, *Dubai, Life and Times* (London: Motivate Publishing, 1997), 97.

20. The phenomenon of Saudi-sponsored Salafism introduced through modern schooling that replaced traditional Islamic learning institutions is extensively studied on the African continent. Such studies can be found in, for instance, David Westerlund and Eva Evers Rosander (eds.) *African Islam and Islam in Africa: Encounters between Sufis and Islamists* (London: Hurst, 1997); and Louis Brenner, *Controlling Knowledge: Religion, Power and Schooling in a West African Muslim Society* (London: Motivate Publishing, 1997).

21. Walter J. Ong, *Orality and Literacy—the Technologizing of the World* (London: Routledge, 1990; second reprint of 1982), 135.

22. An in-depth investigation on the impact of shifts from Islamic orality to a written culture can be found in Jack Goody's *The Interface between the Written and the Oral* (Cambridge: Cambridge University Press, 1987).

23. Salafism from *al-Salaf al-Ṣāliḥ* (the righteous ancestors) is a movement in Islam taking a radical turn toward a reconstructed puritanical foundation based on an imagined early Islamic community that condemns the current society as being in a state of neo-Jāhiliyya (pre-Islamic ignorance). Cf. Hamid Algar, *Wahhabism: A Critical Essay* (Oneonta: Islamic Publications International, 2002), 47.

24. Umm Ibrāhīm, interview/majlis in Umm Ḥrīr-Dubai, 2009.

25. Fāṭima, interview/majlis in Bar Dubai-Dubai, 2009.

26. ʿAlī, interview, in Burjumān Mall-Dubai, 2009.

27. *Shaykh* Wasīm Yūsuf, interview. Studio of Nūr Dubai TV, al-Qusays-Dubai, 2009.

28. Sūrat Yāsīn, 9.

29. *Shaykh* Wasīm Yūsuf, interview. Studio of Nūr Dubai TV, al-Qusays-Dubai, 2009.

30. This is an interesting forum predominantly used by GC members from Dubai. It can be found on http://forum.uaewomen.net/index.php or http://www.alarabyah.org.

31. Antonio Gramsci, *Selection from the Prison Notebooks* (London: Lawrence and Wishart, 1971), 5, 7, and 12–13.

32. For a survey of various schools of thought that investigates dreams from positivist, post-positivist, hermeneutical, symbolic, semiotic, cultural, and psychological paradigms, see Ian Edgar's *Dreamwork, Anthropology and the Caring Profession: A Cultural Approach to Dreamwork* (UK: Avebury, 1995); also in Barbara Tedlock's *Dreaming and Dream Research* (Cambridge: Cambridge University Press, 1978).

33. J. Giles and T. Middleton, *Studying Culture: A Practical Introduction* (Oxford: Blackwell, 1999), 65–66.

PART II

Dreams in Sufi Literature

CHAPTER 9

Dreams and Their Interpretation in Sufi Thought and Practice

Jonathan G. Katz

In 1636, Jean de Brébeuf—a Jesuit priest who was later canonized following his death at the hands of the Iroquois in 1649—wrote an account of the Huron Indians among whom he lived. Discussing their religious beliefs, he accorded particular importance to the role of dreams.

> They have a faith in dreams which surpasses all belief. If Christians were to put into execution all their divine inspirations with as much care as our Indians carry out their dreams, no doubt they would very soon become great saints. They look upon their dreams as ordinances and irrevocable decrees; to delay the execution of them would be a crime.[1]

An aghast De Brébeuf next describes how a person's dream becomes the occasion for public celebrations of all kinds—a feast, a dance, a lacrosse tournament—and that dreams and their public acknowledgment are particularly related to curing certain kinds of mental illness or demonic possession.[2]

I relate this anecdote about the Huron Indians to illustrate the obvious: Although the phenomenon of dreaming is universal, dream interpretation is culturally situated. How people report their dreams and respond to them varies widely. This realization of societal differences has led some students of dreams to speak of *Dream Cultures*, to quote the title of one book devoted to the comparative history of dreaming.[3] The suggestion that there may be different dream cultures within the context of Islamic societies themselves and different discourses about dreams within Islam itself is more recently explored in the collection, *Dreaming Across Boundaries*.[4]

In the context of Islamic societies, it would be difficult to imagine a scenario in which, on the basis of an individual's dream, an entire community devoted itself to a lacrosse tournament (or its Middle Eastern equivalent). And yet, not unlike the Hurons, Muslims in the Middle East and elsewhere obviously did pay attention to their dreams. Accounts of dreams appear in dynastic chronicles and the *ḥadīth* literature; they are a staple of hagiographies; and books of *taᶜbīr* or oneirocritica abound. These are elaborate "keys" for divining the future, many deriving from Hellenistic and ancient Near Eastern antecedents. For Sufis in particular, attuned as they were to the world of intuition and the unseen, dreams naturally had a special significance. Describing the role of Sufi saints in North Africa, the Moroccan historian Halima Ferhat uses language not unlike de Brébeuf describing the Hurons:

> To communicate, the saints often had recourse to a particular language, to symbols and allegories; they used as well gestures and signs of recognition like the kiss on the forehead or between the two eyes. We are in the domain of the secret and the esoteric. Oneiric messages and their interpretation played an essential role in this universe; the dream may be explicit or allegorical but the saint always follows the order received.[5]

For Sufi saint and Huron Indian alike, dreams need to be obeyed. But obvious differences also appear. For example, in his description of the Hurons, de Brébeuf does not say whether the Indians shared the same preoccupation as Muslims with the question of whether a particular dream was *true*. Ascertaining whether a dream was veridical—and therefore either premonitory or in some sense "actionable"—was the major task for Muslim interpreters of dreams, one they shared with their Hellenistic predecessors.[6] And finally, what seems to have scandalized the Jesuit observer of the Hurons was the impact that any one individual's dream could have on an entire community. The dream was not a private communication but the occasion for the performance of an elaborate public ritual.

The relationship between dreams as a private communication and their public resonance is especially intriguing when considering the role dreams played in Islamic societies and particularly for Sufis. Dreams did not engender lacrosse matches for medieval Muslims;

nevertheless, dreams both reflected and shaped the medieval Muslim understanding of the world.

In what sense then do Sufis "believe" in dreams? Do they dream differently from other Muslims? Do they interpret symbolism in a way that can be characterized as particularly "Sufi"? Why are dreams especially important for some Sufi orders or *ṭuruq* and not for others? Does the role of dreams change over time? And what role does the reporting of dreams play in the interaction between shaykh and *murīd,* the disciple?

Over the centuries, dreams and waking visions have fulfilled a variety of purposes for Sufis. These extend beyond the prognostic value normally associated with dreams to include the expectation that dreams provide personal guidance as to one's spiritual state and development. Sufi novices routinely recounted their dreams to their masters, and some *ṭuruq* are especially associated with using dreams as a mechanism for identifying mystical states. Dreams also are the means by which Sufis have communication with deceased shaykhs as well as with the prophet Muḥammad. And not least, dreams and visions have provided some Sufis with a glimpse of what they presume to be metaphysical truth and ontological reality. For those deemed the friends of God, the *awliyāʾallāh,* dreams and visions are a form of *ilhām* or divine inspiration. Although dreams and visions are distinct from *waḥy,* a communication that only prophets experience, they nonetheless offer a continuation in a minor key of the Prophet's original revelation.

The aims of this chapter are twofold. First, the chapter provides a brief, contextualizing survey of the understanding of dreams in Islamic mysticism. In doing so, we examine in passing the doctrines of such well-known luminaries as Ḥakīm al-Tirmidhī (d. ca. 905–910 CE), Abū Ḥāmid al-Ghazālī (d. 1111 CE), and Muḥyī al-Dīn ibn al-ʿArabī (d. 1240 CE). The latter two offer particular insight into dreams as windows on the *ʿālam al-ghayb,* the unseen world to come, and the *ʿālam al-mithāl,* the imaginal neo-Platonic world of ideals. Manuals like ʿIzz al-Dīn al-Kāshānī's fourteenth-century *Miṣbāḥ al-hidāya* and hagiographies like ʿAbd al-ʿAzīz al-Dabbāgh's *Al-Ibrīz* from the eighteenth century provide additional insight into how Sufi shaykhs interpreted the dreams of their disciples.[7] And autobiographical works like Muḥammad al-Zawāwī's *Tuḥfat al-nāẓir* and al-Shaʿrānī's *Laṭāʾif al-minan* from the fifteenth and sixteenth centuries, respectively, offer a valuable glimpse as to how individual Sufis understood and reported their own personal dream experience.[8]

Second, we consider specifically how the reportage of dreams, either by Sufi shaykhs themselves or their disciples, was instrumental in securing popular reputations for sanctity. Particularly in the context of North and Subsaharan African Sufism in the eighteenth and nineteenth centuries, dreams and purported visions enabled individual leaders like Aḥmad al-Tijānī or ʿUthmān don Fodio to validate claims to religious and political leadership. As we demonstrate, the most intimate and private of noetic experience—the dream or vision—could also paradoxically serve a most public role. In the process, dreams and visions extend beyond their customary function as a means of spiritual communication with the unseen to become mundane and highly visible advertisements of the dreamer's *baraka* or charisma.

Two recent monographs that deal with Islamic dream interpretation, one by Pierre Lory and the other by the late Annemarie Schimmel, devote lengthy passages to Sufis and their dreams.[9] Given that dreams are amply reported in Sufi hagiography and autobiography, their inclusion in general overviews of Islamic dream interpretation makes obvious sense, and yet there is a readily apparent difference in the two discourses of popular and Sufi dream interpretation. The popular tradition of *taʿbīr* or dream interpretation fits squarely within the realm of divination. Its chief concern—as manifested in the many so-called "keys to dreams," most famously those authored by pseudo-Ibn Sīrīn, Ibn Shāhīn and ʿAbd al-Ghanī al-Nābulusī—is enabling the dreamer to predict the future. In contrast, the principal concern for the Sufi is confirmation of his or her spiritual state; the Sufi's preoccupation is not the immediate future but his present state or *ḥāl*. Nonetheless, both approaches share the epistemological assumption that dreams in fact do convey certain knowledge from an unseen realm and, for both, interpreting symbolism typically relies on verbal association.

As John Lamoreaux has so ably demonstrated, oneirocriticism—despite its pre-Islamic and Hellenistic origins—emerged early in Islam as a sanctioned *sharʿī* discipline.[10] Passages in the Qurʾān that deal with dreams such as the *sūrat Yūsuf* as well as an abundance of *ḥadīth* encouraged Muslims to view dreams as providing small apertures into what is not readily apparent. According to a famous *ḥadīth*, dreams are good tidings or *mubashshirāt*, a one-forty-sixth allotment of Muḥammad's prophetic experience. They are, to quote Eric Ormsby, the "poor man's prophecy."[11] It is against this common background in which "belief" in dreams in the broadest sense was culturally sanctioned that Sufis crafted their own approach to dreams. However, as the Sufi tradition evolved, Sufis were more concerned with what dreams said about their present spiritual status than their future affairs. This did not necessarily have to be the road taken. The Persian Sufi ʿAbd al-Mālik al-Kharkūshī (d. ca. 406/1015) authored a manual of dreams that derived in part from Ḥunayn ibn Isḥāq's version of Artemidorus, the Hellenistic authority on dreams. Kharkūshī's effort spawned no literary successors. As Lamoreaux notes, "There are no later Muslim dream manuals precisely comparable to that of Kharkūshī, especially in terms of its attempt to fuse dream interpretation and Sufi dream narratives."[12]

Seven hundred years later, the prominent Naqshbandī Sufi and prolific author ʿAbd al-Ghanī al-Nābulusī authored his most acclaimed work, an alphabetically organized encyclopedia of dream symbolism entitled *Taʿṭīr al-anām* or the "Perfuming of Mankind." And yet, despite al-Nābulusī's own career as a visionary, there's little that would characterize his book as especially "Sufi." As one biographer laments, "In it the individual self of ʿAbd al-Ghanī al-Nābulusī has been suppressed to the point of virtual annihilation."[13]

While al-Nābulusī was reluctant to insert his own person into his manual of dream interpretation, dreams nonetheless appear frequently in his autobiographical writings. Indeed, dreams and waking visions—the distinction between the two is not always clear—have generally provided the context for Sufi autobiography. Perhaps the earliest known example of the genre is that of Ḥakīm al-Tirmidhī (d. ca. 905–910 CE). His *Badʾ al-shaʾn,* "The Beginning of the Matter," relates not only his own dreams but the dreams of his pious wife with whom al-Tirmidhī embarked on a "joint spiritual quest."[14] Al-Tirmidhī's writings provided an early elaboration of the concept of *wilāya* or sainthood. In his own dreams he received confirmation from figures like Muḥammad and Jesus of his own high status within the hierarchy of Muslim saints, whereas the dreams he reports from his wife are likewise offered as evidence of his spiritual rank.[15] The initiatory nature of dreams, so prominent in Ḥakīm al-Tirmidhī's account, is a routine aspect of Sufi hagiography. Dreams, as in the case of al-Tirmidhī, can compensate for the lack of investiture by a recognized living master, and so-called Uwaysī Sufis received initiation from the mythical personnage Khiḍr in a vision rather than from a physically present shaykh.[16]

Initiation also figures in the dreams recounted by the twelfth-century Sufi Rūzbihān al-Baqlī in his *Kashf al-asrār,* "The Unveiling of Secrets," a book that is part retrospective autobiography and part diary. As Carl Ernst points out, "The initiatic visions of saintly authority are complemented by a class of visions that illustrate Rūzbihān's authority with images based on kingship."[17] Angels are arrayed like Turkish soldiers serving the sultan. Other dreams and visions derive imagery from the landscape: "Initiatic visions show Rūzbihān drinking an ocean, or receiving a glass from an ocean of wine. Altogether the ocean signifies the vast reservoir of spirit that reveals itself in waves of ecstasies."[18] Ernst links Rūzbihān's account of his dreams and visions to the tradition of "ecstatic utterances." He notes that most of Rūzbihān's subsequent hagiographers, sensitive to the potential damage that some of Rūzbihān's more *outré* visions might do to his posthumous reputation, leave out of their accounts the most extraordinary of Rūzbihān's dreams.[19]

In that it can support a reputation for sanctity, the recounting of dreams is analogous to the performance of miracles or *karāmāt*. The latter are the so-called "gifts" or "graces" by which the Sufi saint's spiritual powers are demonstrated. Not surprisingly, the category *al-ruʾyā* or vision often appears alongside *karāmāt* or miracles in the hagiographical literature and early Sufi manuals. For example, in al-Qushayrī's *Risāla* (and similarly, in Ibn al-ʿArabī's *Futūḥāt al-makkiyya*) the section on visions immediately follows that on miracles.[20] And in a manner similar to the way some Sufis saw the production of supernatural miracles as a distraction from the ultimate path, so too some shaykhs warned against visions for their adepts. The sixteenth-century Egyptian Sufi, al-Shaʿrānī, paid scrupulous attention to his dreams. And yet in doing so, he was mindful of the teaching of his shaykh, ʿAlī al-Khawwāṣ (d. 1532 CE). The dreams of inexperienced mystics are often expressions of wish fulfillment.

> Accomplished mystics (*ʿārifīn*) dream about the manifestations of their deficiency and the badness of their dealing with Almighty God, and the novices dream of the manifestations of their perfection and the goodness of their dealing. Accordingly each of them sees what is suitable to his state (*ḥāl*) with Almighty God.[21]

The *ḥadīth* literature's sanctioning of "glad tidings" enabled pious Muslims to overcome another potential objection to the value of dreams. Islam places a premium on wakefulness and vigilence. Both the Qurʾān and the example of the Prophet encouraged nighttime prayers, and for the Sufi, whose principal goal was an undivided presence with the divine through the constant remembrance of his name, a premium was placed on concentration and focus. To do otherwise was to succumb, both literally and figuratively, to "neglectful sleep," *khwāb-i ghaflat*.[22] The hagiographer, ʿAṭṭār, writes of the Sufi Shāh Shujāʿ of Kirmān who spent a lifetime fighting off sleep only to finally succumb and dream of God. "In love with the pleasure of the dream, Shāh Shujāʿ carried a pillow with him in hopes that he could re-create the experience by falling asleep again."[23]

"Dreams," to cite Eric Ormsby, "come to us with a special imprint of authority, they seem to represent a way of knowledge, and yet at the same time, they involve neither the communications of the senses nor the inborn certainty of a priori knowledge."[24] Where do dreams come from? With a nod to the philosophers, theologians provided at least one answer to this conundrum from whence dreams and their authority—and in so doing redeemed the value of sleep and dreams for Sufis. Drawing on arguments familiar to the Greeks, Abū Ḥāmid al-Ghazālī explains that the soul at rest is freed from sensory interference and therefore susceptible to the imprint of external images and meanings. Al-Ghazālī makes an explicit analogy between sleep and death. As paraphrased by Sara Sviri, "The perception of a dreamer to whom a veridical dream is conferred resembles the noncorporeal peception of the soul in the world to come. Both relate to a mode of inner seeing (*mushāhada*) that is independent of the outer senses."[25]

Images are drawn from the heavenly "well-preserved tablet" (*al-lawḥ al-maḥfūẓ*)—"the heavenly book that records all created and preordained phenomena from the beginning of creation to its end"—and appear reflected in the mirror of the dreamer's heart.[26] The extent to which a dream is symbolic and consequently requires exegesis depends on the clarity of the dreamer's soul. However, the process does not only happen in sleep. In his *Deliverance from Error,* al-Ghazālī claims that, owing to their constant devotion and through spiritual purification, Sufis regularly have waking visions of the prophets and the angels.[27]

Al-Ghazālī's explanation of dreams and visions reflects the experience of the "ordinary" seer. In contrast, the thirteenth-century Andalusian Sufi, Ibn al-ʿArabī—to use the words of one observer—makes "a leap into epistemological arenas far beyond the limits of mental speculation."[28] For Ibn al-ʿArabī, who understands the metaphysical construction of the world to be simultaneously existent and nonexistent, dreams and visions are the ways in which the imaginative faculty gains access to the *ʿālam al-khayāl wa'l-mithāl*. This imaginal world is the interstice or *barzakh,* the intermediary world of incorporeal archetypes that become, through the imaginative faculty, sensibly intelligible.

The language employed by Ibn al-ʿArabī reflects the earlier contributions of the Iranian illuminationist or *ishrāqī* philosopher, Shihāb al-Dīn Yaḥyā al-Suhrawardī (d. 1191 CE). "For Suhrawardī, both visions and their lesser kindred of dreams take place in an intermediate world between that of concrete phenomenal reality and pure intellectual abstraction. Possessing form but not substance, he referred to this world as the world of likenesses (*ᶜalām al-mithāl*)."[29] And much like Suhrawardī before him, Ibn al-ᶜArabī himself depended greatly on visionary experience not only for affirmation of his own spiritual development but for literary inspiration as well. The important work in which he elaborated the relationship between prophecy and sainthood, *Fuṣūṣ al-ḥikam* or "Bezels of Wisdom," was—he maintained—revealed to him in a vision by the Prophet himself.[30]

To return to al-Ghazālī, dreams do not differ from other forms of psychic "occurrences" or "episodes" known as *wāqiᶜāt*. These episodes befall the Sufi when, in isolation, he immerses himself in the recitation of God's name. According to the author of a fourteenth-century Persian manual of Sufi practice, ᶜIzz al-Dīn al-Kāshānī, *wāqiᶜāt* fall into three categories:

1. "Pure unveiling": psychic events that are true and require no interpretation;
2. "Imaginative unveiling": those events that are symbolic and thus require interpretation owing to the interference of the *nafs*, the lower soul, upon the *rūḥ*, the soul; and
3. "Pure imagination": those that are patently false; the product entirely of the *nafs*, the lower soul.

Kāshānī also describes yet another kind of psychic experience or "unveiling" frequently encountered in Sufi writing, *mukāshafa*. According to Kāshānī, unlike dreams and other *wāqiᶜāt* that occur while the Sufi is "absent" to the world of sensibilia, *mukāshafa* occurs while the Sufi is still "present." As "pure unveiling" there is no possibility for deception to occur in *mukāshafa*.[31] For the Sufi Rūzbihān al-Baqlī, who entitled his memoir *Kashf al-asrār,* "The Unveiling of Secrets," this form of *kashf* has a precise technical meaning. "Unveiling," writes Carl Ernst, "is the mystical perception that is the characteristic of the saints. For Rūzbihān this perception is not abstract or philosophical knowledge, but a vision clothed in form, especially human form; it is not cognitive but apparitional, revealed knowledge through divine light."[32]

In the case of Rūzbihān al-Baqlī, *kashf* is associated with the vision of God, the possibility of which in this world was a point widely debated among theologians.[33] Early elaborations of Sufi practice strove to align mystical experience with the dogmas of orthodox sunnism. The Iranian Sufi al-Sarrāj (d. 988) writes in his *Kitāb al-lumaᶜ*, "The Book of Clear Light," that three forms of divine unveiling are possible: First, what everyone sees on the day of Resurrection; second, the miracles produced by prophets and subsequently the saints; and finally the unveiling of hearts directly in the certitude of faith. As such, *mukāshafa* is intimately linked to *mushāhada*, contemplation. But "the use of the term 'contemplation,' suggests al-Sarrāj, is ambiguous because the agent could often be God, and not the mystic. It is God who contemplates Himself, even in the mirror of the soul of the Sufi."[34] Finally, while admitting its possibility, al-Sarrāj "cautions against too readily believing that God is ever visible to the living, noting that Muḥammad's visionary experience (Qur᾽ān 53:11) is a solitary exception."[35]

The concept of *kashf* underwent further elaboration among later Sufis. The Libyan shaykh Muḥammad ibn ᶜAlī al-Sanūsī (d. 1276/1859) summarizes the views of the Khalwatiyya and the Kubrawiyya, two Sufi orders particularly associated with the interpretation of dreams. According to al-Sanūsī, whereas dreams may be interpreted symbolically, the various degrees of *kashf* are precise in their significations and follow a well-defined hierarchical order. Beginning with representations from the material world, the seer finally experiences ever more pyrotechnical displays of light as his soul becomes attuned to the rarified, immaterial world of pure being. There are seven stages along this path in which each human *laṭīfa*, or delicate nature, corresponds to ten thousand lights of a different hue culminating, ultimately, in the colorless light emblematic of the "essence of totality," the highest existential plane.[36]

In the Qur᾽ānic story of Joseph, the dream of the seven cows was beyond the interpretative ability of the Egyptian diviners who declared the dream to be *aḥlām adghāth*, a "muddled" or nonsignificant dream. With its negative connotation, Sufis typically eschewed the word *aḥlām* (sing. *ḥulm*) when referring to their own "true" visionary experience. Similarly, Sufis used the word *ru᾽yā* in preference to the more conventional term for dream, *manām*. Autobiographical accounts of dreams and visions employed the verb *ra᾽aytu*, "I saw." In hagiographies, *ra᾽a*, "he saw," is the familiar introduction to many anecdotes about saintly Sufis. On the face of it then, Sufi visions, whether experienced while awake or asleep, were in fact simple acts of seeing. And yet the problem of how one sees is not clearcut, and the obvious distinction between ocular sight and spiritual sight aroused much discussion. Sufis spoke of an *ᶜayn baṣar*, the actual sight of the eye, and *ᶜayn baṣīra*, the highly developed inner eye of discernment. This "second sight" is purer, less corruptible, and less subject to confusion than actual physical, sensory sight. Along similar lines some

Sufis spoke of the awakened heart as the organ by which one saw, for example, the prophet Muḥammad. By virtue of the seer's soul becoming rarefied, the Prophet's essence can approach it with ease.[37]

The vision of the prophet Muḥammad was understood by Sufis to be *prima facie* true or veridical, a view supported by an oft-cited *ḥadīth*, "Whoever has seen me has seen me truly and Satan cannot take my form."[38] Still, theoretical questions arose about the form that the Prophet took in a vision. For example, in appearance was he young or old, and did his age have special significance for the seer? And what was one to make of his presumed ability to appear in many places simultaneously? Despite these conundrums, for the most part visions of the Prophet assumed a kind of oracular quality; his appearance was understood literally rather than symbolically.

The same was generally true for visitations by departed shaykhs. Pious Muslims routinely sought these visitations from the dead and for good reason: News of the afterlife provided reassurance that the departed's life of faith had been rewarded. Moreover, dead saints were naturally conceived as intercessionary figures for those who would come after them. Appearing in dreams, dead shaykhs provided symbolic robes and other tokens of initiation, and in general their appearance confirmed for the seer his spiritual status. Death was merely the transference from one abode to another. The Shādhilī shaykh Abū 'l ʿAbbās al-Mursī once pungently remarked that the sincere student benefits more from his instructor after the latter's death than during his life.[39] It comes then as no surprise that visionary activity often is associated with pilgrimage to shrines and tombs. The converse is equally true: Shrines and tombs were often built or sited on the basis of dreams. These shrines are "themselves the concrete residue of earlier visionary experiences."[40] Whether the relation is direct or merely tangential, the various rituals associated with pilgrimage to tombs to some degree replicate the pre-Islamic Hellenistic practice of incubation.

Symbolic dreams, that is, dreams that lend themselves to interpretation as opposed to the literal testimony of saintly and prophetic figures, also played a large role for Sufis who were naturally on the lookout for all sources of spiritual guidance. The sixteenth-century Egyptian mystic ʿAbd al-Wahhāb al-Shaʿrānī included accounts of several hundred dreams in his autobiographical *Laṭāʾif al-minan*.[41] In recounting his dreams, al-Shaʿrānī uses conditional sentences, the classic syntactical formula found in ordinary "keys to dreams." Yet despite the fact that al-Shaʿrānī says he assigns a prognostic value to what he calls *tanbīh* or dreams of instruction, the future is not what concerns him. Instead, he scrutinizes his *past* behavior to see what it says about his *current* performance of ritual and observance. Thus, if he omitted his late-night prayers, he dreamt that he was returning to his native village—which he interpreted as meaning that his *maqām*, his spiritual station, was back at the level it was before he migrated to Cairo. If he maligned someone while in a mosque, he dreamt that he was drinking wine there or eating cooked human flesh. In short, the majority of al-Shaʿrānī's instructional dreams are dreams expressing his anxiety over his actions and the correct discharge of his religious obligations.

For al-Shaʿrānī, ascertaining the action that anticipates the dream is the main goal of the interpretative process. He has a dream (usually of a disturbing nature), and in order to assign meaning to it he must examine in detail his actions of the preceding day. Here al-Shaʿrānī diverges from Artemidorus and the Muslim oneirocritics by his willingness to assign instructional status to dreams produced by the day's residues—that is, dreams that ordinary dream interpreters would have rejected out of hand as uninterpretable. By interpreting this category of dreams as an index of a moral imbalance or a flaw in ritual observance, al-Shaʿrānī shifts the focus away from dreams as tools in prognostication to dreams as monitors of interior states.

In interpreting their dreams, Sufis often defer to the superior authority of their shaykh. *Taʿbīr* or dream interpretation plays a role in *tarbīya*, the spiritual guidance offered by the shaykh. In the early eighteenth century, Aḥmad ibn al-Mubārak al-Lamatī wrote a lengthy book entitled *Al-Ibrīz min kalām Sīdī ʿAbd al-ʿAzīz* or "Pure Gold from the Discourse of Master ʿAbd al-ʿAzīz" to memorialize his late master, a shaykh from Fez named ʿAbd al-ʿAzīz al-Dabbāgh.[42] In the *Ibrīz*, al-Dabbāgh elaborates a complicated epistemology that explains visionary experience of all sorts. The latter ranges from simple *kashf*, unveiling or clairvoyance, to *fatḥ*, the illumination that comes with the vision of the prophet Muḥammad, and ultimately, *mushāhada*, the vision of God. Ordinary dreams, the most common form of visionary activity, receive a considerable amount of attention. For the most part, al-Dabbāgh conceptualizes dreams as a kind of spiritual barometer, indicative of the degrees of purity and impurity within the dreamer's psyche.

What distinguishes al-Dabbāgh's treatment is his comprehensive analysis of the way in which moral lapses affect the symbolic content of dreams. According to al-Dabbāgh, humans combine in their persons both a *dhāt*, a corporeal being, and a *rūḥ*, a spiritual presence. These aspects interact both separately and together with the cosmos and reflect to varying degrees the metaphysical and moral dichotomy of darkness and light, *ẓalām* and *nūr*. The symbolic content of dreams correlates directly with the amount of darkness obscuring the individual's *dhāt*. External social factors also determine the significance of any particular dream symbol. As al-Dabbāgh tells al-Lamaṭī:

> Indeed, the whole truth of what you ask me depends on knowledge of the science of *taʿbīr*, and this cannot be perceived through study because it depends on knowledge of the dreamer's condition beyond that of his *dhāt*, for example, is he an urban dweller or a desert dweller, is he educated or common, and as to his profession, is he a grocer or a merchant or an artisan, and is he rich or poor, as well as other circumstances which are almost limitless.[43]

Yet despite al-Dabbāgh's theoretical elaboration, the entire interpretative process is in the last resort essentially intuitive and slightly solipsistic. Is it the content of the dream that throws light on the moral and spiritual status of the dreamer? Or is the opposite the case, that is, only through prior knowledge of the dreamer's character is it possible for the shaykh to interpret the dream?

From al-Lamaṭī's account of his personal interactions with the al-Dabbāgh, it becomes evident that the shaykh's ability to interpret dreams takes its place alongside other displays of his superior intuition. A frequent demonstration of al-Dabbāgh's *kashf*—used here in the more limited sense of "clairvoyance"—can be seen in his ability to reveal the most private details of his disciples' lives. The ability to interpret dreams offered renewed confirmation of a shaykh's superior status vis-à-vis his disciple.

Both the ability to interpret dreams and a shaykh's propensity to have spectacular visions of his own naturally enhanced a shaykh's prestige. It was only a matter of time perhaps that an aspiring Sufi saint would claim to be *walī allāh* almost exclusively on the basis of his visionary experience. This was precisely the case with the fifteenth-century Shādhilī Sufi, Muḥammad al-Zawāwī al-Bijāʾī, who published in his own lifetime an extensive diary of 109 dream conversations with the prophet Muḥammad.

From the fifteenth century onward the veneration of the Prophet attained a special saliency in the practice of Islam in North Africa. In the context of later Sufism, a presumed intimacy with the prophet Muḥammad became a *sine qua non* for almost anyone recognized as a *walī allāh*. This immediate relationship with the Prophet led the founder of more than one Sufi order to forego the normal requirements of a long *silsila* or chain of initiation. As a self-proclaimed *khatm al-wilāya al-Muḥammadiyya* or "seal of the Muḥammadan sainthood," Aḥmad al-Tijānī claimed to be in direct communication with the Prophet through frequent waking visions. His followers, the Tijāniyya, could likewise claim to be *al-ṭarīqa al-Muḥammadiyya* as putative adherents to the proper Sunna of the Prophet. Of course this distinction of being the "Muḥammadan order" par excellence was also claimed by other North African Sufi orders, among them al-Sanūsiyya and al-Kittāniyya. Like al-Tijānī, Muḥammad ibn ᶜAlī al-Sanūsī, the founder of the Sanūsiyya in Libya, also received direct communications from the Prophet. Al-Sanūsī, however, entertained a more egalitarian conception of the Prophetic vision. He held out for all of his adherents the possibility of spiritual communion with Muḥammad.

This democratization of seeing the Prophet was a process already underway in the sixteenth century when Zayn al-ᶜĀbidīn al-Marṣafī (d. 970/1562) wrote a manual with explicit instructions on how to produce a vision of the Prophet.[44] The vision of the Prophet not only had enhanced the worldly prestige of the seer but offered other, eternal benefits as well. A North African tradition dating from the eleventh century if not earlier asserted that whoever *shook hands* with the Prophet (*muṣāfaḥa* or *mushābaka*) would be saved from hellfire. Later this was amended to the effect that whoever *saw* the Prophet would be saved. Eventually, this power to provide salvation was extended beyond the Prophet to the *walī.* According to some texts, anyone who *saw* the *walī* "unto the seventh person" was guaranteed salvation. The notion reached its furthest elaboration in the eighteenth century with the Moroccan shaykh Muḥammad ibn Nāṣir. In a dream the Prophet assured him, "O Ibn Nāṣir, everyone who sees whoever sees you unto the twentieth, God has preserved his body from hellfire absolutely."[45]

The vision of the Prophet was only one aspect of dreaming for Sufis, but it illustrates in its greatest amplitude the expectations that pious Muslims held for dreams. In the mysterious ephemera of these nocturnal and unconscious experiences, pious Muslims paradoxically sought the prospect of certainty. Leah Kinberg has argued that literal dreams of an oracular nature function much as prophetic *ḥadīth*s do. "Voices heard in dreams, which either condone or condemn certain situations . . . have to be understood as opinions which prevailed in the Islamic community and which were expressed as words revealed in dreams to further reliability." She concludes that "all types of dreams are individual by definition, but they most often have wide and general implications for the whole community."[46]

Pierre Lory points to the "social efficacy" that allows dreams and visions to be as accessible to ordinary believers as they are to the elite of the Sufi hierarchy.[47] As this brief survey has shown, whether one calls it confirmation or affirmation or legitimization, Sufi dreams and waking visions all share a common denominator. For the individual in the private and personal realm of his retreat, dreams extend much needed assurance that a chosen course was indeed the correct, preferred route. In the public context dreams provide that ultimate stamp of approval for those deemed to be members of God's elect group of friends. And finally, at the collective level, dreams make the unseen comfortingly real, confirming the existence of an afterworld and the place of the pious in it. In the end, dreams reward those who put faith in them by strengthening the faith of the entire community.

Conclusion

In his account of the Huron Indians, De Brébeuf called attention to their great displays of public ritual, and he saw in the Hurons' response to dreams ample evidence of their naïveté and primitiveness. This is certainly not the way anyone would characterize the Sufi understanding of visionary activity. With their detailed theoretical elaboration regarding the meaning and origin of dreams, Sufis provided sophisticated explanations for the occurrence of what might otherwise be regarded as irrational experience. Rather than question the linkage of "this world" with "the world of the unseen," their explanations reinforced the notion that there was one reality rather than two.

E. R. Dodds, in his brilliant study, *The Greeks and the Irrational*, identifies for the ancient Greeks what he calls the relationship between "dream pattern" and "culture pattern." Much of what he describes is immediately recognizable to anyone familiar with accounts of Sufi and Muslim dreams; in the Muslim experience as in the Greek experience we see the oracular nature of some visitations and the "god-sent" quality of others. We also encounter in both traditions "the self-induced vision" and "the private symbolic dream." Eventually, the ancient Greek philosophical tradition provided a rational explanation for dreaming that had the effect of emphasizing the *individual* experience of the dream and limiting its communal repercussions. In contrast, the Sufi theoretical tradition moved in the opposite direction, placing prophetic revelation, and by extension the dream, at the very heart of *communal* religious experience. Even more convincingly, the sheer abundance of dream accounts in the hagiographic literature provided the weight of empirical evidence and affirmed the epistemological veracity of dreams. Literary reports gained the force of reality, and dreams obtained an objective existence to the extent that the sole notice of a Sufi in a hagiography can be a report of a single dream.[48]

For Sufis, the consequences of their dreams might have been less physically tangible than they were for their Huron Indian counterparts. Nonetheless, the results were no less pervasive. Undoubtedly, to borrow Dodds's terminology, Sufi dream patterns are reflections of Sufi culture patterns, but this observation still leaves us with an unanswerable set of questions: Is the reliance that Sufis put on dreams evidence of the community's certainty in its assumptions about this world and the next? Or does it betray the opposite, an underlying anxiety and a pervasive sense of insecurity that was only assuaged by the added evidence of the dream?

In posing the question, we could be reading into the past a modern wariness regarding the certainty of philosophical and religious truths. We also could simply be acknowledging the discomfiting nature of dreams even in our own day and the human desire to seek meaning in them.

Notes

1. Jean de Brébeuf, "Relation of 1636," in *The Jesuit Relations: Natives and Missionaries in Seventeenth-Century North America*, ed. Allan Greer. The Bedford Series in History and Culture (Boston and New York: Bedford/St. Martins, 2000), 47–48.

2. Ibid.

3. David Shulman and Guy G. Stroumsa, ed., *Dream Cultures: Explorations in the Comparative History of Dreaming* (New York and Oxford: Oxford University Press, 1999).

4. Louise Marlow, ed., *Dreaming Across Boundaries: The Interpretation of Dreams in Islamic Lands,* Ilex Foundation Series (Cambridge, Mass.: Harvard University Press, 2008).

5. Halima Ferhat, *Le Soufisme et les Zaouyas au Magreb: Mérite Individuel et Patrimoine Sacré* (Casablanca: Les Editions Toubkal, 2003), 9.

6. E. R. Dodds, *The Greeks and the Irrational* (Berkeley: University of California Press, 1956), 106–107.

7. ʿIzz al-Dīn Maḥmūd ibn ʿAlī al-Kāshānī, *Miṣbāh al-hidāya wa'l-miftāḥ al-kifāya*, ed. Jalāl al-Dīn Humāʾī (Teheran: Muʾassasah-i Nashr-i Huma, 1367/1988), 171–79. Kāshānī's manual is based largely on *ʿAwārif al-maʿārif* of Shihāb al-Dīn Suhrawardī (d. 1234). Aḥmad ibn al-Mubārak al-Lamatī, *Al-Ibrīz min Kalām Sīdī ʿAbd al-ʿAzīz al-Dabbāgh* (n.p: al-Maktaba al-shaʿbiyya, n.d). John O. Kane and Berndt Radtke have recently published an English translation,

Pure Gold from the Words of Sayyidī ʿAbd al-ʿAzīz al-Dabbāgh: Al-Dhahab al-Ibrīz min Kalām Sayyidī ʿAbd al-ʿAzīz al-Dabbāgh, Basic Texts of Islamic Mysticism (Leiden: E. J. Brill, 2007). See also Jonathan G. Katz, "Dreams in the Manaqib of a Moroccan Sufi Shaykh: Abd al-Aziz ad-Dabbagh (d. 1719)," in *Dreaming Across Boundaries*, 270–84.

8. Abū ʿAbd Allāh Muḥammad al-Zawāwī al-Bijāʾī, *Tuḥfat al-nāẓir wa nuzhat al-manāẓir*, Bibliotheque Générale, Rabat (D209) 509; and Jonathan G. Katz, *Dreams, Sufism and Sainthood: The Visionary Career of Muhammad al-Zawāwī* (Leiden: E. J. Brill, 1996), 215. ʿAbd al-Wahhāb al-Shaʿrānī, *Laṭāʾif al-minan* (Cairo: ʿĀlam al-Fikr, 1976); and Jonathan G. Katz, "An Egyptian Sufi Interprets His Dreams: ʿAbd al-Wahhāb al-Shaʿrānī 1493–1565," *Religion* 27 (1997), 7–24.

9. Pierre Lory, *Le rêve et ses interprétations en Islam* (Paris, Albin Michel, 2003); and Annemarie Schimmel, *Die Träume des Kalifen: Träume und ihre Deutung in der islamischen Kultur* (München: C.H. Beck, 1998). Also see Nile Green, "The Religious and Cultural Role of Dreams and Visions in Islam," *Journal of the Royal Asiatic Society*, Series 3, 13, 3 (2003): 287–313.

10. John C. Lamoreaux, *The Early Muslim Tradition of Dream Interpretation* (Albany: State University of New York Press, 2002).

11. Eric Ormsby, "The Poor Man's Prophecy: Al-Ghazālī on Dreams," in *Dreaming Across Boundaries*, 142–52.

12. Lamoreaux, *The Early Muslim Tradition*, 77.

13. Elizabeth Sirriyeh, *Sufi Visionary of Ottoman Damascus: ʿAbd al-Ghanī al-Nābulusī 1641–1731* (London and New York: RoutledgeCurzon, 2005), 83.

14. Sara Sviri, "Dreaming Analyzed and Recorded: Dreams in the World of Medieval Islam," in *Dream Cultures*, 262.

15. The notion of including other persons' dreams about oneself was an enduring one. The Moroccan shaykh Muḥammad al-Maʿṭī al-Sharqāwī (d. 1766) assembled an entire book recounting his appearance in the dreams of others. *Kitāb al-marāʾī al-Maʿṭī ibn al-Ṣāliḥ al-Sharqāwī.* Bibliothèque Royale, Rabat, 7958.

16. Lory, *Le rêve et ses interprétations*, 234; John Renard, *Friends of God: Islamic Images of Piety, Commitment, and Servanthood* (Berkeley: University of California Press, 2008), 81–83; Green, "The Religious and Cultural Role," 299–301.

17. Carl Ernst, *Rūzbihān Baqlī: Mysticism and the Rhetoric of Sainthood in Persian Sufism* (Richmond, UK; Curzon Press, 1996), 56–57.

18. Ibid., 75.

19. Ibid., 145.

20. Denis Gril, "Le Miracle en Islam, Critère de la Sainteté?" in *Saints Orientaux*, ed. Denise Aigle (Paris: De Boccard, 1995), 75.

21. Al-Shaʿrānī, *Laṭāʾif al-minan*, 415, quoted in Katz, "An Egyptian Sufi," 11–12.

22. Lory, *Le rêve et ses interprétations*, 203–10; and Ferhat, *Le Soufisme*, 55.

23. Renard, *Friends of God*, 78, citing ʿAṭṭār, *Tadhkirat al-awliyāʾ*, ed. Muḥammad Esteʿlāmī (Teheran: Intishārāt-i Zawwār, 2003), 169.

24. Ormsby, "The Poor Man's Prophecy," 142.

25. Sviri, "Dreaming Analyzed and Recorded," 256.

26. Ibid.

27. W. Montgomery Watt, *The Faith and Practice of Al-Ghazālī* (London: George Allen and Unwin, 1953), 61.

28. Sviri, "Dreaming Analyzed and Recorded," 258.

29. Green, "The Religious and Cultural Role," 295.

30. Claude Addas, *Quest for the Red Sulphur: The Life of Ibn ʿArabī.* trans. Peter Kingsley (Cambridge, U.K.: The Islamic Text Society, 1993), 277.

31. Al-Kāshānī, *Miṣbāh al-hidāya,* 171–79.

32. Ernst, *Rūzbihān Baqlī,* 18.

33. Lory, *Le rêve et ses interprétations,* 139–42 and 193–203.

34. Ibid., 199. Henry Corbin describes what he calls the "paradox of theophany." Moses in the Qurʾān could not see God but Muḥammad does ("I have seen God in the most beautiful of forms"). Henry Corbin, "The Visionary Dream in Islamic Spirituality," in *The Dream and Human Societies,* ed. G. E. von Grunebaum and Roger Caillois (Berkeley: University of California Press, 1966), 388.

35. Renard, *Friends of God,* 275–76.

36. Katz, *Dreams, Sufism and Sainthood,* 215. Muḥammad ibn ʿAlī al-Sanūsī, *al-Salsabīl al-muʿīn fī al-ṭarāʾiq al-arbaʿīn,* in *al-Majmūʿa al-mukhtāra* (Tripoli, 1968), 65–67. Sanūsī's table of psychic states is reproduced in both Nicola Ziadeh, *Sanūsīyah: A Study of a Revivalist Movement in Islam* (Leiden: E. J. Brill, 1958), and J. Spencer Trimingham, *The Sufi Orders in Islam* (Oxford: Clarendon Press, 1971). For color symbolism, see Jamal J. Elias, "A Kubrawī treatise on mystical visions, the 'Risāla-yi Nūriyya' of ʿAlāʾ Ad-Dawla as-Simnānī," *The Muslim World* 83 (1993): 68–81.

37. Katz, *Dreams, Sufism and Sainthood,* 216.

38. Ibid., 205–16.

39. Aḥmad ibn Muḥammad ibn ʿAṭāʾ Allāh, *Laṭāʾif al-minan,* ed. ʿAbd al-Ḥalīm Maḥmūd (Cairo: Maṭbaʿ al-Ḥassān, 1974), 167.

40. Green, "The Religious and Cultural Role," 308. Also see Christopher S. Taylor, *In the Vicinity of the Righteous: Ziyāra and the Veneration of Muslim Saints in Late Medieval Egypt* (Leiden: E. J. Brill, 1998).

41. Katz, "An Egyptian Sufi," 9.

42. See note 7.

43. Al-Lamatī, *Al-Ibrīz,* 174.

44. Muḥammad ibn Muḥammad al-Jumrī Zayn al-ʿĀbidīn al-Marṣafī, *Hidāyat al-mushtāq al-mustahām fī ruʾyat al-nabī . . . fī al-manām* (Bibliothèque Générale, Rabat, D157. [Catalogued under Zayn al-ʿĀbidīn ʿAlī ibn Khalīl al-Mawṣilī]. See Katz, *Dreams, Sufism and Sainthood,* 224–25, n. 53.

45. Ibid., 226–27.

46. Leah Kinberg, "Literal Dreams and Prophetic *Ḥadīṯs* in classical Islam—a comparison of two ways of legitimation," *Der Islam* 70 (1993): 279–300.

47. Lory, *Le rêve et ses interprétations,* 249.

48. Ferhat, *Le Soufisme,* 55.

CHAPTER 10

Behind the Veil of the Unseen

Dreams and Dreaming in the Classical and Medieval Sufi Tradition

Erik S. Ohlander

As the now rather passé Victorian-era anthropologist E.B. Tylor famously stated, the very origin of religion itself is to be found in two universal human experiences: death and dreams.[1] For Tylor it was these two basic experiences that, as rationally interpreted by his imagined first "savage philosopher" in the mists of prehistory, lay at the root of "animism" and, in turn, animism at the root of what would eventually evolve into "religion" proper. Although Tylor's unilinear model of cultural evolution is now certainly little more than a quaint "survival" of his own evolutionary moment, his attempt to position death and dreams as major leitmotifs within and across the wide sweep of human religious discourse is not. It is the latter that is of concern here.

Although perhaps no longer serviceable as an overarching category in the comparative study of religion, a sizable body of recent anthropological, historical, literary, psychological, and related scholarship on dreams and dreaming explicated in both localized and cross-cultural religious contexts has set out to theorize the implications of Tylor's observation.[2] The upshot of this literature, divergent as its conclusions may be, is that dreams and dreaming seem to be prominent enough in religious discourses to demand the attention of those who see such discourses as potential structuring elements in human social, cultural, political, and intellectual life in the first place. In this, the Islamic tradition has received its fair share of attention,[3] and if nothing else, the sheer number of premodern Muslim oneirocritical texts alone evince the relative historical importance of the discourse on dreams and dreaming within it.[4]

This brief inquiry seeks to contribute to this discussion by offering a few interconnected observations on the admittedly vast subject of dreams and dreaming among Sufis, focusing in particular on three key markers attendant to what might be called a foundational Sufi oneirology that emerged over the course of the fourth/tenth through the early eighth/fourteenth centuries. The first of these three markers is the "communicativeness of dreams." By this is meant simply that Sufi writers of the period construed dreams and dreaming as a special medium for the disclosure or communication of knowledge otherwise inaccessible. Second, there is the marker of what might be called the "pragmatic nature" of dreams and dreaming, which means that the particular mystical oneirology associated with the period viewed dreams and dreaming as a phenomenon with explicit practicable bearing on wayfaring along the Sufi path. The final marker is that of the "evidentiary value" of dreams and dreaming. Here, classical and medieval Sufi authors saw dreams and dreaming as proof of status and authority, in particular in relation to the claim that among all the social-sectarian groups (*ṭawāʾif*) comprising the Muslim body politic, it was the Sufis themselves who were the true "heirs to the prophets" (*wurrāth al-anbiyāʾ*). Together, these three markers delimit the scope of a wider oneiric discourse from which later Sufi oneirocritics would draw inspiration.

Interpretive and Methodological Considerations

Those familiar with Sufi literature well know that dreams and dreaming have long played a role in Sufi constructions of the Muslim mystical subject, serving as both a salient marker of communal identity and positioning in hagiography and a significant object of experience and analysis in theoretical texts.[5] However, as with other discrete clusters of mystical discourse falling within the descriptive ambit of Sufism, the relatively wide attestation of dream interpretation manuals, visionary diaries,[6] and associated literatures emerging from Sufi milieux in the later-medieval through the early-modern period seems to have depended heavily on a discourse of dreams developed and systematized in the classical and medieval Sufi tradition. In an effort to define and explicate the contours of this foundational discourse, this inquiry seeks to attend to a phenomenology of dreams and dreaming expressed in a representative group of Sufi texts, comprising both theoretical and hagiographic materials, composed or compiled over the course of the fourth/tenth through the early eighth/fourteenth centuries.The method used was simple: Once a fixed body of texts was chosen,[7] they were then probed for explicit references to dreams and dreaming with the goal of developing a descriptive list of recurring lexical, narrative, or conceptual features that could be used to sketch the contours of oneiric discourse within and across the tradition from which the texts emerged. Most of the texts chosen possessed references to dreams and dreaming. Perhaps none too surprisingly, the majority of references occurred in hagiographic rather than in discursive contexts, although the latter did become much more prominent in literature produced toward the end of the period. In summary, this exercise resulted in the identification of the three aforementioned key markers, each of which is considered in turn.

Marker 1: Dreams Are Communicative

Although part of a wider cluster of psychic and visionary phenomena associated with the terms *wāqiʿa* (incident, i.e., a visionary experience), *ilhām* (inspiration), and to a certain extent *mukāshafa* (unveiling), by "dreams" are meant here *manāmāt* (Per. *khwāb*), that is things that are seen or experienced in the sleep state (e.g., Ar. *raʾaytᵘ shayʾᵃⁿ fī 'l-manām*, "I saw something in a dream;" Per. *chīzī-rā bih-khwāb dīdam*) rather than visionary, lucid, or semi-wakeful dreamlike experiences.[8] As expressed in the body of literature surveyed for this inquiry, above all else such dreams are construed as a special medium of communication. In this sense, dreams serve to disclose knowledge not readily apparent to their subject in a waking state. This knowledge can be mantic or confirmatory, can serve to admonish or laude, can be pedagogic or elucidative, and may be communicated in either an obvious or symbolic manner. Generally, such knowledge is taken to be inspired and, on the basis of an often quoted hadith, is understood as being divisible into either one of two types: true and veridical, or false and misleading. The former, properly designated by the substantive *ruʾyā* (vision; or, dream vision), is God sent, whereas the latter, designated by the term *ḥulm* (pl. *aḥlām*), is understood to be satanic or psychological in origin.[9] Here, the value of each type is construed in a manner strikingly similar to the bifold division of dreams posited by the second-century Greek oneirocritic Artemidorus who in his *Oneirocritica*, the only Hellenistic work of the sort to have been translated into Arabic in the early Abbasid period, differentiated between the *enhypnion*, or personal dream, and the *oneiros*, or God-given dream.[10] The former is to be disregarded, whereas the latter demands careful attention.

Although it is often unclear as to which class a particular dream might belong, in the case of hagiographic narratives, dream events occur most frequently in intracommunal contexts, especially in cases where the enunciation, or denunciation, of the relative status or authority of any one affiliate of the *ṣūfiyya* community may be in doubt. Such dream-event narratives typically involve the appearance of either a departed Sufi luminary or the Prophet himself to the dreamer who comes to affirm or correct his spiritual state, and resultant communal status, by addressing unsettled questions among him and his compatriots.[11] A typical example occurs in an anecdote related by Hujwīrī (d. ca. 465/1072) concerning the question of al-Junayd's (d. 298/910) successorship to his acclaimed paternal uncle Sarī al-Saqaṭī (d. 253/867) as public leader of the *ṣūfiyya* of Baghdad:

> It is well known that during the time Sarī was alive, the disciples of Junayd wanted him to discourse to them, but he said that he would not; until one night he saw the Prophet in a dream (*khwāb*) and he said to him: "O Junayd discourse to men because your discourse is a means for making them content, and the Lord has made your words a means for saving the world." When he awoke, the notion that his rank surpassed that of Sarī took root in his heart since the Messenger had enjoined him to preach. At daybreak Sarī sent a disciple to deliver a message to Junayd saying: "When your disciples wanted you to discourse to them you would not speak, and you rejected both the intercession of the masters of Baghdad and my own adjuration as well. Now, when the Prophet gives you a command, you answer him!" Junayd said: "That notion left me and I understood that he (Sarī) knew my inward and outward conditions at any one moment and that his rank is indeed higher than mine because he knows my innermost thoughts, but I am unfamiliar with even his outward condition! Thus, I came near to him and begged his pardon, and asked him how he knew that I had seen the Prophet in a dream." He responded: "I saw God in a dream (*man khudāvānd-rā taʿālā u taqaddus bi-khwāb dīdam*), and He said: "I sent the Messenger to Junayd to tell him to preach to men so that the people of Baghdad would profit by it." This story contains

> clear proof that the Sufi masters are in every case aware of the innermost state of their disciples.[12]

Although it should be noted that the appearance of God in dreams is comparatively rare in this literature in comparison to the appearance of human actors,[13] such narrative constructions of the dream event are not. Additionally, Hujwīrī's interpretive gloss at the end of the above anecdote exemplifies the pedagogic value attached to such narratives in which a clear hierarchy of relative authority, and a warning not to misconstrue it, emerges in relation to the communication of knowledge meaningful to the community addressed by the dream-event narrative. Such "legitimizing" or "legitimizing-edifying dreams" seem to serve much the same purpose as those which Leah Kinberg has described in relation to intercommunal rivalries among the Sunni juridical rites in which the relative status and authority of eponyms such as Abū Ḥanīfa (d. 150/767) or Aḥmad b. Ḥanbal (d. 241/855) was asserted and contested through the production and circulation of *ḥadīth*-like narratives built on stock dream-image topoi.[14]

The hagio-biographic texts surveyed for this inquiry are replete with such anecdotes, often expressed in narratives that place a deceased figure conversing or interacting with a living dreamer from the liminal space of the *barzakh*, the temporal-physical isthmus that plays home to the souls of the deceased awaiting the Day of Resurrection or, in the case of particularly elevated figures, from Paradise itself.[15] At the same time, however, dreams and dreaming are not construed solely as a medium of legitimation frozen in narrative, for the same body of literature also interprets the phenomenon as one possessed of a marked dynamism, particularly in relation to issues concerning mystical praxis.

Marker 2: Dreams Are Pragmatic

Although as a religiously validated communicative medium, dream-event narratives could be made to serve apologetic or pedagogic functions in hagiographic constructions, dreams and dreaming also appear in classical and medieval Sufi literature in the context of the pragmatics of wayfaring on the mystical path. Here, the practice of a Sufi master interpreting his aspirants' dreams and visions (*taᶜbīr*) stands out as being of particular import. Although much better attested in the context of later Sufi literature and the practices attendant to certain *ṭarīqa*-lineages,[16] a recognition (sometimes oblique) of this socially enacted oneirology within the texts surveyed for this inquiry nevertheless exemplifies the relationship between individual mystical experience and the increasingly structured master-disciple relationship associated with Sufi religiosity over the course of this transformational period. This acculturation of a discrete mystico-oneiric theory and attendant lexicon among Sufis of the time is particularly well displayed among the early Kubrawiyya such as, for example, in Najm al-Dīn Rāzī Dāya's (d. 654/1256) confident discussion of "dreams and visions" (*khwāb u vāqiʿa*) in his lengthy Sufi handbook, the *Mirṣād al-ʿibād*.[17]

Another phenomenon attendant to a pragmatic configuration of dreams and dreaming vis-à-vis the Sufi path is found in comments relating to the practice of *istikhāra* (incubation). A well-attested quasi-divinatory practice mentioned in the Hadith, *istikhāra* involves the ritualized performance of two units of prayer followed by the offering of a formulaic supplication in which is included mention of the course of action in question, after which the petitioner goes to sleep in hopes that an answer will be revealed "in a dream" (*fī 'l-manām*) or that the matter will simply turn out for the best.[18] Echoing the earlier instructions lain out by the enigmatic fourth/tenth-century Sufi author Abū Ṭālib al-Makkī (d. 386/996),[19] in a chapter concerning the rules of travel for the Sufi aspirant in his influential handbook, the *ʿAwārif al-maʿārif*, for example, the prominent early-seventh/thirteenth-century Sufi master, and eponym of one of the earliest *ṭarīqa*-lineages, Abū Hafṣ ʿUmar al-Suhrawardī (d. 632/1234), enjoins the practice and gives detailed instructions on how to perform it, saying in part:

> Among the least of steps which the mendicants (*fuqarāʾ*) should take at the commencement of travel is to ascertain the correct reason for their wish to travel by performing the Prayer of Incubation (*ṣalāt al-istikhāra*). The Prayer of Incubation should not be overlooked because it will furnish the mendicant with a much clearer explanation of the constructive reason of his wish to travel than the wish alone. Among the Sufis (*al-qawm*) there are varying levels à propos to clarifying the correctness of a wish, this and higher ones, but in this particular instance one must not neglect the Prayer of Incubation, which is in accordance with the Sunna.[20]

For al-Suhrawardī in fact, the intentional search for practicable knowledge in dreams is not limited to the decision on whether or not to travel, but also extends to other practical elements of wayfaring on the Sufi path such as the oftentimes controversial decision on whether or not an aspirant should marry.[21] As a measured and deliberate process aimed at eliciting a response of practical import from behind the veil of the unseen, discussions such as this underscore the general power and significance of dreams and dreaming among medieval Sufis. At the same time, however, although the basic notion of the communicativeness of dreams and dreaming certainly serve to frame such pragmatic configurations of oneiric experience, it is only linking these two with the third marker—the evidentiary value of dreams—that brings into full relief the particularized oneirology embedded in the body of texts surveyed for this inquiry.

Marker 3: Dreams Are Evidentiary

In his often quoted handbook, the influential fifth/eleventh-century Sufi apologist al-Qushayrī remarked that the sleep state in which dreams are manifest allows the Sufi access to realities not accessible while awake.[22] But what kind of realities did he, and his readers, have in mind? Although certainly not the whole story, a partial answer can be found in considering this idea in relation to wider notions of dreams and dreaming in the Islamic tradition itself. Although deeply familiar to the Abrahamic traditions in general, the potent association between prophetical knowledge and dream visions is particularly visible in relation to Islamic prophetology.[23] Indeed, as the late seventh/thirteenth-century Sunni exegete al-Bayḍāwī remarked in discussing the key differences between a prophet (*nabī*) and a messenger (*rasūl*), the latter is said to receive revelation by way of an angel, whereas the former is said to receive it through dreams.[24] In this regard, a particularly resonant notion for classical and medieval Sufi theorists comes in the often quoted *ḥadīth* in which the Prophet is reported to have said: "The veridical dream-vision is 1/46th a part of prophethood" (*al-ruʾyā al-ṣāliḥa juzʾ min sitta wa-arbaʿīn juzʾan min al-nubuwwa*).[25] In the creedal section of his Sufi handbook the *Miṣbāḥ al-hidāya* the Persian Sufi author ʿIzz al-Dīn Kāshānī (d. 735/1334–35) refers to just this *ḥadīth* to support his implicit argument that among all the social-sectarian groups (*ṭavāʾif*) populating the Muslim body politic, only the Sufis are the true "heirs to the prophets" (*vurrāth-i anbiyāʾ*), saying:

> Everything ascribed to the prophets by way of revelatory inspiration (*vaḥy*) is also ascribed to God's friends (*avliyāʾ*) by way of divine inspirations (*ilhāmāt-i rabbānī*), this distinguishing them from other believers. In visionary experiences (*vaqāyiʿ*) they are given true inspiration by God who

> has made it a saintly marvel (*karāmat*) which occurs while dreaming or awake. Indeed, the veridical dream (*khwāb-i durust*) is one of the parts of prophethood (*jūzī az ajzāʾ-i nubuvvat*).[26]

John Lamoreaux has argued for a certain theology of dreams and dreaming in Islam,[27] and indeed it can be argued further that it is the revelatory character of oneiric experience which is foregrounded in the classical and medieval Sufi tradition. Dreams furnish evidence of spiritual status and divinely sanctioned authority, and in the passage just cited, al-Kāshānī makes the realities referred to by al-Qushayrī explicit, linking them with the *walāya* of those who have successfully traversed the Sufi path in such a way that the status of the Muslim mystical subject, as true heir to the prophets, is reflexively objectified through psychospiritual realities simultaneously present in both an intercommunal prophetology and an intracommunal oneirology. If dream visions are indeed 1/46th a part of prophethood, it would seem that it is the Sufis who lay claim to the greater part of it, for in terms of having access to a persisting suprasensible and suprapersonal knowledge through the medium of dreams and dreaming, the *walī* is but a transposition of the *nabī*—as much his kin as his heir.[28] It is this mark in particular that serves to stamp the Sufi experience of dreams and dreaming as a particularized inflection of the wider experience of dreams and dreaming in the Islamic tradition. Dreams are indeed significant business.

Conclusion

Although the discourse of dreams and dreaming plotted in this group of texts is easily situated within the wider context of oneiric lexica and interpretive schemas available to classical and medieval Sufi theorists for describing, understanding, and analyzing such phenomena, it nevertheless seems that the three markers that emerge therein heavily depended on a particular social vision, ontology, and metaphysics idiosyncratic to the classical and medieval Sufi tradition itself. First, dreams and dreaming were seen to serve an epistemic function, namely communicating knowledge not readily available otherwise. Knowledge of things of direct relevance to the community was of particular significance in this regard. Second, dreams and dreaming were seen to serve a practicable purpose, namely as an experiential element of wayfaring on the mystical path. Finally, dreams were made to serve as a marker of claims to status and authority, in particular in relation to the assertion that among all the self-identified *ṭawāʾif* comprising the Muslim body politic it is the Sufis who fulfill the function of postprophetic heirship for the *umma* itself.

Whereas E.B. Tylor would have most certainly interpreted this discourse as one of but many expressions of a uniform human rationality marked only by increasingly sophisticated abstractions of dubious explanatory value, its ubiquity in this particular expression of the Islamic tradition would seem to assert otherwise. In functioning as a type of "structuring structure" that both frames and yields meaning to the experience of wayfaring on the mystical path, the discussion of dreams and dreaming among Sufis of this period is significant. It is as much a mark of the significance of oneiric experience to this particular expression of human religiosity as it was to grounding wider conceptions, expressions, and assertions of communal identity in a meaningful frame of reference for those who produced it in the first place. There is, in fact, much to be gained from considering such materials as representative of a wider *Gedankenwelt* in which certain forms of textual discourse, as empirically accessible traces of the activities of human actors in time and space, are potentially telling of various subjectivities and social arrangements obtaining in specific historical contexts.[29] As evinced in the body of classical and medieval Sufi texts surveyed for this inquiry, it seems clear that the subject of dreams and dreaming was of more than passing interest to those who produced them. Here, dreams define, explain, and empower—they are real, public, and powerful. As such, the subject itself should properly be of more than minimal concern for those seeking to further their own understanding of those actors, the tradition associated with the literary artifacts they left behind, and with the wider religious, social, and intellectual worlds framing both. As the late third/ninth-century mystic Shāh b. Shujāʿ al-Kirmānī is reported to have said after seeing God Himself in a dream:

raʾayt[u] *surūr*[a] *qalbī fī manāmī / fa-aḥbabt*[u] *al-tanaʿʿus*[a] *wa-l-manāmā*[30]
I found my heart's joy in my bed chamber;
and have come to love sleep and slumber.

Notes

1. E.B. Tylor, *Primitive Culture: Researches into the Development of Mythology, Philosophy, Religion, Language, Art and Custom*, 2nd American edn. (New York: Henry Holt and Company, 1877), 1:424–502.

2. Overview and relevant bibliography in B. Tedlock, "Dreams," in *Encyclopedia of Religion,* Second Edition, ed. L. Jones (Detroit: Macmillan Reference USA, 2005), 4:2482–91. The essays collected by Kelly Bulkeley in idem, ed., *Dreams: A Reader on Religious, Cultural, and Psychological Dimensions of Dreaming* (New York: Palgrave, 2001), are representative of this trend. Prior to this, two other cross-disciplinary collections of some significance should be cited: D. Shulman and G. Stroumsa, eds., *Dream Cultures: Explorations in the Comparative History of Dreaming* (New York: Oxford University Press, 1999), and G.E. von Grunebaum and R. Caillois, eds., *The Dream and Human Societies* (Berkeley: University of California Press, 1966). Each of these three volumes includes essays devoted specifically to Islamic materials.

3. In addition to the relevant contributions in the three volumes cited above, see further: L. Kinberg, "Dreams as a Means to Evaluate Ḥadīth," *Jerusalem Studies in Arabic and Islam* 23 (1999): 79–99; idem, *Ibn Abī Dunyā: Morality in the Guise of Dreams; A Critical Edition of* Kitāb al-Manām *with Introduction* (Leiden: E.J. Brill, 1994); idem, "Literal Dreams and Prophetic *Ḥadīṯs* in Classical Islam—A Comparison of Two Ways of Legitimation," *Der Islam* 70 (1993), 279–300; idem, "The Legitimization of the *Madhāhib* through Dreams," *Arabica* 32 (1985), 47–79; J. Katz, "An Egyptian Sufi Interprets His Dreams: ʿAbd al-Wahhāb Shaʿrānī 1493–1565," *Religion* 27 (1997), 7–24; idem, *Dreams, Sufism and Sainthood: The Visionary Career of Muhammad al-Zawāwī* (Leiden: E.J. Brill, 1996); J. Lamoreaux, *The Early Muslim Tradition of Dream Interpretation* (Albany: State University of New York Press, 2002); L. Marlow, ed., *Dreaming Across Boundaries: The Interpretation of Dreams in Islamic Lands* (Boston, Mass.: Ilex Foundation and the Center for Hellenic Studies, 2008), which includes, among others, chapters by Kinberg, Katz, and Lamoreaux. In addition to these works, of particular importance here one may also cite the relevant portion of the foundational work of T. Fahd on Arab divinatory traditions: *La divination arabe: Études religieuses, sociologiques et folkloriques sur le milieu natif de l'Islam* (Leiden: E.J. Brill, 1966), 247–367; and, idem, "Ruʾyā," in *EI*², 8:645–49. Also of importance in this regard is A. Schimmel, *Die Träume des Kalifen. Träume und ihre Deutung in der islamischen Kultur* (Munich: C.H. Beck, 1998), the overview of H. Ziai, "Dreams and Dream Interpretation (ii. in the Persian Tradition)," in *EIr*, 7:549–51; and P. Lory, *La rêve et ses interprétations en Islam* (Paris: Albin Michel, 2003).

4. Lamoreaux, *The Early Muslim Tradition*, 3–4 and 175–81 (appendix); for which see also Fahd, *La divination arabe*, 330–63.

5. On which in general see Fahd, *La divination arabe*, 303–304; Schimmel, *Die Träume des Kalifen*, 177–228; Lory, *La rêve*, 193–256; and N. Green, "The Religious and Cultural Role of Dreams and Visions in Islam," *Journal of the Royal Asiatic Society*, Series 3, 13.3 (2003), 287–313.

6. Such as the remarkable *Kashf al-asrār* of Rūzbihān Baqlī (d. 606/1209), on which see C. Ernst, *Ruzbihan Baqli: Mysticism and the Rhetoric of Sainthood in Persian Sufism* (Richmond, Surrey: Curzon Press, 1996), index (s.v. dreams, visions); Rūzbihān Baqlī, *The Unveiling of Secrets: Diary of a Sufi Master*, trans. C. Ernst (Chapel Hill, NC: Parvardigar Press, 1997); and, Lory, *La rêve*, 233–40.

7. Namely: al-Ḥakīm al-Tirmidhī, *Badʾ shaʾn al-Ḥakīm al-Tirmidhī*, MS Ankara, İsmail Saib I, 1571, fols. 209b–218a, facsimile in B. Radtke, "Tirmiḏiana Minora," *Oriens* 34 (1994), 268–76, and the annotated translation in idem and J. O'Kane, *The Concept of Sainthood in Early Islamic Mysticism* (Richmond, Surrey: Curzon Press, 1996), 15–36; idem, *Kitāb sīrat al-awliyāʾ*, in *Drei Schriften des Theosophen von Tirmiḏ*, ed. B. Radtke (Beirut and Stuttgart: Franz Steiner, 1992), 1–134 (Arabic text), and the annotated translation in idem and J. O'Kane, *The Concept of Sainthood*, 38–211; al-Junayd al-Baghdādī, [*Rasāʾil*, etc.], in *The Life, Personality and Writings of al-Junayd*, Gibb Memorial Series, n.s., 22, ed. and trans. A.H. Abdel-Kader (London: Luzac and Co., 1962), 122–83 and 1–62 (Arabic text); idem, *Enseignement spirituel: Traités, lettres, oraisons et sentences*, trans. R. Deladrière (Paris: Sindbad, 1983); and, idem et al., *al-Imām al-Junayd sayyid al-ṭāʾifatayn: mashāyikhuh, aqrābuh, talāmidhatuh, aqwāluh, kutubuh wa-rasāʾiluh*, comp. and ed. A.F. al-Mazīdī (Beirut: Dār al-Kutub al-ʿIlmiyya, 2006), 127–360; Anonymous, *Kitāb ādāb al-mulūk fī bayān ḥaqāʾiq al-taṣawwuf*, ed. B. Radtke (Beirut: Orient-Institut der DMG / Franz Steiner Verlag 1991), and idem, *Die Lebensweise der Könige*, trans. R. Gramlich (Stuttgart: DMG / Franz Steiner Verlag, 1993); al-Sarrāj, *Kitāb al-lumaʿ fī l-taṣawwuf*, ed. K.M. al-Hindāwī (Beirut: Dār al-Kutub al-ʿIlmiyya, 2001, and idem, *Schlaglichter über das Sufitum*, Freiburger Islamstudien, no. 13, trans. R. Gramlich (Stuttgart: Franz Steiner Verlag, 1990); al-Kalābādhī, *Kitāb al-taʿarruf li-madhhab ahl al-taṣawwuf*, ed. ʿAbd al-Ḥalīm Maḥmūd (Cairo: Maktabat al-Thaqāfa al-Dīniyya, n.d.), and idem, *The Doctrine of the Ṣūfīs*, trans. A.J. Arberry (Cambridge, U.K.: Cambridge University Press, 1935); Abū Ṭālib al-Makkī, *Qūt al-qulūb*, 2 vols., ed. S. N. Makārim on the basis of the Cairo edition (1306 [1886]) (Beirut: Dār Ṣādir, 1995), and idem, *Die Nahrung der Herzen: Abū Ṭālib al-Makkīs Qūt al-qulūb*, 4 vols., Freiburger Islamstudien, no. 16, pts. 1–4, trans. R. Gramlich (Wiesbaden: Franz Steiner Verlag, 1995); and, pseudo-Makkī, *ʿIlm al-qulūb*, ed. ʿAbd al-Qādir ʿAṭā (1384 [1964]; reprint, Beirut: Dār al-Kutub al-ʿIlmiyya, 2004); al-Mālīnī, *Kitāb al-arbaʿīn fī shuyūkh al-ṣūfiyya*, ed. ʿĀ. Ḥ. Ṣabrī (Beirut: Dār al-Bashāʾir al-Islāmiyya, 1997); al-Sulamī, *Ṭabaqāt al-ṣūfiyya*, ed. ʿAbd al-Qādir ʿAṭā (Beirut: Dār al-Kutub al-ʿIlmiyya, 1998); Muḥammad b. Munawwar, *Asrār al-tawḥīd fī maqāmāt al-shaykh Abī Saʿīd*, 2 vols., ed. M-R. Shafīʿī-Kadkanī (Tehran: Āgāh, 1366 [1987–88]); Hujwīrī, *Kashf al-maḥjūb*, ed. V. A. Zhukovsky (1926; reprint, Tehran: n.p. 1380 [2001–2]), and idem, *The Kashf al-Maḥjúb: The Oldest Persian Treatise on Sufism*, Gibb Memorial Series, 17, abridged translation by R.A. Nicholson (London: Luzac and Co., 1911); al-Qushayrī, *al-Risāla al-qushayriyya*, 2 vols., ed. ʿAbd al-Ḥalīm Maḥmūd and M. b. al-Sharīf (Cairo: Dār al-Kutub al-Ḥadītha, 1966), and idem, *Al-Qushayri's Epistle on Sufism*, trans. A. Knysh (Reading, UK: Garnet Publishing, 2007); ʿAbd Allāh-i Anṣārī, *Ṭabaqāt al-ṣūfiyya*, ed. M.S. Mawlāʾī (Tehran: Intishārāt-i Ṭūs, 1362 [1983–84]); ʿAyn al-Quḍāt al-Hamadānī, *Tamhīdāt*, ed. ʿA. ʿUsayrān (1962; reprint, Tehran: Intishārāt-i Manūchihrī, 1377 [1998–99]); Ibn Khamīs, *Manāqib al-abrār wa-maḥāsin al-akhyār*, 2 vols., ed. S. ʿAbd al-Fattāḥ (Beirut: Dār al-Kutub al-ʿIlmiyya, 2006); al-ʿAbbādī, *al-Taṣfiya fī aḥwāl al-mutaṣawwifa (Ṣūfī-nāma)*, ed. Gh-Ḥ. Yūsufī (Tehran: Intishārāt-i Bunyād-i Farhang-i Īrān, 1347 [1968–69]);

ʿAṭṭār, *Tadhkirat al-awliyāʾ*, ed. M. Istiʿlāmī (Tehran: Intishārāt-i Zavvār, 1377 [1998–99]); Abū Ḥafṣ ʿUmar al-Suhrawardī, *ʿAwārif al-maʿārif*, 2 vols, ed. ʿAbd al-Ḥalīm Maḥmūd and M. b. al-Sharīf (Cairo: Maṭbaʿat al-Saʿāda and Dār al-Kutub al-Ḥadītha, 1971 [vol. 1], and Cairo: Dār al-Maʿārif, 2000 [vol. 2]), and idem, *Die Gaben der Erkenntnisse des ʿUmar as-Suhrawardī*, Freiburger Islamstudien, no. 6, trans. R. Gramlich (Wiesbaden: Franz Steiner Verlag, 1978); idem, *Kitāb aʿlām al-hudā wa-ʿaqīdat arbāb al-tuqā*, ed. ʿAbd al-ʿAzīz al-Sayrawān (Damascus: Dār al-Anwār, 1996); Najm al-Dīn Rāzī Dāya, *Mirṣād al-ʿibād*, ed. M.A. Riyāḥī (Tehran: Shirkat-i Intishārāt-i ʿIlmī va Farhangī, 1352 [1973–74]), and idem, *The Path of God's Bondsmen: From Origin to Return*, Persian Heritage Series, no. 25, trans. H. Algar (Delmar, NY: Caravan Books, 1982); and, ʿIzz al-Dīn Kāshānī, *Miṣbāḥ al-hidāya wa-miftāḥ al-kifāya*, ed. ʿI. Karbāsī and M-R. B. Khāliqī (Tehran: Intishārāt-i Zavvār, 1382 [2003–4]).

8. For which see the references furnished in Ṣ. Gawharīn, *Sharḥ-i iṣṭilāḥāt-i taṣawwuf* (Tehran: Intishārāt-i Zavvār, 1367 [1988–]), 2:27–35 (s.v. *ilhām*) and 10:103–17 (s.v. *nawm*). An approachable overview of the scope and attendant terminology associated with visionary experience in Sufism in general can be found in M. Hermansen, "Visions as 'Good to Think': A Cognitive Approach to Visionary Experience in Islamic Sufi Thought," *Religion* 27 (1997): 25–30. On the differences between dreams and visions in this sense, see further Schimmel, *Die Träume des Kalifen*, 37–38.

9. A.J. Wensinck, *Concordance et indicies de la tradition musulmane* (Leiden: E.J. Brill, 1936–88), 1:504; al-Qushayrī, *Risāla*, 2:714 / Knysh (trans.), *Al-Qushayrī's Epistle*, 392–93; on which see further Ibn Khaldūn, *The Muqaddimah: An Introduction to History*, trans. F. Rosenthal (New York: Pantheon Books, 1958), 3:103–105; al-Tahānawī, *Kashshāf iṣṭilāḥāt al-funūn*, ed. L. ʿAbd al-Badīʿ and trans. ʿAbd al-Naʿīm Muḥammad Ḥasanayn (Cairo: al-Hayʾa al-Miṣriyya al-ʿĀmma li-l-Kitāb, 1963–77), 2:89–99 (s.v. *al-ruʾyā*); Fahd, *La divination arabe*, 270–73; idem, "Ruʾya," 645; Kinberg, "Literal Dreams," 289–92; Katz, *Dreams, Sufism and Sainthood*, 208–209; and Lory, *La rêve*, 18–20 and 59–63.

10. Katz, *Dreams, Sufism and Sainthood*, 209; Lamoreaux, *The Early Muslim Tradition of Dream Interpretation*, 47–51 and index (s.v. Artemidorus); and Lory, *La rêve*, 111–18; on which see further: *Artemidorus, The Interpretation of Dreams: Oneirocritica by Artemidorus*, 2nd edn., trans. R.J. White (Torrance, Calif.: Original Books, 1990), and the critical edition of the Arabic recension (originally produced by the famous Bayt al-Ḥikma translator Ḥunayn b. Isḥāq [d. 260/873]) of the text prepared by T. Fahd (*Artémidore d'Éphèse: Le Livre des Songes traduit du Grec en Arabe par Ḥunayn b. Isḥāq* [Damascus: Institut français de Damas, 1964]); and brief discussion in idem, "The Dream in Medieval Islamic Society," in *The Dream and Human Societies*, 359. On Artemidorus as oneirocritic a readily accessible overview can be found in C. Walde, "Dream Interpretation in a Prosperous Age? Artemidorus, the Greek Interpreter of Dreams," in *Dream Cultures*, 121–42.

11. On which see further J. Renard, *Friends of God: Islamic Images of Piety, Commitment, and Servanthood* (Berkeley: University of California Press, 2008), 68–77 and 275–77; and, Lory, *La rêve*, 211–25 (which adduces a general list of

themes and motifs from the biographical portion of the *Risāla* of al-Qushayrī and the *Rawḍ al-rayāḥīn fī ḥikāyāt al-ṣāliḥīn* of the eighth/fourteenth-century Yemeni Sufi scholar al-Yāfiʿī). On the wider issue of the appearance of the Prophet in dreams see Kinberg, "Literal Dreams," 285–88.

12. Hujwīrī, *Kashf*, 161–62 / Nicholson (trans.), *Kashf*, 128–29; cf. Ibn Khamīs, *Manāqib al-abrār*, 1:319; ʿAṭṭār, *Tadhkira*, 422; and, Jāmī, *Nafaḥāt al-uns*, ed. M. ʿĀbidī (Tehran: Intishārāt-i Iṭilāʿāt, 1370 [1991–92]), 80; and, further a rhetorically similar anecdote related by ʿAbd Allāh-i Anṣārī at the beginning of the entry on Junayd in his *Ṭabaqāt al-ṣūfiyya*: He answered: "Someone saw the Prophet in a dream making haste, and he said: 'O Messenger of God, where are you going in this manner?' He answered: 'I am hastening to the Caliph's funeral.' The next day that man was in Baghdad and he inquired about the Caliph. He was told that he was fine. Later he heard that Junayd had died. The Prophet had been talking about him, 'the Caliph' " (196). Much the same appears in the anecdotes concerning Junayd's dreams collected by A.F. al-Mazīdī as *Bāb fī tafsīr alfāẓ tadūr bayn al-ṭāʾifa min al-kalām sayyid al-ṭāʾifa* in op. cit., *al-Imām al-Junayd*, 291–95.

13. On which see P. Lory, "La Vision de Dieu dans l'Onirocritique Musulmane Médiévale," in *Reason and Inspiration in Islam: Theology, Philosophy and Mysticism in Muslim Thought. Essays in Honour of Hermann Landolt*, ed. T. Lawson (London: I.B. Tauris Publishers in association with The Institute of Ismaili Studies, 2005), 360–61; and idem, *La rêve*, 196–203.

14. Kinberg, "The Legitimization of the *Madhāhib*," 47–79; a strategy which the author also finds playing out among the *muḥaddithūn* concerning establishing the veracity, or lack thereof, of *ḥadīth* transmitters (idem, "Dreams as a Means to Evaluate Ḥadīth," 79–99). On dreams in general as legitimating tools in Muslim scholastic contexts, see idem, "Literal Dreams," 292–99.

15. On which in general see further J.I. Smith, "Concourse between the Living and the Dead in Islamic Eschatological Literature," *History of Religions* 19 (1979): 224–36; Kinberg, *Morality in the Guise of Dreams*, 18–20; idem, "Literal Dreams," 288–89; and Lory, *La rêve*, 77–92; and further al-Ghazālī, *Iḥyāʾ ʿulūm al-dīn* (Beirut: Dār al-Kutub al-ʿIlmiyya, 1996), 4:536–43 (fourth quarter, bk. 10, ch. 8).

16. Such as the Khalwatiyya, where the regular giving of dream/vision-reports and their interpretation is central (on which see the description of al-Sanūsī in *Salsabīl al-muʿīn fī 'l-ṭarāʾiq al-arbaʿīn*, in *Majmūʿa al-mukhtāra min muʾallafāt . . . Muḥammad b. ʿAlī al-Sanūsī* [Manchester: n.p., 1990], 63–68, on which see further Katz, *Dreams, Sufism and Sainthood*, 214–15, and also Schimmel, *Die Träume des Kalifen*, 178).

17. Rāzī, *Mirṣād*, 289–98 / Algar (trans.), *The Path of God's Bondsmen*, 286–93.

18. Fahd, *La divination arabe*, 363–65; and idem, "Istikhāra," in *EI*², 4:259; Schimmel, *Die Träume des Kalifen*, 40–41; and, al-Tahānawī, *Kashshāf*, 4:284–85 (s.v. *ṣalāt al-istikhāra*); cf. Ibn Khaldūn, *Muqaddimah*, 3:213.

19. Al-Makkī, *Qūt al-qulūb*, 2:396 (s.v. *faṣl* 42) / Gramlich (trans.), *Die Nahrung*, 3:431–32 (sec. 42.2).

20. Al-Suhrawardī, *ʿAwārif*, 1:294–5 / Gramlich (trans.), *Die Gaben*, 16.25.

21. Ibid. 1:342–344 / 21.9–13; cf. idem, *Ajwibat ʿan masāʾil baʿḍ aʾimmat Khurāsān*, ed. A.Ṭ. ʿIrāqī as "Pāsukhhāʾi Shihāb al-Dīn ʿUmar-i Suhravardī," *Maqālāt u Barrasīhā* 49–50 (1369 / 1991): 59 (no. 8).

22. Al-Qushayrī, *Risāla*, 2:718 / Knysh (trans.), *Al-Qushayrī's Epistle*, 395; and similarly Kalābādhī, *Kitāb al-taʿarruf*, 103–55 (*bāb* 70) / Arberry (trans.), *The Doctrine*, 157–59; discussed further in Fahd, *La divination arabe*, 304–6; and Lory, *La rêve*, 212–13.

23. On which see further Fahd, *La divination arabe*, 255–89; idem, "Ruʾyā," 645; Kinberg, "Literal Dreams," 283–84; and, Lory, *La rêve*, 20–38. The subject itself is also well reflected in the major *ḥadīth* collections, on which see: M. Hermansen, "Dreams and Dreaming in Islam," in *Dreams*, 74–76; Kinberg, *Morality in the Guise of Dreams*, 35–36; and Lory, op. cit., 39–49.

24. Al-Bayḍāwī, *Anwār al-tanzīl wa-asrār al-taʾwīl*, s.v. Qurʾān 22:52, quoted in U. Rubin, "Prophets and Prophethood," in *Encyclopaedia of the Qurʾān*, ed. J.D. McAuliffe (Leiden: Brill, 2004), 4:289; and further T. Fahd, "Les Songes et leur interprétation selon l'Islam," in *Sources orientales*, vol. 2, *Les Songes et leur interprétation*, ed. A.-M. Esnoul et al. (Paris: Éditions du Seuil, 1959), 137; and Lory, *La rêve*, 55–77.

25. Wensinck, *Concordance*, 1:343, 2:205; and for the range of possible interpretations: al-Tahānawī, *Kashshāf*, 2:95–7; see also Ibn Khaldūn, *Muqaddimah*, 3:209; and further Fahd, *La divination arabe*, 267; Katz, *Dreams, Sufism and Sainthood*, 208, n. 6; and, S. Sviri, "Dreaming Analyzed and Recorded: Dreams in the World of Medieval Islam," in *Dream Cultures*, 252 (and further refs. at 286, n.1).

26. *Miṣbāḥ al-hidāya*, 46, which is, in turn, modeled on the same discussion in ʿUmar al-Suhrawardī's own ten-chapter creed, which Kāshānī used in preparing the initial section of his handbook, viz.: "I believe that the veridical dream-vision (*al-ruʾyā al-ṣāliḥa*) is 1/46th a part of prophethood, and God's intimates (*awliyāʾ*) and the righteous from among the believers have glimmerings (*lawāʾiḥ*) and flashes (*lawāmiʿ*) revealed to them in their dreams which come from the World of Dominion (*malakūt*). If you consider the affair of dreaming to be a strange thing, then know that it is among the manifest signs of God's splendid power. That which will not come into being for a year or a month may well be revealed in a dream. The nonexistent thing that will manifest later is disclosed to you by God before He produces it in order to demonstrate that He is your Creator and your God; He is the knower of unseen things. You know the story of Abraham—God's blessings be upon him—in which God said to His prophet: "Remember in your dream that God showed them to you as few; if He had shown them to you as many you would surely have been discouraged and would surely have disputed" [Qurʾān 8:43]. So you would do well to follow and attain the perfection of guidance" (*Kitāb aʿlām al-hudā*, 82). On this idea, see further al-Tirmidhī, *Nawādir al-uṣūl fī maʿrifat aḥādīth al-rasūl* (Istanbul, 1294 [1877]), 118, quoted in Radtke and O'Kane, *The Concept of Sainthood*, 236; idem, *Kitāb sīrat al-awliyāʾ*, 66–67 / Radtke and O'Kane (trans.), op cit., 136–37; al-Hamadānī, *Tamhīdāt*, 45–6 (no. 63); and,

Rāzī, *Mirṣād*, 290–92 / Algar (trans.), *The Path of God's Bondsmen*, 287–89. On Kāshānī's discussion see further Katz, *Dreams, Sufism and Sainthood*, 213–14.

27. Lamoreaux, *The Early Muslim Tradition*, 79–105.

28. A point explicated in great detail, although not without significant historical conjecture, by Henri Corbin in relation to a distinctive prophetic gnoseology he saw as diffuse across various Islamic esotericisms (Imāmī, Ismāʿīlī, Sufic, and Illuminationst) in which visionary dreams and attendant phenomena figure prominently as modes of accessing, in the mundus imaginalis (*ʿālam al-mithāl*), a persisting and unified hierognosis which is at once prophetic and mystico-noetic. For a synopsis, see: H. Corbin, "Visionary Dream in Islamic Spirituality," in *The Dream and Human Societies*, 381–408. A recent application of this model, here to the case of Ibn ʿArabī, can be found in Lory, *La rêve*, 240–50.

29. The work of Leah Kinberg on the potential of premodern Muslim dream-narrative literature for the writing of the social and intellectual history of the *ʿulamāʾ* during particularly important periods of definition and coalescence, such as the consolidation of the Sunni juridical rites in the third/ninth century, is telling in this regard. The collections of examples adduced by G.E. von Grunebaum in idem, "The Cultural Function of the Dream as Illustrated by Classical Islam," in *The Dream and Human Societies*, 11–20, and, similarly Schimmel, *Die Träume des Kalifen*, 270–96, are instructive as well. A well-reasoned example of the potential of dream narratives to understanding the internal workings of the medieval Arabic biographical notice, as exemplified in an eighth/fourteenth-century biographical dictionary of the blind, is discussed by F. Malti-Douglas in "Dreams, the Blind and the Semiotics of the Biographical Notice," *Studia Islamica* 51 (1980): 137–62.

30. Al-Qushayrī, *Risāla*, 2:717 / Knysh (trans.), *Al-Qushayri's Epistle*, 395; Ibn Khamīs, *Manāqib al-abrār*, 1:399; and, Anṣārī, *Ṭabaqāt*, 237 where the first hemistich is given as: *raʾaytuk[a] fī-l-manām[i] surūr[a] ʿaynī* (as in Jāmī, *Nafaḥāt*, 85); on the significance of which see the brief comments in Fahd, *La divination arabe*, 306, and, F. Meier, "Inspiration by Demons in Islam," in *The Dream and Human Societies*, 422.

CHAPTER 11

Witnessing the Lights of the Heavenly Dominion

Dreams, Visions and the Mystical Exegeses of Shams al-Dīn al-Daylamī

Elizabeth R. Alexandrin

How does a human being "bound to the prison of body, come to know the divine"?[1] In *Dreaming in the Middle Ages*, Kruger examines the development of medieval Christian dream literature and in particular, the emergence of manuals on dream interpretation. He notes that the philosophical concerns of medieval Christian authors reinforced their theological attempts to grapple with the veracity of dreams and visions. By the late medieval period, dream interpretation manuals grew in popularity and began to be written in a multitude of vernacular languages. Medieval Christian society's widespread fascination with narrating, recording, and interpreting dreams led to the production of new literary works and texts, suggesting a notable shift in the social significance of visionary experiences and dreams for individuals and communities.[2]

In terms of different audiences, dreams and visionary experiences held an appeal for scholars interested in philosophical debate as well as Schutz's "man on the street," where individuals from all walks of life began to pose questions in order to decipher the meaning of these experiences. In simple terms, could it be that an individual's dream is merely the end result of something like having eaten a large meal too late at night, and therefore, it could not possibly have any divine origin? Perhaps a person's dream is inspired by the demonic and lacks veracity. Or is it only after much religious practice, in which the individual soul is then purified of its more base elements, that an individual may receive authentic dream visions or an exalted vision of God? In fact, many medieval Christian and Muslim authors of dream manuals grappled with these issues, raising other finely drafted points of debate in the meanwhile: Is the mystical vision an internal process within the individual, for example, or is it a grace received by the individual from without, directly from the divine?

Many of Kruger's theories on the growing popularity of dream manuals are persuasive enough to suggest their usefulness for exploring further the medieval Islamic literature concerned with dreams and visionary experiences in the context of twelfth-century Sufi traditions. This chapter uses select passages from two of Shams al-Dīn al-Daylamī's (twelfth-century CE) unedited works, the Qurʾān commentary, *Futūḥ al-Raḥmān fī Ishārāt al-Qurʾān* ("The Revelations of Divine Mercy in the Allusions of the Qurʾān"), also known as *Taṣdīq al-Maʿārif* ("The Confirmation of Wisdoms"), and the short treatise on mystical visions of time and space, *Mirʾāt al-Arwāḥ wa Ṣūrat al-Wijāh* ("The Mirror of Spirits and the Form of Meeting Face to Face"), to begin to chart his changing hermeneutical approach to the interpretation of dreams, visions, and individual mystical experience.[3] As he negotiates among theological, philosophical and mystical perspectives, al-Daylamī grapples with the veracity and hierarchy of dreams and visions and their implications for the individual's knowledge of God and the divine. His technical lexicon also reveals some of the implicit tensions within the Islamic tradition regarding the relationship between mystical inspiration and prophetic revelation, while it holds in common with the Islamic sciences specific criteria for gauging the content of dreams and the significance of individual visionary experiences. He conceives of a visionary world of the individual that is delineated along parallel lines with the spiritual world, in that the "twins of the inner world of man and the upper world of the unseen provide a mirror for the bipolarity of divine nature, eternal time and space, and intuitive knowledge and direct vision of the Eternal."[4] As this study elucidates, both the symbolic content and significance of al-Daylamī's visionary experiences are read against the text of the Qurʾān.

This chapter explores some of the premises al-Daylamī maintains concerning the narration of visionary experience, as well as how he constructs a model for the individual acquisition of the deep and esoteric meanings of the Qurʾān through key experiences of the divine. After illustrating how the Qurʾān serves as the primary touchstone in the narration of dreams and visionary experiences in the context of al-Daylamī's Sufi teachings, this chapter suggests further avenues of exploration potentially available for examining al-Daylamī's concept of selfhood and the narration of visionary experiences in the broader context of methodological approaches from Religious Studies and Anthropology.

Shams al-Dīn al-Daylamī's Sufi Teachings

The *Mirʾāt al-Arwāḥ* demonstrates the effort to present in written form the dream-world synthesis. It constitutes a relatively early example of a Sufi treatise concerned with the veracity and hierarchy of dreams, visions, and mystical experiences. The manuscript traditions of al-Daylamī's short treatises also reflect a medieval twelfth-century scholar at work, between the different intellectual trends of his day, Sufism (*taṣawwuf*), dialectical theology (*kalām*), and Islamic philosophy (*falsafa*).

Shams al-Dīn al-Daylamī, however, is difficult to situate as an author because of the veritable dearth of biographical information. What little evidence that can be culled from the sources stems from narrative accounts of al-Daylamī's mentorship of Maḥmūd al-Dīn al-Ushnuhī, whose life is discussed by the authors of hagiographical works, such as ʿAbd al-Raḥmān al-Jāmī, among others, concerned with reconstructing the "pre-origins" of the Kubrawī, Naqshbandī, and Kāzerūnī Sufi orders.[5] The works of the Sufi author, Abū 'l-Ḥasan ʿAlī b. Muḥammad al-Daylamī (tenth century), however, constitutes a compelling precedent with respect to intertwining philosophical approaches and mystical doctrines.[6] As R. Walzer and J. C. Vadet first noted, Abū 'l-Ḥasan al-Daylamī incorporated textual citations of pseudo-Aristotle and pseudo-Empedocles into his treatise on mystical love, *Kitāb ʿAṭf al-Alif al-Maʾlūf ʿalā al-Lām* ("The Book of the Inclination of the Letter 'A' for the Unification with the Letter 'L'").[7] The *Kitāb ʿAṭf al-Alif* also serves as an important source for corroborating the Sufi works of Sahl al-Tustarī (d. 896 CE).[8] A brief comparison between the works of the two al-Daylamīs shows an interest in the works of the classical Sufis as well as in taking up certain philosophical and theological questions.[9] It is possible to speculate that Shams al-Dīn al-Daylamī was well-versed in the works of "classical" Sufism because of his citations from such authors as Ibn ʿAṭāʾ, Sahl al-Tustarī, al-Ḥallāj and Junayd. Even if the roughest outlines of his biography are difficult to determine, al-Daylamī's knowledge of the Hebrew

Bible is likewise indicated in his works, such as *Jawāhir al-Asrār* ("The Essences of Secrets"), *Muhimmāt al-Wāṣilīn* ("The Goals of Those Who Have Attained Unity"), and the *Taṣdīq*.[10] The intellectual background of his works, with its synthesis of Islamic mysticism, theology, and philosophy, suggests the diversity of Sufism as an intellectual movement in different parts of the twelfth-century Islamic world.

Concerning al-Daylamī's gradual rapprochement with Sufism, Böwering suggested that the collective manuscript of al-Daylamī's works (MS. Şehit Ali Paşa 1346) contains many internal references to his known short treatises and may therefore represent the revision of the entire corpus of his work towards the end of his scholarly career. Apparently around 589 AH/1193 CE, al-Daylamī undertook some revisions of his short treatises. Al-Daylamī chose to change the title of one of his works, as the result of divine inspiration, from *Kashf al-Ḥaqāʾiq* ("The Unveiling of Realities"), to *Jawāhir al-Asrār*.[11] Other details point to the possible revision or final redaction of al-Daylamī's corpus of works as an indication of his intellectual shift away from philosophy and toward Sufism. For example, in the oldest extant manuscript of his *tafsīr*, al-Daylamī gives it the title *Futūḥ al-Raḥmān*, whereas in both versions of the *Mirʾāt*, it is referred to as the *Taṣdīq al-Maʿārif*. Therefore, the manuscripts of al-Daylamī's corpus may provide more information about significant intellectual shifts in his scholarly career just as his autobiographical statements in his own short treatises speak to his changing intellectual positions on philosophy and Sufism, in particular, the short treatise, *Jawāhir al-Asrār*.[12] Following this line of argumentation, MS. Ismail Saib 4120 of al-Daylamī's short treatises potentially represents an early version of the work, whereas the Şehit Ali Paşa 1346 collective manuscript represents the last version of the work, rewritten toward the end of al-Daylamī's life, at a point when he had thoroughly embraced Sufism. As is discussed here, al-Daylamī's gradual acceptance of Sufism is likewise echoed in the introduction to his commentary on the Qurʾān. The points of correspondence between his *tafsīr* and his short treatises allows for further research into the impact his visionary experiences had on the construction of the dream-world synthesis evident in his works.[13]

It is important to raise one final note on the manuscript traditions of al-Daylamī's scholarly corpus. Taken as a whole, these short treatises speak to another issue that is of considerable importance in terms of understanding better the transition from oral teaching to written text in twelfth-century Sufism. A prime example of this point is how al-Daylamī's *Ghāyat al-Imkān* was recorded and transmitted by his disciple, Maḥmūd al-Dīn al-Ushnuhī.[14] G. Schoeler's contrast between scholars who wrote works with a given form (i.e., as books) and those "who did not put their writings into a fixed form and only transmitted them through lectures" allows us to consider the revision and redaction of al-Daylamī's teachings from multiple perspectives.[15] It also is important to consider how Sufi teachings as well as visionary experiences were recorded or in what instances writing down one's visions and dreams was strictly forbidden. Do al-Daylamī's works, for instance, demonstrate an element of renarration and reconstruction in accordance with culturally conceived expectations of the visionary experience?

Given the complexity of the aforementioned topics, let us now turn to the introduction to *Jawāhir al-Asrār*, which forms a distinctive example of how the mystical experience may impart authorial authority. Al-Daylamī states the following:

> Then I began this book after what I predicted about the future [performed the *faʾl*] with the Qurʾān and I was granted permission from God the Most High, and then came the auspicious omen [*fāl*] and rain fell from the sky, so that through it, the earth came to life after its death. Then I heard a cry of joy in the dark of night of these [words], "O, whoever . . . get up, make a vow, and . . . [obey] your Lord, so strive to become great." So I got up, strove to excel and wrote.[16]

In the course of the history of Sufism, many different attitudes toward writing down and recording mystical experiences prevail. The twelfth-century works of al-Daylamī sketch the parameters of a visionary cosmology for Sufi practitioners. Taken together, his mystical Qurʾān commentary and short treatises chart and re-map the internal schema that individual human being embodies ultimately to explain the visionary and auditory components of dreams, mystical experiences, and prophetic revelation. In the following sections of this chapter, I consider how al-Daylamī reconstructed his visionary experiences as well as aimed to articulate them in culturally expected forms.

The Inner Eye of Vision Gradually Opens

Be it prophetic revelation or mystical visions, the heart (*qalb*) is the locus of experience. Al-Daylamī provides us with a striking image: "[t]he niche of the soul holds the lamp of the spirit, called secret (*sirr*) or inmost being (*khafī*), assisted by the intellect and enshrined in the pure glass of the heart like a glittering star."[17] The prophets and the friends of God (*awliyāʾ Allāh*) may obtain a vision of God (*ruʾyā Allāh*) due to the subtlety of their souls, a vision that is neither through the means of the five senses nor intellect, but through a particular locus of perception and intuition. Because of their pure and peaceful spirits, the heart becomes the inner eye of vision as the "possessors of hearts" (*aṣḥāb al-qulūb*) ascend to the world of spirits (*ʿālam al-arwāḥ*).

Nonetheless, al-Daylamī's discussions of the parameters of individual visionary experience are presented in the format of Islamic theological treatises and include a dialectical component. In the introduction to the *Taṣdīq al-Maʿārif*, al-Daylamī explains that his Qurʾān commentary aims to show that the Sufis, in their discussions of their mystical states, are sound in terms of their doctrines, teachings, and religious practices. Al-Daylamī also divulges that over time, he came to the realization that although many people denied the teachings of the Sufis, or conversely, overly exaggerated their mystical stature, many of their treatises discussed mystical states that were similar to mystical experiences and states he had himself experienced. He claims that the experiences of the friends of God were the same as his own mystical states; as he describes it, a series of visionary experiences in which it was possible to witness the lights of the heavenly dominion (*malakūt*) and where ultimately, pre-eternity (*al-azaliyya*) collapsed into or merged with post-eternity (*al-abadiyya*).[18] In the second half of this short treatise, al-Daylamī reflects on the concept of the time of pre-eternity (*zamān al-azal*), stating, "I saw examples of this many times in visions (*al-waqāʾiʿ*), and each of those is inconceivable in the worlds of sense (*ʿawālim al-ḥiss*), [but] possibly exists in the worlds of the spirits (*ʿawālim al-arwāḥ*)."[19]

In fact, the introduction and the first chapter of the *Mirʾāt al-Arwāḥ* represent al-Daylamī's literary efforts to delineate the visionary cosmology presented in his mystical experiences. The *Taṣdīq al-Maʿārif* likewise provides a framework for his experiences that is based in a mystical reading of the Qurʾān, as is seen later. Throughout the *Mirʾāt al-Arwāḥ*, it is possible to see how al-Daylamī records his experiences autobiographically and employs them as a way of narrating and explicating the themes and concepts contained in this short treatise. One particular experience seems to hold deeper significance for al-Daylamī because of its connection to a set of verses from the Qurʾān (36:1–4), the Qurʾānic verses that perhaps were the original touchstone of several of his visionary experiences. This passage appears in the section concerning space (*makān*): "Know that when I intended to write this section, Satan threw me into doubt." Our author then goes on to explain how he dispelled his doubt by turning to the Qurʾān and receiving guidance from the words he read as he opened it, the opening of the *sūra* of *Yā Sīn*.[20]

In order to explain the individual human being's ability to perceive the lights of the heavenly dominion, al-Daylamī turns to the different theological, philosophical and mystical theories on the body-soul nexus, providing discussions of the divisions between the Sufis, the philosophers and the theologians. Al-Daylamī carefully presents and then refutes in turn both the methods of philosophical and dialectical argumentation in order to support his visionary cosmology.

In fact, the *Mirʾāt al-Arwāḥ* builds on other discussions presented in the *ʿUyūn al-Maʿārif* and the *Tasdīq al-Maʿārif,* to explain the different arguments concerning *nafs* and the separation of body and soul after death, pointing out that in some cases, the theologians and philosophers imply something quite different when they refer to soul by the term *nafs*. Al-Daylamī stresses the distinction between *nafs* and *rūḥ*, as well as the component of the individual human being that he terms the spiritual spirit (*al-rūḥ al-rūḥānī*). What is at the root of this confusion is that the words *nafs* and *rūḥ* often are used interchangeably in the Qurʾān itself or by individuals referring to the verses of the Qurʾān in order to explain their definition of soul. Al-Daylamī is most concerned with explaining that, regardless of this confusion, soul is not the same as body with respect to possessing corporeality. Therefore, when he refers to the spiritual spirit (as he explains a few lines further down in the text), it is actually the secret, a subtle center within the human being.

The knowledge of the divine is therefore possible after the individual purifies his or her carnal soul. The carnal soul (*nafs*) and the spirit (*rūḥ*), the (subtle) soul, use the body and its limbs as extensions, in the sense that the body serves as a "tool" (*ālat*) for the soul in its quest for sensual and corporeal desires.[21] Yet from another perspective, the soul is the "agent" of the body in that it governs over its deeds and actions.[22] It has two aspects.[23] Therefore, the divisions within soul: commanding (*al-ammāra*), reproaching (*al-lawwāma*), and peaceful (*al-muṭmaʾinna*), signify the different states and conditions of one soul. Whereas the soul is corporeal in one aspect, the other aspect is subtle, allowing for actions to be performed through the intellect (*ʿaql*), the secret (*sirr*) and the heart (*qalb*), so that the individual travels on the paths of realities (*al-sulūk fī ṭuruq al-ḥaqāʾiq*) and the world of divine majesty and ascends upward in it to the Highest of the Highest [Heavens].

As an additional note on his concept of the human being, many passages from al-Daylamī's works reflect the Adamology of Sahl al-Tustarī. Beautifully depicted in the *Tafsīr* of Sahl al-Tustarī, the individual souls are like atoms of light that witness the primordial, pre-eternal covenant between human beings (the Banū Ādam) and God.[24] Specific passages in the *Mirʾāt* as well as the *Taṣdīq al-Maʿārif* demonstrate his familiarity with Tustarī's theory of mystical vision as a recapturing of the individual mystic's "moment" with God and the pre-eternal covenant.[25]

In the *Mirʾāt al-Arwāḥ*, it becomes clearer why the soul is a "tool" or "organ" of *nafs*. It is so that the individual is capable of ascending to the highest of the high (*ʿaliyyīn*). Within the human being, the agent of change is "the *nafs* because the goal of everything in the creation of Adam and the commandants of the Banū Ādam is to fulfill the *nafs* created from clay (*al-ṭīn*) attaining to the highest of the ranks of the angels," thus revealing the larger significance of God's creation of the human being in His form.[26]

Dreams and Visions

Now turning to al-Daylamī's treatment of dreams and visionary experience, the first section of the *Mirʾāt* deals ostensibly with al-Daylamī's vision, providing a detailed discussion of the diagram included at the beginning of the short treatise. In the introduction, the title of the treatise is explained: "This is the form unveiled to me in the world of reality (*ʿālam al-ḥaqīqa*) several times in my heart (*fuʾādī*) in order to become aware of it. Then I asked for its name and it said, 'the form of encountering face to face (*wijāh*).' Then I came back to over here with it."[27]

Based on his own visionary experiences, he charts how the first part of the soul, namely the breast (*ṣadr*) of the soul, faces toward the gate that opens up to the heart and the secret, to the inmost worlds (*ʿawālim al-khafī*), the power (*qudra*), and the characteristics (*al-ṣifāt*) because God the Most High, created the soul to ascend to the "Highest of Heavens," not to descend to the "Lowest of the Low."[28] In this context, al-Daylamī makes a marked distinction between the vision of God, dream visions and the exalted inner visions of the Divine rather than discussing the specific content of his visionary experiences. He distinguishes between those individuals who may experience visions in their sleep and those who obtain exalted inner visions. Concerning vision and hearing, the possessors of hearts perceive and sense through the inner senses (*al-ḥawāss al-bāṭina*). A point of contrast discussed throughout al-Daylamī's short treatises is how the "common people" (*ʿāmmat al-nās*) may have something akin to a dream vision during sleep by means of the outward senses (*al-ḥawāss al-ẓāhira*), but the visionary experiences of the possessors of hearts differ due to the fact that their centers of perception are inward and hidden in the locus of the heart. Furthermore, an important distinction lies in his choice of terminology, namely, what is implied by seeing and perceiving.[29] Because the possessors of hearts are the servants and "friends of God," they may perceive the lights of the worlds of spirits and the heavenly dominion by the means of the inner senses.[30]

As suggested earlier, the Qurʾānic paradigm is central in the narration of visionary experiences, especially as al-Daylamī offers up his own definitions of inspiration (*waḥy*) and prophethood (*nubuwwa*), which God bestows on His servants as He wishes, in the course of distinguishing between the degrees and ranks of God's friends and servants.[31] For instance, inspiration may be distinguished from unrestricted inspiration (*al-waḥy al-muṭlaq*), in that it is equated to the external or apparent meaning (*ẓāhir*) of Qurʾānic verses and may be bestowed on in general the "servants of God" (*ʿubbād Allāh*). At the same time, al-Daylamī suggests that the "gnostics" (*ʿurafāʾ*) and the possessors of hearts (*aṣḥāb al-qulūb*), possess the ability to attain to the deeper and esoteric (*bāṭin*) interpretation of the Qurʾānic verses. The Sufis are unique in this respect because, as a result of their inner perception, they are "firmly rooted in knowledge" and possess *taʾwīl*.[32] This latter modality of perception is strictly an internal process: The possessors of hearts perceive through their inner modes of perception (*baṣāʾir al-bāṭina*), in such a way that visionary or revelatory experiences take place in the subtle center of the individual's heart.

The narration of visionary experience is grounded in Qurʾānic interpretation. Daylamī makes a cross-reference to his interpretation of the Qurʾānic passages on the creation and formation of the human being in the *Mirʾāt* before turning to *Sūrat al-nūr* (Q 24). Following his commentary on a select number of verses from this Qurʾānic chapter, he states, "I learned this commentary from My Lord in the world of 'light upon light' (*al-ʿālam al-nūr ʿalā al-nūr*) (Q 24:35) . . . it is also what is called the world of bewilderment (*ʿālam al-ḥayra*). He taught me until I retained it. Then I wrote it down over here."[33] After clarifying what God implied by the "Heavens" and the "Earth" (the worlds of *jabarūt* [*ʿawālim al-arwāḥ*, the worlds of spirits] and *malakūt*

[*ʿawālim al-ajsām*, the world of bodies]), he concludes by stating in reference to his interpretation that, "the likeness of His light is as a niche (*mishkāt*)," which refers to the peaceful, pure soul at rest.[34]

Visions of light are associated with specific Qurʾānic verses in the *Mirʾāt*. In the short treatise *Kitāb Muhimmāt*, the vision of the form of God is a "spiritual light (*nūr rūḥānī*) which is itself a veil (*ḥijāb*) and is variable."[35] In two manuscripts of the *Taṣdīq al-Maʿārif*, al-Daylamī's visionary experience is depicted in the form of a diagram and labeled, "this is the form (*shakl*) of the light (*nūr*) of *Yā Sīn*." In one other manuscript, the diagram was not included though a space was made for it.[36] Notably, the oldest extant version of al-Daylamī's *tafsīr*, the *Fūtūḥ*, includes a small diagram in the right margin.[37] As well, later on in the Qurʾān commentary, our author refers back to the reason for the separate lines that appear in the diagram itself.[38] The text explains that from the three verses of *Yā Sīn*, the light appeared from the *Sīn* of *Yā Sīn* and another light from the *Sīn* of the Praiseworthy One (*Subḥān*), who rules over the kingdom (*malakūt*) of everything and to Him they return."[39] He states, "I saw in myself the chapter *Yā Sīn*. Then three lights ascended from the three verses."[40] The visionary experience is woven together with the prophetic *ḥadīth*, "Everything has a heart and the heart of the Qurʾān is *Yā Sīn*," further clarifying with respect to this section of the *Mirʾāt al-Arwāḥ*, that " . . . the form likewise is the lights that I wrote about here, meaning, the heart of *Yā Sīn* is these three verses."[41]

Perhaps more significantly, the recipients of visionary experiences are granted a special status. In the *Kitāb Muhimmāt*, our author explains that he has discussed the vision (*ruʾyā*) in other works, such as his books on Sufism, like the *Taṣdīq al-Maʿārif*.[42] Summing up his position vis-à-vis the "theologians" and the "traditionalists" on whether or not it is possible to obtain a vision of God in this world, or only after death, al-Daylamī points out that only the prophet Muḥammad was able to see God on the "Night of the Ascension" (*laylat al-Miʿrāj*) with his physical eyes (the pupil of the eye, *bi ʿayn al-ḥadqa*). An implicit hierarchy remains in place as to whom is granted divine vision. As for the *ruʾyā Allāh* in one's sleep, the great scholars apparently claim that it is impossible to see God in a dream. In rejoinder, al-Daylamī uses the impossible dream images that do not exist originally as proof positive that the vision of God in one's sleep occurs by other means than the physical eyes. The *ruʾyā Allāh* is possible through the eye of the secret and the light of faith (*nūr al-īmān*) before death, in this world, because God may grant privilege (*faḍl*) to whomsoever of His servants His wishes, like the Sufis. They see through the "eye" (*baṣīra*) of the heart according to the capacity of the light of faith, not with the physical eye (*bi ᶜayn al-raʾs*). According to al-Daylamī, everyone (i.e., the Muᶜtazilīs, the Ashᶜarīs and Ḥanbalīs) denies this except for the Sufis.[43]

In the oldest extant version of his *tafsīr*, al-Daylamī mentions the common friends of God (*al-awliyāʾ al-ᶜāmma*) and compares them with others who are able to attain in actuality to the types of exalted visions on the higher levels.[44] Here it is possible to see how his mystical commentary on the Qurʾān demonstrates his working theory of how the "possessors of hearts" perceive with the eyes of the heart rather than the physical, external eye. As Böwering has indicated, in the *Futūḥ*, al-Daylamī uses the Qurʾān, *ḥadīth* and passages from the Torah to support the idea that certain individuals, such as Adam, the prophets and the friends of God may obtain the "vision of God."[45] In another short treatise, *Ghāyat al-Imkān* ("The Utmost of the Possible"), al-Daylamī explains that the possessors of hearts are illuminated in terms of their inner perception so that they are capable of perceiving the light of Intellect. This interpretation is correlated with the esoteric interpretation of the *ḥadīth* on how God first created the Intellect.[46]

In the *Mirʾāt*, the role of intellect is important in so far as it clarifies how other loci of perception exist within the individual human being. The visionary cosmology detailed in this short treatise corporealizes the macrocosmic and the microcosmic: the invisible world is mirrored in the components of the individual human being, such as body, soul, heart, faith, intellect, spirit and inmost being. Based on this understanding of the human being as a microcosm mirroring the macrocosm, the example of sleep and how intellect does not function during sleep is used as another proof that the faculty of perception responsible for obtaining visions is likewise not located in intellect.[47] When al-Daylamī's hypothetical opponent poses the argument that what the possessors of mystical states (*aṣḥāb al-aḥwāl*) among the Sufis see in their sleep is false imaginings (*khayālāt bāṭila*), al-Daylamī counters by stating that it is only the case if people are sick and there is an illness or defect in one of their five senses. The verification of visionary and mystical experiences also receives further commentary and elucidation: in terms of mystical states (*aḥwāl*), Satan and the *jinn* may endanger the mystic. For this reason, madness may have either an angelic or demonic point of origin. The Sufi masters can cure the madness of these individuals, rather than physicians.[48] The ability for truthful interpretations (*taᶜbīrāt ṣādiqa*) increases as the individual's capacity for witnessing likewise strengthens.[49] Therefore, the witnessing (*mushāhada*) and vision (*ruʾyā*) he refers to are sound (*ṣaḥīḥ*) in terms of what is set forth in the Qurʾān and the *ḥadīth*. Al-Daylamī then reminds the reader that truthful interpretations are not to be confused with interpretation based on imaginings (*taʿbīr li 'l-khayālāt*).

In the text, another response follows to a question regarding whether or not what someone sees in a dream is similar to what a Sufi sees in a mystical state (*ḥāl*). For some, the example that in dreams it is possible to see a person or animal increase or decrease in size or change into something else is proof that this perception takes place through the faculty of imagination. Al-Daylamī argues that if the individual sees in a dream a spiritual individual (*shakhṣ rūḥānī*), like an angel (*malak*), it is not the result of imagination. The fact that the forms change as one of the distinctions of spiritual spirits (*khāṣṣiyyat al-arwāḥ al-rūḥāniyya*) is supported by the prophetic *ḥadīth* that explains how Gabriel sometimes would appear to Muḥammad in the form of the young man Diḥya Kalbī, and then at other times, in another form.[50]

The visionary cosmology outlined in al-Daylamī's works, as suggested in the transmission of some of his teachings on subtle time and space through al-Ushnuhī, is unique in terms of its multidimensional perspective on mystical experience. In his discussion of the vision in the mirror, al-Daylamī refers to theories of optics in order to explain how it is possible to see reflected in the mirror the varying degrees of subtlety, the light of intellect, the secret, and the heavenly lights. Additionally, just as the mirror serves as a tool (*ālat*), akin to the veil of the tree on Mount Sinai for God's speech to Moses, God may talk to some of His servants by allusion (*ishāra*) in the inmost faculty of perception.[51] In summary, al-Daylamī's elaboration of a visionary cosmology grounded in his individual mystical experiences marks an important contribution to the medieval Sufi tradition.

Al-Daylamī's scholarly corpus in general, and his Qurʾān commentary in particular, alludes to the importance of a specific selection of Qurʾānic verses for the mystics to contemplate and verify mystical experiences against the "touchstone of the Qurʾan." Al-Daylamī thus establishes a Qurʾānic framework for understanding two components of the mystical experience: the visionary and the auditory. Finally, al-Daylamī leaves us with an intriguing statement in the *Mirʾāt* concerning the focus of one of his other short treatises. In the *Kitāb al-Maʿārij*, he addresses the mystical experience and the eschatological realization of the Afterlife in this world as well as the visionary experiences of the subtle soul in the spiritual worlds.[52] Therefore, it may be possible to pinpoint more precisely al-Daylamī's theory of the subtle dream body after additional work on his short treatises in conjunction with his Qurʾān commentary.

Methodological Reflections

Having discussed various aspects of al-Daylamī's Sufi teachings on dreams, visionary experiences, and mystical interpretations of the Qur᾽ān, let us shift our focus to some methodological reflections as a way of bringing this study to a close. Different methodological approaches from the discipline of Religious Studies offer conflicting definitions as to what constitutes "Islamic mysticism" and "mystical experience." The topic of mysticism itself has had a long and varied history in Religious Studies. Early scholars examine mystical experience as psychological phenomena, such as S. Freud, W. James, and R. Otto, or as socially constructed, in the case of E. Durkheim. In some respects, scholars in the field of Religious Studies underscored how there was a "psychological-medical" basis to individual mystical experience. This conceptualization of both mystical and ecstatic religious experiences allowed for scholars such as M. Eliade to advance the idea that there was a universal basis to individual mystical experience. Therefore, Western medical models provided strong reasoning that different mystical traditions could be studied in a comparative context.

The growing impact of the disciplines of Anthropology and Linguistics on Religious Studies in the 1970s and 1980s generated new perspectives on the study of mysticism. Questioning the comparative models in place for the study of non-Western mystical traditions has underscored how cultural values, social expectations, and religious symbolism shape, inform, and articulate individual mystical experience, as is evident in the works of I. Lewis and G. Obeyesekere.

As we have seen, Shams al-Dīn al-Daylamī's works offer numerous interpretative stances on dreams and visionary experiences. It may be suggested here that he frames and narrates his visionary experiences by the means of employing well-known Qur᾽ānic symbols, alluding to the conventions of mystical practices, and drawing on established methods of the esoteric interpretation of the Qur᾽ān.[53] A substantial core of his visionary experience, to which al-Daylamī might have returned for further consideration and contemplation throughout the course of his life and scholarly career, is charted onto a multidimensional depiction of time and space as well as grounded in a mystical reading of the Qur᾽ān. In particular, in the *Mir᾽āt*, the inner world of the mystic and the parallel cosmology of the spiritual world are reflected in diagram form, using, it may be suggested, a religio-cultural template for restructuring mystical experience in the light of Qur᾽anic symbolism. This charting of the individual's inner world reflects the embodiment of the visionary experiences. At the very least, one may postulate that it demarcates the specific loci of mystical apprehension and perception, the subtle centers within the individual human being.

As a final point of reflection, the works of G. Obeyesekere and S. Kugle may help us to reconsider the corporeality of mystics as a key component of their visionary experiences and to gauge in future research to what extent Shams al-Dīn al-Daylamī draws on an already established tradition of narrating visionary experiences and dreams, which commenced with the renowned Central Asian mystic, al-Ḥakīm-i Tirmidhī, as recorded in the autobiographical *Badʾ Shaʾn*,[54] and as is likewise evident in the later works of Rūzbihān-i Baqlī, such as *Kashf al-Asrār*.[55]

Notes

1. S. Kruger, *Dreaming in the Middle Ages* (Cambridge: University of Cambridge Press, 1992), 36; *Dreaming across Boundaries*, Ed. Louise Marlow (Cambridge, Mass.: Harvard University Press, 2008), 1–9.

2. Ibid.

3. Manuscripts of his short treatises are in Istanbul, Ankara, Gotha, Dublin, and Cairo. For additional information, see footnote 11.

4. G. Böwering, "Ideas of Time in Persian Sufism," in L. Lewisohn (ed.), *Classical Persian Sufism* (London: Khaniqahi Nimatullahi Publications, 1993), 227.

5. It is most likely through the vehicle of al-Daylamī's *Jawāhir al-Asrār* that al-Daylamī's discussions of time and space were transmitted to a number of authors of the Sufi traditions in Azerbaijan and Central Asia, in particular, Maḥmūd al-Dīn al-Ushnuhī (or variant spelling Ushnuwī or Ushnuyā) (twelfth century) and Sayf al-Dīn al-Bākharzī (thirteeneth century). Arberry makes note of the fact that al-Ushnuhī is considered to be the student of Shams al-Dīn al-Daylamī, based on the account in ʿAbd al-Raḥmān al-Jāmī's *Nafaḥāt al-Uns* (A. J. Arberry, "The Works of Shams al-Dīn al-Dailamī," *Bulletin of the School of Oriental and African Studies*, 1966; 49–56). H. Landolt, "Sakralraum und mystischer Raum," *Eranos Jahrbuch* (1975), 44: 262, n. 40, has indicated that al-Ushnuhī's work was known to the Central Asian Sufi, ʿAzīz-i Dīn Nasafī (thirteenth century). Al-Ushnuhī's work entitled *Ghāyat al-Imkān fī Dirāyat al-Makān*, is sometimes mistakenly attributed to ʿAyn al-Quḍāt al-Hamadānī, as *Risālat al-Amkina wa al-Azmina*. See H. Dabashi, *Truth and Narrative* (Richmond, Surrey: Curzon, 1999), 72, on this point, that the *Ghāyat al-Imkān* is one of the works whose authenticity, as part of ʿAyn al-Quḍāt's corpus, has been called into question. The *Ghāyat al-Imkān* was first edited by R. Farmanish, *Aḥwāl o Āthār-i ʿAyn al-Quḍāt* (Tehran: Chapkhānah-Āftāb, 1339/1960) and then by N. M. Harawī, *Majmūʿah-yi athār-i Farsī-yi Tāj*

al-Dīn-i Ushnuwī (Tehran: Ṭahūrī, 1368/1989): 9–10; 47–82; Böwering, "Ideas of Time in Persian Sufism," 227–28; H. Landolt, "Sakralraum und Mystischer Raum," 261–62; idem (ed. & trans.), *Le Révélateur des mystères* (LaGrasse: Verdier, 1986), 210, n. 147.

6. Gerhard Böwering, "Deylamī, Abū 'l-Ḥasan ʿAlī b. Moḥammad," *Encyclopaedia Iranica*. Volume VII, 338–39; F. Soberioj, *Ibn Ḫafīf Aš-Šīrāzī* (Beirut: Franz Steiner Verlag, 1998).

7. Böwering, "Deylamī," 338–39; D. DeSmet, *Empedocles Arabus* (Belgium: Verhandelingen van de Koninklijke Academie voor Wetenschappen, Letteren en Schone Kunsten van België, 1998), 31–32, 122, 125, and 128; H. Ritter, "Philologika VII: Arabische und persische Schriften über die profane und die mystische Liebe," *Der Islam* (1933), 21, and 91–92; Soberioj, *Ibn Ḫafīf*; J. C. Vadet, *Kitāb ʿAṭf al-alif al-maʾlūf ʿalā l-lām al-maʿṭūf* (Cairo: Maṭbaʿāt al-Maʿhad al-ʿIlmī al-Faransī li 'l-Āthār al-Sharqiyya, 1962) Introduction; R. Walzer, "Fragmenta Graeca in Litteris Arabicis," *Journal of the Royal Asiatic Society* (1939): 407–22; R. Walzer, "Aristotle, Galen, and Palladius on Love," Reprinted in, *Greek into Arabic* (Oxford: Oxford University Press, 1962), 48–59. See also G. Böwering, *The Mystical Vision of Existence in Classical Islam* (Berlin/New York: de Gruyter, 1980), 86–88; 148–50; and 152–55.

8. Böwering, *The Mystical Vision*, 148–49.

9. Al-Daylamī, *Futūḥ al-Raḥmān*, manuscript Veliyüddin Efendi 430, folio 7b, lines 1–2; *Kitāb Muhimmāt al-Wāṣilīn*, manuscript Chester Beatty 4142, folios 32b–38a.

10. Arberry, "The Works of Shams," 50–51; G. Böwering, "The Light Verse: Qurʾānic Text and Ṣūfī Interpretation," *Oriens* (2001), 36: 140–142. For example, manuscript Ismail Saib 4120–41, 8b.

11. This treatise, *Jawāhir al-Asrār*, is written in Arabic, as are the majority of al-Daylamī's works. Böwering has discussed the two collective manuscripts of al-Daylamī in his 1987 article, "The Writings of Shams al-Dīn al-Daylamī" most notably, manuscript Şehit Ali Paşa 1346 and manuscript Ismail Saib 4120. One manuscript of the *Mirʾāt al-Arwāḥ* also exists in Gotha, manuscript Orient 70. Arberry, "The Works of Shams," 49; C. Brockelmann, *Geschichte der arabischen Literatur*, Vol. II (Leiden: E.J. Brill, 1937–1942), 207. See also, W. Pertsch, *Die arabischen Handschriften der herzoglichen Bibliothek zu Gotha*, Vol. I, Reprint (Frankfurt am Main: Veröffentlichungen des Institutes für Geschichte der Arabisch-Islamischen Wissenschaften, 1987), 127–28 (70, No. 6). See also Böwering, "Deylamī," 341–42; idem, "Ideas of Time in Persian Sufism," 227–28; M. H. Harawī, *Majmūʿah-yi athār-i Farsī-yi Tāj al-Dīn-i Ushnuwī*, 3–6. See also Böwering, "The Light Verse," 140; *Jawāhir al-Asrār*, manuscript Şehit Ali Paşa 1346/1, 1b, lines 3–7.

12. Böwering, "The Light Verse," 140, citing manuscript Şehit Ali Paşa 1346/1, 1b–38a.

13. Whether or not al-Daylamī's commentary on the Qurʾān reflects similar revisions will require additional work on the extant manuscripts. There are six complete manuscripts of the Qurʾān commentary (this includes manuscript Veliyüddin Efendi 430). A provisional list of the manuscripts

is as follows: manuscript Yeni Cami 57 (dating to 430 A.H.); manuscript Köprülü 53/1 (dated to 935 A.H.); manuscript Vahid Efendi 183; manuscript Feyzullah 2163; manuscript Bursa 134 (titled the *Taṣdīq*). Another manuscript of the *Taṣdīq* is part of the collection of Dr. Aṣfar Mahdavī's library (No. 881). I would like to thank Professor Hermann Landolt for kindly providing me with a copy of this manuscript. I also would like to extend my gratitude to Professor Gerhard Böwering for lending to me the microfilm of manuscript Ismail Saib and for his generous assistance on al-Daylamī.

14. For additional information on the unique manuscript of the *Jawāhir*, see Arberry (1966), 50; Böwering, "The Writings of Shams," 26: 231–36; Ḥājjī Khalīfa, *Kashf al-Ẓunūn* (ed. G. Flügel), Vol. II, Reprint (New York: Johnson Reprint, 1964), 640, n. 4263. Böwering, "Deylamī," 341–42; idem, "Ideas of Time in Persian Sufism," 227–28; idem, "The Writings of Shams," 231–36; Harawī, *Majmūʿah-yi Athār-i Farsī-yi Tāj al-Dīn-i Ushnuwī*, 3–6.

15. G. Schoeler, *The Oral and the Written in Early Islam* (trans. U. Vagelpohl) (London/New York: Routledge, 2006), 35.

16. Daylamī, *Jawāhir*, manuscript Şehit Ali Paşa 1346/1, 1b, lines 3–7.

17. Böwering, "The Light Verse: Qurʾānic Text and Ṣūfī Interpretation," *Oriens* (2001), 36: 143. See in particular, *Mirʾāt*, manuscript Şehit Ali Paşa 1346, 63a. The loci of perception are as follows and in the following order: body–soul–heart–intellect–secret–inmost being–power (*badan-nafs-qalb-ʿaql-sirr-khafī-qudra*), whether microcosmic or macrocosmic.

18. Daylamī, *Mirʾāt al-Arwāḥ*, manuscript Şehit Ali Paşa 1346, 3b, lines 1–21; 73a–74b.

19. Ibid., 74a–74b.

20. Ibid., 69a.

21. Ibid., 40a–ff: formation of the body; the body and soul nexus, using the terms *nafs, jism,* and *badan*. Folio 66b: four parts of soul (*nafs*), in the mixture (*mizāj*) of soul, bestial, animal, satanic, and angelic (*sabʿiyya, bahīmiyya, shayṭāniyya,* and *malakiyya*).

22. Daylamī, *Mirʾāt*, 41b.

23. Daylamī, *Jawāhir*, 1b.

24. Böwering, *The Mystical Vision*, 86–88; 148–50; and 152–55.

25. Daylamī, *Mirʾāt*, 43b, ln. 7; Böwering, *The Mystical Vision*, 149–57.

26. Daylamī, *Mirʾāt*, 44a, lns. 20–28. On folio 45a, al-Daylamī presents his view that the *nafs* of the human being, as maintained by religious scholars and teachers [of Sufism], is a mixture of four elements, fire, water, earth and air. This point is addressed in more detail in the chapter on the secret.

27. Ibid., 39b, lns. 8–10.

28. Ibid., 42b, ln. 15.

29. Ibid., 60b, lns. 1–10.

30. Ibid., 61b–62a.

31. Daylamī, *Futūḥ al-Raḥmān*, manuscript Veliyüddin Efendi 430, 17b.

32. Daylamī, *Mirʾāt*, 40–41a.

33. Daylamī, *Taṣdīq al-Maʿārif*, manuscript Yeni Cami 57, 98b, ln. 12; 99b, lns. 13–14; Daylamī, *Futūḥ*, manuscript Veliyüddin 430, 79b, lns. 11–12.

34. Ibid., manuscript Yeni Cami 57, 99b, ln. 14–16. Böwering, "The Light Verse," 142.

35. Arberry, "The Work of Shams," 51.

36. manuscript Bağdatlı Vehbi 185, 119b.

37. manuscript Veliyüddin Efendi 430, 94b.

38. manuscript Veliyüddin 430, 63a, ln. 6.

39. manuscript Veliyüddin 430, 94b, lns. 5–6; manuscript Köprülü 53/1, 81b; manuscript Bağdatlı Vehbi 185, 119b.

40. Bağdatlı Vehbi, 119b, lns. 9–12.

41. Ibid., manuscript Veliyüddin 53/1, 82; Daylamī, *Taṣdīq*, manuscript Tehran, 99a. Daylamī, *Mirʾāt*, manuscript Şehit Ali Paşa 1346, 69b–70a: the section on the degrees of distinction of light (*tafāwut al-anwār*) and the section on space.

42. Daylamī, *Mirʾāt*, 206a.

43. Ibid.

44. Daylamī, *Futūḥ*, 17b.

45. manuscript Yeni Cami 57, 99b, ln. 14–16, 100b, ln.1–6; Böwering, ibid., 142.

46. Daylamī, *Ghāyat al-Imkān*, manuscript Şehit Ali Paşa 1346, 44a–45a. See also *Jawāhir*, 6a; *Kitāb Muhimmāt*, manuscript 4142 Chester Beatty, 1b–2b; Arberry, "The Works of Shams," 52. It may be noted here that in the preface to his Qurʾān commentary (manuscript Yeni Cami 57, 4b, lines 9–10), al-Daylamī briefly comments on how, at one point, the doctors believed he had been overcome by melancholy (*al-sawdā*), and he sought a cure.

47. Daylamī, *Mirʾāt*, 49b.

48. Daylamī, *Kitāb Muhimmāt*, Şehit Ali Paşa, 207b–209a.

49. Daylamī, *Mirʾāt*, 74b.

50. Ibid., 74b.

51. Daylamī, *Kitāb Muhimmāt*, 207b.

52. Arberry, "The Works of Shams," 29; Böwering, "The Writings of Shams," 231–236. See manuscript Şehit Ali Paşa 1346, 68b. The title of this work, as mentioned by Arberry, appears in Chester Beatty manuscript 4142.

53. J. Hirsh, "The Gods Appear," in *The Boundaries of Faith: The Development and Transmission of Medieval Spirituality* (ed. by John C. Hirsh) (Leiden: E. J. Brill, 1996), 47–59.

54. *The Concept of Sainthood* (trans. Bernd Radtke & John O'Kane) (Surrey: Curzon, 1996), 19.

55. Rūzbihān Baqlī, *The Unveiling of Secrets* (trans. Carl. W. Ernst) (Chapel Hill: Parvardigar Press, 1997), 33.

CHAPTER 12

Narrating Sight

Dreaming as Visual Training in Persianate Sufi Hagiography

Shahzad Bashir

This chapter focuses on the fact that when we discuss dreams, the objects of our analyses are not psychic experiences but narratives that purport to relate such experiences. My particular concern here is with representations of dreams in premodern Sufi literature that occur in the context of formalized, genre-bound texts with a highly modulated relationship to the social contexts in which they were produced. I argue that dream narratives need to be treated as literary artifacts placed strategically within larger textual arrangements. It is only after we have established the relationships of dream narratives with other elements of textual representation within a particular work or a genre that we can begin to elaborate on social or ideational functions that can be ascribed to them.

Dream narratives are a common feature of Sufi hagiographic literature, where they perform both descriptive and prescriptive functions.[1] I believe that Sufi hagiography needs to be taken more seriously as a kind of foundational premodern Islamic literature because it constitutes our major access to social contexts for which, otherwise, we have little more than highly theoretical treatises. However, hagiographical texts cannot be taken as straightforward descriptions of the lives they purport to depict. Such texts need parsing at the level of elements such as genre, framing, imagery, predominant motifs, and so on.[2] Descriptions of purported dream experiences provide a particularly useful point of concentration in this regard, with the proviso that we establish correlations between what they contain and other narrative elements of the texts in question in order to draw out larger social and ideological currents running through the literature. This is the task I undertake in this chapter in a limited form.

Dreams and Sufi Hagiography

In what follows, I concentrate on some dream narratives in the extensive Naqshbandī hagiographical work *Rashaḥāt-i ʿayn al-ḥayāt* ("Dewdrops from the Elixir of Life") in the context of the ways in which its author narrates visual experience in general. The *Rashaḥāt*, penned by ʿAlī b. Ḥusayn Kāshifī "Ṣafī" (d. 1532–1533), is a valuable text for this exercise for a number of different reasons. Compiled at the beginning of the sixteenth century CE, it relies on hagiographical narratives pertaining to Khwājagānī-Naqshbandī lineages as well as other hagiographical works produced in previous decades and centuries. In this sense, the *Rashaḥāt* is a summation of a literary paradigm central to Sufi intellectual and social life in Persianate societies during the Mongol and Tīmūrid periods (ca. 1200–1500). But the *Rashaḥāt* also is a compilation with a deliberate and determinate purpose. It aims to promote the figure of Khwāja ʿUbaydullāh Aḥrār (d. 1490) as a Sufi protagonist whose life represents the aggregation of all Sufi virtues. Ṣafī's investment in glorifying Aḥrār is the underlying driving current that makes the *Rashaḥāt* a work with particular rhetorical ends embedded throughout its narrative. My analyses in this chapter presume that what Ṣafī chooses to include in his work is not an unmediated reflection of Sufi lives. Instead, his choices signify a determined agenda with respect to the particular Sufi ideas and practices he wishes to promote within a larger socio-intellectual dialogue alive in his times.

My point of departure is that, for Ṣafī and other authors of Persianate hagiographic works, accounts of dreams amount to narrative tools designed to underscore their overall authorial agenda. On the one hand, these authors can set dreams apart from quotidian vision on the basis of presumed variance in states of consciousness. Seeing a thing with one's eyes while being awake can be inflected differently than seeing something with the eye of the mind while the eyelids are shut. On the other hand, the overall morphology and ideological import of dream narratives correspond closely with other ways in which vision operates in these texts. I suggest that "seeing" in these works is understood primarily metaphorically, and the ways in which this is supposed to happen is depicted quite similarly with respect to dreams and ordinary experience. Most importantly, the texts portray particular sights and ways of seeing as especially beneficial for progress on the Sufi path. What is described to the reader as having been seen, whether as a matter of physical observation or in dreams, forms a kind of prescriptive matrix of sights. In accordance with the overall purpose of these texts, seeing is not a passive activity in which a scene enters the physical or mental eye, but a behavior that needs to be cultivated through deliberate practice. Based on this perspective, dream narratives in works such as the *Rashaḥāt* cannot to be regarded as neutral descriptions of psychic experiences. These narratives are an aspect of Sufi teaching regarding active cultivation of certain types of vision, cycled through experiences ascribed to the elect among Sufis. Textual descriptions of dreaming experience illustrate important aspects of the underlying social functions of hagiographic texts.

The remainder of this chapter substantiates the perspective I have laid out by establishing connections between dream narratives and other visual or visualizing practices to be found in the *Rashaḥāt*. My discussion is divided into parts based on what Ṣafī reports as having been seen in dreams by Sufi figures. I show that the underlying messages regarding what is seen in dreams correlate directly with Naqshbandī Sufi practices undertaken in a waking state that also are described and advocated in the *Rashaḥāt*. The comparison allows me to conclude that, in this and other similar texts, what is most significant about dream narratives is that they represent a concentrated and sublimated form of Sufi prescriptions regarding the cultivation of sight as a mental activity endowed with particular significance in the context of Sufi practice.

Objects of Dreams and Narratives

Historical, social scientific, and even neurophysiological studies have shown that "seeing"' is as much a matter of cultural training as it is of an image being formed on the retina. Because dreams are one segment in an array of visual practices and experiences, analyzing dream narratives requires that we place their contents in the larger context of others things that a source represents as being worth seeing. In hagiographic literature, dream narratives do not always stand out from other descriptions in terms of their contents, structures, or social or narrative functions. Indeed, it often is quite difficult even to specify whether a certain narrative represents a dream or a waking experience.

This ambiguity further enforces the notion that what matters most is not the purported state of the person whose life is being narrated but the fact of seeing, the content of the vision, and interpretive glosses provided by authoritative commentators.

In hagiographic representations of dreams, authors tend to provide information about four elements in particular: the seer, a focal person or being who is seen, the scene surrounding the encounter, and an interpreter who tries to fix the meaning of a vision when it is related to him or her. In the *Rashaḥāt* and other such works, dream narratives preserve the hierarchy of relationships between God and human beings—dead or alive—that one finds replicated in other representations of socio-religious activity as well. In nearly all cases that I have noted in the *Rashaḥāt,* seers of dreams stand in subordinate positions to the individuals or beings that are seen. This is a significant pattern because it marks hagiographic dreaming as an activity through which individuals in lower ranks of spiritual achievement receive guidance in the course of their quests. Whenever dreams are reported to have occurred to men known as great exemplars, the narratives are placed in the early stages of their careers, before their acquisition of high religious status. Dream narratives thus correspond perfectly to hagiography as a genre because it is always written from the perspective of disciples looking up to idealized masters.

Living Masters and Disciples

In the *Rashaḥāt,* dream narratives that contain representations of animate beings include authority figures such as masters or prophets, seen either by themselves or in the midst of interacting with the dreamer. Dreams act as a particularly significant medium for interaction between individuals who are in committed master–disciple relationships but are separated from each other as a result of unavoidable exigencies. In such instances, disciples' obeisance and devotion toward the masters, and the latter's protective roles toward those dependent on them, can be displaced to the dreaming arena because it is precluded from being enacted physically.

An example of dreams mediating a long-term master–disciple relationship can be seen in the depiction of interactions between the Naqshbandī master Saʿd al-Dīn Kāshgharī (d. 1456) and his student ʿAlāʾ al-Dīn Abīzī (d. 1487). The *Rashaḥāt* reports that Abīzī, who had come to Herat from Quhistān, said that once when he was in his company, a messenger arrived from his home town to present a letter that stated that his parents wanted him to come back home in order to get married. This upset him because it would mean leaving the master, and he decided to read the letter aloud in the master's presence in the hope that he would forbid him from fulfilling his parents' wishes. However, the master said that they were calling with such insistence that he must go. Abīzī then went home, got married, and spent eight years there, but always with an interior (*bāṭinī*) connection to the shaykh. During this time, he became subject to harassment by a local official regarding monetary matters, and the situation eventually became so difficult that he felt that he had no choice but to appeal to the shaykh through the *bāṭin* for aid. He states that one night:

> I saw him in a dream carrying a bow and arrow. Suddenly, the [tyrannical] official came into view, and he put the arrow in the bow and shot it in his direction. When I woke up, I wondered about what kind of calamity was going to befall that unfortunate man. Next day, I went to him and told him to be beware that a great calamity was headed his way, but he laughed, scorned me, and said impolite things. After three days, half of his body fell victim to paralysis and he could no longer stand up.[3]

This story's depiction of the master's protection for the disciple hinges on the ability of the two to communicate through interior means across a long distance. Interestingly, the disciple conveys his request through an interior supplication whereas the master replies by appearing in the dream. As seen in this case and other similar Sufi narratives, the ability to project oneself into someone else's dream is the prerogative of the master, the party that holds greater power. The fact that it takes three days for the enemy to succumb gives the impression that the shooting of the arrow was a physical event because it might take the arrow that much time to arrive at the distant location. Abīzī's dream can thus be seen as Kāshgharī allowing the disciple televisual access to his action in advance of the matter becoming clear to him in due course of time. The critical issue in this story is the strength of the master–disciple bond that comes with privileges of access and extraordinary protection. As a matter of authorial rhetoric, this narrative underscores the view that one needs a Sufi master not just as a spiritual guide but also as a protector in the mundane realm.[4]

The *Rashaḥāt* contains dreams that evocate the high station occupied by masters in an abstract sense as well. For example, Ṣafī relates that he himself once saw the master Shams al-Dīn Muḥammad

Rūjī (d. 1499) in a dream in the courtyard of the grand mosque of Herat sitting with both eyes shut. He found this disturbing when he woke up, and went to the master to ask him what this meant. Rūjī replied that among human beings, one eye is fixed on the world of *mulk*, meaning the terrestrial realm, whereas the other is on *malakūt*, the realm of spiritual forms. In a dream, if one sees a person who is blind in the right eye and the left is fine, it means that his sight is hidden from *malakūt* and all his attention is on *mulk*. This is the state of the people who have a veil (*ḥijāb*) in front of them, meaning that they are ordinary people. In contrast, if the right eye is fine and the left is blind, that refers to the station of the people of unveiling (*kashf*), meaning the spiritual elect. If the person seen is blind in both eyes, that means that he is oblivious to *mulk* as well as *malakūt*, both of which are aspects of the nether world that admits internal differentiation between beings. The "sight" of such a person is focused on *jabarūt* and *lāhūt*, the highest realms that reflect divine unity in its most pure forms. This is the station of the elect of the elect.[5]

While the story involving Kāshgharī and Abīzī allowed a disciple to see a master's actions in a direct way, the one involving Ṣafī's own dream reveals a master's status, and that too only in the form of an interpretation. Here the narrative is constructed through the interplay between different types of vision that are nested within each other. Ṣafī's dreaming sight contrasts with Rūjī's insight since Ṣafī finds the dream disturbing but its interpretation reveals something positive. The two eyes of a person whom one might see in a dream are shown fixated on opposing arenas as objects of sight. And in the concluding section, a person who appears completely bereft of sight in the ordinary sense turns out to be able to see things most worth seeing.

Finally, the *Rashaḥāt* also describes a quite enigmatic discussion on dreams that further demonstrates the malleability of meanings that can be ascribed to visual acts in hagiographic narratives. In this case, Khwāja Aḥrār states that he once asked an adept in Samarqand how to interpret a dream in which one sees that God has died. Within the framework of normative Islamic thought which Aḥrār can certainly be presumed to have espoused, it is difficult to imagine how God could be "seen" directly and what could possibly be the scene in which he was dead. Ṣafī does not address this issue but describes three exceedingly divergent opinions on the matter: first, the scholar in Samarqand queried by Aḥrār said that the dream should be understood through analogy with a dream in which one sees the Prophet to be dead: It means that the dreamer's dedication to the Sharīʿa has become doubtful and corrupted. Second, Ṣafī states that Aḥrār himself suggested that it could be that the dreamer possessed tremendous closeness to God that has suddenly left him. Seeing God as dead then refers to the demise of the feeling of closeness. And third, Ṣafī reports that ʿAbd al-Raḥmān Jāmī said that it could be that the dreamer had made a worldly passion his divinity. The death of God then indicates the dissipation of this passion, which implies the betterment of his religious qualities.[6] Aḥrār's question and the three answers are interesting in that they show no concern with the dream's visual content at all and the interpretation of the event remains suspended between mutually exclusive possibilities. Furthermore, it is clear that a dream cannot be interpreted in the abstract; its meaning entirely depends on the general state of the dreamer, which must be available to the interpreter in addition to the dream itself to arrive at any worthwhile conclusions.

The three cases I discussed move the reader away from categorical assessments of any kind of vision as a matter of sensory perception, and toward considerations of metaphorical meanings of "seeing" in all contexts. Moreover, the value of seeing is tied here to the correct understanding of what becomes available for one to see. In the end, in all three cases, dreaming appears as a particular mode through which disciples may receive guidance and protection from masters. Not accidentally, these two things are centerpieces of hagiographic rhetoric, whose chief purpose is to convince individuals that it is in their own greatest interest to become attached to Sufi masters.

Reappearance of the Dead

In the cases just described, dreams enable disciples to continue their vital relationships with masters and become aware of the latter's extraordinary status. In Sufi narratives, a second quite prevalent motif is the traversal of the boundary between the living and the dead through the medium of dreams. This theme occurs prominently where masters claim initiation from members of prior generations of their lineages, whom they could not have encountered in person. For example, in the *Rashaḥāt*, Bahāʾ al-Dīn Naqshband (d. 1389) is shown to receive initiation into the Khwājagānī *silsila* (chain of authority) through a dream of ʿAbd al-Khāliq Ghijduvānī (d. ca. 1217).[7] Similarly, while a novice, Khwāja Aḥrār sees Naqshband acting on his *bāṭin* in one dream, and in another, sees Naqshband's erudite student Khwāja Muḥammad Pārsā (d. 1420) being unable to do the same.[8] In these cases, dreams enable the hagiographers to connect Sufis from different generations on a personal basis when historical noncontiguity makes it impossible for them to have had a relationship in the flesh.

Dreams are able to reconnect masters and disciples immediately after the death of one side of the pair as well. Ṣafī relates that a few days after the death of ʿAbd al-Ghafūr Lārī (d. 1506), a *faqīr* saw him in a dream and only then realized that he had died and was making an appearance from a different realm. He found this to be an important moment to clarify the thorny doctrinal issue of "unity of being" (*vaḥdat-i vujūd*) associated with Ibn al-ʿArabī (d. 1240), which was a major topic of controversy among Sufis in the Persianate world during this period. Lārī's response was unhelpful on this in that he said that he had met the great master since death and had asked him about this matter, but he had responded that whatever needed to be said on it was present in the books he had left behind. Then the same man saw Lārī in a dream again, this time exhibiting illness. When he inquired as to why the spiritual elect experience such tribulations despite their closeness to God, Lārī explained that illnesses and physical exertions act to cleanse the mind and make it strong for apprehending the light that constitutes being. This light can be apprehended by all depending on the level of preparedness of their minds.[9]

In these two instances, the fact that the interaction between Lārī and the disciple happens through the medium of dreams rather than physically seems hardly to matter at all. On the doctrinal question, Lārī's transfer to the world beyond death turns out to offer no greater advantage than while he was living because the disciple is directed back to Ibn al-ʿArabī's writings. And the fact that Lārī appears ill in the dream only provides the pretext for the master to teach that physical discomforts have a deeper purpose. Overall, then, while dreaming is necessary because Lārī is no longer available in the flesh, what occurs in dreams is the continuation of the relationship as it existed before the master's demise.

Masters and Prophets

Constituting a kind of amalgamation of the themes I mentioned earlier, some representations of dreams in the *Rashaḥāt* substantiate interpolation of identities between religious elect of the past and the present. For example, in one instance, Khwāja Aḥrār reports that once a Sufi companion saw a dream in which a large group was sitting together when it was said that the prophet Moses was about to join in the company. The dreamer said that when he surged ahead in order to be able to see the prophet, he realized that he saw the man to be a certain Sayyid ʿĀshiq, a well-known preacher contemporary to him.[10] Similarly, a companion of Khwāja Aḥrār by the name of Luṭfullāh Khuttalānī said that when he was a child, he saw Muḥammad as a beautiful person in a dream and carried this vision with him in his mind the rest of his life. When he became a disciple of Aḥrār, the master mentioned one day that people see the Prophet in many different forms. Khuttalānī said that after this Aḥrār directed his gaze toward him and "appeared to me in the same beautiful form in which I had seen the Prophet that one time. Truly, seeing that form became the cause of my bondage to His Eminence."[11] In these cases, dream narratives allow the hagiographer to draw parity between grand religious figures of the past, such as prophets, and living masters. The attribution of these dreams to disciples solidifies hagiography's overall function as argument for some living individuals to be considered extraordinarily sanctified.

The appearance of Muḥammad in Sufis' dreams is a fairly regular feature of Persianate hagiographical narratives. In the *Rashaḥāt*, one elaborate story related to this theme involves the aforementioned Shams al-Dīn Muḥammad Rūjī who said that as a young man he had great desire to see the Prophet in a dream. One day when he came home, he found his mother and some other elder relatives sitting together reading a book of prayers that was thought to cause one to see the Prophet. This awakened his own desire, and he decided, under his mother's guidance, to recite these prayers and other invocations directed toward the Prophet. While doing this, he fell asleep and saw a dream in which he entered his own house to find his mother waiting in the antechamber and reprimanding him for being late while the Prophet was waiting to see them. She then took him to an inside hall, where he found Muḥammad sitting near a wall with a lot of people surrounding him, including a scribe taking notes from him. Rūjī stated:

> It appeared to me that this [the scribe] was Mawlānā Sharaf al-Dīn Ziyāratgāhī, an exalted scholar and perfected man among the pious of his times. As my mother brought me to him, she did not wait for him to become prepared for her. She pushed me forward and asked, "Messenger of God, is this the child you had promised me, who would be prosperous and long-lived?" His Eminence looked toward me and said, "Yes, this is that child." Then he turned toward Mawlānā Sharaf al-Dīn ʿUs̱mān and said,

> "Write a document (*maktūb*) for him." The Mawlānā took the pen and paper, and I saw that he wrote three lines and, under these, many names separated out in the way when people provide guarantees in the context of giving witness. He folded this up and gave it to me. As I started to leave, I said to myself, "You do not know the content of this document, so turn back and show it to the Prophet so that he may tell it to you." I returned, came in front of His Eminence, and said, "Messenger of God, I do not know what has been written in this document." His Eminence took it from my hand and read it out, and I memorized all three lines from his single reading. Then His Eminence folded the letter back and gave it into my hand. I wanted to ask something else, but then suddenly a voice intervened and my mother, carrying a candle, entered into the room through the door. I then came out of the dream.[12]

When Rūjī and his mother compared their experiences they found that they had been present in the exact same scene, except that the mother's visual experience had been from the vantage point of her own role in the drama.

This narrative aims to establish Rūjī's credentials as one whose birth involved Muḥammad's intervention and who received a written affidavit to this effect in the dream context. Although we are not told the contents of the document he is given, the comment on its form provides a strong indication that it is meant as a kind of certificate. Unlike the cases I mentioned at the beginning of this section, this dream is portrayed as requiring direct observation of the visual and aural content rather than any kind of trick in which one person appears as another. Rūjī and Muḥammad remain separate beings, whereas in the cases I cited earlier, living masters merge into prophets.

Cultivating Visions

In each of the three types of dreams I discussed earlier, the most striking thing is that "seeing" something by itself does not have a fixed meaning. We have, on the one hand, cases that project a thorough realism onto the world of dreams. Thus, Rūjī and his mother are shown to have been present at a localizable event that seemingly occurred in concrete space and time. On the other hand, as in the case of Rūjī appearing to Ṣafī as a blind man, the dream's meaning is the opposite of what is experienced visually. Ultimately, what conjoins the dreams is Rūjī's authority as a master and not a standard position on how their visual content is to be understood in a categorical sense. In the first case, the dream narrative establishes his connection to Muḥammad, whereas in the second, it endows him with the ability to see beyond the world of matter and individual spirits. It appears, then, that dream narratives within hagiographical accounts are keyed entirely to the genre's overall purposes of establishing Sufi masters' authority.

The question of vision within dream narratives can be given further context by comparing it with visualizing practices known to have been cultivated by Persianate Sufis. The most significant example in this regard, which is of direct relevance for discussing the *Rashaḥāt* in particular, is the Naqshbandī practice termed *rābiṭa* that was meant to anchor the relationship between masters and disciples and to maintain a telepathic contact between them.[13] Ṣafī indicates that, in this group, the method of concentration (*tavajjuh*) toward the end of enhancing one's inner reality began by imagining the form of the person from whom one had acquired affiliation with the group (i.e., the master). They would do so to the extent that the image would begin emitting bodily heat and then would continue to hold the image within themselves until it became imprinted on their hearts. The purpose of this procedure was to transform the heart from an ordinary lump of flesh into the organ through which human beings can connect to divine realities. Such a transformation required that the image of the master's body first be absorbed through one's bodily senses and then implanted into the heart using the internal senses. The process of the image settling into the heart went hand in hand with the practice of recollection (*ẕikr*) using the formula *Lā ilāha illā'llāh* (there is no god but God).[14]

The procedure outlined for Naqshbandī practice indicates that vision occupied a particularly significant mediating function when it came to seeking religious transformation. Vision appears here as the sensorial doorway through which one absorbs a master's presence into oneself in order to progress further along the Sufi path. The dreams, as was just mentioned, indicate that this kind of absorption of images into oneself could work as easily from dreams as it would through physical sight. From the perspective of the practice being advocated, the critical issue is not the origin of the image but one's relationship to the person imagined and the degree to which this becomes settled in oneself. Having dreams about Sufi masters and prophets—and, at times, seeing them merging into each other—would thus seem to be part and parcel of the prescriptive program included in a work such as the *Rashaḥāt*.

The fact that dreams were understood as a part of a larger spectrum of visual experience can be substantiated through comments where they are understood negatively as well. The *Rashaḥāt* indicates this when describing the relationship between the Naqshbandī master Yaᶜqūb Charkhī (d. 1447) and Zayn al-Dīn Khwāfī (d. 1435), the eponym of a Sufi community in competition with the Naqshbandīs at the time the *Rashaḥāt* was composed. Ṣafī reports from Khwāja Aḥrār, who was Charkhī's disciple, that the master once asked him if he knew that Khwāfī provided much dream interpretation and that people put great stock in this. When Aḥrār replied in the affirmative, Charkhī went into a trance and came out of it an hour later to recite the following verse

> Since I am a slave of the Sun, all that I say is from the Sun
> I am neither night nor a night-worshipper, to relate things about sleep[15]

The opposition between day and night, and perceptions proper to each, suggests Charkhī's preference for excluding dreams from the array of visual practices relevant for his spiritual method.

Conclusion: The Purposes of Dream Narratives

Based on this partial survey of the *Rashaḥāt-i ᶜayn al-ḥayāt*, I suggest that, in the context of Sufi literature, we should treat dream narratives primarily as exemplary and prescriptive evocations. Virtually everything we see attributed to dreams in hagiographical stories can be seen attributed to waking experience as well, which means that we cannot see dreaming as a privileged mode of consciousness. Quite conversely, the fact that the same "sights" can be relayed from dreams as from physical viewing means that we need to discuss the representations of these two experiences in tandem. Most significantly, we need to see dream narratives as one mode, among others, of training a Sufi's sense of sight in order to progress further on the path. To put this discussion into a larger frame, I would like to go back to the story concerning ᶜAbd al-Ghafūr Lārī appearing in the dream of a disciple very soon after his death. Ṣafī relates that, in addition to seeking clarification regarding Ibn al-ᶜArabī's doctrines, the disciple asked

Lārī whether notions of love and beauty mattered in the metaphysical world where he now found himself after death. Lārī responded with an emphatic yes and then added:

> The beauty associated with the realm of bodies comes about through the mixing of different constituents. It changes and transforms rapidly because of the [natural] opposition between these constituents, leading to the demise of love and the slipping away of the thought [of the beloved]. But the beauties of this world are derived from the combination of subtleties and are incapable of extinction or decay. These are never subject to change or transformation, and since there is no opposition or contention between their constituents, love and loving are established here on a constant basis. The end [of the matter] is that when the relationship between the spirit and the body is severed initially, a consternation finds its way into the essence that is the spirit for two or three days because of its sympathy for the body. But when it becomes purified, it reverts to the condition of [absolute] loving and ardor.[16]

This elaboration regarding the relationship between love and beauty is relevant for the present discussion because it places vision at the center of the way medieval Persianate Sufis became bonded to each other. As I have discussed elsewhere in detail, the question of falling in love through sight is central to the construction of hagiographic representation of relationships between Sufi masters and disciples.[17] In works such as the *Rashaḥāt*, true discipleship becomes operational when masters make themselves available to disciples in bodily forms, and the latter fall in love by absorbing their visions.[18] As presented in Lārī's explanation, this type of love is liable to dissolution because of the material world's inescapable mutability. Such love can be permanent only in metaphysical circumstances that become available after death. This implies that, as long as one is in the physical world, a master must work consciously to keep himself attractive to the disciple, and the latter must focus his senses on the master's form to keep the relationship of love in motion. In the *Rashaḥāt*, Aḥrār cites the earlier Khwājaganī master Niẓām al-Dīn Khāmūsh to state:

> A shaykh is one who can make himself appear beautiful in the sight of disciples. This is because if there is no beauty, the bond (*rābiṭa*) between desirer/disciple (*murīd*) and

> desired/master (*murād*) that is characterized by love—leading to [disciple's] absorption and [master's ability to] work [on the disciple's interior]—cannot become established. Although we know this intellectually, we do not have the leisure to always take pains in this regard and show ourselves as beautiful in order that people's beliefs remain uncorrupted. It is because of this that combing facial hair, tying the turban in a comely way, and other such things concerned with care for appearances have been made the obligatory tradition (*sunnat*).[19]

As seen here, love as a process requires constant visual contact, making all forms of "envisioning" critical to the Sufi quest. This understanding unites physical meetings between masters and disciples, encounters in dreams and trances, and practices such as imprinting the master's image on one's heart components of a single paradigm.

The materials I have discussed in this chapter show that in Sufi hagiographic narratives, dreams are a part of a continuum of experiences and cultivated practices that involve visualization. Their purpose in this context relates to what they accomplish with respect to relationships between masters and disciples, and not to the special character of dreaming as a psychological state or activity. Keeping in view that hagiography is a descriptive as well as didactic genre, the representation of dreams in works such as the *Rashaḥāt* shows dreaming to have been a means for exemplifying and emphasizing the authority of Sufi masters and a medium for training disciples' eyes, minds, and hearts for progress on the Sufi path.

Notes

1. For some recent overviews of dreams in Sufi literature see: Nile Green, "The Religious and Cultural Roles of Dreams and Visions in Islam," *Journal of the Royal Asiatic Society* 13, 3 (2003), 287–313; Jonathan Katz, *Dreams, Sufism, and Sainthood: The Visionary Career of Muḥammad al-Zawāwī* (Leiden: Brill, 1996).

2. For my attempt at such an overall assessment of Persianate hagiography produced during the approximate period from 1300 to 1500 see Shahzad Bashir, *Sufi Bodies: Religion and Society in Medieval Islam* (New York: Columbia University Press, 2011). For a more general treatment of the representation of saintly lives in the Islamic context see John Renard, *Friends of God* (Berkeley: University of California Press, 2008).

3. Fakhr ad-Dīn Kāshifī Ṣafī, *Rashaḥāt-i ʿayn al-ḥayāt*, ed. ʿAlī Aṣghar Muʿīniyān, 2 vols. (Tehran: Majmūʿa-i Mutūn-i Qadīm va Aḥvāl-i Dānishmandān va ʿIrfānān, 1977), 1:220–21.

4. For a detailed consideration of the interdependence between spiritual and sociopolitical and economic matters in Persianate Sufism see Bashir, *Sufi Bodies*.

5. Ṣafī, *Rashaḥāt*, 2:467–68. For a summary discussion of the realms in question in this dream narrative see William Chittick, "The Five Divine Presences from al-Qunawi to al-Qaysari." *Muslim World* 72, no. 2 (1982), 107–28.

6. Ṣafī, *Rashaḥāt*, 2:467–68.

7. Ibid., 1:95. The *Rashaḥāt* mentions this event only in passing. For a detailed analysis of this dream in the context of the generation of Naqshband's hagiographical persona see Devin DeWeese, "The Legitimation of Baha᾿ ad-Din Naqshband," *Asiatische Studien/Études Asiatiques* 60, no. 2 (2006): 261–305.

8. Ṣafī, *Rashaḥāt*, 2:393–94.

9. Ibid., 1:300–301.

10. Ibid., 2:492–93.

11. Ibid., 2:614–15.

12. Ibid., 1:327–28.

13. *Rābiṭa*, literally "bond," is a Naqshbandī practice that requires that the disciple maintain the image of his master in his mind's eye. For a detailed consideration of this technique in Naqshbandī history see Fritz Meier, *Zwei Abhandlungen über die Naqšbandiyya* (Stuttgart: F. Steiner, 1994).

14. Ṣafī, *Rashaḥāt*, 1:169–70.

15. Ibid., 1:120–21.

16. Ibid., 1:300–301.

17. See Bashir, *Sufi Bodies*, 115–21.

18. For a prominent case of this pattern in the *Rashaḥāt* see the story of Khwāja Aḥrār becoming attached to his Naqshbandī mentor Yaʿqūb Charkhī (2:428–30).

19. Ṣafī, *Rashaḥāt*, 2:466–67.

CHAPTER 13

(Re)creating Image and Identity

Dreams and Visions as a Means of Murād III's Self-Fashioning

Özgen Felek

In the early 1990s, when professional tennis player Andre Agassi, with his long hair and flamboyant outfits, boasted "Image is everything!" he reminded us of the fact that we, as modern individuals, had already been preoccupied by "image" for a long time. We live in a time when everything we wear, say, and do is considered part of our image. The image culture dictates even body shapes and hair colors. We have come to the point at which our physical appearance and personalities are not enough anymore; we also need to advertise our image by preparing embellished and even exaggerated resumes, curricula vitae, Web sites, and Facebook pages that all are part of our efforts to sell the image we would like to project to others. In the end, even a new kind of entrepreneur has emerged in order to assist us in this endeavor, the "image consultant."

Although the obsession with image usually is seen as a modern trend, in this chapter I introduce the Ottoman Sultan, Murād III (r. 982–1003/1574–1595), who made a concerted effort both for himself and for others. Yet, before examining how Sultan Murād created his image and identity, it should be stated that he was not alone in this respect. As the Renaissance historian Stephen Greenblatt has demonstrated, there was an "increased self-consciousness about the fashioning of human identity as a manipulable, artful process" in sixteenth-century England.[1] What Greenblatt suggests for sixteenth-century members of the English court appears to be true of Muslim rulers of the age as well. In the first half of the sixteenth century, Bābur (r. 932–937/1526–1530), the founder of the Moghul dynasty in India, penned his renowned memoir, *Bābur-Nāma*, in Chaghatay Turkish. In the second half of the same century, Shāh Ṭahmāsp (r. 930–984/1524–1576) composed his autobiographic *Tazkira* (between 1555 and 1576). Not long after Shāh Ṭahmāsp completed his work, the letters and dream accounts of Murād III that he shared with his spiritual master were collected under the title, *Kitābü'l- menāmāt* ("The Book of Dreams") in 1003/1595.[2]

These three texts are particularly significant, for they indicate an "increased self-consciousness" similar to that which Greenblatt identified in sixteenth-century England. That the rulers of these three great Muslim empires took the time to explore their inner selves, in my view, suggests a deliberate and self-concious effort that, in turn, testifies to a self-awareness in creating one's own identity and image, which appears to have been a "global" fixation for sixteenth-century individuals in both the Muslim and Christian worlds.

Writing about one's self requires a certain level of self-awareness. Murād's dream writings, along with his poetry collection, suggest to us who he thinks he is, and how he wants to be seen by others. We see him being actively engaged in the shaping of his own image rather than leaving it up to historians or anyone else to do it for him. In this sense, what Murād seeks to achieve by having his dreams and visions recorded is not very different from what Shāh Ṭahmāsp and Bābur do. Each of these three sultans uses his dreams to construct his image.

The primary concern of the present study is to examine how Murād III fashioned an image of himself through accounts of his dreams and visions. Dreams have been studied from sociological/anthropological, religious, psychological, historical, mystical, and scientific perspectives, yet there is, to my knowledge, no study that examines dreams as a means of self-fashioning. I argue that Murād, like other individuals of his epoch, turned his dreams into narrative tools through which he also conveyed an image that he wanted people to have about himself at a time when true dreams were seen by his contemporaries as one of the forty-six parts of prophethood. Although Murād made use of other means to paint his self-image, the focus of this study is on his dreams and visions. Before examining Murād's dreams and visions as an image-making device, I first situate him and his *Kitābü'l- menāmāt* in their historical context.

Murād III and Kitābü'l- menāmāt

Sultan Murād was born on 5 *Cumāda* 1 953/4 July 1546 at Bozdağ Yayla near Manisa where his father Şehzāde Selīm, the future Selīm II, served as *sancaḳbeyi* (provincial governor). Following Murād's ceremonial circumcision in 965/1557, his grandfather, Sultan Süleymān I, appointed him *sancaḳbeyi* of Aḳşehir. Then, in 966/1558, when he was eighteen years old and residing in Manisa, the Sultan appointed him *sancaḳbeyi* of Saruhan. When he ascended to the throne on 1 *Ramażān* 982/15 December 1574, following his father's death, he was twenty-eight.[3]

Murād's early life is very nondescript. It is when he had a dream right before his ascension to the throne that his story becomes interesting for us. Seeking its interpretation, he sent it to those who were known for their skills in interpreting dreams. Eventually a poor dervish named Şücā^c, who made his living as a gardener in the vineyards in the Manisa area, is said to have interpreted it as predicting the death of Murād's father and his own subsequent enthronement.[4] After the interpretation of Şücā^c had come true within a few days, Şücā^c Dede was on his way to the position of *ḫünkār şeyḫi* (spiritual advisor to the sultan). Later on, after his enthronement, Murād invited Şücā^c Dede to Istanbul.[5] Over the years, Şücā^c Dede received not only the position of *ḫünkār şeyḫi,* but also a regular salary from the treasure of the dynasty.[6]

Şücā^c Dede is a mysterious figure who has received mixed reports in the Ottoman chronicles. We know little about this obscure man, who was in a position of influence over a powerful ruler for some thirteen years. What is known is that he was one of the disciples of Şa^cbān Efendi of Kastamonu from the *Ḫalvetī* order. Historians provide contradictory accounts of him. Although some treated him as a respected Sufi figure and praise his knowledge of Sufi legacy, despite his illiteracy,[7] a contemporary historian sounds pleased with his death and moreover accuses him of being a charlatan who took advantage of sultan Murād.[8]

The disciple–master relation between the two men lasted until Şücā^c Dede's death in 996/1587–1588. Within this time period, Murād apparently sent accounts of his dreams and visions to Şücā^c Dede in letter form. Murād presumably penned these undated letters between 982/1574 and 990/1582[9] or 996/1587.[10] The letters were compiled, under the title *Kitābü'l- menāmāt,* in 1001/1591–1592, right after the end of the first Islamic millennium, by Mīrāḫūr Nūḥ Ağa, the Master of the Horse to Murād and another disciple of Şücā^c Dede.[11] Although we cannot know with absolute certainty whether or not Murād commissioned Nūḥ Ağa to compile his dream letters, the existence of a fine, gilded, and bound copy of his dreams prepared about three or four years before Murād's death suggests his interest in this project.

Kitābü'l- menāmāt is a 259 folio-bound manuscript, of which the first page is illuminated with gold. The text consists of not only the letters in which Murād relates his mystical experiences, but also of letters, which deal with Murād's daily life as well as political and social affairs.

The relationship between Murād and Şücāᶜ Dede appears to have evolved almost entirely through written communication. In more than two thousand letters, only once is a face-to-face communication between Murād and Şücāᶜ Dede mentioned. Although only one letter from Şücāᶜ Dede has been located up to this time,[12] Murād's statement, "no letter from you has arrived for the last few days,"[13] indicates that their written correspondence was two-way.

Although, in one letter, Sultan Murād scolds Şücāᶜ Dede for sharing his letters with others,[14] Nūḥ Ağa, in his introduction to the text, states clearly that the text was intended to be available to Sufi circles: "O seeker of the Knowledge and the desirer of the Truth! Know and be aware of that. . . ."[15] Furthermore, the compilation of these letters in a clean copy suggests the intention to preserve these accounts for posterity.

Dreams and Visions as a Means of Self-Fashioning

Being a sultan required following prescribed social behavior in the theater of life as witnessed by others.[16] Hence, it was scripted like any other code of social behavior. In his self-fashioning, Sultan Murād was encountering a script handed down to him by generations of sovereigns before him.[17]

The script prescribing how an Ottoman sultan should behave had been socially, culturally, and religiously constructed by many diverse components of group life, including teachers and tutors in the palace, religious scholars and leaders, poets, storytellers within the oral and written culture. The ideal script of the Ottoman sultan became manifest from stories about certain prominent and exemplary figures in Islamic history and well-known heroic figures of the Islamic literature. Although storytellers (*ḳıṣṣa-ḫāns, şehnāme-ḫāns,* and *meddāḥs*) and *ḳaṣīde* poets employed brave, generous, merciful characters in their stories and poems in portraying the ideal sultan, Ottoman chroniclers played a significant role in constructing the image of the *ġāzī* (holy warrior) sultan as a culturally fashioned form of sultanhood.[18] This image was even visually presented in numerous illustrated texts,[19] which not only functioned to legitimize their subjects as great sovereigns who perfectly followed the script, but visually portrayed, for following generations, how the ideal Ottoman ruler should act. Following this script, Sultan Murād was taught to play his roles within the theater of the court.

The script of ideal Ottoman ruler required Sultan Murād to stand out with his bravery as well-skilled in battle and hunting, as well as with his piety, intellectuality, and traits of justice, generosity, and mercy to his subjects. It is with these expectations in mind that Ottoman chroniclers evaluated his performance as a ruler.

In the eyes of the Ottoman chroniclers, Murād III seems to have been a sultanic figure who deviated from the script of a typical Ottoman sovereign in some major ways. Murād's alleged failure in terms of some aspects of this masculine identity was discretely alluded to by the contemporary chroniclers. Murād did not follow the warrior script and "actively" abandoned the traditional *ġāzī* role of the Ottoman sultans. Not only did he forgo the tradition of leading military campaigns, but he withdrew from public interactions as well. He preferred to stay in his palace in the company of a limited number of people and watch performances by dwarves and buffoons. Furthermore, his early alleged sexual failure was interpreted as impotence by the Ottoman chroniclers. Nevertheless, after he became very active sexually, following a treatment, the chroniclers went from depicting him as impotent to depicting him as a sex addict. His close relationship with the Sufis of his time was highlighted by the chroniclers. Although Sultan Murād's general interest in Sufism and his relationship with Sufis seem to have been well accepted, the historian Muṣṭafá ᶜĀlī, for example, expresses his disapproval of certain aspects of Murād's Sufism, in particular, his cult-like submission to Şeyḫ Şücāᶜ.[20]

Although contemporary historians emphasized Sultan Murād's failure to follow the traditional script, Sultan Murād seems to have taken pains to show how he interpreted the "script" to suit his personal self-image. His desired image was drawn by Seyyid Loḳmān, the court historiographer, Naḳḳāş ᶜOs̱mān, the court painter, and Nūḥ Aġa, who collected his dream letters. What follows demonstrates how he, by turning into a storyteller, fashions himself according to what he conceives as the script of ideal Ottoman sultanhood, by using his dreams and visions as a means to that end.

Murād the Storyteller

Indeed, every dreamteller is a storyteller. What differentiates him from the storyteller is the liberty that he has as the *only* one who knows the story he is narrating. Likewise, Sultan Murād turns into a storyteller when he narrates his dreams to an audience. Here, it is noteworthy that when referring to his dreams, Murād prefers the word *vāḳıʿa,* which literally means *event* in Arabic, instead of the words, *rüʾyā* or *düş,* more commonly used for "dream" in the Ottoman dream books and interpretations.[21] Murād the dreamteller's consistent and insistent use of the word *vāḳıʿa* throughout his letters blurs the line between dream and reality. I have discussed Murād as a storyteller elsewhere in detail.[22] Given the connotations of his dream accounts in which he himself is a storyteller, Murād the dreamteller's transformation into a storyteller becomes obvious in an illustration painted by Aḥmed Naḳşī sometime between 1003/1595 and 1008/1600, right before or soon after Sultan Murād's death (Figure). In the illustration, Murād is represented as seated on his throne, surrounded by two dwarves, two janissaries, and two pages, holding a book half-open in his left hand.

By placing himself in the position of storyteller, Murād first splits his self into self and object. The self, as narrator, distinguishes himself from the object, the fictive Murād whom he observes in the *ʿālem-i mis̱āl,* the World of Ideal Images/Forms.[23] Then, he tells us about the adventures of this fictive Murād. The position of narrator provides him with the power and control to shape his stories and characters, and presents his own idealized self-portraiture in narrative form, just as other story and dream tellers do. In a way, Murād is, as Bonnie Melchior would put it, the "self-fashioner . . . who become[s] split by that self-consciousness into a self-who-is-observer and a self-who-is-observed—that is, an observing self who constructs the other self, which becomes a fiction, an artifact or a kind of "Other."[24]

Now, to make it clear: We have two Murād figures in the text. The first one, the protagonist of Nūḥ Ağa, serves as the dreamteller, who reports his own mystical experiences to his Sufi master. The second one is the protagonist of this first-person narrator's narratives in his dreams and visions accounts. In the following passage, the italicized typeface refers to Murād the storyteller, whereas the regular typeface refers to the main character in his story:

> *My fortunate father, after bowing my face to the dust at your feet, the observation of this poor one was that* I was standing on a bridge. Underneath it flows a huge river. This poor

Istanbul Topkapı Palace Museum, H. 2165. Fol. 68r.

> one was throwing some objects like wood and fruits to the water, and the water was taking them away. And then my mother arrived and said "Is it time for the afternoon prayer? I have not performed the noon prayer yet." *The command belongs to my sultan.*[25]

These two Murāds are quite different from one another throughout *Kitābü'l- menāmāt*: Murād the storyteller is a submissive and modest character who puts aside his sultanic identity in addressing his Sufi master. He starts almost all the dream accounts, for example, with the phrase "My fortunate father, after bowing my face to the dust at your feet . . ." and ends with another one ". . . the command belongs to my sultan." Yet, Murād the protagonist appears to be an accomplished Sufi, the *Ḳuṭbu'l-aḳṭāb* (the Pole of Poles), and, beyond this, *pādişāh-ı islām* (the Sovereign of Islam).

Murād the Sufi

The Ottoman chroniclers describe Sultan Murād as a faithful disciple to Şücāᶜ Dede. However, *Kitābü'l- menāmāt* places him in a higher position than a weak and submissive novice. The text mainly functions to relate Sultan Murād's noble deeds and adventures in the *ᶜālem-i mis̱āl* and establish his image as a true Friend of God (*velī;* pl. *evliyāʾ*). It starts with Murād's first meeting with his spiritual master through a mysterious dream, revealing Murād as a divinely chosen figure. As a humble aspirant at the outset, he advances, step by step, to the rank of the Spiritual Pole of Poles *(Ḳuṭbu'l-aḳṭāb)*, the head of saints, the highest level a human being can reach. Each account in the text serves to strengthen Murād's image and identity as a Sufi, to emphasize his mystical qualities, virtues, miraculous gifts, and actions, and to increase his fame and reputation in the public mind as an accomplished, sanctified Sufi. Thus, *Kitābü'l- menāmāt* takes on an increasingly marked hagiographical character, and could thus be renamed as *Menāḳıb-nāme-i Sulṭān Murād H̱ān* ("The Exemplary Virtues of Sultan Murād H̱ān").

His progress in the realm of Sufism can be traced by following two different readings of the material in *Kitābü'l- menāmāt.* First, the Sufi dream interpretations can be used as helpful manuals to follow the journey of the soul from the first state of the soul to the last one. A reader/audience familiar with the Sufi dream culture can grasp the progress of Murād the Sufi by observing the signs such as objects, animal and human figures, places, actions and deeds of Murād, and the colors of lights he experienced. However, even a reader unfamiliar with the Sufi dream symbols can still have a sense of the advancement of Murād the Sufi from Murād the novice to Murād the Pole of Poles. This demonstrates that the image of Murād the Sufi is apparently evident to different types of audience members.

In analyzing Murād's Sufi identity through his dream narratives, it is important to understand how Sufis approach dreams. In the *Ḫalvetī* order, dreams function as a means of communication between the disciples and their spiritual masters. By looking at the dreams of the disciple, the master realizes where his disciples stand and what step they should take next. He decides whether the disciples are ready to pass to the next level, or need a reduction or increase in their daily assignment. Not only specific signs, figures, and actions, but also colors in dreams are examined.[26] Although there are differences in interpreting dreams by different Sufi orders, there is enough agreement that by observing these symbols, one can clearly trace the progress of a Sufi through his dreams.

By using a *Ḫalvetī Taᶜbīr-nāme*, the *Taᶜbīr-nāme* of Şeyḫ Ḳurd Muḥammed Efendi el-Ḫalvetī, a sixteenth-century *Ḫalvetī* master well known for his talent at interpreting dreams,[27] as our guide, we can map out Sultan Murād's journey on the Sufi path. In his *Taᶜbīr-nāme,* one of the earliest of a few *Ḫalvetī* dream interpretations in the Ottoman context, Ḳurd Muḥammed Efendi examines signs in dreams in accordance with the generally accepted seven states of the soul (*nefs*) by looking at certain signs and discusses in which the level of the *nefs* the dreamer stands. Each of these states also corresponds to a specific color.[28] Even though it is impossible to argue that Sultan Murād was familiar with Ḳurd Muḥammed Efendi's text, an audience familiar with *Ḫalvetī* dream understanding can trace these stages in Murād's dream narratives.

In his dream narratives, the signs of each of the stages outlined therein may help us to chart the progress of Murād the Sufi from the earliest stage to the highest. The first stage is the *Nefs-i Emmāre* (the Soul/Self that Dictates Evil), which is the lowest level, and which includes *küfr* (disbelief) and *şirk* (polytheism). This is the *nefs* that directs its owner toward wrong actions, for it resides in the world of senses and is dominated by *şehvet* (earthly desires) and passions.[29] Not surprisingly, the signs of this stage rarely appear in the dream narratives of Murād the storyteller. Of the animals that represent this stage, only elephants and camels emerge in the dream narratives of Murād, but they function to indicate his ability to converse with animals, just like the prophet Süleymān, who is known for his miracle of understanding the speech of animals, and some great Sufi figures who are reported to have been able to converse with animals and birds. There is no mention of the color of blue which indicates the first state.

Horses and camels, among the signs of the second stage, the *Nefs-i Levvāme* (the Self-reproaching Soul), are the most commonly appearing animals in Murād's dream accounts.[30] In the state of the *Nefs-i Levvāme*, the Sufi still struggles between the *Şeyṭānī* (provoked by the Satan) feelings and desires and *Raḥmānī* lights stemming from the Divine. Of the places that signify this state of the soul, such as stores, houses, palaces, and even ships,[31] houses and ships appear only in few dream accounts of Murād.[32] Besides, the color of the *Nefs-i Levvāme*, yellow, is not mentioned in his dream narratives. The relative lack of motifs and symbols from this stage indicates the dreamer's very brief passage through the second state.

The "Arab" motif, which indicates the *Nefs-i Mülhime* (the Inspired Soul),[33] is apparent in Murād's dream accounts.[34] It is in this state that the Sufi's dreams do not include animal figures any more; rather he dreams of Arabs, women, and human beings with deficiencies, indicating that the dreamer's soul is still deficient. Although we don't see the representative color red in Murād's dream accounts, the open areas such as gardens and his being able to walk on water and fly in the air in his dreams correspond to the third stage.[35]

Arches and bows, respected people (i.e., prophets, sultans, learned men), respected places (i.e., the Kaʿbe, mosque, or the cities of Madina and Jerusalem), books and the Qurʾān, which all correspond to the fourth state, the *Nefs-i Muṭmaʾinne* (the Satisfied Self), are the most commonly appearing motifs in Murād's dream accounts. We observe him reading the Qurʾān and some books in numerous dream accounts. Additionally, dreaming of the Kaʿbe, mosque, the city of Jerusalem, the prophets (ʿĪsā, Mūsā, Yaʿḳūb, İsmāʾīl, İbrāhīm, and Muḥammed), and the sultans suggests he has completely liberated himself from worldly ties and reached the state of the *insān-ı kāmil* (perfect human being). He, again, walks on water and flies in the air in his dream accounts. As for the color symbolism, there seems to have been a disagreement on the colors of white and black between the *Ḫalvetī* and the other Sufi orders: Whereas white symbolizes the *Nefs-i Muṭmaʾinne* for the *Ḫalvetī*s, it is black that indicates the *Nefs-i Muṭmaʾinne* for other orders.

The fifth state, the *Nefs-i Rāżiyye* (the Consenting Self), indicates that the Sufi has been able to abandon all his worldly desires and carnal passions, and has submitted himself to the Divine will. That is, he is now at the level of angels and *ḥūrīs*. We don't see green, the color of this stage, in Murad's dream accounts,[36] but his walking on water, and flying in the air indicate he has reached the level of angels. Yet, because these motifs are considered as the signs for the third and the fourth levels as well, the importance of consulting with an expert, *mürşid*, on dreams rather than simply looking up dream interpretations and trying to figure out the hidden meanings behind the symbols becomes clear.

It is in the sixth state, the *Nefs-i Marżiyye* (the Consent-given Self), that the Sufi dreams of seven skies, the Sun, stars, fire, lit candles, lightning, thunder, and such. A flame that comes out from him and wraps around the belly of a horse, and a big fire that appears during his circumbulation around the Kaᶜbe[37] suggest that the soul of Murād has reached the *Nefs-i Marżiyye*, the sixth state. For the *Ḫalvetī*, white is the color of the *Nefs-i Marżiyye*.[38]

Ultimately, Murād's dream accounts include rain, snow, a black sea and a white sea next to each other, and the colorless light[39] which are considered as the signs of the seventh, last, and most advanced state of the soul, the *Nefs-i Ṣāfiyye*, also called *Nefs-i Tezkiyye* (the Purified Self).[40]

However, it is not that easy to argue what each of these signs and symbols refer to. As the dream interpreters emphasize, each dream account deserves a unique interpretation based on the social, cultural, religious, and economic background of the dreamer. For example, some dream narratives include symbols and motifs that may belong to different levels of the self. Obviously, such complex and mysterious dreams can reveal their meanings only to those who are experts on the Sufi dream culture. Thus, not everyone who has the access to these manuals can easily claim to locate where the dreamer is standing in his spiritual journey. This indicates that being able to use these dream manuals requires a specific talent and training process. Therefore, as this specific dream account demonstrates, it is not easy to locate which state Murād has reached, but it is meant to be obvious to a certain kind of audience members.

Moreover, each Sufi order has its own understanding of symbols in dreams, and dreams require an independent and unique interpretation. Sultan Murād's dream accounts thus would be interpreted differently by representatives of different Sufi orders. However, by looking at the *Ḫalvetī* dream interpretations, the states Murād the Sufi passes through can be detected in accordance with the dream culture within the *Ḫalvetī* circle, for his *şeyḫ*, Şücāᶜ Dede himself, was a *Ḫalvetī*.

Although these Sufi dream experts could identify the symbols in Murād's dreams, much of the intent of his dreams easily could be followed even by those not familiar with this symbolism. Murād's evolution in the spiritual hierarchy clearly can be traced not only through the symbols, metaphors, or colors, but also through the deeds and actions of Murād, the protagonist of Murād the storyteller. In short, Murād can be observed in three different states of sainthood: *mürīd* (disciple), *ḫalīfe* (successor of a spiritual master), and the *Ḳuṭbu'l-aḳṭāb* (the Pole of Poles).

The first phase of Murād as a Sufi is as a disciple, *mürīd,* which is the beginning step of the process. As a *mürīd,* Murād appears to be a submissive and modest disciple. His relationship with Şücā ᶜ is in the mode of regular *mürīd-mürşid* relationship. Sometimes they appear in a face-to-face setting during which Murād receives advice and instructions from his *şeyḫ*[41]; sometimes some mediators, who are probably other disciples of Şücā ᶜ, bring instructions from the *şeyḫ*. Yet, for the most part their communication is through letters as it was in real life.[42]

Their relationship occasionally goes beyond verbal instruction, and turns into a physically controlling one. When Murād is in the state of *vecd* (ecstacy), for example, Şücā ᶜ Dede, as his spiritual master, holds him tightly,[43] suggesting the physical manifestation of Şücā ᶜ's spiritual authority over Murād.

The second phase of the evolution of Murād as a Sufi is when he takes on the role of spiritual mentor to his sisters, as the "successor" (*ḫalīfe*) of his *şeyḫ*. With the spiritual authority he received from his *şeyḫ,* Murād the *ḫalīfe,* provides them with instructions regarding the spiritual path. He teaches them how to perform *ẕikr,* and even commands them to bring their dreams to him for his interpretation, which demonstrates his maturity, placing him now as an advanced Sufi master over them in the hierarchical structure of Sufism.

> Your majesty had given *dest-i tevbe* (hand of repentance) for my sisters and appointed this poor one as the successor (*ḫalīfe*) over them. You told me to interpret all of their dreams, and left. I gathered all of them around me, and said, "Now, each of you, tell me. Each of you, go and find an empty place and occupy yourself with, 'There is no god but God.' Take 'There is no god but God' from your right side and give it to your left side. And whatever dream you have, come and tell me. But never take your dreams to someone else. Bring them only to me. Beware! Otherwise you become infidels." I advised them in this manner.[44]

In fact, Murād, the Sufi master or *ḫalīfe* of women, appears again when he gives specific assignments to some women whose identities are not clearly stated.[45]

Upon reaching the level of *"veliyyullāh"* (a friend of God),[46] Murād finds himself in the realm of the invisible hierarchy of saints, and he is even elevated to a highest position in the Sufi hierarchy by a written statement given to him in a dream.[47] It validates his position as the Pole of Poles (*Ḳuṭbu'l-aḳṭāb*), the highest spiritual rank in the invisible hierarchy a saint can hope to attain. After being called "the crown of the saints and the superior of the purified ones/saints," confirming his status,[48] he is ultimately turned into Ḫıżır, one of the four pillars (*evtād*) in the Sufi spiritual hierarchy.[49]

His being granted the position of *Ḳuṭbu'l-aḳṭāb* is vividly depicted, in his words, in a "strange" dream scene in which he "observes" that all the saints on the earth have gathered in a dome and are sitting with the current Pole of Poles:

> and then I arrived. When I approached the Pole of Poles, he embraced me. Once he held me tightly, a drop of sweat came out of his right cheek, and I drank this drop. Another drop of sweat came out again, and I drank that one too. A drop of sweat came out from his left cheek, and I also drank that one. And then the Pole of Poles said, "Now, it [your sainthood] has exceeded mine and that of the other saints." Then, the Pole of Poles continued, "Both keep your sultanate and be the Pole of Poles."[50]

This dream account is obviously framed as a clear confirmation that Murād is both the temporal ruler and the religious guide. His status of the *Ḳuṭbu'l-āḳṭāb* is further demonstrated through the pledge of allegiance (*bīᶜat*) of other Sufis who thereby submit themselves to him. An unnamed Sufi in a white dress, which symbolizes purity and heavenly acceptance, kisses his hand,[51] and the celebrated Sufi Ẕü 'n-nūn-ı Mıṣrī prostrates himself at his feet.[52] As the *Ḳuṭbu'l-aḳṭāb*, Murād is granted the *ᶜilm-i ledünnī*, the knowledge that is not learned but revealed by God only to his elect servants.[53]

On the other hand, Murād takes his claim even further by asserting to have received Divine revelation from God (*vaḥy*).[54] He replaces the Prophet in the Islamic declaration of the *tevḥīd*:

> a letter fell down. It was written that "Messenger (*Resūl*)! Call people to Allāh. He who disobeys you will be sent to

> Hell eternally." Immediately after I read this, I woke up. There is no god, but God; Muḥammed is His Messenger. A *nidā* (call) came saying, "There is no god, but God; You are His Messenger." This has happened a few times.[55]

Murād's seeming assertion of prophecy, however, presents certain problems, because Muḥammed's being the last prophet is one of the pillars of Islam. This assertion is clarified as sainthood in the same dream account by relating another visionary experience in which Murād is given the "possession of sainthood."[56] Furthermore, the obscurity over the meaning of "*nübüvvet*" (prophecy) is explicitly clarified without leaving any doubt in the following Divine inspiration that occurs in his heart:

> What I mean by "I gave you prophethood" is that I merged the secrets of the saints and prophets in you. I gave you all of what I gave to the prophets and saints, except for the office of the prophethood (*nübüvvet*) and messengerhood (*risālet*). The prophethood and messengerhood are sealed. Yet, you are my chosen beloved. I merged the secret of messengerhood (*risālet*) and sainthood (*velāyet*) in you. All these states are in you. I gave you the observance and union that I gave them too.[57]

Murād's claim to prophecy needs to be discussed in the light of Ibn el-ʿArabī's understanding of sainthood, which encompasses *nübüvvet* and *risālet*.[58] Seen from this perspective, this is not a declaration of prophecy, but rather reinforcement of Murād's status as the foremost heir of the Prophet.[59] In fact, these references identify Murād with the light of Muḥammed (*Nūr-ı Muḥammediye*), the most exalted representation of his primordial substance, and the sublime reality of Muḥammed (*ḥaḳīḳat-i Muḥammediye*).[60]

Sultan Murād's spiritual journey, however, does not end with his arrival at the stage of messengerhood (*risālet*). He ultimately reaches the level of *vaḥdet-i vücūd* (Unity of Existence or Oneness of Being), the ultimate goal of Sufi gnostics (*ʿārifūn*), in which God and the created world are united in one undifferentiated entity. In a flash of divine inspiration (*ilhām*), Murād the dreamteller declares that his hero has ultimately reached the stage of *vaḥdet-i vücūd*: "O My beloved, you are Me, and I am you. There is no difference between Me and you," "I am One, and you are One," or "I am He. You are He. I am the True Reality [Ḥaḳḳ]." Say, "I am the True Reality [Ḥaḳḳ]."[61]

Murād the *Pādişāh-ı İslām*

Throughout *Kitābü'l- menāmāt,* the protagonist of the narrative is described as the Sovereign of the Muslim world (*pādişāh-ı islām*). It should be noted that, although the historical Murād III kept the titles of the *Ṣāḥib-ḳırān* (Lord of the Auspicious Conjunction) and the *Ẓıll'ullāh* (Shadow of God) as the Sultan of the Empire, Murād the dreamteller ignores these titles, except for a single statement in which Murād is called the *Pādişāh-ı ᶜālem-penāh* (Sovereign of the Refuge of the Universe).[62] Rather, Murād the protagonist's role as the Sultan of the Muslim world is emphasized. Moreover, although Murād is never named as the awaited Mehdī, he is implicitly portrayed as a messianic figure whose signs recur throughout the text.[63]

In fact, Sultan Murād had reasons to assume that he was the chosen one. When he ascended to the throne as the twelfth sultan of his Ottoman dynasty on 1 *Ramażān* 982/ 15 December, 1574, there were only seventeen/eighteen years left until the end of the first Islamic millennium. Due to a widespread belief that world would not last beyond one thousand years, throughout the sixteenth century certain Muslim groups were anxiously awaiting its last days. This millenarian worldview was vividly and imaginatively described in the pictorial *Fāl-nāme*s (Books of Omen) "that can be read as one such manifestation of the millenarian history."[64] Such apocalyptic anxieties seem to have led people to anticipate the coming of a Mehdī, who would put the world in order and unify the mutually hostile strands of Islam. Murād's dreams make the Sultan Murād the focus of apocalyptic expectations, as is evident from the following dream account:

> I was given a book in which it was written "*elif elif elif elif.*" I was told that this is how much time was left before the end of the world. It was also written "*elif be te s̱e cim* (the first five letters in Arabic alphabet)." Then, a witnessing (*müşāhede*) occurred that I was traveling towards Jerusalem on a ship.[65]

Murād's visionary journey to Jerusalem is crucial, since it mirrors the *ḥadīth* account, according to which the Mehdī and his men will travel to the city of Jerusalem on a thousand ships.[66] However, Murād encounters a major predicament, which his ancestors had faced earlier when they claimed the caliphate.[67] The Mehdī has to be a descendant of the Prophet, which the Ottoman dynasty could not claim.[68] Yet Murād the dreamteller resolves this problem by establishing a spiritual connection that verifies Murād as the direct successor of the Prophet. The Prophet's mantle is put on Murād,[69] along with the Prophet's amulet, scimitar and copy of the Qurʾān,[70] in an act that confirms his special status and the bestowal of prophetic blessings on him. He is ultimately called "the inheritor of the knowledge of the Prophet."[71] This is particularly significant because the Shīʿa tradition holds that before his death, the Prophet passed a sacred and secret knowledge (*ʿilm*), inaccessible to ordinary human beings, as well as his political and religious authority onto ʿAlī, although the Sunnis deny this. It is through this knowledge that the Shīʿa imams claimed to have been the "the infallible interpreters of God's will," a claim that established them as the true authorities over the Muslim world.[72] Our narrator, however, asserts that this authority and sacred knowledge was passed onto Murād by the Prophet himself in his dream, reinforcing his claims to be the true political and spiritual leader of the Islamic world. Ultimately, his image as the living embodiment of the Muḥammedan knowledge is completed by his transformation into the Prophet himself.[73]

Furthermore, Murād is also transformed into ʿAlī, thus verifying his supremacy as a divinely ordained ruler in order to gather the Shīʿī Muslims as well as the Sunnis under his governance. First, the *velāyet* (Sainthood) and *kerāmet* (Miracle working) that ʿAlī is believed to posses is passed onto Murād.[74] Then, just as he turned into the Prophet, he turns into ʿAlī.[75] This allows him to establish himself as the hybrid of both the Prophet and ʿAlī, under whose authority both the Sunni and Shīʿī communities of Islam can be united. To these already impressive credentials, Murād adds another one, that is his being the twelfth sultan in his Ottoman dynasty, identifying himself with the twelfth Imam who is believed to be the Mehdī in the Shīʿa tradition:

> I was given a letter. It was written, "The Ottoman caliphs are supposed to be twelve. There have been eleven so far. The twelfth is 'Hāẕā Murādu'l-Murād.' That is, it is you." It was written: "May God grant goodness to you."[76]

These credentials make Murād's claims to be the awaited Mehdī truly unassailable. As the Sultan of Islam (and the awaited Mehdī), Murād the dreamteller assigns two major responsibilities to his hero: He is both the protector and restorer of the religion. For example, a dream shows Murād, in the middle of a desert, leading a prayer for more than ten thousand people. This scene establishes him as the foremost religious leader and authority of the age.[77] Yet, he is not only the leader of the believers, but also the protector of Islam par excellence. We observe him on the battlefield, fighting against infidels,[78] or in the role of a fatherly figure taking the religion onto his lap, as described in the following dream account, in which the religion is symbolized by a beautiful little boy:

> in a desert, there was a black curtain. I opened that curtain. A boy with a bejeweled crown on his head was sitting there. Yet, this boy was so beautiful that he could not be described. I took him and made him sit on my lap. While wondering who he could be, a voice came from the unknown, "It is not a boy, it is the religion of Muḥammed and the religion of Islam; it is the religion of Muḥammed."[79]

Not surprisingly, Murād receives Divine inspirations that promise him triumph and victory in the West and the East.[80] He is even specifically granted "the disposal of all the sovereignty of the province of the Persian Lands."[81] These divine inspirations are particularly remarkable because they may have been the reasons behind Sultan Murād III's insistence on relaunching military campaigns against the Safavids in 987/1578, despite the strategic disadvantages faced by the Ottoman armies and his viziers' objections.[82] In this way, *Kitābü'l-menāmāt* functions not only to create an image of Sultan Murād, but also to legitimize his political and military decisions.

As mentioned, Murād is also depicted as the restorer of the religion (*müceddid*), who is promised to the Muslims to arise in order to revive Islam at the dawn of each century.[83] Given the fact that Murād's letters were compiled toward the beginning of a new millennium, in 1001 A.H., Murād's claims sound particularly pertinent, as the following dream account seems to suggest:

> I had arrived at the *Ravża-i Resūl*[84] . . . while visiting it, someone came and took me to the door, saying "The Well of *Zemzem* is here. Let's go see it." Then, he said, "Let's lower a bucket to see if it comes back full." We lowered it again and again. Each time it came back full. Yet, its bucket and rope were worn out. I exchanged it with a good/strong bucket.[85]

Just as the protagonist of Murād the dreamteller is symbolically presented as a restorer of the religion in this dream, the historical Murād III busied himself with the restoration of the *Ḥarem-i Şerīf* (the Noble Sanctuary in Jerusalem). He ordered its domes to be covered with marble, to clean the water channels, and to renovate the walls of the Kaᶜbe.[86]

In fact, it was not only for spiritual reasons, but also for political ones that Murād sought to assert his supreme religious authority. Apparently, both outside and within the Empire, he was not alone in such claims. At the beginning of the sixteenth century, Shāh Ismāᶜīl (r. 907–930/1502–1524), the Safavid monarch, claimed to have a semi-divine status. He also identified himself with the awaited Mehdī.[87] Following the death of Shāh Ismāᶜīl, his son Shāh Ṭahmāsp (r. 930–984/1524–1576) abandoned his father's claims to divinity, yet he continued to insist on having "a special stature (*makhṣūṣ, mumtāz*) designed and protected by the grace of God to maintain temporal and moral order as the shadow of God on earth."[88] A few decades later, Shāh Ismāᶜīl's great-grandson ᶜAbbās I (r. 995–1038/1587–1629) revived Shāh Ismāᶜīl's self-depiction as the "Shadow of God," and transposed it onto his own persona.[89] About the same time, another Muslim ruler, the sultan of the Moghul Empire, Akbar (963–1014/1543–1605) also was described as both the Spiritual Pole (*ḳutb*) and the Perfect Man (*insān-ı kāmil*) of his time by his courtiers, who spoke of him as "the type-symbol of God, as the sun is His type-symbol in nature . . . the fulfillment of divine destiny," as asserted by Ebū 'l-Faḍl ᶜAllāmī in his *Akbar-nāma* ("Book of Akbar").[90]

Conclusion

Like modern men and women, sixteenth-century individuals cared deeply about their image and self-representation. Unlike modern individuals, they employed dreams and visions to project the image they wished others to see. This study has analyzed how one of these individuals, the Ottoman sultan Murād III, made use of dreams and visions to fashion himself.

This self-image stands in sharp opposition to the ways he was portrayed by the chroniclers who faulted him for deviating from the generally accepted script of sultanhood. Through his dream accounts, Murād creates an image of a sultanic figure whose sovereignty is blessed and directed by God. He is a divinely ordained sultan, destined to restore Islam and unite the Muslim world under his sovereignty. Throughout the text, he turns into three major figures: Ḫıżır, Muḥammed, and ᶜAlī. His transformation into these three grand figures of the Islamic tradition, not only verifies him as the embodiment of *velāyet*, *nübüvvet*, and *risālet*, but also presents him as unifying all

Muslims under his sovereignty at a time perceived by some to be the end of the world.

We will never know if Sultan Murād indeed had these dreams and visions, or if he was deliberately creating this fictive character to further his spiritual and political career. Yet, these dream accounts were particularly useful for him, because in contemporary Muslim lore the sound dream (that is, a dream that comes true) of a righteous man was considered to be one of forty-six parts of being a prophet. By recounting his dreams to Şücā ͨ Dede, his spiritual master, not only did he reach a certain audience, whom he perceived as receptive, but he also sought a confirmation of the authenticity of his dreams as "valid dreams." It is true that, like other dreamtellers, he was the only one who knew what really happened in his dreams; however, his position among his subjects helped him to present his dream accounts as genuine and veridical. Which of his subjects would dare to assert that the Sultan of the greatest empire of the time, the Caliph of Muslims, the Lord of the Auspicious Conjunction (*Ṣāḥib-ḳırān*), and the Shadow of God (*Ẓıll'ullāh*), the Sultan Murād Ḫān, had not had any of these dreams? After all, did the Prophet not say that the worst lie is when "a person claims to have seen a dream which he has not seen"?

Notes

This article is a shortened version of my UM dissertation which has the same title as the article. I am grateful to Alexander Knysh, Gottfried Hagen, Walter G. Andrews, Kathryn Babayan, Karla Taylor, Rudi P. Lindner, and Shahzad Bashir for their insights, feedback, and suggestions during the writing process of the dissertation. I also thank Erdem H. Çıpa for his comments and suggestions on the final version of this article.

1. Stephan Greenblatt, *Renaissance Self-fashioning: From More to Shakespeare* (Chicago: University of Chicago Press, 1980), 2.

2. For more on the autobiography and self-narrative in Ottoman context, see Cemal Kafadar, "Self and Others: The Diary of a Dervish in Seventeenth Century Istanbul and First-Person Narratives in Ottoman Literature" *Studia Islamica* 69 (1989), 121–50; and Derin Terzioğlu "Man in the Image of God in the Image of His Times" *Studia Islamica* 94 (2002), 139–165. The other collection of a disciple's dream letters to a Sufi master belongs to Āsiye Ḫātūn of Üsküp, a seventeenth-century woman dervish of the Ḫalvetī order. See Cemal Kafadar, *Rüya Mektupları/Asiye Hatun; Giriş, Çevrimyazı, Sadeleştirme,* (Istanbul: Oğlak Yayıncılık, 1994).

3. Faris Çerçi, *Gelibolulu Mustafa Âlî ve Künhü'l-ahbâr'ında II. Selim, III. Murat ve III. Mehmet Devirleri* (Kayseri: Erciyes Üniversitesi Yayınları, 2000) vol. 2, 225.

4. Ibid., 249; *Kitābü'l- menāmāt*. Nuruosmaniye, nu. 2599, 1v–2r.

5. ᶜAṭāʾī, ᶜAṭā Allāh ibn Yaḥyā, *Ḥadāʾiḳü 'l-ḥaḳāʾiḳ fī Tekmileti'ş-şeḳāʾiḳ: Ẕeyl-i şeḳāʾiḳ* ([Istanbul: s.n.], 1268 [1852]), 364.

6. *Kitābü'l- menāmāt*, 176r.

7. ᶜAṭāʾī, *Ḥadāʾiḳü 'l-ḥaḳāʾiḳ*, 364.

8. Çerçi, 248.

9. Ibid., 249.

10. ᶜAṭāʾī, 364.

11. Although we have no information about Nūḥ Ağa's mystical affiliations, the fact that he prefers the phrase "Ḥażret-i Şeyḫ" when he addresses Şücāᶜ in the introduction of *Kitābü'l- menāmāt* suggests that he was also one of Şücāᶜ Dede's disciples (2r–2v).

12. Ibid., 159r.

13. Ibid., 13.

14. Ibid., 158v.

15. Ibid., 1r.

16. See Erving Goffman, *The Presentation of Self in Everyday Life* (Garden City, N.Y.: Doubleday, 1959); *Interaction Ritual; Essays in Face-to-Face Behavior* (Chicago: Aldine Pub. Co., 1967); *Frame Analysis: An Essay on the Organization of Experience* (Cambridge, Mass.: Harvard University Press, 1974).

17. Here, in developing the script of an Ottoman sultan I use the term in reference to Simon and Gagnon's theory of sexual script that approaches sexual behaviors as a sociocultural process. I expand this process beyond sexual conduct to rulership as a social behavior. Laumann, E. O., Gagnon, J. H., Michael, R. T., & Michaels, S., *The Social Organization of Sexuality: Sexual Practices in the United States* (Chicago: University of Chicago, 1994). I thank Walter G. Andrews for introducing me to scripting theory through his forthcoming article "Ottoman Love: Preface to a Theory of Emotional Ecology."

18. On the construction of "*ġāzī* sultan" image, see for example, Colin Imber, "Ideals and Legitimation in Early Ottoman History," in *Süleyman the Magnificent and His Age: The Ottoman Empire in the Early Modern World*, eds. Metin Kunt and Christine Woodhead (London; New York: Longman, 1995), 138–153.

19. On visualization of the ideal sultan in the illustrated manuscripts, see Serpil Bağcı's "Visualizing Power: Portrayals of the Sultans in Illustrated Histories of the Ottoman Dynasty" in *Islamic Art* VI (2009), 113–27.

20. For a thorough discussion on the negative image of Murād III and Şücāᶜ Dede presented by the Ottoman chroniclers, see Chapter I in Özgen Felek, "(Re)creating Image and Identity: Dreams and Visions as a Means of Murād III's Self-fashioning," Unpublished PhD dissertation, University of Michigan, 2010.

21. See, Hasan Avni Yüksel, *Türk İslâm Tasavvuf Geleneğinde Rüya* (Istanbul: Millî Eğitim Basımevi, 1996).

22. See Özgen Felek, "Re-narrating Islamic Lore: The Dream Writings of Sultan Murād III," in *Journal of Turkish Studies* (eds. Cemal Kafadar, Gönül

Alpay Tekin, and Mehmet Kalpaklı) (Harvard Univ. Dept. of NELC, 2010), vol. 34/II, 1–19.

23. William C. Chittick, *The Sufi Path of Knowledge: Ibn al-ʿArabi's Metaphysics of Imagination* (Albany: State University of New York Press, 1989), 112–21.

24. Bonnie Melchior "Gender and Self-fashioning" in *Studies in the Humanities,* June 2000. See also Thomas C. Heller, Morton Sosna, Christine Brooke-Rose, David E. Wellbery, *Reconstructing Individualism: Autonomy, Individuality, and the Self in Western Thought* (Stanford, California: Stanford University Press, 1986), 12.

25. *Kitābü'l- menāmāt,* 20v.

26. Specifically in the *Kübreviyye* order, an elaborate color symbolism, which is welcomed in the *Ḫalvetī* tradition as well, was developed. See A. Schimmel, *Mystical Dimensions of Islam* (Chapel Hill: University of North Carolina Press, 1975), 255–56, and Alexander Knysh, *Islamic Mysticism A short History* (Leiden: Brill, 2000), 234–39.

27. For Ḳurd Muḥammed Efendi see, Mustafa Tatçı and Halil Çeltik, *Türk Edebiyatında Tasavvufî Rü'yâ Ta'bîr-nâmeleri: Kurd Muḥammed el-Halvetî, Niyâzî-i Mısrî el-Halvetî, Karabaş-ı Velî el-Halvetî, Yiğitbaşı Ahmed Marmaravî el-Halvetî* (Ankara: Akçağ, 1995), xix–xx; and Peçevī, vol. II, 36.

28. For a detailed explanation of the association of colors with certain stages of mystical progress, see Yüksel, *Türk İslâm Tasavvuf Geleneğinde Rüya,* 190–212.

29. Tatçı and Çeltik, *Türk Edebiyatında Tasavvufî Rüyâ Ta'bir-nâmeleri,* 6–7.

30. *Kitābü'l- menāmāt,* 3r–3v; 4r; 7r; 12v–13r; 37v; 75r–v.

31. Tatçı and Çeltik, *Türk Edebiyatında Tasavvufî Rüyâ Ta'bir-nâmeleri,* 7–8.

32. *Kitābü'l- menāmāt,* 5v, 6v, 8v, 43v, 48r, 123r, 37r, 39v, 75v.

33. Tatçı and Çeltik, *Türk Edebiyatında Tasavvufî Rüyâ Ta'bir-nâmeleri,* 8.

34. *Kitābü'l- menāmāt,* 13r–13v.

35. Ibid., 3r, 37r, 94r, and 137r.

36. Tatçı and Çeltik, *Türk Edebiyatında Tasavvufî Rüyâ Ta'bir-nâmeleri,* 10.

37. *Kitābü'l- menāmāt,* 75r and 121v.

38. Ibid., 10–11.

39. Ibid., 49r, 36r, and 22v.

40. Tatçı and Çeltik, *Türk Edebiyatında Tasavvufî Rüyâ Ta'bir-nâmeleri,* 11.

41. Ibid., 3r–3v; 31v; 69v; 125v–126r; 137r–137v.

42. Ibid., 3v–4r; 88r–89v; 132r–v; 33v–34r; 36r.

43. Ibid., 52v.

44. Ibid., 73r–73v.

45. Ibid., 5v; 37v; 83v.

46. Ibid.

47. Ibid., 119r. The concept of the *Ḳuṭb,* literally "pole" or "axis," was elaborated on by ibn el-ʿArabī. For a detailed discussion of the hierarchy of the saints, see Muḥyi'd-dīn ibn el-ʿArabī, *el-Futūḥāt el-Mekkiye* (Beirut: Dār el-Fikr, 1994/1414), vol. 3, 9. The ideas of ibn el-ʿArabī, about the *ḳuṭb* are at

some points contradictory and confusing. Michel Chodkiewicz did his utmost to systematize ibn el-ʿArabī's thoughts regarding the concept of the Pole. See, Michel Chodkiewicz, *Seal of The Saints: Prophethood and Sainthood in the Doctrine of Ibn ʿArabī*, translated by Liadain Sherrard (Cambridge: Islamic Texts Society, 1993), 92. The *ḳuṭb* refers to either the Perfect Man (*insān-ı kāmil*), or the Reality of Muḥammed *(Ḥaḳīḳat-i Muḥammediye)*, which manifests itself in the Perfect Man (*insān-ı kāmil*). Although neither in the Qurʾān nor in the earliest Sufi tradition is the term *insān-ı kāmil* mentioned, it was developed by ibn el-ʿArabī, and it reached its perfect and finalized form in ʿAbd el-kerīm el-Jīlī's (d. 820/1417) *el-Insān el-kāmil*. ʿAbd al-Karīm al-Jīlī, *Universal Man Extracts*, trans. with Commentary by Titus Burckhardt; English translation by Angela Culme-Semour (Paris: Beshara Publications, 1983).

48. *Kitābü'l- menāmāt*, 45v.

49. Ibid., 102v; 12v. According to ibn el-ʿArabī, the other three are Ilyās, ʿĪsā and Idrīs. See ibn el-ʿArabī, *el-Futūḥāt*, vol. 3, 9. Ḫıżır is also believed to be the spiritual guide of Moses. While Moses has the Şerīʿat (Divine law), Ḫıżır has the *ʿilm-i ledünnī*. Thus, Sufis perceive Ḫıżır as not only their own spiritual guide, but also Moses'. For more, see Ahmet Yaşar Ocak, *İslâm-Türk İnançlarında Hızır yahut Hızır-İlyas Kültü* (Ankara: Türk Kültürünü Araştırma Enstitüsü, 1985).

50. *Kitābü'l- menāmāt*, 119r.

51. Ibid., 127v.

52. Ibid., 60r.

53. Ibid., 8r; 255v.

54. Ibid., 85v.

55. Ibid., 21r.

56. Ibid., 112v.

57 Ibid., 90r.

58. Chodkiewicz, *Seal of the Saints*, 52.

59. For a discussion of saints as the heirs of the prophets, ibid., 74–88.

60. Quoted in Uri Rubin, "Pre-Existence and Light," in *Israel Oriental Studies* 5 (1975), 62–119. For a thorough discussion about the light of Muḥammed (*nūr-ı Muḥammedī*) and reality of Muḥammed (*ḥaḳiḳat-i Muḥammedī*), and for the discussions on the nature of Muḥammed's pre-existence, see Rubin's "Pre-Existence and Light."

61. *Kitābü'l- menāmāt*, 14r, 28v, 46r, and 74r.

62. Ibid., 142r.

63. On the anxious anticipation of the Last Days and a Messianic figure in the early modern Islamic era, see Sanjay Subrahmanyam, "Connected Histories: Notes Towards a Reconfiguration of Early Modern Eurasi," in *Modern Asia Studies* 31, 3 (1997), 735–762; and Cornell H. Fleischer, "Mahdi and Millennium: Messianic Dimension in the Development of Ottoman Imperial Ideology," in *The Great Ottoman-Turkish Civilization*. Editor-in-Chief, Kemal Çiçek; Chief of the Editorial Board, Halil Inalcık, (Ankara: Yeni Türkiye Yayınları, 2000), v. 3, 42–54; idem, "The Lawgiver as Messiah: the Making of the Imperial Image in the Reign of Süleymân," in *Soliman le Magnifique et son*

temps, ed. G. Veinstein (Paris: La Documentation Français, 1992), 159–177. I thank Erdem H. Çıpa for bringing Subrahmanyam's article to my attention.

64. For the description of the millenarian view in the Safavid context, see Kathryn Babayan, "The Cosmological Order of Things in Early Modern Safavid Iran," in *Falnama the Book of Omens*, ed. Massumeh Farhad (Washington, DC: Arthur M. Sackler Gallery Smithsonian Institution, 2009), 246–55.

65. *Kitābü'l- menāmāt*, 39v.

66. Shaykh ʿAlī ibn Ḥusām al-mashhūr bi-al-Muttaqī al-Hindī, *Kitābü'l-Burhān fī Kitāb al-burhān fī ʿalāmāt Mahdī ākhir al-zamān*; dirāsah wa-taḥqīq Jāsim ibn Muḥammad ibn Muhalhil al-Yāsīn (Kuwait: Dhāt al-Salāsil, 1988), vol. 2, 778–782.

67. See Colin Imber, *Ebu's-suùd: The Islamic Legal Tradition* (Edinburgh: Edinburgh University Press, 1997), 103–106.

68. On the *ḥadīth* accounts that establish the Mehdī as the descendant of the Prophet, see el-Muṭṭaḳī, *Kitābü'l-Burhān*, vol. 2, 565–594.

69. *Kitābü'l- menāmāt*, 14r. This dream account also alludes to the well-known story of Veysel Ḳaranī (Üveys el-Ḳaranī), a contemporary of the Prophet, who was desperately passionate for the Prophet, yet could not meet him in his life time. The Prophet, knowing Ḳaranī's burning desire to meet him, sent his mantel to Ḳaranī. Ahmet Yaşar Ocak, *Veysel Karanî ve Üveysîlik* (Istanbul: Dergâh Yayınları, 1982); J. Baldick, *Imaginary Muslims. The Uwaysi Sufis of Central Asia* (London; New York: I.B. Tauris & Co., 1993).

70. *Kitābü'l- menāmāt*, 75r; 96r.

71. Ibid., 96r.

72. Alexander Knysh, *Islam in Historical Perspective* (Upper Saddle River, NJ: Pearson and Prentice Hall, 2011), 162.

73. *Kitābü'l- menāmāt*, 112v; 252r.

74. Ibid., 8r.

75. Ibid., 33r.

76. Ibid., 98r.

77. Ibid., 130v.

78. Ibid., 42r, 104r.

79. Ibid., 62r.

80. Ibid., 6v.

81. Ibid., 162v.

82. The historian Peçevī details the Grandvizier Soḳullu's efforts to stop the military campaigns against the Safavids. Peçevī, vol. 2, 37–38. Interestingly, this dream account reminds us of the divine inspiration that Meḥmed Çelebi mentions in his *Şecāʿatnāme*, commissioned by Sultan Murād. The author justifies the military campaigns against the Safavids, saying it is not a result of Sultan Murād's personal insistence, but of a Divine inspiration Murād had. Meḥmed Çelebi's text is in a way a companion work to the *Kitābü'l- menāmāt*. Âsafî Dal Meḥmed Çelebi (Bey, Paşa), *Şecâ'atnâme: Özdemiroğlu Osman Paşa'nın Şark seferleri, (1578–1585)* (haz., Abdülkadir Özcan) (Istanbul: Çamlıca Basım Yayın, 2006), 25.

83. Quoted in Gerald T. Elmore, *Islamic Sainthood in the Fullness of Time: Ibn al-ʿArabī's Book of the Fabulous Gryphon* (Leiden: Brill, 1999), 3, n: 2.

Also see E. van Donzel, "Mudjaddid," *Encyclopaedia of Islam,* Second Edition. Edited by: P. Bearman, Th. Bianquis, C.E. Bosworth, E. van Donzel and W.P. Heinrichs. Brill, 2010. http://www.brillonline.nl

84. *Ravża-i Resūl,* also known as *Ravża-i Muṭaḥḥara,* is the Garden of the Prophet, where the tomb of the Prophet is located in Medina.

85. *Kitābü'l- menāmāt,* 129v.

86. H. Ahmet Kırkkılıç, *Sultan Üçüncü Murad: Hayatı, Edebî Kişiliği, Eserleri ve Divanı'ndan Seçmeler* (Ankara: Kültür ve Turizm Bakanlığı, 1988), 7.

87. Kathryn Babayan, *Mystics, Monarchs and Messiahs: Cultural Landscapes of Early Modern Iran* (Cambridge, Mass.: Harvard University Press, 2002), 295–348.

88. Ibid., 324.

89. Ibid., 357.

90. Marshall G. S. Hodgson, *The Venture of Islam: Conscience and History in a World Civilization* (Chicago: University of Chicago Press, 1974), vol. 3, 78.

CHAPTER 14

The Visionaries of a *Ṭarīqa*

The Uwaysī Sufis of Shāhjahānābād

Meenakshi Khanna

One day, in the assembly of *Shaykh* Sayyid Ḥasan, there was a discussion about the appearance of the ennobling vision of the Prophet. The *Shaykh* related, "As, by the grace of God, this circumstance often appeared to me, therefore in order to confirm the legality of this matter, I dressed myself in distinguished robes and accompanied by a few other men visited the house of *Shaykh* ʿAbd al-Ḥaqq Muḥaddith Dihlawī. He asked me, "Where have you come from?" I replied, "From the East." He then questioned, "What is your intention in visiting this city?" I answered, "For my livelihood." He further enquired, "What is your name?" I responded, "ʿAbdallāh." All this was true. . . . Then he asked, "What is the purpose of your visit?" I submitted, "There is a person who often sees his holiness, the refuge of prophecy, may God bless him and grant him salvation. Kindly verify this matter with an appropriate *ḥadīth*." He responded, "The fact is, in whatever form the Prophet is seen, and if the seer is confident that the vision is the Prophet, may God bless him and grant him salvation, or if the apparition itself claims to be the Prophet, then undoubtedly the vision is of the Prophet. There is no interference of the Devil in this matter."[1]

This episode is recorded in the hagiography of a seventeenth-century Sufi, Sayyid Ḥasan, who lived in Shāhjahānābād. In the medieval sources he is mentioned invariably by his *laqab* (title) "*Rasūlnumā*" (One who shows the way to the Prophet).[2] Although this dialogue signifies the gravity of concern over the appearance of the Prophet in visions, it also hints at the tension between two alternate methods of spirituality that co-existed in Hindūstān (northern India) in those days. On the one hand, ʿAbd al-Ḥaqq (1551–1642 AD), the renowned scholar of the Prophet's traditions and practicing Sufi in the *Qādirī ṭarīqa*, epitomizes the idea of spiritual authority structured around the concept of *silsila* (initiatic genealogy). Sayyid Ḥasan, on the other hand, subverts this scheme of spiritual-genealogical authority and challenges its historical frame of reference by forging direct association with the principal source of authority of the Prophet through the *Uwaysī* technique. The appellation "*Uwaysī*" is inspired by the story of Uways al-Qaranī, the Yemeni contemporary of the Prophet who never met him, but communicated with him through telepathic means, thereby becoming deeply devoted to him. Later, Sufis who were initiated by the spirits of Muḥammad or of pre-Islamic prophets, or by the spirits of the Sufi saints from the past, were known as *Uwaysī*.[3] Because this *ṭarīqa* (spiritual method) was marked by the absence of a physically present *shaykh* (master), initiation and instruction along the Sufi path was mediated through visionary means. When compared with the more conventional formulation of the *silsila* as Sufi organizational behavior, the *Uwaysī* notion leaves the individual Sufi, notwithstanding his spiritual status, essentially unable to guide and teach others.

The Sufi described in this chapter, however, proves himself to be a capable instructor of disciples by inducing dreams and visions. This study attempts to understand the method and significance of Sayyid Ḥasan's *ṭarīqa* through an analysis of dreams and visions that are recorded in his principal hagiography, *Malfūẓāt-i Ḥaḍrat Sayyid Ḥasan Rasūlnumā* ("Discourses of the Venerable Sayyid Ḥasan Rasūlnumā"). I concentrate on two aspects of visionary experiences mentioned in this work. First, this chapter is concerned with the mode in which the visionary narratives highlight some formative aspects of an *Uwaysī* community established by Sayyid Ḥasan *Rasūlnumā*. Dream episodes play a vital role in the initiation and elaboration of relationship between the master and disciples, but in the *Uwaysī* tradition this relationship gains added strength due to the *pīr's* (guide) immediate relationship to the Prophet. As is seen here, Sayyid Ḥasan not only communicated with the Prophet but also enabled his disciples to partake in his visions. Second, this chapter explores the contemporary Muslim intellectual concerns for dreams and visions through the lens of Sayyid Ḥasan's hagiography. This context gives meaning to the alternate strategies used for inducing dreams in the Sufism of Sayyid Ḥasan and ʿAbd al-Ḥaqq Muḥaddith Dihlawī.

The Historiographical and Hagiographical Context of Sayyid Ḥasan: Exploring a Community of *Uwaysīs* in the Age of *Silsilas*

The history of Sufism has been written primarily from the perspective of the *silsila,* which represents continuous chain of master–disciple relationship stretching back to the prophet Muḥammad. This was the dominant style of organizational behavior among Sufi fraternities settled in the subcontinent since the twelfth century. Each *silsila* is identified by distinctive rituals of initiation, spiritual practices, ideals, ethical and social norms controlled by the *shaykh* who assumed an extraordinary position as an intermediary, linked to the Prophet and God. By the seventeenth century, which is the focus here, the Indo-Persian sources, especially Sufi literature from Mughal north India, promote the *Chishtiyya, Naqshbandiyya* and *Qādiriyya* as leading orders that developed considerable complexities in their functional modes in response to the changing historical circumstances, especially the changing Mughal Imperial attitudes.[4] The *silsilas* also experience significant changes in their structural organization. For instance, within each Sufi order there were frequently suborders sometimes designated by composite names indicating branches or teaching sublineages within the *silsila.*[5] Furthermore, during the seventeenth century, many Sufis preferred multiple rather than singular affiliations, while showing ascendancy of their principal order. Such variations in lineage-based Sufism are shown to be symptomatic of great "spiritual conflict" and "contested authority" between *shaykhs* who belonged to the same *silsila,* as well as between *shaykhs* belonging to different brotherhoods.[6]

An alternate pattern of Sufi behavior is noticed in the *Uwaysī ṭarīqa* of Sayyid Ḥasan. Even though students of Indian Sufism and scholars elsewhere have identified individual Sufis as *Uwaysīs,* relatively little scholarly attention in this direction may be a result of academic inclination for *silsilas* that are associated with tangible social structures.[7] It is assumed that the *Uwaysiyya,* on the other hand, operate only in a nonphysical and transhistorical sense, and therefore fail to consolidate institutional structures worthy of historical analyses. In fact, this limitation is a major consideration in resisting the notion of a *silsila* for the *Uwaysīs*. Furthermore, the proclivity of contemporary sources toward narrating *silsila*-based fraternities also explains the relative marginalization of the *Uwaysiyya* in academic discourse.

Malfūẓāt-i Ḥaḍrat Sayyid Ḥasan Rasūlnumā[8] is the detailed biography[9] of an *Uwaysī* Sufi Sayyid Ḥasan that was written by Mīr Sayyid Hāshim Sirhindī in AH 1104/AD 1693. The compiler along with other fellow disciples was part of an *Uwaysī* community established by his *Shaykh* in Shāhjahānābād. The Urdū translation bearing the same structure has an alternate title, *Manāqib al-Ḥasan wa Fawāʾiḥ al-ʿIrfān* ("Virtues of Ḥasan and Fragrances of Knowledge") and gives the author's name as Muḥammad Hāshim bin Muḥammad Kāẓim Ḥasanī Ḥusaynī Najafī. The Persian text of the *Malfūẓāt* available to me is imperfect toward the beginning and end, which explains loss of some information and the alternate title as referred by the translator. The work is, however, extremely valuable in drawing our attention to an alternative pattern of Sufi behavior, because unlike other contemporary sources the *Malfūẓāt* does not project the *silsila* but casts the *Uwaysī* technique into focus. In order to do this the hagiographer attributes a role model to his subject. The life-telling of Sayyid Ḥasan copies the character and events from the life of Uways al-Qaranī, the prototype *Uwaysī,* at the beginning of the first millennium of Islam. This is further endorsed by Sirhindī's appellation for his *Shaykh* as *"sar-i ḥalqa-i fuqarā-i Dihlī Ḥaḍrat Sayyid Ḥasan Rasūlnumā Uways-i thānī"* (The venerable leader of the group of mendicants of Delhi Sayyid Ḥasan *Rasūlnumā,* the Second Uways.)[10] Also, Sayyid Ḥasan is repeatedly projected as an *Uwaysī* who had no earthly master, and thus received initiation, instruction, and guidance from the "*ghayb*" (invisible world) in numerous visions.[11] Additionally, the *Malfūẓāt* contains notices of several disciples of Sayyid Ḥasan, who were inducted in to his *ṭarīqa* through visions induced by him.

In the *Malfūẓāt,* Sayyid Ḥasan's life is embedded in diverse urban locales in northern India. He belonged to an influential family of Nārnaul (in the Mughal province of Agra and later Delhi), but at the age of eighteen was cheated out of his official position (*manṣab*) and landholding by scheming relatives. He journeyed eastward from Akbarābād (Agra) to Jaunpur, an established center of Islamic learning, to acquire scholarship in order to avenge himself and regain his lost position at the Mughal court. This journey transformed Sayyid Ḥasan, and he returned to Nārnaul after fourteen years as a scholar and mystic deeply devoted to the Prophet. Twelve years later, following Muḥammad's instruction in a dream, he left for Shāhjahānābād where he lived for nearly fifty years till his death (22 *Shaʿbān* AH 1103/9 May A.D. 1692).

The new Imperial capital of Shāhjahānābād was then under construction (AD 1639–48) in proximity to the older cities of Delhi that had accommodated scholars and mystics of phenomenal reputation for nearly four centuries. Many of them lay enshrined in tombs that were popular pilgrimage centers, often linked to the *Chishtiyya* and the *Naqshbandiyya*. From these older cities devout individuals continued to influence lives of people as teachers, preachers, jurists, healers, and diviners. Later, after the Court left with Emperor Awrangzēb for the Deccan (AD 1679), Shāhjahānābādīs continued to draw religious and cultural sustenance from the older sacred symbols, while also extending patronage to recent Islamic institutions within and outside the precincts of the city wall.[12]

The nascent circumstance of Shāhjahānābād offered opportunities of livelihood for individuals like Sayyid Ḥasan who aspired for a career in spirituality. He settled in his dwelling and *darsgāh* (seminary), where his shrine still stands, in Kulālī Bāgh, a quarter near Pahārganj where the principal grain market was located outside the city's Ajmerī gate. Disciples from diverse ethnic, social, and economic backgrounds, including *Naqshbandī* Afghans, Indo-Tūrānī notables at the Court, and mendicants visited him seeking his intercession, primarily, to enable the vision of Muḥammad. He too ventured inside the city, often disguised as a cloth market broker (for the sake of anonymity), to call on *murīds* (disciples) or to attend local festivities at various shrines. At a time when the spiritual and intellectual surroundings of this city favored the tradition of lineage-centered *silsila*s, Sayyid Ḥasan's lack of a formulaic genealogy signified absence of the necessary hallmark for validation of spiritual credentials. He, however, possessed an alternative source of power that sanctified his aspiration in this direction. He was an *Uwaysī* and frequently "saw" the Prophet who was his initiator and guide in various states of sleep and wakefulness. This extraordinary ability could not have earned him much commendation for surely there were other Sufis who claimed similar experience. What was unique to Sayyid Ḥasan's practice was his ability to "show" the Prophet to whomever he desired.

Pīrī-murīdī Discipline in the "*ṭarīqa*" of Sayyid Ḥasan *Rasūlnumā*

Before examining the significance of visionary phenomena in the Sufism of Sayyid Ḥasan, I mention some features that have shaped my approach in analyzing this material. Sufi literature in general and biographical notices of the Sufis in particular, frequently mention accounts of visions experienced in state of sleep and wakefulness, as well as visualization experienced between the state of sleep and waking. The mystics consciously distinguished these categories with specific terminologies.[13] They also developed elaborate taxonomies and interpretative strategies, largely worked within the framework of various Islamic dream traditions, to explain the diverse functionality of visionary occurrence in religious and social modes. Nevertheless, the recitation in Sufi texts often blurs these distinctions, and creates complications of an analytical nature.

Furthermore, such accounts along with other paranormal occurrences, are compiled either in an independent chapter, or are found scattered as separate narrations, usually, interspersed with other biographical notices. In the *Malfūẓāt*, for example, although visionary anecdotes are mentioned throughout the text, many dreams and visions of God and His Prophet are clustered together in chapter 5 dedicated to the *mukāshafāt* (spiritual unveilings) and *khāriq-i ᶜādāt* ("contrary to custom" in reference to a particular type of miracles); and chapter 11, devoted to the *kamālāt* (perfections) of Sayyid Ḥasan. The location assigned to these narratives is significant. Sirhindī explains that his *shaykh*'s greatest extraordinary ability was to enable people to perceive visions of God and the Prophet. Whereas such capacity is conferred on the *awliyā*ᵓ (saints) of high rank, his *shaykh*'s *tawajjuh* (master's ability to focus on disciples' heart and to control mystical states) and *ṣuḥbat* (the master's immediate and physical presence) achieved similar affect for his disciples.[14] In the Sufi worldview articulated by Sirhindī, miracles reflect the perfections of divinity bestowed on an ideal *shaykh*. The display of miracles is normally restricted, lest it lead to mystic's indulgence in false pride. God, however, lifted this constraint when he appointed a *shaykh* for teaching and instruction of the community. The *shaykh* was then obliged to relate these miracles before his students and disciples to inspire their confidence in him, and for purpose of strengthening faith.[15] Accordingly, Sayyid Ḥasan communicated God's perfections, as reflected in him, by narrating his experience perceived through visual, auditory, and sensual modes to an audience. His audience perceived such narratives as a proof of the *shaykh*'s spiritual authority. Furthermore, the *shaykh*'s followers frequently reported their own visions, claiming that they were induced and mediated by him. This explains the utility of dreams and visions as a legitimate mode of communication among the *Uwaysīs* of Shāhjahānābād. The accounts that follow are concerned with the appearance of the Prophet. Scholars have classified such dreams as literal because the content and message conveyed in them is the same, and they require no interpretation.[16] However, in the *Malfūẓāt* each dream and vision, whether literal or symbolic, accumulates further significance that relates to the larger context of the work. In the *Malfūẓāt* we find dreams that appear in the entries about of the dreamer as well as dreams that appear in the entries about the dreamed. The latter fact suggests that dreams can be incorporated into an entry not only by the biographical fact that a certain person has dreamed them but also by the content of the dream itself.[17] This shows that the dream is not merely subjective to the dreamer but has an objective existence as well. Furthermore, as biographical notices, like that of Sirhindī, are arranged in a thematic rather than in a chronological order, visionary anecdotes are not related in a historical sequence. This arrangement gives the hagiographer an opportunity to use the dream or vision as a subterfuge for conveying something at strategic points in his narrative that he would not have been able to do otherwise. Finally, these descriptions are located within the cultural patterns of dreaming in Islam wherein the dream is treated as a privileged sign by the dreamer. Sirhindī's predilection for availing himself of such narratives in his composition has a legitimizing function that is intimately linked to the self-perception and self-identity of Sayyid Ḥasan *Rasūlnumā* and his community of *Uwaysīs*.

At several points in the *Malfūẓāt*, Mīr Hāshim Sirhindī mentions that his *shaykh* did not have an earthly master. Sayyid Ḥasan did not give his hand in discipleship to any instructor; in fact, he had differences with his teachers of Islamic sciences, Ustād Muḥammad Jamīl and Maulānā ʿAbd al-Rashīd Jaunpurī, over matters concerning appropriate conduct for Sufis. Therefore, he tutored himself by emulating the practice of Uways al-Qaranī—combining ascetic conduct with ecstatic devotion toward God and His Prophet. He thus developed a distinct style of piety called the *ṭarīqa-i Uwaysiyya,* in which visions played a major role.[18] Following are some narratives that sketch an image of Sayyid Ḥasan in the eyes of Shāhjahānābādīs before whom these descriptions were related.

Sayyid Ḥasan narrates a *wāqiʿa* (literally "incident" that can be seen in a dream or a waking state) to Sirhindī and others present in the gathering. This is a literal vision where the auditory content and message conveyed are essentially the same:

> I saw in a *wāqiʿa* (vision) that the prophet Muḥammad, may God grant him peace and salvation, is standing on my left side, and all the prophets preceding the coming of Islam are lined up on my right. And before me God most

> pure is manifest. God blessed me and said, "I have kept you under my protection. You have the row of pre-Islamic prophets on one side. And the prophet Muḥammad, the seal of the prophets, is present on your other side." In this manner, this *bishārat* (good tiding) was repeated several times. After this, the Prophet repeated this *bashārat* several times. A thought occurred to this *faqīr* ["poor/mendicant," as the author calls himself] that since the heart is on the left side, it was tutored by the purified and sanctified person [of Muḥammad] who is the origin of higher cognition (*maʿrifat*). Therefore, the Prophet fixed his auspicious gaze on the left direction for the purpose of teaching and affecting (*taʿlīm wa taʾthīr*) [Sayyid Ḥasan].[19]

The imagery evoked in this vision is a figural representation of two basic precepts of Islamic tradition. First, the idea that God perfected prophecy by sealing it with Muḥammad who is the last prophet. Second, the idea that even after the demise of Muḥammad and cessation of prophecy, the Muslim community continues to receive divine guidance through true dreams that are harbingers of good tidings (*mubashshirāt*) and thus part of prophetic knowledge. Thus, in his visions, Sayyid Ḥasan receives instruction and the effects of prophecy directly into his heart through the gaze of Muḥammad. In this way, Sayyid Ḥasan is a continuous source of guidance for the community. Since this vision occurs in the notice of Sayyid Ḥasan, it also symbolically displays the virtue of an *Uwaysī shaykh*'s direct contact with the Prophet who is his instructor and guide.

The following dream narrative is significant for the self-identification of Sayyid Ḥasan with Uways al-Qaranī:

> Once I [Sayyid Ḥasan] saw the prophet Muḥammad in a dream. He said to me, "You will become Uways Qaranī." I implored, "I am not deserving of any [such] thing, but God is very generous toward this worthless one." He [the Prophet] repeated this. This weak author says that from this indication and some other gestures, like the plucking out of his teeth, and besides what has been written before [in the *Malfūẓāt*], it is known that he had acquired the exalted stature of *Ḥaḍrat* Uways Qaranī, and was the guardian of the *ṭarīqa-i Uwaysiyya,* the principal consideration of which was purification of the heart and enlightenment of the soul;

and in the external way (*dar ẓāhir*) did not have the mediation of *ṭarīqa-i mashaykhat* (way of the masters).[20]

This dream and Sirhindī's commentary in the narrative, encapsulate the idea of Sayyid Ḥasan's spiritual method. The *shaykh* was contemptuous of *mashaykhat* that refers to the formalized relationship between *pīr* and *murīd* in his day. As the *pīrān-i zamān* (shaykhs of the age) falsely claimed to be *ahl-i kamāl* (perfect people), the credulous folk got caught in the net of their deceit and were led astray. Such pretenders were not capable of leading anyone to the ultimate goal of attaining proximity to God, nor can they intercede for Muslims on the Day of Judgement. Even though the so-called masters themselves had not traversed stages of *murīdī* discipleship, they accepted disciples and boasted about their spiritual prowess. To remedy this deplorable situation, Sayyid Ḥasan recommended the discipleship of the Prophet who is the most virtuous and universally acknowledged mentor. Even though the Prophet was dead, it was possible to establish a spiritual connection with him. In the method prescribed by Sayyid Ḥasan the seekers were advised to focus directly on the Prophet, thus circumventing the necessity of an intermediary *pīr*. And, if there was need for a mediating *pīr*, the solution would come from the *ghayb*.[21]

Sayyid Ḥasan, on the one hand, did not encourage *murīds*. If someone approached him with request for *taᶜlīm-i ṭarīqat* (instruction in spiritual method), he would dissuade them from seeking his companionship. In his opinion, mysticism, like any other science, should be cultivated step by step. The first step required the suppression of the *nafs* (animal soul), followed by the renunciation of material possessions, and then the *talqīn* (implanting) of the *dhikr* (the recollection of God), *lā ilāha illā'llāh*,[22] in the heart of the disciple by the *shaykh*. He ordered *murīds* to diminish their food, sleep, speech, and dress; he also recommended that they avoid association with strange women and the rich, favor knowledge of Islamic sciences over philosophy, and adhere to the custom of the Prophet.[23] On the other hand, he demanded absolute submission of his disciples and expected them to share with him everything—even their offensive thoughts and actions. In this way, he achieved absolute control over their personalities.

The following narratives are characteristic of this pedagogy. In chapter 15, there is an account of the relations between Sayyid Ḥasan *Rasūlnumā* and Shāh Ilāh Yār Ṣāḥib Sākin of Bajwārā (a town in the Mughal province of Lahore) who was initially a *murīd* of Shāh ᶜInāyatallāh Qādirī. Being the longest narrative of its kind in the *Malfūẓāt,* it provides an illuminating description of the *shaykh*'s spiritual method. After Shāh ᶜInāyatallāh Qādirī had initiated Shāh Ilāh Yār into the *Qādirī, Chishtī,* and *Naqshbandī* orders, he embarked on a pilgrimage to Mecca.[24] Before his departure, he advised his distressed pupil to seek further guidance in Delhi. A wiseman of this city reassured Sayyid Shāh Ilāh Yār about finding a *pīr* and advised him to follow a certain course of action (not defined by the author) that would enable him to receive beneficence from the spirit of the Prophet. Within a few days, Sayyid Shāh Ilāh Yār had a dream:

> On a Thursday, I saw *Ḥaḍrat Murshid* [Sayyid Ḥasan], may his secret be sanctified, in a dream. He held both shoulders of this slave with his hands, and, placing his lips on my lips, he breathed with extreme concentration on them. I felt the impact of this in my entire body; in fact, I felt it in the roots of every hair. For twelve days, I could not enter into his presence. I again saw in a vision that I had arrived at a river. I came up to the bridge of that river with the intention of doing ablution. As I went to the steps of that bridge and started performing ablutions, suddenly my foot slipped and I fell into the river. All of a sudden, a person appeared, and by the bank of the river there was a horse. He mounted me [on the horse], pulled its reins, and took me to the august *madrasa* (school of Islamic learning) of *Ḥaḍrat Murshid.* [I saw] several people who were taking leave from his presence. This *faqīr* [Shāh Ilāh Yār] was also summoned and asked to state his condition. I petitioned, "What is the order for this *faqīr*?" He said, "Whoever wishes to taste my *khichri* [a dish made of rice] should come tomorrow in the afternoon."[25]

This story is clearly one of initiation, and the manner of its occurrence defines the *Uwaysī* phenomenon as observed in the practice of Sayyid Ḥasan. Although the symbolism of the dreams is not complicated, nevertheless, their explanation requires acquaintance with certain themes that have been referred to elsewhere in the text. Shāh Ilāh Yār's anxiety about finding a guide for himself in Delhi and observing a certain unnamed exercise prescribed to him by a wiseman of that city creates the context for this dream. Although the nature of this exercise is not explained, one may assume that it is something akin to *rābiṭa,* a technique whereby a Sufi concentrates on the inward as well as the outward image and personality of his master, whether present or absent, living or dead. Having done this, the master enters into his heart, as the bearer and transmitter of "divine emanation" (*fayẓ*). This technique opens up the adept to his master's *fayẓ*. Perhaps the wiseman had revealed the identity of Shāh Ilāh Yār's future guide to him, and the latter exercised *rābiṭa* with him. What is significant is that prior to any physical association, a spiritual bonding takes place between Shāh Ilāh Yār and his *Uwaysī shaykh* as the latter breathes into his mouth in a dream. This action is symbolic of *tawajjuh* in the course of which the master funnels his energy into the disciple. This "funneling" is complementary to observance of *rābita*.[26] Furthermore, Sayyid Ḥasan had kept a firm hold of the adept's shoulders while touching and breathing into his mouth. It is quite evident that this represents the *shaykh*'s bodily presence in the dream and conveys the idea of *ṣuḥbat*, a technique used by the master to transmit his qualities and attributes to a willing recipient. The dream is a perfect example of *Uwaysī* style initiation.

When Shāh Ilāh Yār tarries in following the instructions, according to the Urdū text, the Prophet appears to him in another dream, instructing him to visit Sayyid Ḥasan's seminary. It is significant that the Prophet's vision occurs to Shāh Ilāh Yār only after his dream initiation at the hands of Sayyid Ḥasan, and after he has secured the benefit of the latter's *tawajjuh* and *ṣuḥbat*. The dream continues, and the dreamer sees a river, which alludes to his journey to the *shaykh*. His desire for ablution signifies the purifying impact of his forthcoming visit. But his own lack of conviction in this matter is illustrated by his fall in the river. In the method of Sayyid Ḥasan, when a disciple is firm in his desire for a *pīr*, the *ghayb* ensures the realization of his yearning. Further, an invitation to share food is symbolic of partaking in a spiritual repast with Sayyid Ḥasan. Shāh Ilāh Yār continues to tell us about transformation of these visions into reality:

> In the morning . . . I presented myself before the *Shaykh* and told him about my condition. He said, "Take your two *nān* (bread) and *khichri*. Study and pay attention!" People were surprised at how easily you had admitted me in the circle of your servants.[27]

It was not uncommon practice for *shaykhs* to serve food to their visitors. In this particular context, the distribution of *khichri* seems to be a part of the initiation ritual of the *madrasa* of Sayyid Ḥasan, where the rite symbolizes transference of the *shaykh's* spiritual energy to the initiate. In the Urdū text, this idea is illustrated by the reverence displayed by other students who receive the *khichri* as *tabarruk* (blessing). The somewhat envious response of other students here is understandable in view of the *shaykh*'s reluctance to recruit disciples. Sayyid Ḥasan's own response, however, was motivated by the appearance of the Prophet in a dream. The Prophet had advised the dreamer to instruct Shāh Ilāh Yār in the teachings of his *ṭarīqa*.[28]

This narrative informs us that the *shaykh* first and foremost instructed his disciples in the traditional Islamic sciences—*tafsīr* (Qurʾānic exegesis), *ḥadīth* (sayings or traditions of the Prophet), *fiqh* (Islamic jurisprudence), and *uṣūl* (sources of Islamic law)—and then trained them in Sufism (*taṣawwuf*).[29] According to Shāh Ilāh Yār, Sayyid Ḥasan had an unusual method of instruction. The *shaykh* spoke little but in his thoughts remained absolutely engrossed in the person of Muḥammad, thereby affirming his faith in the Oneness of God and in His Prophet. Shāh Ilāh Yār further narrates his experience:

> I brooded, in what manner would I conceive the person of the Prophet? In the morning in a state of wakefulness, I was sitting in the chamber facing the *miḥrāb* (prayer niche). He [Sayyid Ḥasan] said, "Behold! Be devoted to the noble presence." When I looked, the two pure and sanctified eyes, which were extremely beautiful and perfect, appeared from the blessed face [of the Prophet]. I was [absolutely] spellbound, and from that very day I made [that] condition my vocation.[30]

As Shāh Ilāh Yār sat facing the *qibla* (direction of prayer) Sayyid Ḥasan *Rasūlnumā* appeared before him and showed him the vision of the Prophet.

Dreams further elaborate on the nature of relationship between Sayyid Ḥasan and his disciples. Mīr Hāshim Sirhindī had doubted Sayyid Ḥasan's claim: "God has told me that the one who shuns you (Sayyid Ḥasan) has shunned Me, and the one who defies you has defied the Prophet."[31] The compiler confesses that he verified the truth of this statement during the days of his studentship when he had not yet given up his profession to become a *darwīsh*. Once the *shaykh* dismissed someone from his gathering for no apparent reason. This disturbed the compiler who thought to himself that if the *shaykh* did not wish to enlist *murīds*, then it was no use visiting him. This resulted in fearful thoughts that continued to perturb him despite his seeking God's forgiveness. Crying bitterly in repentance, he went to sleep, and saw the following dream:

> In a dream I saw that I was standing in a house that was full of people. Suddenly a person appeared with a pair of shoes tucked under his arm. That keeper of shoes addressed himself to someone in the gathering: "The Prophet is present in this house. These shoes have been removed from the blessed feet [of the Prophet]." That person, the carrier of shoes, dusted the shoes so that dust is separated from these. He gave a little of that dust as blessing to each one [present] in that gathering. When it was the turn of this weak one, I put my hand forward. That dear one withdrew his hand [and said], "There has been a feebleness in your belief, therefore, I will not give [it to] you." I woke up due to the horror of that thought and the terror of this dream. Crying and trembling, I reached the court (*dargāh*) of *Ḥaḍrat Murshid*. By chance, I came upon Miyān Muḥammad Jamāl Khān, a scholar of philosophy and science. I related the entire incident to him. He asked me: "Is it that your faith towards Mīrān Jīu [an endearing form of address for Sayyid Ḥasan] has weakened?" My infirmity became evident to me, and I had earlier experienced a similar incident. I said, "Indeed, some languor is evident in the past relation." He said, "Quickly, repent for there is great fear." It was Thursday, I repented in my heart and left to be in the *Shaykh*'s presence. Before this, due to the weakness of my faith, when I greeted him, he did not acknowledge me. This time he immediately responded to [my] greetings and asked about my past condition. And, despite my lack of confessing any sin or repentance, that condition was set aside.[32]

This dream has to be analyzed with reference to other events mentioned by the hagiographer, while also taking into account the importance of dreams in the pedagogical method of our *Uwaysī shaykh*. In Chapter 6, the compiler explains that for thirteen or fourteen years he had visited the *shaykh* without ever being granted the benefit of his *tawajjuh*.[33] The reason for this was compiler's preoccupation with thoughts of his livelihood rather than complete devotion to God. Disappointed with his own inability to pursue the requirements of spiritual discipline, he even criticized his *shaykh*'s actions in frustration. Apparently, it was the *taṣarruf* (exercise of the *pīr*'s power in the affairs of the *murīd*) of the *shaykh* that created fearful thoughts in his mind. In the dream, the Prophet's presence is only alluded to and at best is represented through the shoes that his servant carries. The message of this dream is clear: One who has a weak faith in Sayyid Ḥasan shall be denied the good fortune (represented by the shoe-dust) of the Prophet's blessing. The Prophet will not appear in the dream of a person who doubts Sayyid Ḥasan's ability as a guide.

Distressed on account of his dream, Sirhindī went looking for his *shaykh*. Fortunately, he met Miyān Jamāl Khān, another *murīd* of Sayyid Ḥasan, who advised him to repent of his feeble faith in the *shaykh*. Jamāl Khān recalled his own apprehension with regard to the *shaykh*'s utterances in the early years of their association, and how his conviction was reinforced in a vision that he narrated to alleviate the uneasiness felt by Sirhindī:

> One day, I saw God and the Prophet, may God bless him and grant him salvation, and *Ḥaḍrat* Shāh [Sayyid Ḥasan] was standing before them. He had a light in his hand. Every time he opened his fist, the light came out, entered my heart and enlightened it. And, every time he closed his fist it fell out from my heart and returned into his blessed hand. The Prophet said, "This is the light of faith that has been given into his [Sayyid Ḥasan's] hand. If he desires, it will remain in you, and if he does not so will, it will disappear from you."[34]

Sirhindī has not specified the nature of this vision. Jamāl Khān simply introduces his vision with "I saw" (*man dīdam*). Nevertheless, the vision is self-explanatory. Since the Prophet's speech is sacrosanct, his words in a dream are the law. Sayyid Ḥasan's position as keeper of Muḥammad's faith is placed above doubt, and his will in the matter of Jamāl Khān's faith is absolute. Recalling his own repentance and the subsequent strengthening of his belief in Sayyid Ḥasan on account of this experience, Jamāl Khān renders the same advice to Mīr Hāshim Sirhindī. Repentance for doubting one's guide, especially on the auspicious day of Thursday, secures the *shaykh*'s attention for our compiler.

These anecdotes demonstrate that visions of Muḥammad define the structure of Sayyid Ḥasan *Rasūlnumā*'s belief and practice as an *Uwaysī* Sufi. In an age when elaborate chains of initiation commanded great respect, Sayyid Ḥasan's one-link connection to the Prophet, claimed on the basis of his visionary experience, was an attempt to create an alternative to *silsila* association wherein physical contact between the master and the disciple were to be replaced with an extra-physical spiritual link. The visionary perceptions of Sayyid Ḥasan's disciples, however, continue even after his death. These narratives either state a premonition of the *shaykh*'s death or focus on informing us about his condition in heaven. The compiler has discussed these visions in the conclusion of his work, where he notes the circumstance of the death and burial of Sayyid Ḥasan.

A couple of days before the death of the *shaykh,* his devoted *murīd,* Sayyid Raḥmatallāh Sāmānī, saw the vision that he described to the hagiographer as follows:

> I saw in a vision that *Ḥaḍrat* Mīrān Jīu is girdling his waist and pointing towards the sky saying, "Raḥmatallāh, I am going." He brought down the red and white striped *tāqī* (hat) from his head and put it on my head.[35]

This vision refers to Sayyid Ḥasan's journey to the other world, but also symbolizes the transmission of spiritual authority to his disciple. Unlike most other *silsilas* where the *shaykh* defined his principal successors by granting them *khilāfatnāma* (document of succession) inscribed with details of the *shajara-i ansāb* (genealogical tree) all the way back to the Prophet, Sayyid Ḥasan's *murīds* have no such proof. Therefore, the dream of Raḥmatallāh Sāmānī is of considerable significance, defining the mode of succession to Sayyid Ḥasan. This aspect is elaborated in another dream description that appears in the notice of Muḥammad Hāshim (Sayyid Ḥasan's eldest son), and is related by Raḥmatallāh Sāmānī to the compiler. In a dream, the *shaykh* had seen the Prophet who ordered him not to interfere with the tutoring of Muḥammad Hāshim, because the Prophet himself wished to instruct him.[36] Sirhindī also mentions that as his death had drawn near, Sayyid Ḥasan instructed his grandson, Muḥammad Qāsim, son of Muḥammad Hāshim, to convey to his father in Lahore that he should take over the task of looking after the *shaykh*'s followers in Shāhjahānābād and Nārnaul.[37] Bearing in mind that Sayyid Ḥasan possessed no spiritual pedigree, the principle of hereditary succession proved persistent, perhaps due to the natural tendency to retain the material and spiritual prerogatives of religious authority within a given family. This is, however, not unusual as hereditary *shaykh*s were the norm, rather than the exception, even in the *silsila* conscious *Naqshbandiyya* and other Sufi fraternities by the seventeenth century.

Contextualizing the Dreams and Visions of Sayyid Ḥasan *Rasūlnumā*

From the descriptions of dreams and visions presented here it is evident that the author of *Malfūẓāt-i Ḥaḍrat Sayyid Ḥasan Rasūlnumā* has used these narratives as a legitimizing tool to substantiate the spiritual authority and method of his master. This treatment is certainly not unique to Sirhindī, because visionary narratives conventionally serve as vehicles of authority in Sufi hagiographies and in other Islamic literary traditions as well. What is remarkable in the *Malfūẓāt* is the hagiographer's ability to analyze these visionary narratives by means of sophisticated vocabularies of diverse Islamic discourses on this subject. In providing a brief overview of them here, I show the significance of these phenomena in the mentality of seventeenth-century Indian Muslims in and around Shāhjahānābād. It is in this context that the episode related at the beginning of this chapter will be rendered more meaningful.

Shaykh ʿAbd al-Ḥaqq Muḥaddith Dihlawī[38] was perhaps the most respected, influential, and widely known scholar of Delhi at the end of the sixteenth and beginning of the seventeenth centuries. This period coincided with the end of the first one thousand years of Islam, and the beginning of a new millennium. At that time, bold religious claims were made by certain men of religion, and the *shaykh*'s opinion had great influence on acceptance or rejection of such claims. A case in point is the *Naqshbandī shaykh* Aḥmad Sirhindī. He claimed, among other things, to share the perfections of Muḥammad, to enjoy direct proximity to God without the mediation of His Prophet, and promised to "renew" Islam in its second millennium. ʿAbd al-Ḥaqq had his own vision of how Islam was to be "renewed." He suggested the assertion of the primacy of the Prophet and his Sharīʿa (code of conduct for Muslims) and the dissemination of Islamic sciences, especially *ḥadīth* in the *Ḥanafī* tradition, from his seminary positioned at the periphery of courtly power located in Shāhjahānābād. He rejected Aḥmad Sirhindī's claims.[39] ʿAbd al-Ḥaqq had some influence with the Mughal courtiers, although he was critical of the policies of the Court itself, which was one of the reasons for his popularity.[40] His image as a great authority on Islamic traditional sciences is repeatedly emphasized in the *Malfūẓāt,* which enumerates his works alongside major writings on Qurʾānic, *ḥadīth* and Sufi sciences. As Sayyid Ḥasan claimed to be able to "see" the Prophet frequently, it was only natural for him to seek endorsement from ʿAbd al-Ḥaqq.

Mīr Hāshim Sirhindī has quoted extensively from *Ashiʿat al-Lamaʿāt fī Sharḥ al-Mishkāt al-Maṣābīḥ* ("The Rays of Effulgences in the Commentary on the Niche of Lights") which is ʿAbd al-Ḥaqq's Persian commentary on a fourteenth-century collection of the Prophet's traditions in Arabic by Muḥammad Tabrīzī. The *Sharḥ* provides a detailed discussion of the Prophet's sayings to prove the veracity of a particular type of dreams. In other words, he uses the *ḥadīth* to legitimize the role of dreams in the Islamic community.[41] He asserts that all dreams are basically ascribed to God, except for those in which Satan exercises his influence. A set of the Prophet's traditions identifies these two different types of dreams: *ruʾyā-i ṣādiq* or *aḥkām* (true, good, or sound dreams inspired by God and therefore subject to interpretation) and *ḥulm* or *aḍghāsu'l-aḥlām* (bad or confused dreams that are instigated by Satan to lead a pious Muslim astray). Another set of traditions instructs about appropriate action to ward off the effect of bad dreams.[42]

Mīr Hāshim selects those prophetic sayings from the "Commentary" that confirm two basic ideas: dreams are a part of prophecy, and the vision of the Prophet in dream is equal to his appearance in reality. The first idea is expressed in Muḥammad's words that after prophecy ended only *bishārāt* (tidings), which he explained as true dreams, will remain. In other words, prophetic guidance continues for Muslims through true dreams that are bestowed on some special people after the demise of Muḥammad. ʿAbd al-Ḥaqq counsels that the person who is favored with true dreams is a carrier of Prophet's virtues, and even if he is not a prophet, he is akin to one. It is in this sense that dreams are continuation of prophecy. Sirhindī advocates this recommendation of ʿAbd al-Ḥaqq Muḥaddith Dihlawī for his *shaykh.*[43]

The commentator then opines that if the Prophet speaks in a dream, his words should be viewed as equivalent to *ḥadīth-i ṣaḥīḥ* (sound tradition). If, however, something improper has been uttered, then the dreamer's hearing ability is at fault.[44] That is, it is not merely the actual meeting or seeing of the Prophet that instructs people about their behavior. The Prophet's words heard in a dream also may have the same impact. Physical appearance of the Prophet, therefore, is no longer the only source of advice. His appearance and speech in dreams is sufficient and may have the same effect. This is but a restatement of the message that dreams are a continuation of prophecy. The *Sharḥ* cautions pretenders with another *ḥadīth* that although it may be possible for the Devil to appear to the dreamer and mislead him about the visionary presence of God, it is not possible for him to fake the appearance of the Prophet.[45]

These traditions raised theological debates about the authenticity of the Prophet's appearance in state of sleep or wakefulness. In his *Sharḥ al-Mishkāt* ʿAbd al-Ḥaqq expresses conformity with the views of Muḥammad al-Ghazālī AD (1058–1111) regarding this issue as discussed in his *Al-Munqidh min al-Ḍalāl* ("The Deliverer from Error"), and states that the vision of the Prophet either in the state of sleep or wakefulness is possible. Al-Ghazālī praises the Sufis for being able to contemplate the image of the angels and the spirit of the prophets, hear their voices, and receive instructions from them. Al-Ghazālī answers some fundamental questions like: When the Prophet died and his soul was separated from his body and buried, how can he be perceived in the absence of his physical form? How is it possible for hundreds of people to see him in different places at the same time? Al-Ghazālī answers these questions in terms of the symbolic representation of the reality of the formless essence of Muḥammad or his incorporeal soul (*rūḥ-i mujarrad*) and not the vision of his body that is perceived by the dreamer. Now, the symbolic forms in which the Prophet is perceived vary according to the inner condition of the hearts of the perceivers, because they reflect the essence of the Prophet like the surface of a mirror.[46] ʿAbd al-Ḥaqq elaborates that to perceive Muḥammad in a beautiful form signifies the dreamer's commitement to his faith. On the contrary, seeing him in an unhappy or angry form indicates the weakness of the dreamer's belief. The Sufis, therefore, use visions of the Prophet to diagnose and treat their spiritual condition (*ḥāl*), as well as to determine their spiritual station (*maqām*).[47] Even though traditionalist scholars denied the credibility of waking visions of the Prophet, ʿAbd al-Ḥaqq validates these through al-Ghazālī, whose admiration of Sufis' visualization of angels and souls of prophets in wakefulness is also recorded in *Al-Munqidh min al-Ḍalāl*. Since these visions are special kind of miracles, ʿAbd al-Ḥaqq observes, questioning their trustworthiness is tantamount to disregarding the Qurʾān and the traditions of the Prophet.[48]

Elsewhere in the *Malfūẓāt*, the hagiographer draws a comparison between the reliability of those who transmit *ḥadīth* and those who narrate the dreams of Sayyid Ḥasan *Rasūlnumā*. This is another proof, in addition to the testimony of ʿAbd al-Ḥaqq, that the *ḥadīth* and dreams are treated as equal by the *Uwaysī* community of Shāhjahānābād.[49]

In the medieval Muslim belief, *ruʾyā-yi ṣāliḥa* besides being treated as *bishārāt* and continuation of prophecy, also is treated as a mark of strength and the perfection of faith of a Muslim. Most of the dream accounts in the *Malfūẓāt* belong to a special category of true dreams that are concerned with the visionary appearance of God and Muḥammad. According to ʿAbd al-Ḥaqq Muḥaddith Dihlawī's *Takmīl al-īmān*, one who sees God in a dream should be relieved of sadness and preserved from the corruption of faith; in the same manner, to be blessed with the vision of the Prophet is a mark of the integrity of one's faith.[50] Now, despite the sanctity of dreams in general, it is the Prophet's dream that is taken to be a sign of the greatest blessing for Muḥammad Hāshim.

The belief that true dreams, especially dreams of the Prophet, were a source of divine communication obviously enjoyed wide acceptance in Islamic civilization, and this belief developed to an extent that scholars of Islam prescribed special formulae for inducing such dreams. Mīr Hāshim Sirhindī informs his readers about some of these methods prescribed in the epilogue of ʿAbd al-Ḥaqq's biography on Muḥammad, *Madārij al-nubuwwat* ("The Stairs of Prophethood").[51] According to ʿAbd al-Ḥaqq, there are two methods for inducing dreams of the Prophet. The first technique involves invocation of constant *dhikr* of the Prophet; or the invocation of his physical form; or that of his grave; or else invocation of constant prayers for the Prophet. ʿAbd al-Ḥaqq's second prescription instructs Muslims to invoke *ḥaqīqat-i muḥammadiyya* (reality of Muḥammad which, being a composite of all the qualities of the Divinity and creation, serves as a connecting link [*barzakh*], between God and the material world).[52]

In contrast to the arduous technique involving prayers and devotional rituals prescribed by ʿAbd al-Ḥaqq, Muḥammad Hāshim's own *shaykh* recommended a simpler procedure for visualising the Prophet. The *shaykh* advised the seekers of prophetic vision to acquire the *tawajjuh* and *ṣuḥbat* of a *shaykh-i kāmil* (perfect master).[53] Evidently, the latter technique is preferred by Sayyid Ḥasan, who through the exercise of *tawajjuh* and *ṣuḥba* could induce such visions. Unlike the method of ʿAbd al-Ḥaqq Muḥaddith Dihlawī, which was open to any Muslim, the way of Sayyid Ḥasan was totally controlled by him, and the beneficence of the Prophet's vision was bestowed as a mark of his favour on those whom he desired.

Conclusion

In the thirteenth century, Farīduddīn ʿAṭṭār was the first to mention *Uwaysī* Sufis as a group of people who have no need of a living *pīr,* because they obtain spiritual knowledge directly from the Prophet, in the same way as Uways al-Qaranī had done. In the fifteenth century, Jāmī had elaborated on the definition of *Uwaysī*s: They are not only individuals guided by the spirit of Muḥammad, but also by the spirits of "God's friends" (*awliyāʾ Allāh)* who walk in the footsteps of the Prophet. Therefore, their disciples are in no need of a living *pīr*; they are also *Uwaysī*s. By the seventeenth century, there is a considerable expansion in this definition: *Uwaysī*s are not only guided by the spirits of Muḥammad or dead saints, but they can also receive instructions from a living *shaykh* by evoking his *tawajjuh*. Sayyid Ḥasan's spiritual experience is of the same category as that of Uways al-Qaranī. Hence it is considered as the purest of its kind available amidst various styles of *Uwaysī* connections suggested by later definitions. However, Sayyid Ḥasan's own conduct vis-à-vis his followers creates the possibility of conveying his own spiritual affiliation with the Prophet to his disciples. In the process, he goes on to expand the scope of *Uwaysī* style of Sufism.

In the view of Sufism and sainthood presented in *Malfūẓāt-i Ḥaḍrat Sayyid Ḥasan Rasūlnumā,* the *ṭarīqa* is dependent on the single founder's sanctity and charisma and not on legitimization through a *silsila* that links the founder or his followers to the sacred origins of Islam. Sayyid Ḥasan redefines the structural notion of the *silsila.* In his case, it is the vision of the preceptor and not the genealogy that functions as the source of legitimacy. In the teaching of Sayyid Ḥasan, the only *pīr* worthwhile in his day is the Prophet. Given the context of seventeenth-century Islam in India and the attempts to revitalize it, Sayyid Ḥasan's prophetic visions acquire a truly tremendous significance. Sayyid Ḥasan's own association with the Prophet is akin to that of Uways al-Qaranī, and therefore, the necessity of a spiritual genealogy for connecting to the Prophet is excused. In fact, he is the second Uways al-Qaranī at the beginning of the new millennium of Islam.

The *shaykh,* however, required scriptural justification for his unique method of re-connecting the community to its founder. To this end, his hagiographer marshals the authority of prophetic traditions. In the pedagogical system of Sayyid Ḥasan, the revitalization process is achieved by emphasizing the personal authority of the Prophet who is positioned as the indispensable guide.

Notes

1. See Mīr Sayyid Hāshim Sirhindī, *Malfūẓāt-i Ḥaḍrat Sayyid Ḥasan Rasūlnumā,* Persian text in manuscript, microfilm (I.I.I.S No. 52) vol. I/53. For details, see note 12; and Urdū translation called *Manāqib al-Ḥasan Rasūlnumā yaʿnī Fawāʾiḥ al-ʿIrfān* by ʿUmar Bakhsh, Lahore: 1921, reprint Karachi, not dated, 124–25.

2. For example, Khāfī Khān, *Muntakhab al-Lubāb,* Bibliotheca Indica, vol. 60/2a (Osnabruck: Biblio Verag, 1983), reprint of Calcutta edition (1868–1874), 552–53; Chaturman Kāyastha and Rāi Khān Munshī, *Chahārgulshan,* manuscript (I.I.I.S No. 37), Central Library, Jamia Hamdard, New Delhi; Ḥabīb Allāh, *Dhikr-i Jamīʿa-i Awliyā-i Dihlī,* ed., Sharīf Ḥusayn Qāsimī (Delhi: New Public Press, 1987–1988), 102–104, 107, 119, and 121; Ghulām Sarwar Lāhorī, *Khazīnat al-Aṣfiyā,* vol.1 (Kanpur: Nawal Kishore, 1312/1894), 180.

3. For the legend of Uways al-Qaranī and the notion of the *Uwaysī* Sufis see, A.S. Hussaini, "Uways al-Qaranī and the Uwaysi Sufis," *The Muslim*

World, 57/2 (1967), 103–13; Julian Baldick, *Imaginary Muslims. The Uwaysi Sufis of Central Asia* (London: I. B. Tauris, 1993); Devin DeWeese, "An 'Uvaysī' Sufi in the Timurid Mawarannahr: Notes on Hagiography and the Taxonomy of Sanctity in the Religious History of Central Asia," in Yuri Bergel, ed., *Papers in Inner Asia* (Subseries: Central Asia) No. 22 (Bloomington: Indiana University Research Institute for Inner Asian Studies, 1993), 1–36.

4. For example, the controversy triggered by Akbar's *Dīn-i Ilāhī* received a mixed response from many Sufis which determined their social and political engagements. In this regard, see S.A.A. Rizvi who attributed great significance to the Islamic "revivalist" and "reformist" movements initiated by the *Qādiriyya, Naqshbandiyya* and *Chishtiyya* in his works, *The Muslim Revivalist Movements in Northern India in the Sixteenth and Seventeenth Centuries* (Agra: Agra University Press, 1965); and *Shāh Walī Allāh and His Times* (Canberra: Maᶜrifat Publishing House, 1980).

5. For a discussion of the development of sublineages within the *Chishtiyya*, see Carl W. Ernst and Bruce Lawrence, *Sufi Martyrs of Love: The Chishti Order in South Asia and Beyond* (New York: Palgrave Macmillan, 2002), 18–24; Bruce. B. Lawrence, "Biography and 17th century Qādirīya," in Anna Libera Dallapiccola and Stephanie Zingel-Avé Lallemant, eds., *Islam and Indian Regions* (Stuttgart: Steiner, 1993), 399–415.

6. Lawrence, "Biography."

7. For a discussion of *Uwaysī* Sufis in the Indian subcontinent in pre-colonial times, see Meenakshi Khanna, "The Dreams and Visions in North Indian Sufic Traditions, ca. (1500–1800) AD," Unpublished PhD Dissertation, Centre for Historical Studies, Jawaharlal Nehru University, 2001, Chapters 4 and 5. For *Uwaysī* developments in Central Asia see DeWeese, "An *'Uvaysī'* Sufi in the Timurid Mawarannahr," 1–36; idem, "The *Tadhkira-i Bughrā Khan* and the "*Uvaysī*" Sufis of Central Asia: Notes in Review of *Imaginary Muslims*," *Central Asian Journal*, 40/1 (1996), 87–127.

8. A copy of *Malfūẓāt-i Ḥaḍrat Sayyid Ḥasan Rasūlnumā* is preserved as inventory (I.I.I.S No. 52) in the Central Library, Jamia Hamdard, New Delhi. The original manuscript (Acc. No. 3791) from which this microfilm is prepared was not available for consultation. There is some confusion about the untraced manuscript, as the published catalogue: *A Descriptive Catalogue of Persian Manuscripts in the Library of Jamia Hamdard* (New Delhi: Iran Culture House, 1999) identifies this title as Acc. No. 2185, which was untraced and missing for consultation. Nevertheless, the manuscript (Acc. No. 3791) in microfilm, copied by Sayyid Muḥammad Niẓāmuddīn Ḥanafī Naqshbandī Hāpurī, is dated 28 Rabīᶜ al-thānī A.H. 1300/8 March A.D. 1883. The text is paginated and divided into two volumes containing 333 pages, fifteen chapters of unequal length—each called *fāʾiḥ* (fragrance). A comparison with the Urdū translation highlights some discrepancies and missing detail from the manuscript. For example, the first chapter of the Persian original is briefer than its translation. This is explained by the copyist's notes on the *shaykh*'s early circumstance concerning his travels on an un-numbered leaf of 18 lines attached before the *Bismillāh* page, which could not be incorporated fully in

the first chapter. Hāpurī also makes a marginal note on page 129 of the second volume informing us of a few missing pages that he hopes to incorporate if discovered. Furthermore, the author's preface and introduction are also missing in the manuscript. Therefore, it is necessary to read the Persian and Urdū texts simultaneously. As such, all references to *Malfūẓāt-i Ḥaḍrat Sayyid Ḥasan Rasūlnumā* (henceforth *Malfūẓāt,* and the volumes indicated in Roman numbers I and II) in this chapter will be to the microfilm, along with references to the reprint of the Urdū translation (hereafter *Manāqib*) mentioned in note 1. All translations from these two texts are mine.

9. A shorter Persian hagiography is *Fayżān-i Ḥasan Rasūlnumā* by Sayyid Najīb al-Dīn ibn Mīr Muḥammad Hāshim, translated into Urdū by Sharīf Ḥusayn Qāsimī, Karachi: not dated.

10. This is an honorific mentioned in the titles of chapters 1, 2, 9, 10, 11, 12, 13, 14, and the epilogue of the *Manāqib*, 40, 95, 318, 348, 363, 379, 383, 390, and 422.

11. S.A.A Rizvi in *History of Sufism in India*, vol. 2 (New Delhi: Munshiram Manoharlal, 1983), 101, mentions Sayyid Ḥasan's initiation in the *Qādirī* order by his teacher ʿAbd al-Rashīd at his seminary in Jaunpur, but I found no such reference in the *Malfūẓāt/Manāqib*.

12. For spatial and cultural ambiance of Shāhjahānābād, see Hamida Khatoon Naqvi, "Shāhjahānābād: The Mughal Delhi, 1638–1803: An Introduction," in R.E. Frykenberg, ed., *Delhi Through the Ages. Essays in Urban History, Culture and Society* (Delhi: Oxford University Press, 1986), 143–151; Stephen P. Blake, *Shahjahanabad: The Sovereign City in Mughal India, 1639–1739* (Cambridge: Cambridge University Press, 1991), 26–82 and 150–56; Jamal Malik, "Islamic Institutions and Infrastructure in S̲h̲âhjahânâbâd" in Eckart Ehlers and Thomas Krafft, eds, *S̲h̲âhjahânâbâd/Old Delhi, Tradition and Colonial Change* (New Delhi: Manohar, 2003), 71–92.

13. Here, I differ with Professor Hermansen's view that Sufis "rarely formally distinguished" between different categories of visions, as expressed in "Visions as 'Good to Think': A Cognitive Approach to Visionary Experience in Islamic Sufi Thought" in *Religion*, 27 (1997), 27. See Khanna, "Dreams and Visions," Chapters 2 and 3.

14. *Malfūẓāt* I/46–47; *Manāqib*, 118.

15. *Malfūẓāt* II/64; *Manāqib*, 363–64.

16. See for instance Leah Kinberg, "Literal Dreams and Prophetic *Ḥadīṯs* in classical Islam—a comparison of two ways of legitimation," in *Der Islam*, vol. 70 (1993), 279–300.

17. As observed by F. M. Douglas, "Dreams, the Blind, and the Semiotics of the Biographical Notice," in *Studia Islamica*, vol. 51 (1980), 146–47.

18. See descriptions in Chapter 1 of *Malfūẓāt* I and *Manāqib*.

19. *Malfūẓāt* II/63; *Manāqib*, 364. In the translation the vision is included in Chapter 11 with slight variation in Sirhindī's interpretation.

20. *Malfūẓāt* II/67; *Manāqib* 367.

21. *Malfūẓāt* I/121–122; *Manāqib*, 199–201.

22. *Malfūẓāt* I/107; *Manāqib*, 182.

23. For details see Chapter 6 of *Malfūẓāt* I/119–132; *Manāqib*, 197–214.

24. According to *Dhikr-i Jamīʿa-i Awliyāʾ-i Dihlī*, Shāh ʿInāyat died on way to the Ḥijāz in AH 1101/ AD 1690, 143.

25. *Malfūẓāt* II/118–119; *Manāqib*, 415.

26. For explanation of *rābiṭa* and *tawajjuh* see Jürgen Paul, "Doctrine and Organization. The Khwājagān/Naqshbandīya in the first generation after Bahā'uddīn," *ANOR*; 1 (Berlin: Verlag Das Arabische Buch, 1998), 34–46.

27. *Malfūẓāt* II/120; *Manāqib*, 416; the Urdū text gives a more elaborate version of this account.

28. *Malfūẓāt* II/118; *Manāqib*, 413–414.

29. Sirhindī also indicates this balance between Islamic sciences and mysticism with reference to *Naqshbandī* practice mentioned in Kāshifī's *Rashaḥāt ʿayn al-ḥayāt*, *Malfūẓāt* I/123; *Manāqib*, 203.

30. *Malfūẓāt* II/ 119; *Manāqib*, 416.

31. *Malfūẓāt* II/74; *Manāqib*, 374.

32. *Malfūẓāt* II/74–75; *Manāqib*, 374–75.

33. Cf. *Malfūẓāt* I/74; *Manāqib*, 158.

34. *Malfūẓāt* I/49; *Manāqib*, 120.

35. *Malfūẓāt* II/127; *Manāqib*, 424.

36. *Malfūẓāt* II/109–10; *Manāqib*, 406.

37. *Manāqib*, 410. Some text is missing from the manuscript as explained above.

38. For biography of ʿAbd al-Ḥaqq, see Rizvi, *Muslim Revivalist Movements*, 148–75; M.S. Akhtar, "An Introduction to the Life and Works of Sheikh ʿAbd al-Ḥaqq Muḥaddith Dihlawī," *The Muslim World*, 68/3 (1978), 205–14.

39. For ʿAbd al-Ḥaqq's criticism of Shaykh Aḥmad Sirhindī, cf. Rizvi, *Muslim Revivalist Movements*, 268–71; Yohanan Friedmann, *Shaykh Aḥmad Sirhindī. An Outline of His Thought and His Image in the Eyes of Posterity* (Montreal and London: McGill-Queen's University Press, 1971), 87–89.

40. For ʿAbd al-Ḥaqq's relations with the Mughal court, see Rizvi, *Muslim Revivalist Movements*, 155–56, 160–67, and 173–74; and Lawrence, "Biography and 17th century Qādirīya."

41. For an excellent discussion on the *ḥadīth* and dreams as a parallel source of authority in Islam, see L. Kinberg, "Literal Dreams and Prophetic *Ḥadīṯs* in Classical Islam" in *Der Islam*, vol. 70 (1993), 279–300.

42. *Malfūẓāt* I/71–72; *Manāqib*, 145.

43. *Malfūẓāt* I/63; *Manāqib*, 131–32.

44. *Malfūẓāt* I/67; *Manāqib*, 140.

45. *Malfūẓāt* I/63; *Manāqib*, 135.

46. *Malfūẓāt* I/66; *Manāqib*, 138–39.

47. *Malfūẓāt* I/66; *Manāqib*, 139.

48. *Malfūẓāt* I/68; *Manāqib*, 141.

49. *Malfūẓāt* I/47; *Manāqib*, 121.

50. *Manāqib*, 124.
51. *Malfūẓāt* I/ 77–78; *Manāqib*, 150–54.
52. *Malfūẓāt* I/77–78; *Manāqib*, 150–54.
53. *Malfūẓāt* I/74; *Manāqib*, 122.

Contributors

Elizabeth R. Alexandrin is Assistant Professor of Islamic Studies at the Department of Religion, University of Manitoba. She holds a Ph.D. from the Institute of Islamic Studies, McGill University (2005). Her recent publications have appeared in *Reason and Inspiration* ed. by B. T. Lawson (2005), and in *The Prophet Explores Other Worlds* ed. by F. Colby and C. Gruber (2009).

Shahzad Bashir is Professor of Religious Studies and Director of the Abbasi Program in Islamic Studies at Stanford University. He is the author of *Messianic Hopes and Mystical Visions: The Nūrbakhshīya Between Medieval and Modern Islam* (2003), *Fazlallah Astarabadi and the Hurufis* (2005), and *Sufi Bodies: Religion and Society in Medieval Islam* (2011). He is currently working on the way the past is made an object of knowledge in Persian literature produced during the period 1400–1600 CE.

Özgen Felek is a Mellon Postdoctoral Fellow in Religious Studies at Stanford University. She received her first Ph.D. from Fırat University in Turkey, in classical Ottoman poetry with a focus on the *Sebk-i Hindī* (Indian Style) poetical movement (2007), and her second Ph.D. from the Near Eastern Studies Department at the University of Michigan with emphasis on Ottoman dream culture and Sufism (2010). With Walter G. Andrews, she is the co-editor of *Victoria Holbrook'a Armağan* (2006), which is a collection of essays in honor of Victoria Rowe Holbrook.

Omid Ghaemmaghami is currently a Ph.D. candidate in Islamic Thought and Sessional Instructor of Arabic at the University of Toronto. His doctoral dissertation addresses the narratives of encounters with the Hidden Imam in early Twelver Shi'i Islam. He received his M.A in Islamic and Near Eastern Studies from Washington University in St. Louis, Missouri (2005).

Gottfried Hagen is Associate Professor of Turkish and Ottoman language and culture at the Department of Near Eastern Studies, the University of Michigan. He is interested in the way Ottoman culture constructs the globe and the universe, space, self, and others. He is the author of numerous publications that include his book *Ein osmanischer Geograph bei der Arbeit. Entstehung und Gedankenwelt von Kātib Çelebis Ǧihānnümā* (2003). He has contributed chapters to such volumes as *Evliya Çelebi-An Ottoman Mentality*, ed. by Robert Dankoff (2004), *Legitimizing the Order: The Ottoman Rhetoric of State Power*, ed. by Maurus Reinkowski and Hakan Karateke (2005), and most recently, *Exploring Other Worlds: New Studies on the Prophet Muhammad's Ascension (Mi'raj)* ed. by Christiane Gruber and Frederic Colby (2009). Other aspects of his study of Ottoman intellectual history include translations, myths, as well as Western travel and Orientalism.

Jonathan G. Katz is Professor of History at the Oregon State University. He is the author of *Dreams, Sufism and Sainthood: The Visionary Career of Muhammad al-Zawawi* (1996) and *Murder in Marrakesh: Émile Mauchamp and the French Colonial Adventure* (2006). Katz is also a contributor to *Dreaming across Boundaries: The Interpretation of Dreams in Islamic Lands*, ed. Louise Marlow (2008). His current research concerns Jewish conversion to Islam.

Fareeha Khan is an affiliated scholar at Willamette University. She received her Ph.D. from the Department of Near Eastern Studies at the University of Michigan (2008). She focuses on issues related to women and gender, the classical Islamic tradition, and approaches to reform among Muslim religious scholars in the modern period. Khan has taught as assistant professor of Islamic Studies at Willamette and at Georgia State University. She is completing a manuscript on the legal-spiritual approaches to reform of Ashraf 'Alī Thānawī and is also serving as advisory editor for the Oxford Encyclopedia of Islamic Law.

Meenakshi Khanna is Associate Professor of Sufism at the Department of History, Indraprastha College for Women, Delhi, India. In April–July of 2011, she held an Annemarie-Schimmel professorship at the University of Bonn, Germany. In addition to several articles and book reviews, her publications include an edited volume of essays, *Cultural History of Medieval India*, and the forthcoming English translation of the *Catalogue of the Microfilms of the Persian and Arabic Manuscripts (vol. 3) of Hakeem Sayeed Zillur Rehman.*

Leah Kinberg is Professor of Islamic Studies at the Department of Middle Eastern and African History at Tel Aviv University. Kinberg's research focus is the function of dreams in Medieval Islam, the interaction of this world and the next in classical Islamic literature, as well as Qur'an exegesis. In recent years, she has also studied the uses of classical Islam in contemporary media and the functioning of the Islamic Law (*Sharīʿa*) in non-Muslim countries. Kinberg is the author of numerous articles as well as *The Book of Death and the Book of Graves by Ibn Abī al-Dunyā* (1983) and *Morality in the Guise of Dreams: Ibn Abī al-Dunyā's K. al-Manām* (1994). She is also the co-editor of *Studies in the Linguistic Structure of Classical Arabic* (together with Kees Versteegh).

Alexander D. Knysh is Professor of Islamic Studies at the Department of Near Eastern Studies, University of Michigan. His research interests include Islamic mysticism and Islamic theological thought in historical perspective as well as Islam and Islamic movements in local contexts (especially Yemen, North Africa and the Northern Caucasus). His publications on these subjects include *Ibn ʿArabī in the Later Islamic Tradition: The Making of a Polemical Image in Medieval Islam* (1998), *Islamic Mysticism: A Short History* (2000), translated into Russian in 2004, *Al-Qushayrī's Epistle on Sufism: An Annotated Translation* (2007), and *Islam in Historical Perspective* (2011). Knysh is also the section editor for "Sufism" on the editorial board of the *Encyclopedia of Islam* (3d edition).

Derek J. Mancini-Lander is a Ph.D. candidate in the Department of Near Eastern Studies at the University of Michigan where he studies Islamic History. He received an M.A. in Medieval Studies from the University of Toronto (1997) and a B.A. in English from Kenyon College (1994). He is generally interested in cultural history in the early modern Islamo-Persianate world and his dissertation focuses on local traditions of history writing in Iranian cities during that era. In particular, he explores how the authors of these local histories used memories of their city's past as a way of constructing a particular sense of the "local" in relation to broader or more inclusive categories of spatial and social organization.

Sarah Mirza is a Visiting Fellow at the College of Wooster, teaching in History, Philosophy, and Religion. She received her Ph.D. in Islamic Studies from the Department of Near Eastern Studies at the University of Michigan (2010), and her M.A. in Modern Middle

Eastern and North African Studies from the same university in 2004. She is presently working on historical documents associated with the prophet Muhammad and his mission. She is interested in orality and literacy and the transmission of learning in pre-Islamic Arabia and the early Muslim community.

Erik S. Ohlander is Associate Professor of Religious Studies and Director of the Religious Studies Program at Indiana University–Purdue University Fort Wayne. He received his Ph.D. in Near Eastern Studies from the University of Michigan (2004). A specialist in the history of Islamic mysticism, he is author of *Sufism in an Age of Transition: 'Umar al-Suhrawardī and the Rise of the Islamic Mystical Brotherhoods* (2008). He is a frequent contributor to the 3d edition of Brill's *Encyclopedia of Islam*, the *Encyclopedia Iranica*, and other scholarly reference works in the field of Islamic studies. At present, he is working on a project exploring the history of Sufi communities and trans-regional networks during the Later Medieval Period.

Maxim Romanov is a Ph.D. candidate in the Department of Near Eastern Studies at the University of Michigan. He holds an M.A. in Sociology from St. Petersburg State University, Russia (2001); he has also completed a graduate program in Islamic Studies (Classical Islam with the focus on Traditionism, Ḥanbalism, and the Ḥanbalī critique of Sufism) at the Institute of Oriental Manuscripts of the Russian Academy of Sciences, St. Petersburg, Russia (2004). His dissertation is an interdisciplinary study of the theory and practice of Islamic preaching (medieval *waᶜẓ* and its equivalents in present-day Muslim societies). In particular, it focuses on preaching as a socio-religious mechanism that creates and perpetuates "imagined communities" of religious commitment.

Muhammad alZekri is a Lecturer and Post-doctoral Research Fellow at International Graduate School of Heritage Studies, BTU Cottbus in Germany. He was until very recently Director of Center for Cultural Diversity in Bahrain. He obtained a Ph.D. in cultural anthropology from the University of Exeter in England (2005). In addition to his contributions to the Gulf Region section of the "1000 Women for the Nobel Prize," he has been publishing a semi-monthly book review column in the popular Bahraini newspaper "Akhbar al-Khaleej." He is currently working on a book entitled *Majalis of Bahrain: Sites of Religio-cultural Negotiation*.

Index